PROBING HEAVEN

Key Questions on the Hereafter

JOHN GILMORE

BAKER BOOK HOUSE

Grand Rapids, Michigan 49516

The New International Version, NIV, (© 1973, 1978, 1984 by International Bible Society, used by permission of Zondervan Bible Publishers), serves as the basis for this Bible study. Other translations used are New American Standard (NASB), Good News (GNB), King James Version (KJV), New English Bible (NEB), and Revised Standard Version (RSV).

The following publishers have granted permission to use copyrighted material.

Thomas Nelson Publishers for use of chart from *The Lamb and the Lion: The Gospel in Revelation* by Graeme Goldsworthy, 1984.

Yale University Press for use of quotations from *Heaven: A History* by Colleen McDannell and Bernhard Lane, 1988.

The Zondervan Corporation for use of materials from *A Student's Dictionary for Biblical and Theological Studies* by F. B. Huey, Jr., and Bruce Corley, 1983.

Harvest House Publishers for use of chart from *New World Coming* by Hal Lindsey, 1973.

Library of Congress Cataloging-in-Publication Data

Gilmore, John.
    Probing Heaven: key questions on the hereafter / John Gilmore.
      p. cm.
    Includes bibliographical references.
    ISBN 0-8010-3833-2
    1. Heaven—Christianity. I. Title.
    BT846.2.G55 1989   89-17588
    236'.24—dc20   CIP

In Loving Memory of
My Parents

Haydn Gilmore (1898-1971)
born in South Wales
rose from being a pit-pony boy
to
shift superintendent of the Harding Power Plant
selfless father, patient parent
model of wisdom

and

Anna Lewis Gilmore (1900-1985)
second-generation Welsh girl
school teacher, loving mother,
enthusiastic exhorter of four happy children
model of kindness

both believers
both Baptists
both beloved
both alive
both at home

Contents

Part 3
Midcourse Corrections
INFERENTIAL

Preface

Going to heaven has always appealed to me as the greatest adventure I could imagine. I have had the hard-breathing excitement of a boy climbing a forbidden fence to see what was on the other side. (You may be like me in this.) I have never lost my eagerness to learn as much as I could about heaven.

My investigation spans several decades. I was taught one eschatology as a teenager, which, through extended study, I have found partially right and partially defective. What I have presented may enable others to begin to sort through alternative views on the hereafter rather than blindly following an elaborate eschatology of a recent tradition. I think we grow in our Christian understanding of the future when we realize that current popular positions on the hereafter are sometimes forced on the Bible rather than an outgrowth of the biblical text.

I have put down what I consider the most compelling arguments on twenty-one of the major topics on the hereafter. It is an individual contribution to the debate that continues. Admittedly, my reasons may not convince all. Nevertheless, I hope what follows provides a solid bridge to more exegetical studies and further theological dialogue. New clues are yet to be uncovered in continuing biblical research. I have tried to face—head-on—the central issues.

Except for one chapter, I have not dealt at length with salvation-assurance, the subject in which I earned my doctorate, and the subject (which I see) has next importance when the hereafter comes up. Lord willing, my next project is a work on the topic of salvation-assurance. I believe the two subjects belong together as parts of a whole.

Moreover, some readers may notice, perhaps with a degree of disappointment, that the present study on heaven does not deal at length with infant and child immortality. The scarcity of my comments on this matter does not mean I think this topic is less important than the issue of the fate of adults. Indeed, my early eschatological research focused mostly on that subject and my interest in it has run parallel with what I have dealt with in this book. Bereaved parents certainly have a lot of questions regarding the unexpected deaths of their children. I decided, however, to deter temporarily getting involved in this topic. And I am not entirely convinced there is a need for my kind of presentation on the subject because I feel the greater problem is not that few children will be in heaven, but that few adults will be there. In my pastoral work the chief challenge has been to wean adults away from childish fantasies about the hereafter.

After reading this book on heaven one should junk forever the notion that all faiths can agree on the subject of heaven. Certainly, the Bible's view of heaven differs from other world religions. The purpose of what follows is to deal with how and where it differs. Also it intends to provide evidence for the views presented here.

Three distinguishing features of the present study should add to its value:

It is reader-oriented. Rather than beginning in Genesis and working through the Bible to Revelation I have begun with the questions readers most often ask. Then I have brought to bear pertinent scriptural passages on the points of quandry and supplied some elementary but essential responses.

It is interactive. I have tried to relate the biblical perspectives to significant ancient philosophies and modern cults. Exegetical substance is followed by biographical applications. I have drawn from historical, dogmatic, and biblical theology, from psychological studies, even from medical history. I have used poetry and science. Christians cannot truly enter into the distinctives of the Bible on heaven unless they know what others have written and proposed. Only in contrast do we appreciate what is uniquely Christian.

It challenges to further study. Some may feel what follows is too detailed. In fact it is abbreviated, condensed, and preliminary. Much more work needs to be done in most of what is covered. (The work should challenge younger men and women to continue the subject in greater depth.) The notes are sometimes lengthy. These were intended for those who want to go into the subject a little further. But the notes are hardly exhaustive. I have tried to keep the material in manageable form because I realize the modern Christian often is too pressed to engage in extended study.

Many colleagues urged me to publish this material. The late "Pat" Swallen, founder of the Cincinnati-based Swallen Stores, was an early reader and admirer of this manuscript in its original form. He is now with Christ. Members in my present pastorate, Madisonville Baptist Church, Cincinnati, Ohio as well as friends in Tamaqua, Pennsylvania, have taken a keen interest in its appearance as a book. And the couple, which was earliest convinced it should be published and who kept after me to submit it, is Evelyn and Jim Reinke of Okeana, Ohio.

A word of appreciation is due to the Bible study groups in

Pennsylvania, where the midchapters have been used for spiritual profit by new converts from my ministry in Tamaqua. Also, I would be remiss not to thank several persons who have interacted with earlier versions of the manuscript. These include Gary Habermas, Ph.D.; Newton Bush, Th.D.; Donald Leggett, Th.D., John Owen Gilmore, M.S., who is in a scientific doctoral program at Stanford University, Susan Poncavage, R.N.; Cincinnati physician Tom Dryer, M.D., and Tim Hensgen, M.A. I wish to thank Tom Wells for calling my attention to some overlooked dispensationalist material, my brother for pointing out the appearance of the McDannell/Lang volume, and Sarah Lyons Miller, Librarian of Carey S. Thomas Library at Denver Seminary for special assistance. Vernon Grounds, Ph.D., of Denver, Colorado, graciously gave me a block of time in his busy schedule to read the entire manuscript. Of course, none is finally responsible for what I have written. Interpretations, conclusions, and any errors are mine alone. This study is only one man's attempt to come to grips with the biblical heaven.

My initial curiosity about heaven came through the influence of my older brother, Haydn Gilmore, Th.M., M.A. In our country home of Mount Zion, Pennsylvania, he first sparked my interest in the Celestial City. Without his early guidance, like Mr. Evangelist of *Pilgrim's Progress*, this presentation would never have been possible. Finally, as many have found before me, good wives are gifts from God. My companion and fellow pilgrim, Roberta, has encouraged me to strive for clarity, simplicity, and excellence every way.

Dr. John Gilmore
The Keruxkabin
P.O. Box 24064
Cincinnati, OH 45224-0064

May 16, 1989

Introduction

*C*hristian parents are eager to tell their preschool children of "heaven." They want them to know that there is another world, another life. After "God," "heaven" is probably the next theological word learned. And, as God would have it, it is undoubtedly our last theological thought as a tottering adult.

But thinking about heaven is not necessarily heavenly any more than reflecting on hell is hellish. Eventually, however, everyone thinks about heaven—if only to deny it.

The word *heaven* remains popular. It doesn't seem to have suffered the fate of fad expressions. Certain words in our society are socially "in" for a time, but they fade out as fast as they catch the attention of the public. *Heaven*, however, is a word which has constancy and lasting appeal.

Credit for the continued popularity of heaven is partly due to the hymns of the church which eulogize and enhance it.[1] Ironically, heaven's transcendence and triumph permeate traditional church music, whereas contemporary preaching largely ignores it.

Sermons play down certainties about the hereafter. This has taken away poetic inspiration as evidenced by a diminution of heaven references in late twentieth-century hymns. Some notable exceptions, of course, would include the Blackwood Brothers who sing "Heaven's Sounding Sweeter All the Time," and an earlier chorus "Heaven Is Better Than This."

Vagueness tires listeners, tempting some to trash "heaven" as a meaningful expression. Today's usage has been severed from its biblical richness. "Scarcely any other word," commented Hans Küng, "has been so defiled, so abused, so torn to shreds."[2]

Few fault calling earthy ecstasies, such as a romantic kiss, "heavenly." Despite its overuse and misuse, however, there is an unwillingness to completely reject the word's validity. On special occasions, when lost for another word, people fall back on picking "heaven" to describe their ultimate pleasure. In our most euphoric moments *heaven* mirrors microcosmic glimpses of harmony, joy, and pleasantness. But have we ever stood back to check the word *heaven* for its contents? Circulation without certification is bad theological business.

The problem is that people differ as to what *heaven* means for their own reasons. Some would like heaven ornate; others, like the Shakers, would prefer it simple. Some expect there to be literal golden streets; others anticipate a nonmaterial experience, leaving the symbols of wealth and greed to our former earthly existence. Some anticipate sitting on clouds; others look forward to clear skies. Some believe that heaven will be solitary contemplation; others hope it will be ceaselessly social. Some say the millennium is the Intermediate State in heaven; others think it a literal one-thousand-year period on earth. Some would like to go to heaven as soon as possible; most wish to postpone their entrance.[3]

Tragically, in our adulthood not enough attention has been devoted to this subject to which we were introduced in our toddler years. And, sadly, our original acquaintance with the topic may have prejudiced us to retain comfortable conceptions which fail to agree with and take into account the full range of Scripture.

The danger for an adult is to drift back to those sketchy and unsubstantiated views passed on by an early teacher whose understanding was distorted by his/her own lack of biblical conformity. Shaking off the nostalgic pull of youthful views need not be a venture of disrespect, but is required by those committed to striving for a more complete conformity to God's self-revelation (Scripture).

Too many grown-ups prefer to feed and follow their hunches of heaven without dipping into bunches of books. Childhood fantasies about heaven, to them, may be more comforting than dealing with what the Bible says. Because the Bible is an old book, they would prefer to consult something more recent, something shorter. The public will eagerly buy up thin books on near-death experiences but never give the Scriptures second thought.

Are near-death encounters superior to scriptural teachings? Some would prefer to swap near-death stories or watch videotaped testimonies of out-of-the-body experiences. Many are satisfied to compute the reality and nature of the hereafter on the basis of the debriefing of the resuscitated.[4]

Before one's excitement becomes excessive, we need to enter a discussion, headfirst, on what is actually retrieved and how much faith we can have in what is reported. Surprisingly the most elementary fact about these accounts should be the main obstacle in accepting them as trustworthy sources. Hans Küng noted that of the 150 cases of dying persons investigated by the American physician, R. A. Moody, "not a single individual really died."[5] What bearing does this have on the value of what is said? It pointed up that dying is not death. Dying is the way out of life, death is the "destination."[6]

This distinction reduces the impact of the testimonies, because no one has actually returned from the dead to tell what the other side is like. What has been reported is one's impressions in the act of dying. Theologically, this has enormous importance, for it means one is supplied provisional, introductory impressions. One is not given factual final findings. It means that the impressions are about a process; they are not conclusions about eternity. Therefore, the insights derived must not be given eternal value and personal trust.

How is one to know what predisposing factors distort what was perceived? For instance, can we really bank on an atheist's impression in the act of dying? His recall powers may be sharp and his reporting honest, but that does not mean they are reliable perceptions. The person's impressions can be steered, unconsciously, to affirm what he wants, and therefore what he says is misleading both to himself and to others. How much confidence should one venture from what he says? Why should he be believed that there is nothing dangerous on the other side of the death line? He went into dying believing in some sort of universalism or in an amorphous, nonthreatening power. No wonder he came out believing the same things. No wonder he returns to his philosophical presuppositions without a trace of terror.

In reading the present study on the hereafter one notices a virtual absence of references to published recollections of those who have had near-death experiences. Near-death reports aren't near enough to heaven to warrant basing beliefs on them. There is just as much likelihood that the atheist, mentioned above, who was flooded with light at the gateway of death, was met, not by the Lord in welcome, but by Satan, his true master, who appears as an angel of light.

Maurice Rawlings, M.D., and others have noted that hidden drives and satanic forces can deliberately disguise what is *ahead* as well as obscure what is *within*.[7] Thus, individual reports are unreliable as standards of the hereafter. The safest touchstone of truth is the biblical text. The Bible is taken as our final authority. It is not human speculation about God, but God's self-disclosure in Scripture. Contemporary testimonies are interesting, but finally inconsequential. When the two sources conflict, which one we accept as authoritative reflects our truer orientation.

Attempts by those who have minimal desire to sift Scripture to discover truths about the afterlife will come up with precious little to go on from near-death testimonies, for the conclusion of those who have tabulated out-of-the-body experiences recorded in various cultures is that they offer only glimpses rather than full-scale accounts and long-term narratives. Near-death testimonies show many similarities. Their focus, however, is always on the gate of heaven; they can't describe its interior. They have not gone that far.[8]

The tendency to relinquish the Bible as one's final authority is not just a recent phenomenon. In other generations people put similar weight on the fatuous findings of telepathic experts and the fulminations of tent evangelists. Making clergy spokesmen spiritual norms has resulted in rivaling Scripture as rule. Stereotypical revivalists have been depicted spending more time on the torments of hell than on the pleasures of heaven. That excess, real or imagined, justly lowered their credibility. In a comment which is now a popular quip in clergy groups, Reinhold Niebuhr (1892-1971) said that we can know as little about the furniture of heaven as we can calculate the temperature of hell.[9]

Others voice a guarded, mild skepticism about the possibility of knowing about the hereafter in depth. Some evangelicals are of this persuasion, such as the second successor of D. Martyn Lloyd-Jones at London's Westminister Chapel, R. T. Kendall. On the subject of heaven he hesitated to wager a specific position. "I agree with the man who said that we will know a lot more about heaven five minutes after we are there than all the speculation can tell us this side of heaven."[10] Wait a minute. That sounds like a dodge. Should we draw conclusions in eschatology from off-the-cuff comments of someone who hasn't bothered to search the Bible in a thorough manner?

Pervasive skepticism regarding arriving at sure knowledge may explain why segments of scholars have neglected the theme. Jürgen Moltmann, the German Reformed theologian, may have referred to both European and English churchmen, when he wrote, "Present-day Christian theology has not paid enough attention to the way heaven is talked about; and the Protestant theology of modern times has positively neglected heaven altogether."[11]

How we interpret the futuristic passages of Scripture is the crux of the problem. In 1986, Peter Toon of Britain published a valuable book, *Heaven and Hell: A Biblical and Theological Overview.* Colin Brown, Professor of Systematic Theology, Fuller Theological Seminary, found much value in the work, but took exception to some conclusions. The chief weakness of the book, he thought, was that Toon gave "exegesis without hermeneutics—or rather, exegesis which does not attempt to come to terms with hermeneutical questions."[12]

Brown's terms, of course, are household words in seminary halls, but they may be unfamiliar to the average reader. *Exegesis* is an exact reading out of what the biblical text says, and *hermeneutics* are the interpretative principles which stand behind meanings advanced. (Whenever you come across an unknown term, check the Glossary at the end of this book.)

Brown's questions go to the heart of differences in interpreting the Bible on heaven: "What is the nature of the language used? How do space-time concepts apply? How do we think of God in relation to heaven and hell?"[13] Moltmann and Brown expressed the same concern.

Neglect of an interpretative agenda in a book on heaven may lessen its value as a definitive treatment of the subject. And what Brown commented on Toon certainly applies to whole library shelves on heaven. Toon's book was framed for and pitched to those who have a background in theology. Even at that he saw no need to begin with a thorough hermeneutical *prolegomenon* (jargon for a technical introduction).

In this book, at select points, the matter of genre (the mode of writing being interpreted) and other interpretative issues have been raised, but not on the scale or depth which Brown and Moltmann desire.

Hermeneutical debates on how to interpret the symbols of Revelation can get heated. Our views of the future life are going to be off unless we interpret apocalyptic literature consistently as apocalyptic. Too many times Revelation is interpreted selectively apocalyptically. (This problem arises especially in the big numbers such as 144,000 and 1,000.)

Therefore, we ask ourselves, "When is the language to be taken literally? When are the expressions to be taken figuratively? Are fulfillments in the future or have they been progressively fulfilled? Need fulfillment be a once-only fulfillment? And what is the meaning of specific symbols?" These are some of the issues we eventually face. And underneath these are space/time questions, which mire all futuristic discussions. In chapter 4 (space) and in chapter 8 (time) fresh solutions to these problems have been offered.

Exegesis has not been done without hermeneutics, but neither have debates among professionals been allowed to deter us from coming to reasonable conclusions. Whether this is a success or failure, whether we conform or depart from the biblical standard and credible critical hermeneutics, is an outcome and future judgment one cannot fully anticipate. If what is presented enables the reader to understand the biblical teachings on heaven a smidgen better and enables us to integrate our view of heaven with what we have on earth, this will be regarded as a successful effort.

A more serious neglect, however, is to abandon the subject

altogether or to dismiss it as something that occupies a fanatical fringe in Christianity. Denominational representatives are so caught up hammering out yearly resolutions and in strategizing against social injustices that they have neglected to articulate a world view that includes how history is going to turn out.

We need more promoters of heaventalk. Even more, we need to return to the Scriptures and vigorously shake its branches for its heavenly fruit. But before we can be creatively engaged in serious interaction, we will need to familiarize ourselves with standardized terms.

The old excuse that we can't learn some new vocabulary has been pretty much blown away by the fact that our medical vocabulary has significantly increased without much pain. If we know medical words—as *carcinoma, osteoporosis, aneurysm,* and *emphysema*—why don't we learn some theological words? (In stretching our minds in a new direction there is no danger that they will snap.)

We should be willing to familiarize ourselves with the chief word for the future life. The word is *eschatology* (pronounced: es-ka-tology). Get used to using this word. Get the feel of it. Pronounce it. *Forever* is a street-smart partial equivalent for *eschatology. Forever,* however, is inadequate, for it is concerned with length, not with quality. *Eschatology,* on the other hand, is all about the *quality* of the future life. In expanding your mind, your assumptions may be challenged, which, in turn, will result in your coming into a new perspective.

If understanding eschatology is a snag or drag, avoidance of the subject of heaven is a more serious problem. Part of the neglect comes from those who discourage heavy reliance on the Scriptures. Consequently, we are lazily drifting to a medieval level of ignorance.

Scripture is God's Word on heaven and we turn to it before any book. The Bible is our compass here. We appeal to its descriptions over all others, for it is God's self-revelation.[14] The task we face is to compile biblical teaching, to sift through interpretive options, and to draw provisional conclusions that commend themselves to us because they are derived from solid evidence, sound scholarship, and a careful scrutinizing of the biblical text.

To retreat from exploring heaven with the excuse that our test procedures are incapable of producing trustworthy results is to give up too easily on the Bible, which is more rewarding than we realize. Though heaven appears in the Bible sparingly, it is not the kind of scarcity that justifies silence. As we shall see, God has supplied us with ample revelation on what heaven is about, but it takes patience to fit the pieces into a meaningful, faithful, coherent whole. Twenty-one often-asked questions are discussed in this book. What bothers people seems a good place to start.

Silence on heaven by clergymen is puzzling. The pulpit is where one would expect to hear more about heaven. Yet, to the loss of the flock, the matter is passed over briefly, if mentioned at all. Some preachers overcompensate with relentless talk about the future. "Prophetic" topics (by which they mean futuristic topics), such as the "rapture," "the tribulation," "Ezekiel's temple," and "the millennium" are their trademark. To focus on heaven itself, we have not dealt in depth with these matters. However, comment on them has been unavoidable. Some of them impinge on our subject. Extra reflections and resources are found in the notes. An Appendix on the millennium has been provided, because, in our view, the millennium of Revelation 20 is a description of the Intermediate State of heaven (which is the time between Christ's first coming and his final second coming).

Ministers need to address future-life questions with more courage. Some may avoid the subject as an unconscious compensation mechanism. Perhaps their reluctance to tackle the subject is a reaction against those whose futuristic timetables are absurdly absolutistic and subtly arrogant. In seeking a balance they may have slipped into a verbal brownout and may have ended with a complete blackout.

In other cases, the neglect is a sign that the biblical roots of the Christian faith are regarded as unreliable. If the Bible is not trustworthy, then nothing of finality can be said about anything, including God and Christ, as well as the hereafter. The argument goes: since everything in the Bible is time-conditioned, then we must give Scripture qualified authority and limited usage. Thus, many neo-Protestants are unashamedly silent on heaven or they take positions colored by eastern religions and New Age speculations.

As they see it, the very introduction of heaven in the Bible was to take a man's mind off his problems and miseries. The slaves of the eighteenth century sang about heaven because it helped ease the pain of their servitude. This form of debunking, however, lacks credibility, for according to the biblical perspective heaven existed before man or pain.

Although many black congregations both retain and revel in "heaven" in the late twentieth century, other blacks, especially but not exclusively in the late 1960s, felt the focus should be more upon cleaning up the hell of earth. Joblessness, malnutrition, unfair housing practices, drug dependency, and the plight of single parents, they argued, should preempt heaven talk. James H. Cone, for instance, wrote in 1969, "The idea of heaven is irrelevant for black theology."[15] The critical downplaying of heaven, he felt, was necessary for blacks to address their economic suffering.

The author of Revelation had a similar feeling of helplessness in facing his adverse circumstances. The isle of Patmos was John's prison (Rev. 1:9). But his troubles did not scare him from the heaven cause. He was pursued by heaven in the midst of his hell. Revelation did not come to him as an escapist safety valve, nor did he devise the visions as a technique to make his readers feel better. It was Christ's own disclosure of the dynamics of human behavior and of the destiny of the church, under God's hand. Because of God's control of history they would both survive and surmount the ordeals occasioned by their witness for Christ.

A dosage of biblical eschatology, which honors the contribution of Revelation, will do much to prepare the modern Christian for ongoing and imminent trials.

Disinformation on Revelation's alleged pointlessness has been detrimental and a disservice. Hans Küng has written that Revelation is too complex, too much a conglomerate to make study of it fruitful.[16] (Yet at another time he did not abandon images entirely.[17]) Küng stated that images in Revelation are too inexact to warrant conclusions about heaven. He considered arriving at any reliable information about heaven from studying Revelation hopeless. He never bothered, however, to substantiate his claim that nothing certain could come out of Revelation. Therefore, his advice should not be gulped down but spit out.

The last book of the Bible is not as baffling as Küng would make out. Admittedly, some of the images are hard to fathom, yet others, through checking previous reflections on the matter, yield helpful insights and trustworthy anticipations.

A large number of conflicting meanings are due to lack of theological focus and to a failure to grasp the presence and importance of the book's repetitions. Thus, before we try to make sense of the visions, we must work through the matter of how the visions are to be perceived. "Do they follow like ducks in a row, or are they layered like a wedding cake? Do they talk of events as sequential, or are the same events and forces, covering the time between Christ's first and second coming, looked at from different perspectives making them seem like different events?"

Some have argued that Revelation follows a strict chronological sequence. For them after 4:1 everything is future. Others disagree. We shall present evidence in the next chapter why a strict chronology is *not* used in Revelation. An overlap of various periods of time emerge in Revelation, rather than a tight chronological log.

Against consistency and rules of polished prose, John did not hesitate to mix his metaphors, to reverse logical sequences, even to switch genders and cases (known as "solecisms"). He took freedom to use words evocatively and elastically rather than one-way-only exactly. Therefore to take his book "literally" we must *not be* literal, for apocalypse form is misused and the meaning distorted when we take literally what is used symbolically. Conversely, Scripture's historical and hortatory sections should be interpreted literally rather than symbolically.

The evocative material past Revelation chapter 3 is not straight prose! Shifting interpretive gears is probably the hardest task facing each reader. We know it is a difficulty we find disagreeable because even popular theological writers lapse into straight-line literalism in the interpretation of Revelation. What John described had a depth that defied all speech. Therefore, he felt justified in ignoring proper Greek grammar and in not repeating the same truths the same way throughout the book.

What we find, therefore, in Revelation is what American football players would call ball-carrier cut-backs and reverse-field running with themes, for the author returns to truths time after time but with different twists. This includes not only chronological back tracking (which we will deal with in chapter 1), but even departures from logical order within verses (such as 3:17, where the result of getting rich is put before the process of getting rich, and 10:4, where the sealing up is before the writing).

In space terminology John's apocalypse resembles zero gravity. Movement is effortless from one enigmatic form to another. Linear time lines, as in outer space, are not adhered to.[18] A literalistic mind-set would prevent us from following his prophetic acrobatic maneuvers. G. E. Ladd wrote,

> [Revelation] retraces history under the guise of prophecy. [For example] the beast is Rome and at the same time an eschatological antiChrist which cannot be fully equated with historical Rome.[19]

In dealing with Revelation we find confirmed an established hermeneutical rule that biblical predictions are fulfilled, then fulfilled again (biblical promise always has an overflow element), and beyond the serial fulfillment there is the final consummation. In concrete terms, this means that the shadow of the final Antichrist has impacted on the world throughout its history, and the dirt clouds of Armageddon have been swirling throughout the confrontations of the Gospel with unbending, spiritually alienated humans. Reduplication of the Revelation record both suggests and requires this approach.

The multi-dimensional, bizarre, esoteric combinations witness to a reality greater than what data sifters can detect. *En toto* the Book of Revelation witnesses to a reality greater than human capacity to describe or comprehend. The bottom line of the visions is that a spiritual dynamism runs through all that has been, all that is, and all that will be.

> Our ideas about heaven may be vague, insubstantial, and one-dimensional, but when we compare the real heaven with earth, it is earth that is vague, insubstantial, and one-dimensional.[20]

Scripture's cross-cultural and paradoxical phrasing on heaven makes meanings multiple rather than murky and misty. It is not the mystery of fog but of sunshine. It is more complexity than confusion. Its depths come clearer, not by the neglect of detail but by attention to it. Some of its intimations tease more than tell and some of its sketches are of the nature of prototypes and prods. Nevertheless, we are encouraged to find nourishment, stimulation, and comfort in Revelation.

Admissions by authors, speakers, and readers that our views, at best, are provisional would inject a healthy modesty and foster even-temperedness vital to mutual understanding. Otherwise dogmatism can escalate into demagoguery, and demagoguery can degenerate into donnybrooks. Sometimes televangelists, who strut and sweat on the stage, express a dogmatism on heaven that the critical listener finds more disgusting than disturbing.

We should never let intemperate futurist presentations cause us to back off or shy away from one of the grandest themes of theological inquiry. Nor should we pull up short from the hot pursuit of truth because of the skepticism of others.

Those with a low view of Scripture have an analogy that goes: heaven is a jigsaw puzzle with most of the pieces missing. Their bottom line: drop the subject. Supporters of the saying come across as having a picture of heaven in mind, for how would they know what pieces are missing? In addition, wouldn't one have to have a total picture in mind to know when it is incomplete? The real problem may be that the pieces that are contained in the Bible don't fit into what they want!

Though God's self-revelation in the Bible is partial (not even sixty-six books can fully contain God!), what we have provides reliable parameters and safe guides. What Scripture says about the future deserves our closest attention and serious acceptance.

Appreciation of heaven is frequently highest among those nearing death. Suffering both increases our desire for heaven and prepares us for it. John Bradford (1510-1555), less than five months before his fiery departure from life for preaching the gospel in violent times, wrote to a friend of the glories of heaven he anticipated:

> I am assured that though I want here, I have riches there; though I hunger here, I shall have fullness there; though I faint here, I shall be refreshed there; and though I be accounted here as a dead man, I shall there live in perpetual glory.
>
> That is the city promised to the captives whom Christ shall make free; that is the kingdom assured to them whom Christ shall crown; there is the light that shall never go out; there is the health that shall never be impaired; there is the glory that shall never be defaced; there is the life that shall taste no death; and there is the portion that passes all the world's preferment. There is the world that shall never wax worse; there is every want supplied freely without money; there is not danger, but happiness, and honour, and singing, and praise and thanksgiving unto the heavenly Jehovah, "to him that sits on the throne," "to the lamb" that here was led to the slaughter, that now "reigns;" with whom I "shall reign" after I have run this comfortless race through this miserable earthly vale.[21]

We wrongly imagine that heaven is a subject that concerns only those with a mystical bent or bias. Heaven is the Christian's favorite land, the beatific vision, *visio Dei*, the ultimate sight. Whether living in tranquil or troubled times, the Christian should have heaven on his mind. The Bible encourages us to consider our glorious future with God. If heaven is not considered worthy of attention before we read Scripture, we cannot read the Bible without being rebuked for that neglect, for there the saints were inspired by its reality, cheered by its rich relationships, and motivated to endurance by its promises. It is when we look to men too much that we look up to heaven too little.

Why we have an interest in heaven is explained differently by the Bible compared to every other religion. According to the

Bible heaven reaches us before we reach heaven. Our search is initiated by God. He reaches inside us as we reach out to study his Word. In the Bible, it is not that we discover God but that he discovers us. It is never that we penetrate heaven, but that heaven first penetrates us. That is the only way the quest will begin. Biblical religion is not man getting hold of God, but God getting hold of man.

Heaven comes to us, before we come to heaven. Not only are we promoting heaven's filling when Christ is heard, but in the overflow of heaven's power we are drawn into its orbit. Heaven probes us more thoroughly than we probe heaven. God loves us before we love him. He accepts us before we receive him. The Christian life is as much an expression of heaven as a pursuit of heaven.

Scripture, therefore, is not another way of man's viewing God, but God's self-revelation, God's giving to man what he could not uncover on his own. In Christianity the biblical text is the theological given, the source book of our information about heaven. Heaven has revealed heaven, otherwise we cannot know it as a reliable reality. This perspective, therefore, raises what follows above the level of another man's speculation. I have tried to have my mind brought into conformity to what God has revealed in the Bible. Otherwise, guesswork proliferates and the reader thinks his word is equal to the writings of the apostles.

We may not agree together on some details of the afterlife, but one purpose of this study is to compel dealing with essential matters we have not addressed with enough enthusiasm in the past.

This book presents heaven from the questioners' viewpoint. In responding to twenty-one knotty questions on heaven, valuable comments have been culled from a wide expanse of church history and from various theological writings. Thus, this approach is a blend of apologetics and dogmatic theology and differs from the approach of a systematic theologian who would amass all the verses in the Bible on heaven and present a system. Nor is this approach that of the biblical theologian, who subsectionally examines the relevant texts author by author and book by book. These disciplines are drawn on but are not represented here.

The book is composed of three basic divisions. The first, titled, *The Ignition Stage,* SITUATIONAL, deals with the matter of how Revelation is best approached. The launch determines the outcome. Unless we agree how Revelation was meant to be taken, we shall differ widely on the nature of the hereafter. Differences on hermeneutical principles in the study of Revelation account for the fact that Christians have not agreed on what heaven will be like and what other aspects of the future hold.

Crucial to this approach is seeing the book as a pastoral document, rather than a horoscope for earth. The immediate situation of the readers is infrequently or slightly referred to by futurists. But, just as importantly, from our viewpoint, the immediate situation of the readers had vital bearing on the future expressions of God's wisdom, sovereignty, and justice. I don't deny the future elements of the unveiling (the meaning of "apocalypse" or Revelation) but neither do I think the immediate situation is minimal. First-century applications do not rule out overlap fulfillments and climactic conclusions.

The middle portion of the book addresses those questions about which the Bible has most to say with one exception. *The Booster Stage,* EXPOSITIONAL portion, deals with the most important questions, though not always the most popular ones. The eleven questions in this section are more basic than the final nine (including the Appendix). And one of the questions (time in eternity) is included here because it is foundational to the discussion on music in heaven (chap. 9). Chapter 8 (time) touches many aspects of the book. It has definite ties, too, with the interpretation of Revelation as well as with the understanding of the final heaven discussed in Part 3.

The final section, called *Midcourse Corrections*, INFERENTIAL, examines the questions frequently avoided by many Christians. The avoidance is often due to the hesitation to indulgence in drawing inferences.

The questions in the INFERENTIAL section are among the most frequently asked. They are the knottiest of the knotty questions. Christians should be unafraid to face them.

After our most industrious inquiries we confess that on earth "we know in part." Our anticipations of heaven are surely less than proximate. Of heaven Godfrey Thring wrote: "Where in joys unthought of, saints with angels sing." Bernard of Cluny wrote: "What radiancy of glory, what bliss beyond compare." What is presented here is in the right direction, although I concede there will be many surprises when I, by grace, join the company of the church triumphant.

We would miss out on much to leapfrog the first two sections to delve into the last nine questions. The earlier chapters provide a better basis for addressing the final ones. By working through the first twelve chapters we meet facts and factors which would enable discussions on the final nine chapters to be more productive and profitable. Therefore, the discipline of working sequentially should be encouraged.

Christians should refuse to cruise below the ozone layer of popular speculations. We should probe and penetrate the outward-bound biblical given.

1

The
Ignition
Stage

SITUATIONAL

1

But Isn't Revelation Too Difficult to Follow ?

*R*evelation is the all-time Christian masterpiece on the hereafter. It is a ride into worlds unknown, but without the bitter side-effects of chemically induced hallucinations and without the distortions of sin-infused psyches. Near-death "revelations" cannot begin to improve, supplement, fortify, or replace the finest Christian vehicle that has penetrated spiritual space.

Revelation is a trip that enabled John to see history in a new light. It is not world history laid out end-to-end. Its canvass is not of world movements but of other-world movements, and how God resolves them. John is in the book, but it is not his diary. It is not a dated document with only minor significance for our time. It is not bad dreams put on paper, but it is a dramatization of sin's failure to put out the Light of the World, of how God preserves his church and pulverizes the wicked, and of how Christ triumphs, reigns, and vanquishes evil.

The first eleven chapters of Revelation describe a life-and-death struggle of Satan for spiritual supremacy. Satan is on the attack against Christ's agents. But chapters 12-20, on a deeper level, show Satan's focus of hatred is against the personage behind the church—Christ himself. John saw behind the political scenes to detect horrendous power struggles. The conflicts were cosmic.

The larger picture of spiritual forces enables the reader to identify with the cause of Christ, rather than view it as an attempt to isolate prominent personalities as "fall guys." It is not a first-century expose of political figures (athough some rulers are alluded to), but the disclosure of God's determination to validate and vindicate those in Christ's care—his afflicted church—who have been victimized by institutions and individuals infected with evil.

The reader becomes attached to the book to the degree that he sees himself in it. We are *in* it. "All well and good," someone says, "but what do we get *out of* it?" The practicality of the book is a modern reader's first concern. But that requires that the reader settle his own spiritual direction. If we are not on the side of Christ, then the detailed symbolism is lost even on the erudite scholar.

For those who know whose "side" they are on, to insure personal gain in reading Revelation we should get our minds used to, if not into, the apocalyptic gear. As every space launch requires preparation, so we cannot board John's Revelation vehicle and expect to go along for a nondizzy ride without some in-flight, if not preflight, knowledge. Those who have aborted reading past, say, the fifth chapter, may have done so because they haven't been prepped with an overview.

Need the book be closed to us? Do we have to wait until we

take a course in the future life before we read Revelation? Will we be kept in the dark until the world's last day dawns?

None of the above. After all the original readers were ordinary people. Admittedly, the apocalyptic genre ("genre" means form of writing) is strange to us in our hard-data world. There is some getting used to "apocalypse" form. We should acquaint ourselves with the characteristics of apocalpyse. To make sense of the flight plan and to have some idea about its intended purpose, preparation is advisable. Time spent in becoming acquainted with apocalyptic style and with the intentions of the writer is time well spent. (The Introduction gives an idea of how apocalypse is to be distinguished from historical writings.)

A frequent response is to back away from the Book of Revelation. The seven bowls of Revelation may have all the frustration and unreasonable task of trying to unravel a bowl of spaghetti. To others the book is like a Gordian knot best cut with a butcher knife from an editor's kitchen and left as a worthless heap. But, Revelation is more a timber-hitch knot, which most tenderfoot Christians can learn to untie, if they are persistent enough. We let our fears unduly tie our hands from receiving the blessings of the book.

Of course, inquiring into heaven puts us on the spot. Are we willing to make the effort to learn John's way of expressing ideas? Will we risk the transition from the gravity pull of historical interpretations to the zero gravity of apocalyptic space? Too many have been willfully victimized by a Catch-22 situation. "People do not understand prophecy, simply because they do not study it; and then they refuse to study it because they do not understand it."[1]

Understanding the book is not an insurmountable task. By determining the main issues, the parts more easily fall into place and break forth with fresh, lasting, and vital meaning. It is when there is no overview that confusion rules. We need to realize that a grasp of the book is a manageable challenge. It need not be a frustrating task, a fatiguing experience, ending as a fruitless time-waster.

What I present is not a commentary on Revelation but a perspective. We must have a justifiable perspective regarding apocalyptic writing for our understanding of it to "fly."

We cannot escape this demand. We may not wish to take side trips, tracing out an Old Testament allusion or pondering over each fascinating figure, but we cannot avoid dealing with the overall directions of the various visions. Heaven and Revelation are all-of-a-piece. It is impossible to arrive at a Christian view of heaven without considering specific passages in Revelation. But we cannot make sense of specific passages until we see them in the total context of the book.

At the start we need to allay some fears. Revelation arose, originally, to answer questions, not to increase them. Unlike Paul in Romans, who in the fashion of Jewish diatribe style, anticipated eleven key questions of his readers, Revelation is an indirect answer to the troubling questions that came to Christians as they faced the hostility of anti-Christians. Why were those chosen for heaven having a hard time? Why were loyal followers of Christ abused? How is Jesus in control of churches, and what will be the outcome of moral history? Where will it all end, and who will overcome? What forms will the hereafter show?

The best procedure to begin with is to recognize that everything in Revelation is not tangled. Some of the symbols are too obvious for comment (1:8, 17; 19:11, 13, 14). At other times, the meanings are given (1:12 [see 2:1, 5]; 1:18 [see 9:1,2]; 1:20; 2:11 [see 20:6; 21:8]; 3:12 [see 21:2, 9, 10]; 4:5; 5:6; 7:13, 14; 8:3, 4; 12:3, 9 [see 20:2, 7]; 14:8 [see 16:1, 19]; 14:20 [see 19:15]; 17:9, 10, 12, 15; 19:8; 20:2, 8; 20:14, 15). Admittedly, some of the figures are gruesome (9:7-11; 12:3, 4; 13:1); others are grandiose (11:8; 16:21; 18:12); others are garbled (15:2);

still others are grotesquely humorous (16:13, 14—an army led by three frogs; 17:9—a woman sitting on seven mountains).

Everyone agrees that Revelation is a book about the future. But the question is *which* future? Does it describe a more immediate future or a more remote future (1:3; 3:11; 4:1; 12:10; 22:7, 12, 20)? In checking the latter references one discovers that the author was writing primarily for what was soon to be—impending happenings. Some of what was future for the writer, of course, now is past.

Our own lift-off into the same thought territory will be stalled or aborted unless we have settled on which trajectory John took so that we can follow him in our simulated reliving of what he saw. Which way we approach the book partly determines what we make of it. How we use the book determines what we say about heaven. Before we can explore John's vantage point on heaven, we need to settle on how the seven visions in Revelation fit. How are they coordinated?

There are two basic ways Revelation is perceived.[2] One approach is to stress that the visions were meant to be kept end to end, and that the book should be read like an airline flight schedule. Those who follow this approach see the book as a development, in linear fashion, from past to present to future. Chart A (after the Glossary) represents this viewpoint. Hal Lindsey represents the *chronological* approach.

Is Revelation a divine time line spelled out? The other approach (which doesn't get as much attention as it should) is the *contrapuntal* approach. "Contrapuntal" is a musical term. It describes the style of music made famous by Johann Sebastian Bach (1685-1750), in which there are tiers of melodies going on at the same time, but they present a harmonious whole. Charts B and C illustrate this approach. This other approach sees the visions as overlays. In a contrapuntal layout there is deliberate overlap.

Advocates of both approaches find justification in the key

verse, Revelation 1:19. To see how the two approaches interpret this verse, we shall have a better grasp of how they view the entire book.

> Write therefore the things which you have seen, and the things which are, and the things which shall take place after these things (1:19, NASB).

The Chronological Approach

Revelation 1:19 is said to contain the author's own outline of the book, and that the book proceeds from (1) things seen to (2) things present to (3) things to come. Chapter 1, in this view, deals with what the author had seen. Chapters 2-3 dealt with matters in the present, and chapters 4–22 deal with things future. Hal Lindsey's books carry the detailed arguments of this approach. John Walvoord's writings, though less flamboyant, provide better argumentation for the chronologists.

There are serious flaws with the chronological approach, although it first seems the best way. A quick glance at the various chapters shows its weaknesses. Notice that Christ in 1:12-18 is seen as powerful and glorious, similar to Christ as he appears at his second coming (19:12, 15, 16). One of Jesus' names is "The Last" (1:17; 22:13). The Last *(eschatos)* has come. The end is the Person of Christ. Jesus came into history at Bethlehem. He began the last days, because he was, is, and forever shall be last. (Incidentally, the word *eschatology* comes from the Greek word *eschatos,* which means "last.") The continuity of Christ comes through Revelation. What he was in chapter 1, he is in chapter 21 and 22. Christ continues to be the thirst quencher (21:6; 22:17) and the healing agent (22:2).

Revelation has a back-and-forth motion. If the book were wired to a medical oscillograph, which shows physicians the action of the human heart, we would notice in Revelation a repeated pattern with variations. The oscillations of the book can be charted, but they are charts of similar things with dissimilar intensity and detail. In addition, what is said to be ended in one section, reappears in another. For instance, take the displacement and reappearance of Christ's enemies. The final "shoot-out" or "fire fight" said to begin with a mustering of men by Satan to attempt the overthrow of Christ's rule is early indicated in 16:14, alluded to again in 19:19, but phrased more specifically and finally in 20:8. The wicked nations are said to be destroyed in 16:14-16 and in 19:21, yet they reappear as not destroyed in 20:7-9. There is no contradiction when one realizes that the book repeats itself and the three descriptions are not meant to be understood as sequential. This is one indicator that the chronological approach is flawed. There are others.

Chapter 4 is said by advocates of this view to be the beginning of the exclusively future section of the book. But chapter 4 describes the pre-Christmas heavenly state, before Christ was born of a woman. Chapter 5 is a description of the heavenly scene immediately following Christ's enthronement following his ascension. Note: he had already overcome death (5:9, 12).

Moreover, chapter 12 should have the effect of a bop on the head for those who sleepily, unthinkingly, and complacently have accepted the contention that everything beyond chapter 4 is future. The chronological approach, after one reads the references to Christ's earthly life, should fall flat, for chapter 12 depicts in dramatic form the saving of David's offspring, Christ, out of the ordeal of death. The escape Christ experienced came after his death and was in his resurrection-ascension (12:5). His resurrection-ascension was in the past!

The repetition of the themes of the judgment and annihilation of the wicked argue strongly for readers to abandon a strict chronological scheme. To spread out Revelation, as so many prophecy charts do, with neat divisions, time-table precision, assuming that different names and descriptions mean different events, is patently forced. Whatever charts are used, they should never be made of cement and used as concrete mindwalks. Any chart aims to simplify and, by the same token, falls prey to oversimplification.

Theological considerations apart, the grammar of Revelation gives additional embarrassment and damage to the chronological approach. For instance, take the futuristic aorist or the proleptic future tense (*see* the Glossary) in Revelation which was used by John in his vision telling. It appears in several key places and has ramifications for the issue of the chronological vs. the contrapuntal approach: 7:9-17; 10:7; 11:15; 15:1; 19:6-10; 20:6.[3] The feature of this tense is that it speaks of the future as already done, past. The proleptic future underscores the certainty of the victory Christ will secure. To the writer the future triumph was so sure that in his mind it had already happened. Traditional time was clearly an embarrassment to the writer John, for he had crossed the time line. The grammar of the book militates against a strict chronological interpretation.

Apocalypse has no respect for chronology. Not only is this seen in the use of the proleptic tense, but it is also seen in the writer's anticipation of events through the interludes that intersperse the major visions. For instance the vision beginning at 8:1 is preceded by the anticipation of God's people being brought through safely from the coming crisis (7:9-17). Again, after the judgments of the six trumpets and before the seventh final one, there occurs an extended or a double preface, covering chapters 10 and 11:1-13, in which John seeks to encourage Christians not to give up by assuring them by presenting both deliverance of the persecuted and the following heavenly victory party.

What was originally suggested in good faith by chronologists to help make Revelation understandable, therefore, doesn't do justice to the book's genre, grammar, style, and arrangements. As the British evangelical Donald Guthrie concluded, "It is impossible to trace [a chronological] order throughout the whole book."[4]

The Contrapuntal Approach

Again, look at Revelation 1:19. Instead of it describing three categories, it is mentioning two.

What you have seen, that is, what is now.

What will be hereafter or after these things.

The middle phrase—"what is now"—explains the first phrase (this feature is called "epexegetical"). Others, however, see that the explanation is given in the last two phrases. "What you have seen" is described as "what is now and what shall be hereafter."

In either case, it ought not to be overlooked that the significance of *"shortly"* in verse 1 by the author makes it probable that he did not think of his writing as applying exclusively to late time as much as to his own time (1:3; 22:6, 7, 12, 20). Too many Christians minimize this feature.

How do the two approaches compare as methods of interpretation? In the chronological approach, the purpose is telescopic, that is, seeing down the time tube. In the contrapuntal approach, the purpose is kaleidoscopic, that is, all the little pieces are the same throughout, but take on different shapes. Another way to view the contrapuntal school of interpretation is that it is like Scotch plaid. It is all the same, but with different patterns. It is based on the principle of repetitions with differences, recapitulation with variety, review with progress. Thus, the recognizable variety establishes that the repetitions are not unthinking redundance or hackneyed restatements. They allow the reader to view eschatological reality from various camera angles, thus making Revelation the most dialectic book in the entire New Testament.

Several themes are recapitulated. The final battle between good and evil is found in 16:14-16, 19:19, 20, and 20:7-9. These are not separate events, but the same confrontations appearing in different parts of the book. As on other matters, it is characteristic of Revelation to refer to the same phenomenon by different expressions, such as Armageddon and Gog and Magog. The book describes the final judgment at the concluding portion of the seven sections: the final judgment is found in 6:12-17, in 11:15, 18, in 14:17-20, in 16:20, 21, in 19:11-21, and in 20:11-15.

Martyrdom is another recurring reference (2:7; 3:12, 21; 5:9; 7:4-9, 13-15; 11:9; 12:17; 13:7, 15; 20:6). American Christians, who are accustomed to prosperity and peace, cannot easily accept that their rights under the Bill of Rights may not always be secure. But where will upper middle-class, tranquil Christians stand when Satan organizes and unites both secular and religious authorities against Christians just prior to Christ's second coming (Rev. 20:7-9)? We would like to put these matters out of our minds, but we cannot put them out of Revelation.

Yesterday's history, today's reality, and tomorrow's probability would end with Christ and his own on the victory side (16:12; 19:19; 20:8), which is the overall theme of the book. The final heavenly state (Infinite) is anticipated in the Intermediate State (4:10, 11; 5:11-14; 7:9-17; 12:9-17; 15:1-4; 20:1-10). Chapters 12 and 20 are specifically on the Intermediate State and chapters 21 and 22 form the top stones of the final heavenly state, which issues into the new heavens and the new earth.

Because American evangelicalism is dominated by the chronological approach, few seem to know that the reduplication approach has a long history and has much more to commend it over the straight-line methodology of dispensational explanations.

Recapitulation was used by John in the first century. Interpreters didn't verbalize about it until the third/fourth centuries, represented by Victorinus of Pettau, a Christian writer who died under Emperor Diocletian (284-305). Victorinus commented that Revelation presents a series of events from a variety of viewpoints. Augustine (354-430) and Dutch exegete Campigius Vitringa (1659-1722) used this approach. The symbols differ, but they cover the same events. Because the recapitulation format of Revelation is not rigorously followed, the evangelical public has been deluged with a bewildering assortment of chronological eschatological speculations. When recapitulation is recognized and applied, it has the effect of Occam's razor, that is, it cuts off a lot of unnecessary ideas. Happily, on occasion, one finds a historical premillennialist who acknowledges the recapitulation principle.[5]

One of the easier charts to follow is Chart C. John's seven visions are compared to seven weeks.[6] Each set of seven ended with a Sabbath, and each was interspersed with interludes that both anticipate what is to follow and give hymnic responses to the power and grace of God to be demonstrated in the next sequence. Keep in mind these seven weeks are not end to end, but like a movie cartoonist, use a series of overlays that add more color, detail, and show movement. The end result is the feature film, the sum total of the separate frames.

We must step back from this discussion for a moment to consider what John assumes of the readers of Revelation. John intended readers to know what Christian theology is being symbolized, else symbolical associations are lost. He builds on established inferences from the body of theology.[7] Read Romans and the Gospel of John to get grounded in the main tenets of apostolic Christianity.

The blessing promised in 1:3 is not really a *carte blanche* blessing, for John takes it for granted that informed believers are the readers. The invitation should override and allay fears that Revelation fosters and sanctions weird opinions. Some people recoil from reading Revelation because of the wild conclusions Charles Manson drew from it.

Charles Manson, obviously, showed no acceptance of the gospel before August 1969, when, according to those inside the Manson gang, he drew the inference that the locusts of Revelation 9 were the Beatles and the seal (9:4) on the forehead, which protected people from the deadly sting, designated Manson supporters. The third part of mankind that would die (9:15) would be those who would die in Helter Skelter.[8]

Where we begin spiritually determines where we come out in our understanding of Revelation. The book begins with a blessing (1:3) and ends with a warning (22:18, 19). We reap blessings if we read the book aright, and we reap personal loss if we read into the book (adding) and read out of the book (deny what it says as having truth value). In both cases inferences are involved. Some are valid; others are invalid. What runs through both the blessing and the warning is the same belief that the words of Revelation are from Christ—not just about Christ. It is the *revelation* of Jesus Christ to John. Readers must be alert not to trespass Christ's word (that is, supplementing, which results in contradicting him) and must be careful not to fall short of Christ's word (by not following through the implications).

Given Revelation, we should not impose on it draftsman expectations. We should not expect it to have the precision of an architect's blueprints, nor the accumulated travel data of a captain's log. A consistently literalistic approach distorts the message of the book. Take, for instance, its use of numbers. Seven is a recurring symbolic number. The number 666 has a symbolic meaning. So does 144,000, and 1,000! Literalists will have no problem in seeing the lower numbers symbolic, but when it comes to 144,000 and 1,000, then, all of a sudden, they switch back to thinking in terms of literal 144,000 and literal 1,000.[9] Some people are not rigorous enough in seeing that *all* numbers in Revelation are to be seen in the apocalyptic framework. This is especially true following the more hortatory (injunction) section of Revelation (chapters 1 through 3). Not assigning mathematical value to 1,000 years, for instance, best honors the intentions of the author.

Many will disagree with me on this point. But it seems to me that there must be consistency in approaching all of the Revelation, which is more apocalypse than prophecy (declaration) after chapter 4. Essential in making sense out of Revelation is that it is not meant to be interpreted in a literalistic fashion.

Revelation 20 is probably the most controversial chapter in the Bible. The chapter cannot be understood correctly in isolation from the rest of Revelation. Especially important is the bearing of chapter 12 on chapter 20. By comparing 12:9 with 13:1 and 20:1-3, one finds the multifaceted way Satan's reduced freedom was described. In 12:9 Satan is thrown down, in 13:1 he is stranded on the shoreline of God's decrees, and in 20:1-3 he is chained. Before we look into these matters in more detail, we need to allay fears readers have about inference drawing.

Weird interpretations may cause some readers to shy away from drawing inferences and forming conclusions. We should beware of deceptively attractive but unfounded inferences on the subject of heaven;[10] however, we should not throw out inference drawing.

Inference drawing is not a disrespectful meddling into areas where God has barred human inquiry. The refusal to draw inferences in Scripture does not honor Scripture, but is in violation of Scripture. The writer of Revelation urges his readers to draw conclusions. He says so in the phrase literally translated "hither [or here is] the mind with wisdom" in 17:19. The same idea appears more cryptically in 13:18 and 14:12.

We are not to suppose that John is encouraging wild guesses. Responsible coming-to-grips with what is said and that validly argued, rather than radical speculations, are commended. To call a conclusion "an inference" is not to overthrow it, anymore than to call an opinion "a theory" overthrows the theory. Don't forget, whereas some theories of origin lack evidence, atomic theory has worked consistently.

A green light for inference drawing is found throughout the book. John, for instance, fully expected his readers to infer that the twenty-four elders have left their thrones (4:4) to throw themselves down before God's throne (4:10), although it does not specifically say they left their seats.

The writer forces us to draw an inference about the takedown of Satan in Revelation 12 and of the binding of Satan in Revelation 20. From comparing these verses, we cannot rightfully infer that Satan's binding is total. From a comparison of the representative functioning of the satanic "bad guy" beasts (13:1 and 11) we infer that both the figurative hurling (12:9) and stranded voyager (13:1) are not meant to mean that Satan's curtailment is total. The rage of the Prince of darkness against the saints is unabated (12:10, 12, 17). In the light of 12:10, 12, 17; 13:7; 20:7 the forces of evil are presented as still working but in a reduced capacity. And it is said they will continue to be in operation until the powers of evil are fully and finally destroyed.

Don't deplore inference drawing, but be aghast at the action of unnoticed assuming. Assumptions are what force Scripture into preconceived notches. At least in validly drawn inferences, some attention is given to the text. But assumptions are unproven ideas imported from elsewhere. In assuming, however, omissions of the text are filled in with concepts from outside. Though the text doesn't have what they claim, the assumption is that the author meant what the interpreter says. Interpretations are first assumed, then imposed, then said to be taught by the passage being considered.

One of the results in reading through this book on heaven, we hope, will be that we have discovered that views we once held as sacrosanct have no basis in the Scriptures, and that we have been kindly but unwittingly conned. We may wake up to having ingested from our particular traditions and training an eschatological scheme, and accepted it without question, only to be shocked that it isn't really in the text.

Die-hard literalists, however, are not going to roll over and admit having misinterpreted. People do not easily eat crow. Few would openly admit to having been misled. Some have career investments to preserve. But we will be forced to restudy what we once accepted as the only position. Perhaps reading this book will open our eyes to what we haven't been told and thus begin a new leg in our spiritual journey.

To get that journey in Revelation headed right, realize one part of the book helps to explain another part. We have been dealing with the important twelfth chapter. Chapter 12 is pivotal for interpreting chapter 20, the famous chapter (indeed, the only chapter in the Bible) where Christ's one-thousand-year reign is mentioned. The parallels between chapters 12 and 20 are significant, but too frequently missed or denied. To understand chapter 20 we need to understand chapter 12. Both are in the nature of reviews or recaps regarding the messianic age (inaccurately referred to by some as the "Church Age," as if the church were not in the Old Testament).

Chapter 12 is said, by dispensationalists, to refer to Israel, that is, the national entity.[11] This assertion is partially based on their prior assumption that the church was "raptured" at Revelation 4:1.[12] In their approach to Revelation 12, where

Satan is said to be cast down, they take to mean that Satan is cast down to the earth to be active, not cast down to the earth as a sign of defeat. But defeat was the intention of the phrase "cast down" (mentioned four times in 12:9, 10).

"Hurled" meant defeat, not just a new location of operation. The frenzied fury of the dragon was proof of his having lost the war. Satan's defeat was being celebrated. Otherwise, if it were a mere "going down," it would be absolutely ludicrous to sing about it (which is the form of 12:10-12). Thus Satan's defeat was witnessed two ways. First, as a slanderer Satan's abusive mouth was shut up in heaven, (12:10) and, secondly, as a slayer Satan was shut off on earth (13:1).

Calvin R. Schoonhoven pointed out that Jewish eschatological expectations are absent in chapter 12, and that it is totally occupied with the spiritual conquest of Satan. The birth signified the incarnation (12:2), the snatch signified the ascension (12:5), consequently, the casting down signified the defeat of Satan in Christ's atonement (12:7-12).[13] Satan's defeat was the guarantee of the church's safety (12:14-16) and in Satan's isolation from the church, pictured in 13:1, he was as a downed dragon stuck on the shoreline of God's decrees.

Dispensationalists stress the literal location where Satan is hurled and miss the point that the hurling was a defeat. Because of this, they do not identify the throwing down of 12:7-9, 13 with the binding of 20:1-3.

A literalistic approach affects other matters in Revelation 12. For instance, the meaning of "desert" (12:14). "Desert" is not seen to be solely symbol. They insist the sandy wilderness-reality must be taken along with any symbolic significance. (Presumably the desert is in Israel rather than in America or in Africa.) Instead of seeing "desert" or "wilderness" solely as an emblem of safety, in which case it could apply either to heaven or to earth, they are inclined to require an earthly, possibly mideastern location.[14]

Therefore, because of a literalistic mind-set, they cannot grant that inclusion of Gentiles into the church would allow the woman to be Israel. To them the woman is nothing but ethnic Israel in the future. They imagine that Gentile additions would diminish, and therefore disqualify, the expression "woman" of Israelite association.[15] By this process dispensational representatives dismiss the applicability of Revelation 12 to Revelation 20. But this misses the emphasis on the woman being the representative of those of faith and destroys the emphasis of Christ being longed for and being channeled through the faith-filled Israelites prior to and at the time of Jesus' arrival.

If, however, reduplication is a prominent feature, and therefore a preferred interpretive tool of Revelation, then the similarities between chapters 12 and 20 need to be rigorously pursued. Without each other the two chapters are more likely to suffer extensive distortions both in terms of their applications and also in terms of a total eschatological picture.

Chapter 12, as chapter 20, covers the times between the first and second comings of Christ. Chapter 12's triumphalism is less pronounced than that of chapter 20. Chapter 12 shows God's safe keeping of his own, Son and followers, however, the believing church is definitely on the run; but in chapter 20, although it describes the same time slot (between Christ's two comings), it details the cause, the proof, and the nature of the church's victorious preservation. In chapter 20 the church is preserved to participate in the agenda of Jesus for humanity.

A comparison between 12 and 20, however, does not completely remove or dissolve the complexities of Revelation 20. No other chapter in Revelation seems to have produced as many inferences. One of the most popular ones is that Christ's reign is on the earth and that the city of Jerusalem is his locus. Extraneous details are factored into the text in this approach. The passage is not allowed to stand in its own right, but (illegally shipped in) are gregarious animals and attack beasts.

And, additionally, resurrected saints are mixed in with unresurrected sinners. Read into the twentieth chapter are spearheads melted down into plow tips. Among their imported ideas are a so-called postponed kingdom of Israel, the elevation of earthly kingdom over the heavenly (making the church a parenthesis instead of the main subject of redemption), and the dubious hypothesis of resurrections at different times. Additional arguments regarding the interpretation of chapter 20 are found in the appendix on the millennium.

Dispensational theology unashamedly claims adherence to the hermeneutics of literalness. One wonders whether a Zionistic cast attributed to Revelation 20 is justifiable when the prime premise of literalness is contradicted by them. Literalness, as a hermeneutical principle, requires that one accepts what is in the text and does not import what is not there. Jamming the biblical text with concepts that are novel is to bruise and abuse the Bible. Inferences should not be accepted at the expense of ignoring or overriding the wording. Ironically, some who decry inferences in eschatology are precisely the ones whose theology is replete with them.

The only practical implications for the earth in this famous passage is that over a long period Satan is unable to get going a coordinated effort of diverse political entities to completely silence the gospel and crush the church. Satanic influence is partially curtailed. Christians in heaven with Christ and because of Christ are loosed from the limitations of the body and further threats to their lives. Now Satan's working through his agents (beasts) goes on, and after an extended time (a thousand years, figuratively) Satan will organize a revolt in and through those nations he was not able to arouse and motivate for a final push to destroy Christ during the time he was bound.

So far our probing of heaven has been an initial probing of Revelation. We have been introduced to some hefty questions.

But by facing them head-on and honestly we can begin to grasp the broader picture. And only as we see the larger picture will the individual scenes make sense. The reason why so many have found the Book of Revelation too difficult to follow is that they have not been exposed to the key interpretative options.

Thus, we submit that the decisions we make at the entrance to Revelation have a crucial bearing on what we make of the book and of heaven. Also, we have warned the reader of the hazards of literalism. Keep in mind that we misuse apocalypse by trying to squeeze it into the dimensional framework of pure history. Many people mangle apocalyptic form by forcing a historical perspective on the text. Worse, they act as if their imported inferences are the biblical text! Literalness is abandoned when assumptions are imported, and at the same time, literalness—in the sense of the literal verses—is ignored.

Our pauses of reflection are as important as the pauses in the Book of Revelation, for only in thoughtful examination of various inferences are we brought closer to the message of the book.

One of the functions of thinking in accordance with biblical fact means we test our inferences by the textual given. The key to understanding the millennium and the secret to avoiding false inferences in eschatology is when we deliberate, take mental precautions, and apply trusted rules in the study of the Book of Revelation.

In summary, these rules include the following:

1. Begin with what is in the text. Inadvertently and unconsciously, we have a tendency to smuggle in ideas that are not there!
2. We should begin testing inferences by comparing them with the nonsymbolic sections of Scriptures.
3. Next in order, genre should act as our interpretative gyroscope. Revelation will be distorted if we interpret it like Romans.

4. In interpreting Revelation let the context of the book and its repetitions guide our understanding of a portion which is less clear.

5. Check to see if our conclusions follow validly from the premises, which, in turn, are checked for being textually accurate. A conclusion cannot be valid unless it validly follows from the preceding premises.

We should seek defensible and reasoned conclusions based on the biblical text. Scripture must be allowed to speak in its own voice, else we make it say what it doesn't say.

Reexamination is necessary to refinement of ideas. With an increase in biblical cross-checks the greater chance there is for erroneous conclusions to be caught and discarded. First John 4:1 urged the early Christians to test the spirits. The call is for Christians in all ages. It was a call, in essence, to test *our* inferences and reevaluate *our* conclusions. What we say should be placed against what Scripture says.

Probing heaven begins and continues when Scripture probes us, and since our views need continuous readjustment, the probe must go on.

The
Booster
Stage

EXPOSITIONAL

2

Is There a Heaven ?

"Burma Shave" signs were in abundance along roadsides when I was a boy. These, some may recall, were slender, painted-on-fence-slats signs spaced out, roughly, fifteen yards apart. They were a good source of chuckles for those "out riding." Sometimes they had biblical subjects, such as:

Moonlight and roses, whiskers like Moses,
   just don't go together, Burma Shave!

Noah had whiskers, in the ark, but he wouldn't get by,
   on a bench in the park, Burma Shave!

One I have always liked went:

The bearded devil, is forced to dwell, in the only place,
   where they don't sell, Burma Shave!

My all time favorite, however, is this one:

The whale, put Jonah, down the hatch, but coughed him up,
   because he scratched, Burma Shave![1]

Ecclesiastes has something in common with Burma Shave signs. It reads along like a winding road, then periodically sayings appear similar to the Burma Shave ads of years ago. If the writer had chosen to write in limericks, Ecclesiastes might have sounded something like this:

> The dog, the cat, the cow;
> The chief, the king, the sow;
> Every bod turns to sod, Ecclesiastes!

Or,

> The smart man in his library,
> the rich man near his vault,
> the big man on the throttle,
> All men come to rot, Futility!

The punch lines "vanity" or "emptiness" appear thirty-seven times, and the refrain "under the sun" occurs twenty-nine times in its twelve moderate-length chapters.

Ecclesiastes's refrains are almost as well known as Burma Shave slogans. Of course, the lines from Ecclesiastes are much older. The book is ancient, but its message is current. It deals with death, and death is still very much part of modern life. Life eventually comes to an abrupt—some think absolute—halt. The question arises, "Is there life after all this?" "Is there a heaven?"

Many people believe there is a heaven, but a significant number of meat-and-potato atheists, for instance, are unmoved by Christianity and answer a firm "No!" Still others are not sure who to believe. Propagandizing skeptics who say Christian claims about the reality of the hereafter convey only emotional energy themselves often want only a material heaven.

Though a person may reject a Christian concept of heaven, that does not mean he does not pursue a heaven on this side of the death line. The secularist may unashamedly admit that for him earth is heaven.

Earth heaven? The only heaven some seek is entirely on earth. A heaven which is *unearthly* is held to be fictitious. How is this viewpoint arrived at and justified?

Sometimes a person will hold that the only reality is what we presently know. Because he limits his data and has a need to deny God, heaven is lumped with fantasy. To him, death is followed by nothingness. The late Dr. Loyal Davis (1896-1982), the foster father of Nancy Reagan, was a Welsh-American neurosurgeon who became skeptical about the Christian hereafter in medical school. In his autobiography this renowned surgeon, who taught neurosurgery at Northwestern Medical School, told how his work in the hospital's dissecting room led to his questioning man's capacity to survive death. "Here was plain, matter-of-fact evidence that made belief in a physical hereafter impossible, certainly not in the same form."[2]

Similarly, in today's autopsy rooms medical students may be examining and questioning theological assumptions. There is nothing, however, in a cadaver that postulates Christianity's claims are erroneous. It is what we bring to the examining room, not what is there, that pushes a person into skepticism. The seventeenth-century writer-surgeon, Sir Thomas Browne (1605-1682) wrote, "Man is a noble animal, splendid in ashes, and pompous in the grave, solemnizing nativities and deaths with equal lustre."[3]

Life is tragic when we have plenty to live on, but little to live for or to look forward to. Surely our potential is more than meeting our bodily needs. We have a transcendent dimension that needs fulfillment. We may know supreme happiness in our secular pursuits, and have enviable luxuries, but feel a nagging, restless hunger yet unsatisfied.

Some would rather let go of entering heaven so long as they could still hold onto earth. Exclusion of heaven without completely shunning God signals, however, a shortsightedness which concludes in inevitable disappointments. Puritan

Richard Baxter (1615-1691) saw a secularistic life as radically inverted, needing to be righted. "Whoever loves earth above heaven, and fleshly prosperity more than God, is a wicked, unconverted man."[4] Was Baxter's approach too heavy-handed? Or was he on to something which, like Ecclesiastes, hits a responsive chord in the reflective? If we were more truthful life has not provided answers, and material things, in becoming "God" to us, have left us empty.

Put on a value scale, then, where we end after death has greater importance than lifestyles of the rich and famous. We are meant to devote our best hours and greatest energies, not to trivial pursuits, but to God's revelation. One cannot take pride in not being an official atheist when one lives like a functional atheist. If God is objectively real and we are answerable to him, and assuming heaven is our final place and our most fitting company, why then do we live as if heaven doesn't matter and as if God were just another fine idea?

Accumulation of goods and the power of wealth are still all that some people seek, making the message of Ecclesiastes as relevant as when first penned. It becomes a dangerous obsession to be caught up with the means of living yet to be oblivious to the ends for which we were made! More evil than the denial of immortality is the evil of creating our own new earth, and of the substitutions or replacements of forms of heaven without Christ—private heavens independent of a personal spiritual search.

Warning about materialism is not outmoded tent-meeting rhetoric or revivalist cant. Those within the mainstream have confessed to the inadequacies of secular interests. Jeremy Rifkin has written: "The more steeped a world view is in the material side of life, the less conducive it is to the human quest for spiritual transcendence."[5]

Ecclesiastes shows a profound understanding of how objects become evil. Objects are not intrinsically evil, but we can exalt

objects into God's place. Things have obscured ideas. Possessions have obliterated God. Productivity has replaced receptivity to God's gift of eternal life. Our idolatrousness has been so
well camouflaged that we scarcely realized that we manage images calculated to blind us to spiritual realities, including
heaven.[6]

> There are a number of us who creep
> Into the world to eat and sleep;
> And know no reason why we're born,
> But only to consume the corn,
> Devour the cattle, flesh and fish,
> And leave behind an empty dish.
> And if our tombstone, when we die,
> Be not taught to flatter and to lie,
> There's nothing better can be said
> Than that he's eaten up all his bread,
> Drunk up his drink, and gone to bed.
>
> ISAAC WATTS

To ignore our ultimacy is a form of unreality. John Calvin
(1509-1564), whose own life itself was relatively short, saw
through the blindness of his contemporaries who were as dedicated to buttressing their financial resources as moderns are in
increasing their riches. He wrote, "As if no inkling of [immortal-
ity] had ever reached us, we return to our thoughtless assurance of an earthly immortality."[7]

Ecclesiastes contains powerful slogans warning us of im-
mense dangers. The author called himself *Koheleth*, which
could have meant master of ceremonies, debater, or preacher.
Some say "philosopher" best sums up the meaning of the word.

Before he turned philosopher, he was a superachiever. Along
with that, too, he was superdisappointed. Modern celebrities
sometimes have their own version of the same track. The enjoyments of life's best (*see* 2:24; 3:12, 22; 5:18; 9:7; 11:9) for him
produced only frustrations and emptiness. Letdowns followed

let-live as being laid out in death was a follow through of being laid up in sickness. Enjoyments ended in exasperation. Yet these disappointments did not end with extinction. His outlook was not an annihilation wish as some have supposed.

The writer reveals a progression in his spiritual development. He took up new ventures, but these ended with the feeling that he had wasted life and cheated himself. That is why the book is so modern. It speaks to those who feel "being had."

The book reflects an elementary theological interest and shows a healthy progression.

Immortality is a tendency resulting from intuition.

Immortality is a tradition suggested by inference.

Immortality is a truth given by divine inspiration.

Three key texts show this progression: 3:11; 3:21; and 12:7. They read as follows:

3:11, NIV: He has made everything beautiful in its time. He has also set eternity in the hearts of men; yet they cannot fathom what God has done from beginning to end.

3:21, NIV: Who knows if the spirit of man rises upward and if the spirit of the animal goes down into the earth?

12:7, NIV: And the dust returns to the ground it came from, and the spirit returns to God who gave it.

The first text (3:11) clearly affirms that the belief in immortality is endemic or common to man as man. The word *eternity* (Hebrew, *ha-'olam*) used here occurs elsewhere in Ecclesiastes as "eternity." *See* 1:4; 2:16; 3:14; 9:6; 12:5. If one is allowed to dig deeper, it may become apparent that the desire to continue after death is not just an idea found in church people, but is found in those who avoid God. Beneath denial of God, beyond substitutions for God, is a quest for God which takes different directions and expressions.

The second text (3:21) expresses both a doubt and a point of belief. He acknowledged the doubt that man's spirit returns to God at death. Yet he doubted that. The text suggests that a human being is better than animals, though sharing their mortality. He tended toward reconsideration of the finality of death, if not reaffirmation of hope for the hereafter.

The third text (12:7) contains an allusion to Genesis 2:7. There God is said to have breathed life into soil, thereby, making the original human. The spirit of man, being more than breath, is said to survive in a way simple expelled air does not. Some objectivity of personality seems to be implied.

The quality of his existence, the problems of living, and survival occupied the author. That is why Paul Tillich (1886-1965) described Koheleth "the great existentialist of his period."[8] But to say that is not to say enough, for there are existentialists who see man's plight differently, from radically different perspectives. There is the atheistic existentialist, who interprets life as absolutely hopeless and one's death as fulfilling nothing. Then there is the believer who has had an authentic, personal encounter with the Lord. He also is existential.

I disagree with Hans Küng who saw Ecclesiastes "very remote from *any sort of hope in a joyous hereafter. . . .*"[9] Another German scholar, Gerhard von Rad, has cautioned, "Ecclesiastes is anything but a nihilistic agnostic."[10]

Certainly, we would dishonor the book by putting a New Testament perspective where it cannot be found. Again it would not overstate his contribution by seeing that what he ends with is a theological vamp (introductory notes) to a much later joyous theme of ultimate reunion guaranteed in the resurrection. Karl Barth (1886-1968) recognized that "To perceive the absolute vanity of life under the sun in the light of the heavenly life of God is also to perceive its relative potentiality."[11] Much earlier Ernest W. Hengstenberg (1802-1869), aware of the limited teaching on immortality in the Old Testament, felt nevertheless that here was a positive statement which formed "the anthropological basis of the doctrine of the immortality of the soul."[12]

The mature writer, whoever he may have been, spent much of his adult life apart from God. What he wrote in Ecclesiastes was the confession of having made earth a materialistic heaven. He had immersed himself in things, a life apart from God. He was the sounding board of a philosophy of life in which man is central and God peripheral. That orientation brought him first to experience, and then to express disillusionment. In a sense, the book shows him struggling to escape secularism. His emergence and emancipation from the grip of a materialistic lifestyle probably explain the origin of the book. It has, therefore, become a testament *against* a hedonistic or pleasure-geared approach to life.

By chapter 3 of Ecclesiastes the author admitted God's involvement in time. For years I thought that Ecclesiastes 3:1-8 was a list of etiquette rules (convenient ammunition for teachers to use against unruly students). I got this idea from the fact that in morning chapel (which was compulsory) our public-high-school principal frequently read Ecclesiastes chapter 3, I suppose, to reinforce good deportment in the student body.

But the point of the passage is something entirely different. It is not about what man can do to be a better man, but what God does for, through, and in man. It's more a lesson on history than a lesson on etiquette. "God cannot be excluded from history" is the theme of Ecclesiastes 3:1-8. The reference to "a time to" is not about the appropriateness of "what" to do "when," but it has to do with "set time," which ironically, of course, turns out to be appropriate. Whenever we view time as set, we view it as settled. And to the writer God fixed and set time without consulting man. To determine time meant, of course, he deter-mined events. In other words Ecclesiastes 3:1-8, rather than being a series of exhortations for insensitive creatures, was an affirmation of the involvement of God in phases of life over which man previously thought he was in complete control. Its bottom line is predestination. [13]

A degree of moral wobble is detectable in 3:21. But that must be tempered with the long introductory section of the chapter on divine sovereignty, mentioned in the preceding paragraph. Indeed, because God's control of life is ignored, man denied, decried, and degraded his own immortal nature and wasted his time on fruitless ventures. His statement of 3:21 is not a flat denial that man is immortal, but a recognition that the bulk of humankind didn't believe it. [14]

Though he moved under the sun, he moved *toward* the sun's source. The bleak shades of chapter 1 show a dramatic turn by chapter 12. On a much larger scale, this progression is discernable between the two testaments, Old and New. Francis Patton (1843-1932), a former president of Princeton University, observed that whereas the high watermark of the Old Testa-ment was Psalm 23:4, that of the New Testament was Philip-pians 1:23. David was willing to go, but wanting to stay, but Paul was willing to stay, but wanting to go. [15]

The debater/philosopher was giving a resume of his spiritual history. His life direction showed a definite spiritual upturn or rollover. He went from being an idealist to being a materialist to being a realist. Intuition nudged his secularism out of the way. The futility of his to-the-hilt pleasure principle became a lever-age point for his new spiritual realism. Then, finally, in chapter 12, he was on the runway to theism and belief in man's immor-tality.

Our particular faith journey may not have followed the grooves left by Koheleth. Our struggles may have been more practical than philosophical, less wrenching, less wrecking. Surely the apostle John did not go through the turmoil of Koheleth, for he was on the Son side for a long time, and happy to say, "The world is passing away with all its allurements, but he who does God's will stands forever." (1 John 2:17, NEB).

Philosophically, there is a giant step between Koheleth and the apostle John. Koheleth sought God out of despair; John sought God out of delight. Yet God, whether reluctantly admitted to or ardently pursued, has a reality as either subject seeking or object sought. God as real and capable of a relationship with man requires place and can make place. And one of the paradoxes of divinity is that God does not require space to have place.

Of course, a more concrete influence brings conviction about the reality of heaven and a willingness to defend it. For the Christian the prime mover is Jesus Christ who came from heaven. A tangible, talking Person claimed to be from that intangible region.

What the philosopher went through was not without value. We learn through negative findings. What may propel a person Godward is the feeling of helplessness and hopelessness in human energy and endeavors. Belief in heaven may begin at the end of the garbage heap.

Ecclesiastes presents a unified thesis and not just a lot of aphorisms strung together. Life has lost the key to itself. Meaning is not conveyed by matter. Meaning is not self-imposed or self-emerging. Nature won't supply it. History doesn't have it. To find the key to life the author, finally, turned to the locksmith.[16] The need for having God involved is anticipated not only in 3:11, but also in 7:14, and again in 8:17. We misjudge the book by making it entirely pessimistic.

To say heaven has not been experienced is not to say that there is no heaven. Whole cultures have sometimes been chained to a cosmology that concrete fact has overturned. Similarly those who have concluded science will allow no heaven need to be more scientific by recognizing the presence of One who came from heaven, Jesus Christ.

This is illustrated in the attitudes toward sea travel before Columbus and sea travel after Columbus. I am impressed how a pivotal historical event can radically change the outlook of the human species. Recall the time when sailors feared sailing too far, lest they fall off the ocean's edge?

The strength of the belief that it was a dangerous risk to go too far on the seas is illustrated in an inscription on a monument near the Rock of Gibraltar that dates back to the fifteenth century.

One time Spain controlled both sides of the narrowest part of the strait of Gibraltar. At that narrowing of the two land masses (Africa and Europe), there was a huge marker called the "Pillar of Hercules," and prior to Columbus' voyage in 1492, it carried a three word Latin saying chiseled into stone: NE PLUS ULTRA, which, translated, said, "No More Beyond."

Coins, like stamps, can tell us about a country. They celebrate victories, praise founders, sloganize ethnic styles, and advertise scientific breakthroughs. "No More Beyond" was the standard belief of that time. No one would dare question the prevailing conviction that the western horizon contained nothing new.

After Columbus's discovery of a new world beyond Spain, recognition of the revised outlook was pressed into its coins. Coins were struck with a simple Latin slogan, two words: PLUS ULTRA: which meant "More Beyond." Coins in circulation in Florida in 1796, still had that slogan!

Jesus came to tell us and show us that there was more beyond! What he won and showed was more beyond what Ecclesiastes's author dreamed of. Jesus, in his birth, life, and resurrection assures us that though our experiences may not have been of heaven, that there is nevertheless a real one. His resurrection assures us that we are not meant to perish.

The Book of Ecclesiastes says there is nothing new under the sun, but that is not all it says. It says, however shyly and slightly, what Christ confirmed with gusto, *that heaven is real.* Christ brought the answer Koheleth could never arrive at on his own. The Son of God had to show and shine before heaven could be fully known. The message of the New Testament is that the enormous eternal Son of God has come. With his coming, through his mediation, and in his shining, we find he makes everything *new* under the sun and everything beyond the sun everlastingly secure and attractive. [17]

3

Is Heaven Created ?

*H*eaven is both a loan word and a loaded word. We have borrowed it from the Bible, but we have loaded it with our own meanings—meanings that sometimes prevent the biblical perspective from being heard.

We have packed it as if it were a cosmic sausage. What we have put into it are stray scraps picked from childhood memories, tidbits from intellectual chopping blocks, and choice cuts from poetic doublespeak. Mixed in with the eclectic mass are down-home anecdote spices to add aroma and individual flavor.

The typical American, possibly for lack of time, ends with a hodgepodge of theological views. Tragically, what we demand in industry we decline to enforce in religious thought. For instance, food products can't be marketed without meeting stringent FDA standards. Inspections are conducted to make sure manufacturers comply. Yet we refuse to hold our thinking up to the standards of Scripture, when we wouldn't allow anything to go out the factory door unless it measured up to superior product specs.

Interstate transports must conform to load regulations. State-code restrictions prohibit carrying, for instance, hazardous chemicals with healthful foods. Knowledge is the shipment of ideas.

"Heaven" is a load of ideas. Yet anything is allowed to be tied down or hang over our mental flat-bed. Safe-carrying limits are ignored in the business of word cargo. Because we endlessly accommodate the craziest notions of afterlife, the axles of "heaven" are near collapse, making it a rig more dangerous than a cyclist zigzagging down a steep street on a stormy day.

Churches encourage creative ideas on heaven. Out of fear of seeming repressive, exclusive, or restrictive, few ideas are dismissed. Class members are encouraged to share their views. In a dialogic, democratic setting divergent views are both invited and said to be legitimate expressions of Christian opinion. But a *carte blanche* approach to theology, in fostering openness, invariably cosponsors deceptions. Often the result differs little from conclusions drawn from national polls.

The USA Weekend, a supplement to many regional Sunday papers, carried results of a poll on heaven. In late 1986, across the nation random interviews of 604 American adults were conducted. It was found that 80 percent of those polled believed in heaven and 67 percent believed in hell. The 1986 *USA Weekend* poll should be compared with the *Newsweek* poll conducted in December 1988 in which 77 percent of the respondents believed there is a heaven and 58 percent believed there is a hell. (Note the slippage in the percentage of those who believed in hell.) Both the *USA Weekend* and the *Newsweek* poll showed a slight increase over the larger-sample Gallup poll published in 1982 in which 71 percent of the American public expressed belief in heaven. [1] In the 1986 *USA Weekend* poll the question "What are your chances of going to heaven?" produced some ingenious responses. We will get to what the Bible says in response to this question in chapter 11 and more in chapter 12.

Poll results are said to contain a plus or minus 4 percent margin of error. From a biblical perspective, opinions solicited from sinful creatures are necessarily replete with errors. Our sinfulness predisposes us to screen out Scripture. Our self-centeredness prevents our unthrottled exaltation of God. The Holy Spirit must change us so what Scripture speaks we receive as the Word of God.

The most fundamental question, however, which unfortunately is far down any list (and rarely asked), concerns what sources are reliable in arriving at a concept of heaven. Is it prudent, for instance, to devise and develop ideas on heaven independent of the primary source material of Christianity, the Bible?

Uppsala born, Emanuel Swedenborg (1688-1772), for instance, proposed dead infants first go to be with the angels, then after they become wise, they "become angels."[2] Swedenborg's elaborate speculations/inspirations apparently had cross cultural-theological appeal, for humans-into-angels was not confined to the infrequently read writings of the Swedish mystic. Lay theological beliefs rarely get printed, but occasionally they do show up on tombstone epitaphs. Consider the one in Saint Albans, England:

> Sacred to the memory of Martha Gwynn,
> Who was so very pure within,
> She burst the outer shell of sin,
> And hatched herself a cherubim.

If belief that people become angels galloped through Christian cemeteries, it crept into Christian hymns. Here is a hymn fragment some may accept as coming from the Bible.

I want to be an angel and with the angels stand;

A crown upon my forehead, and a harp within my hand.

The contention that a person becomes an angel in heaven not only infected literate hymn writers in the Eastern United States, but it became part of the saddle-bag theology of the American cowboy of the Old West.

It seems the influence of Swedenborg traveled far from his native Sweden. It turned up in the most unlikely place of Dodge City. There an English duke and a weathered cowboy struck up a conversation. After they bent their elbows together at a local "watering hole," the English duke reached into his pocket to pay. He pulled out an English coin. Reminded by it of his heritage, the duke held the coin before the cowboy.

"You see the likeness of His Majesty, the king, on this coin? He made my grandfather a lord."

The cowboy looked over the coin solemnly, then dug into the pockets of his breeches and came out with a copper penny.

"Un-huh," he said. "An' see the likeness of thet red Injun on this here penny? He made an angel outa my grandpappy!"[3]

Even today a lot of people imagine in heaven they will be transformed into angels. These instances regarding belief in becoming angels illustrate that having thoughts that are religious is not enough to make them true. We need to ask, "Is this what Scripture says? (Turn ahead to chapter 15 on the question of equality in heaven for an answer.) We need to ask if our conceptions of heaven are genuinely biblical or superficially spiritual. Do *we* create them or has God revealed them? Are our views of heaven from us or from God? Have we absorbed them from accumulated speculations or are they scripturally authenticated?

Space fiction is sometimes thought little different from biblical material. "Star Wars" or other space ventures are considered equally as valid as the Bible. Theater audiences and home-video users may agree with the sentiment in the first of two popular films on ghost hunting in which comment was casually dropped to the effect that each religion attempts to unravel what the end of the world will be like. Despite star talk and the talk of movie stars, the greatest heavenly spectacle of all, the biblical heaven, is neglected.

Excessive emphasis on space fiction and an overdependence on movies for truth inevitably results in a self-isolation from the Bible. To confine heaven to sky and stratosphere rather than encompassing inner dimensions, to think only of altitude rather than attitude, to see galactic forces rather than spiritual warfare, to focus solely on stellar objects rather than intangible powers, to quote a movie line rather than a Bible verse means we have limited heaven to what is visible, sense-verifiable, and culturally popular.

Yet the Bible tells us some things about heaven ahead. To significantly if not completely fill that gap, God gave the Bible. Although some delight in beginning with their own projections about what will constitute the greatness of the final heaven, we must not. God will startle us and set us straight in his own time. Of the fullness of heaven ahead, Paul wrote "Eye hath not seen, nor ear heard, neither have entered into the heart of man, the things which God hath prepared for them that love him" (1 Cor. 2:9, KJV). We actually distance ourselves from the real heaven, the kingdom of heaven, by attributing reality to space fantasies. In concentrating on movie versions of heaven and their commentary dialogues we trivialize heaven and threaten our own futures in it.

Yet allowance must be made for individual integration of biblical principles. A foundational premise for all reflections about the final heavenly state is the matter of a spiritual body (1 Cor. 15:40, 44). Three-dimensional resurrected bodies are more than spent air and intangible thoughts. To postulate bodily resurrection requires future space or place. Where and how will the resurrected glorified function?

Some expect heavenly pleasures to resemble or catch something of what we have known on earth. Traveling to unspoiled parts of our world may give us a glimpse of heaven. An enchanting vacation may broaden our outlook as well as widen our eyes (and empty our savings). Renaissance people used to think of heaven in terms of Elysian Fields. Now in an age when commercial jets are common carriers, we think of it as a tropical island.

Hawaii is one place that draws tourists. It has an attractiveness which inspired one Chicago business executive to exclaim on his first visit to Honolulu (which means "sheltered haven"): "If heaven isn't like this, I don't want to go there."[4] Not coincidentally, in the closing years of the apostle Paul's life, since death was shoving off from the earthly shore, heaven by implication was a *peaceful* port (2 Tim. 4:6c).[5]

Earlier Paul spoke of having made contact with God in a third heaven in 2 Corinthians 12:2. It seems unlikely that he was giving credibility to the rabbinic parceling of heaven into stages or tiers. (*See* "Third Heaven" of the Glossary). More than likely it was an expression of the rapturous expansiveness, defying explanation, of what he experienced.[6]

In view of the fact, therefore, that even an apostle groped for words in describing heaven, we feel both a kinship in our limitations and the enormous difficulty of the task in trying to convey the grandeur and greatness of what Scripture says of all that heaven contains. In this light, author and reader alike share a degree of inadequacy in struggling with the present subject.

Nothing is more open to speculation than the idea of heaven. Options range from the sublime to the ridiculous, from fictitious dreaming to meaningless verbiage, from heaven as pleasure palaces from which none desire to vacate, to open territories where outdoor recreations dominate one's leisure. We must be on the guard against the importation of ideas which contradict Scripture. We must question whether ideas expressed by Christians today as well as by Christians in earlier ages really reflect the Bible or whether they are only perpetuating personal and cultural anticipations.

Do the nine ideas below stem from Scripture?

We will meditate rather than act in heaven.

Wc will sit on clouds in heaven.

All heavens are perfect.

Peter guards the entrance of heaven.

He stands before the pearly gate.

Halos and wings are worn in heaven.

We become angels in heaven.

We are reincarnated in others.

We survive in a mind without body.

Can we trace these assumptions to biblical texts? If we cannot, we should doubt them. It is amazing how often we assume the Bible teaches something, when it does not. *None* of the above is taught in Scripture.

Take the first two to start. (The first two are related.) Will heaven be nothing more than silent meditation without action? Is action less heavenly than thought? By reading medieval writers one would think so. We may be surprised to find that it is not a biblical, but a medieval idea of heaven as absolute and exclusive meditation. Heaven, if anything, is perfected action: doing more, doing it better, and having more space in which to do it. We contend that heaven is pell-mell, reflective exploration and not occupied with immobile contemplations. Occasionally, one finds modern Roman Catholics questioning the medieval picture.[7]

False assumptions about heaven arose when there were undue non-Christian influences. This was especially evident in the first three centuries when clerics were overawed with pre-Christian intellectual giants. The early church fathers felt some pressure to look respectable by incorporating insights from Greek philosophy. They tended to be less critical of non-Christian philosophers than they ought. Especially dangerous was their willingness to adapt Plato's approach to knowledge.

Early Christian apologists endorsed Plato's (427?-347 B.C.) theory of knowledge. Plato argued that there is no absolute separation between the world of ideas and the world as we know it—earthly reality. He said every object on earth was matched by an idea in heaven. Each thing has a pattern above and harmony is achieved below when it matches the pattern above. The temporal must imitate the eternal to attain true goodness. The Greek Fathers thought Plato's concept was compatible with Christianity.

Origen (185c-254) went afoul by following the Platonized views of his teacher, Clement of Alexandria (150c-220). Origen ended up believing that neither heaven nor hell existed, "but only the gradual education and purification of the universe and its beings until once more God was all in all."[8]

To propose that a World of Ideas existed that had a form for every earthly object, explaining individual existence of sense objects, was in conflict with the Christian exaltation of God as the originator of all things. God, not forms in the World of Ideas, explains where things came from. Ideas are not earlier, stronger, or greater reality than sense phenomena. Plato did not postulate a Supreme Being but asserted an absolute World of Ideas. At best "God for Plato [was] an intermediary being distinct from the Idea of the Good."[9] But the determining premise for the Christian is the reality, objectivity, superiority, and personality of God. It is this God who is in charge of history—not absolute ideas.

Our lives conform to God's decrees. They are not the outworking of our compliance with absolute ideas. It is God's concern for us as individuals that his ideas were expressed in

writings through choice servants. Finally, he sent his only be-
gotten Son.

> Heaven is a concrete state of perfection of all creation. It is
> more concrete than the heaven of Plato, richer and more pure
> than Augustine's City of God. [10]

Equally detrimental to Christianity has been the nineteenth-
century philosopher, Ludwig Feuerbach (1804-1872) who
claimed that Christian concepts of heaven were nothing but
human projections. This automatically meant the subject of
heaven was an intellectual illusion, for a projection is an attribution and imposition on reality a set of beliefs not in reality.

Feuerbach said man, not God, created heaven. To him
heaven, like God, was a disguise of our idealized self. Feuerbach
claimed God was nothing more than man looking in the mirror
and seeing the man he would like to be. He wrote:

> The divine being is nothing else than the human being, or
> rather, the human being purified, freed from the limits of the
> individual man, made objective, i.e., contemplated and revered
> as another, a distinct being. All the attributes of the divine
> nature are, therefore, attributes of the human nature. [11]

Karl Marx (1818-1883), the prime architect of atheistic com-
munism, was greatly influenced by Ludwig Feuerbach. [12] But,
closer to us, we should not fail to note that Feuerbach infiltrated neo-Protestantism. Carl F. H. Henry has pointed out:

> Leading theologians of the nineteenth and twentieth cen-
> turies alike were unable to forge an effective reply to Feuerbach's
> dismissal of all religion as illusion because they shared his belief
> that God is not the source of our concepts of God, but that
> man's conception of God is the product of the human mind. [13]

Feuerbach objected to confessions of Christian faith beginning with the apostles. Feuerbach wanted his readers to believe
him in preference to believing the Bible.

We have, however, no good reason to buy Feuerbach's thesis. The main fault with Feuerbach's *Essence of Christianity* (if one looks closely) is that he offers no proof that the God of the Bible does not exist. He began by assuming God does not exist and then went from there to develop his projection theory. It may strike one as plausible that theology (the study of God) is nothing more than anthropology (the study of man) and for those who can't bother with the Christian Scriptures, indeed, what some say is God is only God recast in the image of the speaker.

Certainly Feuerbach projected his own wishes. Many agree with Feuerbach because they want a world without God and without heaven. They actually live the way they speak. Heaven, God, and Christ impinge on them from history, and they are not happy with the intrusion on their independence. They may speak of an open view of the universe, but in their private lives they live by the view of a closed system, denying that there is a transcendent world. To admit God, to admit a self-revealing God, to admit the Bible is God's self-revelation are thoughts too disturbing to entertain. Yet, at the same time, wanting to appear progressive and openminded, they speak of an expanding universe. But what kind of expansion do they have?

Jürgen Moltmann observes that the only transcendence followers of Feuerbach grant is material self-transcendence which would seem to guarantee an indefinitely endless universe. However, "the qualitative infinity of heaven [that is, the Christian case] is replaced by the quantitatively indefinite endlessness of the universe's extension."[14]

If Christianity has no objective basis, then Feuerbach's hypothesis seems compelling. It would mean, then, that rather than God creating man in *his* image, man has created God in *man's* image!

A preliminary Christian response to Feuerbach is not to say that the real God corresponds to our projections, but that the declarations of Scripture on God are from God and, therefore, authoritative (2 Tim. 3:16). Heaven's reality is as much attested as earth's.

In real life, on a subjective basis, Feuerbach's approach has been shown to be inadequate. Occupation with the "here" and ignoring the "hereafter" does not fit us to handle life's traumas.

Heinrich Heine (1797-1856), a famous German lyric poet, illustrated the emptiness known by those who embraced Feuerbach's conclusion. He was an ardent atheist and outspoken mocker of religion. Heine contracted an incurable spinal disease which confined him to bed. For eight years he was in his "mattress tomb."[15] It gave him time to rethink many things. When pressed against the fact of his impending demise, he reversed himself and published his changed view of God, as a postscript to *Romancero,* published in 1851. He wrote,

> I have returned to God, like the prodigal son, after a long time of tending swine with the Hegelians. [He didn't stop there.] Was it my wretched state that drove me to go back? Perhaps there was a less wretched reason. A heavenly homesickness overwhelmed me and drove me on, through woods and chasm and over the vertiginous mountain paths of the dialectic. [He concluded,] When one longs for a God who has power to help— and this is the main point, after all—then one must also accept his persona, his otherworldliness, and his holy attributes as the all-bountiful, all-wise, all-just, etc. The immortality of the soul, our continuance after death, then becomes part of the package so to speak.[16]

We are confronted through Feuerbach with a primal question: "Is heaven created?" So far we have examined Feuerbach's answer to that question. He said that man created the idea of heaven. The Christian, however, says God created heaven, God has revealed heaven.

Feuerbach, of course, was speaking of the *concept* of heaven. We have yet to direct the question to *the physical reality* of the heavens. We wonder whether the heavens always were or were they made. "Have the heavens always been?"

The first verse in the Bible answers this question. "In the beginning God created the heavens and the earth" (Gen. 1:1). Yet Psalm 123:1 (NIV) says, "[God's] throne is in heaven." This seems to suggest the heavens always were. "If God always had a throne, wouldn't heaven always have had to be?" Or the question could be phrased: "If God always was and he needed a locus, a place, a residence, then wasn't God in heaven always?" Allowance must be made for an uncreated heaven, for "God is his own world of being; he fills it and nothing can share it."[17] The problem is this: "Must heaven be confined to observable nature? If heaven is nothing other than God's own presence, then is it not absurd to talk of God creating heaven?" From one side or another, then, the question still remains, "Is heaven created?"

Two understandings of heaven stand out. One is that heaven always was because God always was. The second view is that heaven had a beginning. (But as we shall see these positions are not incompatible.)

Heavens, heaven-as-mass, have not always been. Genesis 1:1 is joined with a bundle of other texts which say the same thing. (*See also:* Ps. 33:6; Isa. 42:5; Acts 4:24; 14:15; 17:24; Rev. 10:6; 14:7.)

Obviously, these verses are not about heaven as atmosphere where God always was. The starry heavens are the result of God's creative action. Space is real, for God made it. The biblical texts on God's creation of the heavens do not mean that before that God was homeless. What Genesis 1:1 is affirming is that God made the physical heavens as well as the physical earth. "If heaven is pushed out of the doctrine of creation," warns Jürgen Moltmann, "it becomes difficult to go on interpreting the earth as God's creation at all."[18]

Creation is important because it rules out the eternity of

matter. In one sense, it would be wrong to argue that all heavens always were. The eternity of the heavens cannot be established by arguing that in the Bible God always was and "heaven" is just another word for "God." There are the heavens God made, and there is the heaven which is God's presence. We must not confuse the two.

On the matter of *heaven* being another word for *God*, we need to note how it developed. In the thinking of the Hebrews "heaven" was a substitution for God. Frequently, in the Bible "heaven" took the place of God's name. Jews were reluctant to speak the name of God. And that same reserve continues in some branches of Judaism. In everyday speech we may substitute "heaven" for "God," as when we say "for heaven's sake," or "heavens—no!"

Heaven became an important substitution for God's name. The Gospels use "the kingdom of God" and "the kingdom of heaven" interchangeably.[19] Matthew, the Gospel geared to Jewish readers, is the only Gospel to use the phrase "kingdom of heaven" (*see* 3:2; 5:10; 6:20). In Matthew 19:23, 24, the two expressions are shown to be equivalent. The other New Testament documents made "the kingdom of God" their standard expression (*see* John 3:5 [the word *kingdom* rare in John]; Acts 1:3; 8:12; 19:8; 28:23, 31; Rom. 14:17). In a real sense Jesus brought the realization of God's kingdom, yet there are still future aspects of it. (In the next chapter we treat this in greater detail).

The cosmos is both less than God and originated by God. "Heaven is neither God nor is it divine; it is part of the created world. . . . If God is its Creator, then his creation has its unity in him, not in itself."[20]

A random, evolving universe would seem to outlaw God's firm hold of his property. Heavenly realms, in Scripture, are not pictured reproducing themselves. At a point in time God made one earth and many heavens.

God created the starry heavens, where the planets are and all galaxies farther out. And there are texts that say Christians dwell with Christ in heavenly realms where their inheritance is (Eph. 1:3, 20; 2:6). This is separate from earth, a place less noted for its geography than for its stability and authority.

Sandwiched somewhere in the spirit world is another heavenly realm invaded, controlled, and filled with destructive spiritual "squatters." In this section of the heavenly realms are the foes of Christ and of Christians. Satan occupies this area and from it he oversees his opposition to the mission of Christ on earth. It is a realm of heaven charged with hatred against God and his Christ. It is a realm from which assaults are made on the church on earth.

The rulers of darkness reside in this divisive, negative heavenly realm (Eph. 6:12).

> We wrestle not against flesh and blood, but against principalities and powers in high (Greek: heavenly) places. But our adversary is no material or corporeal foe. Hence, "in the heavenlies" is an immaterial, unseen world that lies behind, above, outside the world of sense. Even the words "behind, outside" are incorrect. It is a world of minds or spirits, not bodies. Nor does the phrase mean "heaven" in the commonly accepted usage. Heaven as we think of it, does not contain evil spirits. These "heavenlies" do. Nor must we think of this spiritual world as up toward the moon or Saturn. It is right here on earth also. The descent into and the valley of the shadow of death, where the goblins whisper in our ears, is our mind itself. We too are members of the supra-sensory world of spirits.[21]

The "principalities and powers" in Paul's phraseology are the inhabitants of the abyss of Revelation 9:1-12. The locusts are the demonic powers and they torment the church from their place of darkness and dreadfulness.

In summary, we have noted that God created the starry heavens. In himself, however, the eternally existing God carries about his own atmosphere. Wherever he was the ultimate heaven was.

Concepts of heaven must also include other kinds of heaven. There is also the kind of heavens where our spiritual inheritance is reserved, safe from hostile assaults. We are not sure whether our future inheritance is preserved separately from God or is part of his immediate presence. More than likely, it is part of his eternal mind. At least we can be confident that the heavenly realm from which Christ's spiritual foes operate— from which they advance and retreat—are distinct from God's special presence.

The latter heavens have a hand in channeling and fueling the destructive actions of humans on earth. The physical earth and heavens are impoverished by satanic forces. Man's disobedience of God contributes to the moral pollution of our world, which in turn contributes to further contamination, destruction, and erosion of the universe's assets.

God plans the re-creation of the heavens and the earth at the end of time. Because of various corruptions the created heavens and one part of the heavenly realms need re-creation.

Thus, the heavens, starry and spiritual, stand in need of redemption as much as earth. It is wrong to assume that heaven is intrinsically pure and removed from the need of cleansing. Although the heaven of romanticism has only silver linings, and is a place of pure delight, one spot free from pollution, the Bible does not say that. An idyllic heaven we may have imagined belongs more to Greek-Hellenistic writings than to the New Testament.

To many people "heaven" is intrinsically immaculate. Scripture, however, never makes that claim. Rather, it says parts of the heavens are dominated by and headquarters for demonic forces, satanic agents, and sinister personages.

An imperfect heaven is to be expected because of the fundamental antithetical structure everywhere given between this evil

age (heaven and earth) and the age to come. It must be emphasized that this total age experiences turbulence, disquiet, and
flux; both heaven and earth experience the wrath of God, the
powers of evil, personal incompleteness, and temporality. The
age to come is alone "heaven" in the idyllic sense.[22]

Scripture speaks of a new heaven and a new earth (2 Peter
3:10-13; Rev. 21:1, 2). It is interesting to note that in the eschatological anticipation of Isaiah the prophet there is the
strong theme of retaining earth in a revised form, of its preservation by recreation (Isa. 34:4; 51:6; 65:17; 66:22).

> The new order for them did not involve a different kind of
> existence in "which a non-bodily, non-material, heavenly or spir-
> itual mode of being takes the place of the material world of solid
> reality," but they anticipated the "then" as terrestrial bliss on a
> transformed earth.[23]

Paul saw a cosmic reformulation at the conclusion of history.
Christ's crowning achievement was to be the remolding of the
universe. Christ's death was "to reconcile all things to Himself
. . . whether things on earth or things in heaven" (Col. 1:20
NASB). "In Christ the space of heaven and the region of the earth
are to be united. The result of their union will be a new communication between them, and the outcome of this communication will be new life."[24]

The remaking of the heavens and the earth does not mean
something entirely new, but something qualitatively better
than the old. The word *new* is the word *kainos*, which refers to
something of superior value, functionally superior, a rejuvenated form.[25] Age does not automatically disqualify the attribution of the adjective *new*, for the new Jerusalem used old-world
jewels. (More on this in chapter 5.) In at least one place "new"
was used of something relatively new, not of something absolutely new. "New wine" or fresh wine was still wine. In Mark
2:21, 22 the idea of sewing a new leather patch on an old

wineskin wasn't wise. Whereas the new skin was flexible, the old was rigid. The new had more "give." The old couldn't stretch.

The re-creation of the heavens and the earth is not to be identified with Jesus' promise to go and prepare a place for his disciples, which was a reference to believers going to the Intermediate State or to the second coming of Christ (John 14:2, 3).[26] Nor is the re-creation of the heavens and the earth identical to and to be identified with the millennium mentioned in Revelation 20. The new heavens and the new earth come *after* the millennium, and their sharp contrasts make it impossible to consider them identical.[27] On the millennium of Revelation 20 consult the Appendix.

An earthly millennium is frequently confused with the new heavens and the new earth. The Bible presents postdeath heaven as the Intermediate State and the postearth phase as the new heavens and the new earth. In concentrating on the bliss of heaven now and in the Intermediate State (the time between death and resurrection) we ought not miss the distinctive feature and central truth of restored creation for which nature yearns (Rom. 8:22, 23).

All of nature is to be purified and reused, heaven as well as earth. The cataclysmic events described in Second Peter (also described in Mark 13:31; Rev. 21:1) initially produce destruction, and yet that is only the preparation for renovation. It does not end in annihilation.

> Since God will make the new earth his dwelling place, and since where God dwells there heaven is, we shall then continue to be in heaven while we are on the new earth. For heaven and earth will then no longer be separated, as they are now, but will be one (*see* Rev. 21:1-3).[28]

Jesus alluded to this happening, however indirectly, in the Sermon on the Mount. He said "The meek will inherit the earth" (Matt. 5:5). Oscar Cullman has reminded us:

The Christian hope relates not only to my individual fate, but to the entire creation. . . . God in a new act of creation will not *destroy* matter, but set it free from the flesh, from corruptibility.[29]

The promised spiritual body involves real people. Real bodies take up real space. We have misconstrued the final heaven if we see it as a place where bodyless spirits float and where the resurrected sit motionless through eternity in thoughtful contemplation. The teaching of a new earth and new heaven involves the participation of redeemed bodies. We shall have access as Christ's body to all that is his, including the new heavens and the new earth.

Supercolossal, the doubled-up adjectives now misapplied to man's extravagances, will be surpassed by the greater reality of our fondest hopes in his new creations. If the splendor of the spoiled world still can take our breath away, what can we expect in the world to come! To think that heaven will only be mildly interesting is to misjudge the capabilities of God to astonish and amaze puny humans. Our yearning for exploration of God's new and vastly improved, purged property will not be frustrated by the limitations most of God's children know on the present globe because of budget and body restrictions.

Glorified bodies will, doubtless, involve glorious action and enormous enjoyment. It would seem that some form of the pleasures of sight, sound, touch, and (less so) taste will be part of the new earth. The New Jerusalem, the city, is the bride. The redeemed will enter and enjoy a new earth rid of both moral and chemical pollutions. If there is no utilization of the new heavens and new earth, then holding out the promise of heaven to people amounts to "indeed an evangelical purgatory, denying the full glory stored up for the sons of God."[30] The Bible does not envision a future without a changed heaven and full earth or saved souls without new bodies. Adventures in the kingdom of heaven await the ransomed church. What agenda these truths will entail are left unstated in the New Testament, but it would be demeaning to think of it as an enormous play area for the saved.

Retired Jesuit Professor of Theology, Edmund J. Fortman, Hyde Park, Chicago, speculated that the transfigured earth will accommodate the latest scientific and artistic achievements of the past, involving structures to house them. This would make the new earth a monument to human achievement, when the focus of the new earth will be the glorification of God rather than individual men going apart and doing what they like to do, alone or with others.[31] In fairness, it should be noted that the Rev. Fortman cautioned, "Wherever we go in the cosmos, whatever we do there, we shall always have in us the beatific vision, love and enjoyment of the divine essence and persons and be utterly impeccable and supremely happy."[32] All activities will realize the goal of glorifying God in all things. What will be there we have no way of knowing, and how we shall view interests of time has not been revealed.

"Is heaven created?" has led to the question "Is heaven re-created?" In the first instance, there was no heaven to begin with and God brought the heavens, with all their marvelous complexity and immensity, into reality. Just as impressive in his power to recreate and reclaim what has been spoiled by the fall of man and its consequent curse.

Christians need to realize that the implication if God did not create the heavens is that matter is eternal. And if matter is eternal, then there is something as equal as God. To have any object as old or coexistent as God diminishes God's greatness. Scripture clearly shows how God still owns what is spoiled by sin and that he intends by his creative power to reclaim and remake the heavens and the earth. The result of insisting on God's priority to the heavens and his superiority in their creation bears on the outcome of history and the final form of reality.

The establishment of the vast heavens by God overthrows the faulty philosophy of Ludwig Feuerbach who attempted to dismiss God as a human projection that has no reality. His theory, which would destroy both the concept of God and of heaven, is a philosophic hypothesis far more unreal than any space fiction conceived.

Yet one must grant that there is a problem for those within Christianity in projecting on the Bible what they would most like to be there. This is evident in which emphases most appeal to us.

To compile views on heaven is a study of humanity. Human expectations reflect those who have them. What is voiced is not necessarily reality so much as the reality wished. Little publicized heaven beliefs provide points for self-identification. For such Colleen McDannell and Bernhard Lang's *Heaven: A History* is a treasure house for exploration. After sifting through centuries of opinions on heaven from within the Judeo-Christian tradition, Colleen McDannell and Bernhard Lang, concluded that most views of heaven fall within one of two categories: either a theocentric model of heaven in which God and the individual's relationship with God are stressed or an anthropocentric model of heaven in which human ties (friends, family, community) play a greater role. Whereas the former model seems to be vague, mystical, and idealistic, the latter model has an optimistic and more positive view of the world, and projects the better qualities of social and physical life into heaven.

These models are the major conclusions drawn by McDannell and Lang in their encyclopedic work mentioned above.[33] A significant flaw in this, however, was that they didn't see a third or moderating model, a model which was both theocentric and anthropocentric at the same time. A closer attention to the eschatological writings of theologians may have produced that for them, for a theocentric heaven does not exclude new uses on a new earth and physical activity. They found this true in late Augustine (pp. 65, 66, 68), in Luther and Calvin (pp. 147, 152, 154), and in Isaac Watts (pp. 207-209). Instead of seeing this as part of the theocentric model, they interpreted it as atypical, if not an aberration of the theocentric model. What wasn't made emphatic in their book summation was that those whose theologies and eschatologies were theocentric articulated a full life for the resurrected just. While they recognized this emphasis in some Reformed Protestant writings, they missed it in subsequent Protestant theologies. It is questionable that "by the mid-nineteenth century, the static theocentric heaven of the reformers was favored only by a handful of Protestant writers" (p. 287). No references are made to evangelical theologians such as Charles Hodge, Augustus Hopkins Strong, W. G. T. Shedd, B. B. Warfield, Louis Berkhof, and their multi-thousand pastoral representatives. This oversight may have been due to an unfamiliarity with the span of Protestant theology in the last two centuries and with the breadth of support for an evangelical orientation in the churches.

We have shown in this chapter that the biblical theme of "new heaven and new earth" requires a magnificent full-scale active life in the habitation, use, and governing of the new earth by those who are part of the blissful eternal state. Focus on this phase of eschatology was more the result of the Word of God than personal whim.

Various Christian representatives downplayed or denied this theme, partly because of the confusion between the millennial life as amillennialists see it and the new heavens/new earth. The premillennialist's view of the millennium makes it a thousand literal years with Israel prominent in Christ's reign on earth. Whereas the amillennialist view (argued in the Appendix) is that the millennium is now and in heaven.

What had been attributed to a physical millennium, minus a geophysical Israelite enclave, properly belongs to life on the new earth. Admittedly, another reason for this oversight is due to the fact that amillennialists can be faulted for not having sufficiently expanded on the new earth scenario for the blessed in the eternal state. According to McDannell and Lang, "in early seventeenth-century Protestant theology, belief in a 'new earth' virtually disappeared."[34]

A case can be made that the two approaches (spiritual vs. physical views of heaven) arise more from commitment to the biblical text, rather than from the psychological needs of the inquirers. The theocentric (God-centered) emphasis is credited as having started in the New Testament.[35] But the anthropocentric (man-centered) emphasis was also in Scripture. Irenaeus (140-200) was excited by a physical millennial theme even more so than he was about the theocentric theme of heaven as a state.[36]

The anthropocentric emphasis struck a responsive chord in the superheated atmosphere of persecution during Irenaeus' lifetime. Great comfort for potential martyrs arose from the thought of heavenly compensation for earthly assets likely to be lost in their stand for Christ. But the biblical text had clues that God was going to restore the earth to its pristine condition and have his saints populate it and derive pleasure from it. Irenaeus failed to see the distinction between millennium as a spiritual phase and the new heavens/new earth as a spiritual/physical stage. It was the confusion of the two entities which perpetuated the illusion that there would be an earthly paradise before the new heavens/new earth.

If it is true that people choose a position mainly because it satisfies their psychological needs, then to compile lists of the benefits of the other viewpoint would seem to make the compilation an exercise in futility. For if people choose the spiritual (theocentric) versus the physical (anthropocentric) aspects of the afterlife because of psychological preference, then why even consult or compare the history of ideas? It will only result in what one wants, not in what God wants.

What may slip by the casual reader of *Heaven: A History* is the fact that its operating premise was to begin with man rather than with God. It was not their starting point that the only God has revealed himself in meaningful language, but that men, even the apostles, must check their own "inner effervescence" and react to their own cultural environment to arrive at some idea of what is ahead.[37] Thus, their approach was itself anthropocentric (man-centered), rather than theocentric (God-centered). Their whole approach was anthropocentric from the start. They did not begin with the premise that Scripture is the authoritative guide to what will be.

> The earth is the LORD's and everything in it, the world, and all who live in it . . . (Ps. 24:1 NIV).

> Blessed are the meek for they will inherit the earth. (Matt. 5:5 NIV).

These affirmations, one from the Old Testament and one from the New Testament, underline an overlooked fact that Christians can be proheaven without being antiearth. The biblical heaven is not antimatter, but for restored and revised matter. Those committed to a biblical heaven do not despise the physical world. Because of the biblical vision of a new heaven and new earth, there is no cause to reject the anthropocentric over the theocentric models, for properly understood, they show two sides of the same reality, two orientations which are not incompatible. Therefore, for the Christian, the choice is not between heaven and earth, but the dual prochoice of heaven and earth in renewal.

4

Where
Is Heaven
❓

There is a land of pure delight,
Where saints immortal reign;
Infinite day excludes the night,
And pleasures banish pain.

We can admire Isaac Watts's (1674-1748) poetry in his "*A Heavenly Canaan.*" It appeals to our romantic side. But it may not pass with realists. What lasting value is there, if the sentiment doesn't have geography to back it up? Many react this way: it is not enough to say heaven is nice if it is nebulous. If heaven exists, what is the address? If skyward, plot it. Every traveler has a destination point. Knowing *where* heaven is would seem to make a journey there desirable, easier, surer.

Where is that land? Above, beneath, around us?
Lost in all space, or to a star confined?

F. M. FORD

One answer is that heaven is more a condition, sphere, or state rather than a place. It can't be plotted, for by definition it is extraterrestrial, otherworldly, inaccessible, uncharted terrain. How far is one to take Revelation's concrete descriptions of heaven?

The heavy symbolism of Revelation seems a strong argument that heaven is not a place. The abundance of rare jewels, the crystal river that never floods or runs dry, and the perpetually bearing fruit tree that never dies but gives life makes Revelation seem a jumble of fantasies to tantalize the poor and the hungry. Gigantic pearly gates that never close and golden streets that never tarnish may strike advocates of honesty in advertising as garish.

Another objection discourages belief in heaven as place: God's nature. God is too big to be in one place. The Jews recognized that long ago (1 Kings 8:27). God's longstanding omnipresence (latinized word for "everyplace") appears to overturn a place fixation.

Even within evangelical Christianity doubts have been raised about heaven as a place.[1] Some say insisting on heaven's locality is to urge an unreality, because God takes up every place and because the imagery of Revelation is too elaborate to be real and is deliberately paradoxical. Those who take this position argue that the figure of Christ returning to the Father's right hand militates against heaven as a place. "Right hand" is a metaphorical description of a place of honor, authority, and bliss; it is not a literal place. And "heavenly realm" is spiritual, not spatial.

Three serious arguments, however, commend and make credible heaven as a place. First, God is said to have created heaven as well as earth. How could God have created something that can't be located? The second reason adds more weight to the argument that place is not a slippery path not worth risking to follow: Christ ascended with a resurrection body. How can a body that was tangible, that took up space, not exist in a heavenly place? Third, there are specific texts, both in the Old Testament and in the New Testament, which speak of heaven as place. Isaiah 57:15 (NASB) says, of God, ". . . I dwell on a high and holy place. . . ." Jesus' statement regarding preparing a "place" (John 14:1,2) would make him utter a malapropism, using the wrong word.

What do we have left if the concept of place, which requires some sort of space, is abandoned?

> If heaven is completely non-spatial, then (we used to say) the heavenly life must be a fearful sea of feeling, a shapeless ecstasy; or anyhow, nothing you could fairly call the resurrection state of man. Whereas if heaven has any form of spatial dimension, then it falls somewhere in the field of space; a telescope might record it, an astronaut might reach it. And so heaven is pulled back into the perishable universe.[2]

Place should not be quickly abandoned. It is more profoundly rooted in the biblical material than first appears. And space need not be "pulled back into the perishable universe." Another alternative is to keep it where it is in an independent existence. Modern science is open to alternative explanations of space. New attitudes toward reality conclude that a static understanding of reality is self-limiting and incapable of accounting for some phenomena that cannot fit into our present concepts of multi-dimensional reality. The world of antimatter, of superspace, and subatomic particles has gone far in shaking up staid conclusions about how heaven has to be or cannot be.

Director of the Institute of Nuclear Studies at Oak Ridge, Tennessee, physicist William G. Pollard, proposed that in a space of a higher dimension reality is less restricted. He wrote:

> In that event the supernatural domains of heaven and hell, which have been so universally acknowledged in human experience, have as much claim on reality as does the restricted

spacio-temporal boundary between the natural and the supernatural is then rather differently drawn, and in a manner much more agreeable to modern views of the natural universe. Heaven, instead of being above us in ordinary space, is perpendicular to ordinary space, and the eternal is perpendicular to the temporal dimension. The transcendent and the supernatural, instead of being pushed farther away from us with each new advance in astronomy, are again everywhere in immediate contact with us, just as the dimension perpendicular to a plane surface is everywhere in contact with it, though transcendent of it.[3]

If what Dr. Pollard has proposed is right, then "heaven does lie about in our infancy." Place for heaven is less radical or ridiculous than some have thought, especially in view of modern astronautical physics. In fact, Jesus' use of the "above" and "below" references may be to the same effect.[4]

The likelihood that heavenly place is different from earthly place increases when one recalls how Jesus, in his resurrected form, had no problem in functioning in either earthly or heavenly realm. There has been only one resurrection like Jesus'. His resurrected body had the unique feature of being able to function in both the natural and supernatural dimensions.

Biblical resurrection requires us to retain concreteness as a characteristic of the afterlife. Christianity is based on Jesus' historicity, that is, that he was a real Person. In Jesus God was localized (his name "Emmanuel" means "God with us"). Also Jesus' tangibility in his resurrection-ascension should cause denouncers of heaven as place to reconsider their position. Where he went in his ascension reinforces and perpetuates the theme of heaven as place (Acts 1:9-11).

Rudolf Bultmann (1884-1976) considered Jesus' ascension myth, not fact. He dismissed Jesus' ascension as a historical event. It was (to him) the projection of the church, an early attribution of glory to Christ.

The resurrection stories in the Gospels are neither thin-air theatrics nor thin-ice imaginations. All evidence points to the objectivity and corporeal reality of Jesus' resurrection and ascension. Thomas Torrance replied to Bultmann:

> The ascension sends us back to the incarnation, and to the historical Jesus, and so to a Word and Act of God inseparably implicated in our space and time. It sends us back to a Gospel which is really accessible to frail creatures of earth and history, and a Gospel that is relevant to their bodily existence day by day in the structures of space and time.[5]

The biblical argument that heaven is a greater reality than earth (Heb. 8:3-5; 9:24; 10:1, 2) would mean that we should not easily discount heaven as place.

The fact of Jesus' bodily ascension not only established heaven as place, but at the same time it obligates us to recognize that Jesus' authority is above that of human seers:

> Because it is the historical and risen Jesus who is ascended, what Jesus says to us, the Jesus whom we meet and hear through the Witness of the Gospels, is identical with the eternal Word and Being of God himself.[6]

In reading the Gospels we meet heaven in print. The recorded deeds and sayings of the Lord are not man's words about God so much as God's Word about man. No wonder George Herbert (1593-1633) exclaimed that heaven lies flat in the Bible.[7]

Jesus in the Scriptures reminds us that heaven as atmosphere has arrived and that Jesus as heaven's administration acts. In Jesus heaven has come to us, and what he has said and done pulls back the curtain on the mysteries of the eternal. It is far more comforting for some people, however, to think of heaven as a space station, because it pushes heaven far enough away that it does not intrude into our lives now.

Jesus didn't get stalled on place questions. More important matters occupied his time. He strongly urged his audiences to get away from a geographical mind-set. He asked them to focus on heaven as a "kingdom," even before a "house."

Kingdom was Jesus' favorite word for heaven. Jews of his day thought of "kingdom" in terms of God's intervention for Israel and the recovery of their standing as a nation. The messianic hope was for the restoration of Israel's fortunes. They wanted to get out from under Roman domination. They thought of heaven in terms of physical and political freedom. The Pharisees were looking for signs of the arrival of God's kingdom.

> Some Pharisees asked Jesus when the kingdom of God would come. His answer was, 'The Kingdom of God does not come in such a way as to be seen. No one will say, "Look, here it is!" or, "There it is!" because the Kingdom of God is within you' (Luke 17:20, 21, GNB).

Luke 17:21 can be translated two ways and both have linguistic legitimacy: "within you" or "among you."[8] The translation "within you" is preferred by many translations and, in my estimation, it is to be preferred, not only because of manuscript evidence, but also because it logically leads to "among you," whereas if translated "among you" "within you" does not necessarily follow. The chief objection to the "within you" is that the total remark was addressed to skeptical Pharisees and to allege the kingdom was within them would be unlikely.[9]

But the recognition of the negative attitudes of the Pharisees, however, does not necessarily make "within you" out of place, because Jesus was inferring that their emphasis on external signs—"Here it is" and "There it is"—to which they were addicted, was the mistake of looking in the wrong place.

Where they didn't look was where the kingdom was to be. The Pharisees, who first heard the words of Jesus in Luke 17:21, unfortunately, denied themselves the thrill of coming into the kingdom. In belittling Jesus (the kingdom among them) they showed he was never within them. Christ was definitely among them, but because they wanted external manifestations and not the Person who embodied the kingdom, they missed it. By rejecting Jesus' ministry they could not possibly experience the kingdom of heaven.

Jesus' statement, "The Kingdom of God is within you," redirected his audience away from spatial concerns. He put the stress on the presentness of the kingdom. The rationale for the stupendous claim that heaven had arrived is traced to Christ's nature and stature. The kingdom had come because the King of the eternal ages had arrived.

The place question, finally, is a person question. The New Testament locates the kingdom in Jesus' person and ministry. "Jesus brought the kingdom."[10] And, with Jesus, the time question was answered with the place question. "Since Jesus, mankind has been freed from the question of when the end will come."[11] Jesus brought heaven. Jesus was heaven. Wherever Jesus is, there is heaven. "Jesus Christ is . . . God's place in the world where he is really present to us in our place."[12]

What happened, then, when Jesus was crucified? Wasn't heaven destroyed or displaced when Jesus died? If permanency was one of the characteristics of heavenly reality, then was Jesus evicted from his place when he died? His death, however, was neither heaven's destruction nor Jesus' displacement.

On the cross Jesus stayed in place to establish a new place. Jesus was opening heaven for sinners all the time his executioners were bringing down the curtain on his life. Where heaven was thought least likely, there it reached its zenith in operation.

"Where is God?" inquired the mind:
"To His presence I am blind. . . .
I have scanned each star and sun,
Traced the certain course they run;
I have weighed them in my scale,
And can tell when each will fail;
From the caverns of the night
I have brought new worlds to light;
I have measured earth and sky
Read each zone with steady eye;
But no sight of God appears
In the glory of the spheres."
But the heart spoke wistfully,
"Have you looked at Calvary?"

THOMAS C. CLARK[13]

Jews were accustomed to thinking of heaven ahead, not heaven now. But Jesus relentlessly stressed the here-nowness of heaven (Matt. 6:33; 11:12; 12:28; Mark 10:15; Luke 12:31; 11:19ff). The arrival of the kingdom in Christ, however, did not rule out a future expression of it.[14] In Jesus' arrival is heaven's extension. Heaven is where Jesus is. Where Jesus reigns, heaven resides.[15] The translations "within" and "among" underscore the truth that the kingdom of heaven arrived in the words and works of Jesus. This perspective was radical in Jesus' day. It continues to rattle us, especially if we ask ourselves whether heaven has begun in us in time.

Heaven is meant to be an inward reality for us. Our searching is the result of his finding us. When Christ enters a life there is a remarkable remaking. This comes through in the often overlooked synonym for heaven "eternal life," which appears most frequently in the Gospel of John. Ordinarily, people think of "eternal life" as something following death, a kind of automatic state that every person enters. But that concept was never taught by Jesus. On the contrary, he taught that "eternal life" was to be an in-time, predeath experience and was shared only by those who believed in him. John 5:24 (GNB) is one of many verses which shows this:

> I am telling you the truth: whoever hears my words and believes in him who sent me has eternal life. He will not be judged, but has already passed from death to life.

Our search for heaven's location should begin with the Christ of the New Testament. Our inability to locate heaven in space is not due to the fact that evidence for heaven is scarce or faulty. Expressions of heaven are right under our noses. Both in the Bible and in the transformed lives of Christians about us are ample instances that heaven is in our midst. Once Christ steps out of the New Testament into our lives by the power of his Word, we are transformed. Then we begin to think differently about heaven.

> One who believes himself reborn does not think of eternity as a norm outside of time. . . . No one can deprive the believer of his faith in the *here and now* of the eternal, the here and now of salvation.[16]

Entrance into heaven now, without death, strikes the average person as farfetched. To him heaven follows an earthly life; it is not in this life. But heaven is astride us. Amazing! Just as amazing is the audacious truth that the believer on earth is automatically a resident of heaven ahead or heaven above, "deep heaven."

We are in eternity now. Eternity is parallel to time, not after it. That is what Paul meant when he wrote that we are "seated with [Christ] in the heavenly places" (Eph. 2:6 NASB, *see also* Col. 3:3). Unlike God, we cannot be in two places at the same time. But that restriction is overridden, because in God's mind we are viewed as already there. What God perceives in the presentness of eternity will surely become reality. "We are in heaven but only in the sense of a mystical incorporation in the life of Christ who is in heaven."[17] The same truth is celebrated with a string of certainties in Hebrews 12:22-24 (NASB).

> [Notice the stress on the present] You have come to Mount Zion and to the city of the living God, the heavenly Jerusalem, and to myriads of angels, to the general assembly and church of the first-born who are enrolled in heaven, and to God, the Judge of all, and to the spirits of righteous men made perfect, and to Jesus, the mediator of a new covenant, and to the sprinkled blood, which speaks better than the blood of Abel.

Therefore, heaven is in the believer *before* the believer goes to heaven and the believer has already been to heaven *before* he settles in heaven. The Christian has this double dwelling: heaven's prepresence in the believer and the believer's prepresence in heaven ahead. God, thus, gives us a double assurance.

Shirley MacLaine, an award-winning actress, in an attempt to make Jesus seem to agree with her view of human abilities to find God, cited Luke 17:21 as one which "taught that the purpose of life was to work one's way back to the Divine Source of which we are all a part."[18] Two years later she argued similarly. She wrote,

> I spent most of the weekend rereading parts of the Bible, once again reminded of what a metaphysical document it really is, each teaching referring to the Kingdom of Heaven existing within each of us, and a New Age of recognition coming that would attest to that.[19]

Was Jesus saying in Luke 17:21 that God is in everyone? Within organized Christianity, there are some who say just that. To them Jesus' statement, "the kingdom of God is within you," means that everyone is in touch with God, that heaven is in every man making each an anonymous Christian.

Does heaven enter everyone? Is God present in every human

being? Some say so. Listen carefully in church groups, pay attention to small talk on golf greens, or listen to the comments of guests on talk shows, or better still check the resolutions of mainline denominations. What one hears gives the impression there is no urgency for people to seek heaven, for everyone is already in it or will get to enjoy it.

An increasing number of nominal church people hold views similar to those of Albrecht Ritschl (1822-1889), who wrote:

> The kingdom of God is the people of God conceived in the totality of their ethical activities, under the impulse of love.[20]

Boiled down, Ritschl's formulation meant that everyone would be saved. He characterized the kingdom of God as "the moral unification of the human race, through action prompted by universal love to our neighbor."[21]

True mystics don't need to read to learn. They do read (and they publish!) mostly to confirm what they already intuitively feel. Shirley MacLaine is a prime example. It is needless for the genuine psychic or mystic to look to others. All they need is to consult their "higher self," as they see it. The heart has its own reasons. They will fall back on logic if by it they can gather new followers. They will argue, "If God is everywhere, isn't heaven, therefore, everywhere?" The creative moment[22] or the crunch of conscience[23] are viewed as sufficient indicators of the presence of God's kingdom. If so, then consulting Christ's words is not really necessary. British poet William Blake (1757-1827), spoke for them all, when he wrote, "There is a full and entire heaven in every man."[24]

This approach means that the kingdom of God is a moral realm into which each person can put himself. It is blatant distortion to say that Jesus implied that man was devoid of evil or that the kingdom of God was in every person. Jesus' words have been given a new heading and destination by those who seek to have his statements endorse their feelings.

Plane hijacking has become a tool of international terrorists. In the fashion of innocent tourists, many thought, on boarding (that is, joining) a church, that they were going to heaven. In fact, unknown to them, the crew has been given new directions and instead of landing in heaven, they are due to dock in hell. More and more churches have been hijacked by errorists. There are not enough spiritual security checks for those boarding churches! Once errorists are in the cockpit, they detail their own midcourse corrections, diverting the flight to an unwanted destination.

Tragically, the words of Jesus are turned around to establish the very opposite of what he said. Jesus' insistence was that he was the substance and source of divine power, a claim which falsifies the boast that humans, without distinction, are God-possessed. Peter T. Forsyth (1848-1921) put it in sharp focus:

> The idea we are offered is a kingdom of men, with God to serve it, rather than a kingdom of God, with man to serve it. It is a consecration of the natural man by God instead of redemption by God.[25]

The alternate translation has been used to redirect Christian belief into a path which leads farther from God. "Among you" or "in your midst" in Luke 17:21 has been taken as a justification that the kingdom and church are identical. In this case *you* is stressed out of proportion, to the denial of the importance and initiative of Christ. By emphasizing the recipient of the kingdom the centrality of Christ is obscured or obliterated.

George E. Ladd (1911-1982) has given one of the better summaries:

> Men can enter the kingdom (Matt. 5:20; 7:21; Mk. 9:47; 10:23, etc.), but they are never said to erect it or to build it. Men can receive the kingdom (Mk. 10:15; Lk. 18:17), inherit it (Matt.

25:34), and possess it (Matt. 5:4), but they are never said to establish it. Men can reject the kingdom, i.e. refuse to receive it (Lk. 10:11) or enter it (Matt. 23:13), but they cannot destroy it. They can look for it (Lk. 23:51), pray for its coming (Matt. 6:10), and seek it (Matt. 6:33; Lk. 12:31), but they cannot bring it.[26]

The church "belongs to His kingdom, but is not yet the whole of this kingdom";[27] "the community of the kingdom but never the kingdom itself."[28]

The case for heaven's reality is not helped by ambiguity in hymns. Some early twentieth-century hymns on heaven abandoned specificity in describing heaven. Generalities were popular. Four hymns in particular lapsed into vagueness: J. P. Webster's "Sweet By and By," Charles H. Gabriel's "Some Bright Morning," and Tullius C. O'Kane's "The Home Over There." But the most ambiguous hymn of all on heaven was the 1897 hymn "Beautiful Isle of Somewhere."

> Land of the true, where we live anew,
> Beautiful isle of somewhere.

Somehow (if I am permitted to perpetuate this indefiniteness a little more), the words may reflect an inability to resolve the place problem. But doesn't "somewhere" end "nowhere" every time?

Jeremiah Burroughs (1599-1646) grasped the true significance of "the kingdom within."

> Before death, there is a Kingdom of God within the soul. . . . He need not wait till afterwards, til he goes to heaven; but certainly there is a heaven in the soul of a godly man, he has heaven already. . . . There is a heaven within the souls of the saints [he means, living Christians J.G.]—that is a certain truth; no soul shall ever come to heaven, but the soul which has heaven come to it first. . . . If you will go to heaven when you die, heaven will come to you before you die. Now this is a great

mystery, to have the kingdom of heaven in the soul; no man can know this but that soul which has it. The heaven which is within the soul for the present is like the white stone and the new name, that none but those that have it can understand it. [The last sentence is a reference to Rev. 2:17.)[29]

At issue is our attitudinal position, rather than heaven's precise location. It matters little *where* heaven is, but it matters very much where *we are in relationship to Jesus.* If we began asking "where" heaven is, we should progress to inquire "where" we are spiritually.

The first focus should not even be where we are, but where Christ is, for he epitomizes heaven. This deeper question has more practical bearing than a navigator's curiosity about heaven's address and apogee. No one likes to be put on the spot. It makes people back off from self-inquiry entirely.

On our own, however, we should, nevertheless, consider the question. God will bring it up again, if we don't face it in time. Our reflective moment may come at any time. God doesn't remind us of it only when we encounter failure. He may nudge us into self-evaluation at the pinnacle of success. Pat Williams, the General Manager of the Philadelphia 76ers, who organized Sunday chapels for the Phillies and '76ers, said:

> Athletes have been goal-setters all their lives. . . . As soon as they reach what they have been striving for, there is a momentary ecstasy. But it usually lasts as long as it takes the champagne to dry up. And then there is this nagging question: "Is this all there is?" They have this restlessness, this emptiness. There is a real void in their life. They may try to fill that void with fame or power or fortune or sex or drugs or alcohol. But that isn't the answer either. Maybe it is for a while. But it is never lasting. . . . And they feel cut off from God by the sin factor. So, recently, a lot of them have been rededicating themselves. They find God again . . . they discover something that, in this world of turbulence, they can count on. . . . What it amounts to is they give up the ego drive.[30]

To have eternal life in eternity we must have it in time. If Jesus is not part of our lives today, he will not be in our futures later. Jesus in the heart is heaven in the heart. Our interest in heaven must return to *who* Jesus was. That should be the chief motivation. However our own lack of consistency should stimulate us to engage in self-examination.

During pre-Civil war days blacks were very aware of and angry with the injustices perpetuated against their race. They were also able to see through the hypocrisy of their masters. One time when a master died, a slave expressed doubt about the master's heavenly arrival. When asked why, he said, "When Massa go north, or go on a long journey to the springs, he talked about it for a long time and got ready. I never heard him talking about going to heaven. I never saw him get ready to go."[31] Our heavenly journey, though close at hand, is no less real than a trip to a distant city or to a foreign country.

> The trip to heaven or hell is surer, longer, and more certainly one way than a trip to Australia. For every earthly trip, you at least make some inquiries at the travel bureau. The church claims to be the heavenly travel bureau as well as the ship, the Noah's ark, in which we go.[32]

Only in a loose sense is the church a vehicle to heaven. Churches have strayed. Christ is the only reliable way. A traveler in the Swiss Alps once asked a boy where a certain town was. (Maps don't always show small towns.) The boy replied, "I heard of that town, but I don't know where it is. But I do know that people who go there go by this road."

We can't fix heaven on an astronomer's chart, but we know that people who go there go by Jesus the Way. The decision to follow Christ leads where we want to go. "Unto him shall the gathering of the people be" (Gen. 49:10 KJV).

Christ is the heart of heaven
Its fullness and its bliss;
The center of the heavenly throng,
The object of the ransomed's song,
Is Jesus in the midst.[33]

Therefore, the answer to the question "Where is heaven?" boils down to two further questions: Where is Christ? and, just as importantly, What is our relationship with him?

5

What
Is Heaven
Like
?

*T*his question is not always asked out of a desire to go, but just a desire to know. People are as curious about heaven as they are about reports on any distant place yet to be visited. A person's desire to go anywhere is conditioned by how it is perceived.

Before we attempt to answer the question we should seek to know which heaven is meant. There are several "heavens" (*See* Glossary, "Heaven—in Old Testament and New Testament").

Once we get past the upper air and starry heavens, three others stand out:[1]

An Immediate Heaven

An Intermediate Heaven

An Infinite Heaven

"Immediate Heaven" was dealt with in the preceding chapter. When Jesus enters our lives heaven has begun. Heaven is in the Christian before the Christian is in heaven. First John 5:12 says it all: "He who has the Son has life. . ." (NIV).

"Intermediate Heaven" refers to those who die before the culmination of history. It concerns those who on death go to be with the Lord. The final form of heaven differs from the Intermediate Heaven the way a bud differs from the full flower.

"Infinite Heaven" is the final heaven. It is the subject of Revelation 21. C. S. Lewis's expression "Deep Heaven" is an apt way of referring to it. When a person asks, "What is heaven like?" I assume that the person is asking about the final phase of heaven, the infinite heaven.

Chapter 21 is widely recognized as the most extended treatment of the final phase of heaven in the Bible. Indeed Revelation 21 is the culmination of descriptions of heaven in the entire book of Revelation.

The last book of the Bible shows a progressive parallelism in describing the hereafter. This is true of its depiction of judgment, which began with less detail (6:12-17), and ended with the climactic scene near the end of the book (20:11-15). It is true, also, of heaven.

> Though the final joy of the redeemed in the life to come has been hinted at in 7:15-17, it is not until we reach chapter 21 that we find a detailed and elaborate description of the blessedness of life on the new earth (21:1—22:5).[2]

Revelation 21 is not just one among many sources on heaven, little different from the imaginative visions of William Blake or Emanuel Swedenborg. The Book of Revelation is the revelation of Jesus Christ (1:1). As a descriptive guide it is worlds apart from other mystical writings. Because of its originator, Jesus Christ, Revelation is the Christian's measure to evaluate other views. Revelation 21 is the central passage for a Christian in any discussion on the subject. Therefore, we must examine it carefully.

Heaven Moves

One unique feature about John's vision was the way heaven emerges. The church itself, massive and magnificent, moving downward, descending, coming to a new earth.

> And I saw the holy city, new Jerusalem, coming down out of heaven from God, made ready as a bride adorned for her husband (Rev. 21:2 NASB).

Central in this description is that John did not journey up to the church, but the church came to the new earth. Its action was special not because of its speed. The motion of a bride to her beloved is more deliberate and determined than fast. The spiritual significance of the New Jerusalem's movement was that it—the bride, the church—moved toward Christ. Size aside, its greatest significance was that the total body wanted to be with Christ.

Here was a powerful symbolism, yet frequently passed over. Of all heaven's symbols, it was this symbolism which is missed the most. That heaven came to John illustrated not only a church God intended for occupancy of earth, but also it dramatized the origin of John's vision and the initiative of God in saving man. The bride complete descended to Christ, the groom. John did not strain heavenward, nor did he use psychic stimulation to push himself into the beyond. The movement was from God. The motivation was not John's. This feature sets John's vision apart from human-generated trances.

In contrast to John's vision was Dante's (1265-1321) epic journey to paradise, combined with his trips to purgatory and hell, in *The Divine Comedy.* Written in 1300, it remains today a classic model of the Italian language. Dante had something in common with John, for he was also an exile. For nineteen years he was a vagabond from his native Florence. In his banishment, like John, he recorded his visions.

The Divine Comedy is a famous source for concepts on heaven, but it is not something which should shape our views of heaven. The poetry is unassailable, but its theology is misguided and misguiding.[3] We should hesitate turning to it for guidance about heaven, for the following reasons:

(1) Christ didn't reveal heaven to Dante, but Beatrice, his love, did. He began seeking for a tour guide outside Christianity, begging Apollo himself, the patron of the Muses. (See his introduction). Jesus Christ, the Alpha and the Omega, was not petitioned, nor was his revelation considered adequate. In the end, a human figure grown to god-like proportions was used. Love for Beatrice drew Dante to heaven. In the vision of John, however, it was the Christ's love which lowered heaven itself. For Dante, it was the grip of Beatrice. For John, it was God's initiative. John stayed still; heaven moved to him. But in the *The Divine Comedy,* however, Dante went to heaven.

(2) In Dante good behavior was made the basis for entrance into heaven. Augustus Hopkins Strong said, "As the soul laden with sin experiences a downward" motion, "so the soul possessed of purity experiences an upward gravitation."[4]

Revelation 21 says the opposite. There God does not set conditions for seeing heaven, nor does any meritoriousness cause heaven's doors to open. Rather the reader is encouraged to "drink without cost" (21:6 NIV). The freeness of heaven is clearly stated in Revelation 22:17: ". . . take the free gift of the water of life" (NIV).

Dante saw man going through eight stages or eight heavens before he got to heaven's deepest interior. In the lowest heaven, he saw nuns who got married. Doctors of divinity were found on level four. To pass through to the final state Dante had to pass the tests of faith, hope, and love. These tests were administered by Saints Peter, James, and John respectively. Only "when he has shown himself expert in these prerequisites to heavenly bliss" was "the poet carried up to the 9th or highest heaven."[5]

John of Revelation, however, was handed no requirement list to pass on to his readers. The ground for entrance into heaven for John was acceptance of heaven as a gift.

> (3) The third reason why the poem is theologically lacking is because it showed man moving to heaven, rather than God coming to man with heaven. John showed heaven descending. Dante showed man ascending. Heaven was possible, in Dante, because of human achievement. In Revelation heaven was reality, because of divine action, because of supernatural grace. In Revelation 21 God is pictured as receiving all the glory, and whatever good man enjoyed was the result of a grant to undeserving man.

Dante reflected the medieval view that man can have moral merit before God. There are still many supporters of this view. Today it is as much alive in forms of Protestantism as in contemporary Catholicism. What may stun some nominal Protestants is the fact that Catholic theology is more willing to credit a larger portion of salvation to Christ than do some neo-Protestants.

In the Bible man cannot get to heaven by self-propulsion. According to some forms of Christianity, the new Jerusalem does indeed "come down from heaven, not as a bride adorned for her husband, but as the domestic servant of omnipotent man."[6]

> (4) A fourth reason why Dante's *Paradise* can't pass as evangelical is that the degrees or stages in heaven reflect more neo-

Platonic emanation (via Albertus Magnus, the teacher of Thomas Aquinas) than they do Scripture. The order of value that Dante pressed should not be overlooked. As with other medievalists he put contemplation over action. But it is not a biblical prioritization to have "thought" considered better or more important than "doing."[7]

At the very beginning of John's vision of heaven in Revelation 21 is the emphasis that heaven "owes its existence to the condescension of God and not to the building of men."[8] The motion is *to* man, not *from* man. This approach fits the New Testament picture of man immobilized in sin and in need of God beginning in him what he is incapable of initiating himself.

Heaven as the Ultimate Model City

Cities are more than masses of population, they are citadels for mutual safety, conduits of commercial enterprise, and centers of artistic and scientific creativity. The representation of heaven as a city was intended to suggest "intensity of life, variety of occupation, and closeness of relation to each other."[9]

Upkeep and maintenance of city life and structures are major challenges to modern cities. Through intentional management and resourceful funding some cities are able to keep their attractiveness, wonderful healthiness, cleanliness, and collective decency. Without purposeful and persistent attention to tendencies of decay, earthly cities develop notoriously tough neighborhoods, urban blight, and pockets of violence, crime, and risque entertainments.

Those cities which have been winning their fight over crime, crumbling housing, and declining quality education become known as "model cities." One city, devoid of detractions, perpetually clean, eternally nonthreatening, will be heaven. John called it "the new Jerusalem" (Rev. 21:2).

Originally, Jerusalem was called "holy" because God came to the city, made the city, chose the city (Ezek. 43:2; Zech. 2:5; 14:4). It reflected God's intention to have a city totally dedicated to himself. It was not called "holy" because its citizens were better or because its politics were freer from corruption, but it was "holy" because God picked it, because God's Word was channeled through it, and because God's love was set on it.[10] Heaven ahead was exemplified by old Jerusalem in its initial spiritual orientation.

Famous cities of the world have been chosen because of the advantages they provided. Paris was chosen because of its centrality. Moscow was chosen because of its defensibility. But Jerusalem was chosen neither because of its commercial value nor because of its political importance.[11]

Old Jerusalem had no military advantage and was economically dependent on its neighbors. That accounted for the ease by which she was besieged, broken, taken, and retaken. She stood in contrast with man's first city, a city which reflected human self-reliance.

Genesis records the erection of the first city. Cain built a city and made it his personal monument of achievement and independence from God (4:17). He intended it to praise the builder. It was undertaken to free man from God and to proclaim his ability to live apart from God. Jacques Ellul's analysis is worthwhile:

> The city is the negation of the omnipotence of God; it is the closed door of man's walling himself up against any relation with the Creator. The original city was "a creation . . . to exclude God."[12]

Jerusalem, on the other hand, was the city of God. In Jerusalem, God was wanted. In it God worked. Its theological value eclipsed its cultural and commercial ventures.

WHAT IS HEAVEN LIKE?

John of Revelation saw the secular city of Jerusalem as sinful as old Babylon (11:8), for it was there that Christ was made captive, condemned, and crucified. Jerusalemites were as uncaring toward Christ as the Babylonians were unfeeling toward the Jews. Old Jerusalem had degenerated to the level of Cain, which was the prototype of Babylon.

The church was the replacement of Old Jerusalem. It had to be made "new," for it had turned against Christ. Of the two Greek words for our one word *new*, *kainos* was chosen. It meant something qualitatively better than the old, something superior in value. The other Greek word, *neos*, not used here means recently new, something lately made, even if a reproduction. *Kainos* is new in kind; *neos* is new in time.[13] Throughout Revelation *kainos* is used.

The New Jerusalem, ironically, had some old objects in it. Precious metal and stones made it sparkle in the light of God. There may be a problem in some minds with inclusion of vintage figures to describe the city's wealth and worth. But age will not cause its value to drop. *Kainos*-new can refer to being unused, such as unused wineskins (Mark 2:21, 22). Untapped and undiscovered glory resides in ore reserves of old earth. In heaven as there can be new beauty in old substance, so there will be new joy in old (and remade) sinners and new peace in old (and remade) bodies. Another aspect of heaven's newness will be the matter of the "new songs" of Revelation (ahead in chapter 9).

The joy of heaven will be a group experience. With the pain, sorrow, and suffering being eliminated, heaven's joys will be undiluted and unending. The Beatitudes of Jesus will be fulfilled. The pure will see God, the poor will possess the imperishable, the persecuted will have losses restored, the deprived will have immediate access to all parts of the renovated earth.

Heaven—A Marvel of Design, Spaciousness and Efficiency

William Penn (1644-1718) laid out the first streets of Philadelphia. God designed the heavenly city. The city was described as a huge cube with a homogeneous stable population. It was shaped and sized a perfect cube (1,500 miles [calculated from stadia; a stadion was 600 feet] wide, high and deep [21:16]). It had a symmetrical number of sides, gates, and foundation stones (4 sides, 12 gates, 12 foundation stones), and lumination which would never need replenishment (21:23). God will pervade every part of it (21:3, 11). "The Lamb is the light" (21:23 KJV) is better stated in the NIV: "The Lamb is its lamp."

It would dishonor the heavenly Architect to contend that its dimensions were meant to be taken literally. Graphic figures, presented in apocalyptic fashion, thundered forth theological truths. A certain reserve was maintained and some vagueness accompanied its enticing emblems. The intention was to allow the element of surprise for those privileged to enjoy it.

The oversized New Jerusalem was only a fraction of what it would finally become. It had the shape of a cube (Rev. 21:16). Its cube shape was a carry-over from Old Testament worship specifications for the Holy of Holies (1 Kings 6:20). Heaven was portrayed as one gigantic Holy of Holies (Rev. 21:22), where God would be worshiped freely and without end by the redeemed. That was what would set it apart from every human enterprise. That was how it would function, endure, and enthrall.

Moderns are not conscious of seeing, handling, or using cubes. Occasionally, we may try to solve the maddening challenge of the Rubic's cube (a mind-memory toy), or structural engineers may use the cube, hopefully with more certainty than a casino dice-thrower. In most civilizations the cube is a mathematical article that represents balance, togetherness, and peace. To be in God's presence eternally is not to be confined in a cell, but to be surrounded by One whose nature, gifts, and glory are of the essence of liberty, variety, and symmetry.

We desire to dwell in heaven, not because of its cubic shape, its jasper walls, its golden streets, its pearly gates, or its dazzling light. Christians want to go to heaven to be with Jesus and to live forever with the Lord.

Popular opinion likens heaven as having one pearly gate, whereas Revelation 21:12, 21 mentions twelve, three on each of the four points of the compass. Notice that Peter is not the attendant, but twelve angels (21:12). Have we noticed, also, the size of the gates? The individual pearl gates match the height of the walls (21:12, 13, 15, 16, 21). The walls were given a height of 200 feet.[14] If the pearl gates are taken literally, then one is left thinking of the ludicrous notion that some gigantic oysters produced them. And considering that there will be no more sea (21:1) God would have a double handicap!

Seriously, it should be noted that the gates of pearl were not an artistic whim, but had a theological purpose. They represented the Pearl of Great Price, a figure from the Gospels, which pointed to Jesus Christ. The message of the twelve gates was that access to heaven was not limited to people from any one geographical location. Conversion stories show how varied the vehicles God has used to bring people into eternal life, and how different their emotions are in the process.

> From opposite divisions of the theological compass, from opposing standpoints of the religious world, from different quarters of human life and character, through various expressions of their common faith and hope, through diverse modes of conversion, through different portions of the Holy Scripture, will the weary travelers enter the Heavenly City, and meet each other—"not without surprise"—on the shores of the same river of life.[15]

Everyone must pass through Christ to get into heaven. Unless we go through Christ we cannot get into the New Jerusalem. Regrettably, earth dwellers are under the delusion that passage into heaven can be achieved by avoiding Christ. They may scramble in haste, struggle in pride, even scratch in panic to tunnel through the walls of glory, failing to realize that the only thing they have to do is go through Christ, the door always open. An invitation to use the gates is one of the concluding portions of the Book of Revelation.

> Blessed are those who wash their robes, that they may have the right to the tree of life and may go through the gates into the city. Outside are the dogs, those who practice magic arts, the sexually immoral, the murderers, the idolaters, and everyone who loves and practices falsehood (22:14, 15 NIV).

Heaven's dimensions were not meant to be taken literally. The calculations are precise, but only to convey the sense of immensity. They are meant to convey how huge, how grand, how glorious and how lavish life in heaven will be. The river of life (22:1, 17) and the tree of life (22:2) are meant to suggest never-ending and totally satisfying refreshment by the Spirit through the gospel of grace.

The accommodations sketched were the finest, befitting God's flawless excellence. The literal details by which they are described show how God's hospitality could not be improved. It is tragic that some Christians question the spiritual commitment of those who emphasize the symbolic intentions of chapter 21. If anything should disabuse of insisting on literal fulfillment, it is twelve gigantic pearls!

If some Christians are puzzled by the size and style of gates, others are turned off by the use of walls. Why would heaven need walls, and how would jasper enhance them (Rev. 21:17)? The wall feature was a mild spinoff from Isaiah 54:11, 12.[16] With the banishment of all evil the walls hardly seemed necessary. Inside the New Jerusalem all the old conversational walls the redeemed felt on earth were to be dismantled, symbolized by Christ who through his death purposed to break down the cultural wall between Jew and Gentile (Eph. 2:14). Walls, in this case, were unnecessary for defense, but they were reminders to those inside of how once they were on the other side, reminders of their inability to penetrate or be allowed the privilege of access to God apart from Christ's high priestly action who established free communication with God through the torn curtain of his flesh on the cross.

If some are annoyed by the fact of the walls, even more are mystified by the variety of gigantic gems mentioned as named after the apostles (Rev. 21:14-20).[17] It is doubtful that the writer wished to impose a burden on the reader to try to come up with some special mystical meaning to each variety of stone, since the ancient manner of identifying precious stones was imprecise, positive identification is problematical, even prohibitive. Rather, the intent seems to have been to leave us with the overwhelming wealth buried in the teachings of the apostles, of the variety, superior quality, range of beauty, and enormous wealth in their body of writings.

The foundation stones were less significant for size than for their strategic importance for the stability of the city. There were twelve (and no more) on purpose. Ultimately, they were more essential than the gates. Enormous importance was placed on the limited writings of twelve apostles. For the message of the twelve precious stones, which had inscribed the names of the twelve apostles (21:14), was that heaven's first and finest interpreters laid the conceptual groundwork of the New Jerusalem. "The twelve foundations of the city are a symbolic resume of the whole revelation."[18] God's revelation through the apostles, not in those who followed them, formed the basis for Christian hope hereafter. God does not continue to reveal himself, but his revelation ended with the last apostle. If one grants that Revelation was Christ's Word to John, then we cannot dismiss the significance of this symbolism as an ego-tistical elevation of the last of the apostles. What John wrote was what Jesus said. This explains the conclusion of Revelation where the warning goes:

> I testify to everyone who hears the words of the prophecy of this book: if anyone adds to them, God shall add to him the plagues which are written in this book; and if anyone takes away from the words of the book of this prophecy, God shall take away his part from the tree of life and from the holy city, which are written in this book (22:18, 19 NASB).

The population of heaven, unlike any other city, will neither gain nor lose. The ones who are there do not leave, nor do they want to leave. ". . . and no one who practices abomination and lying, shall ever come into it, but only those whose names are written in the Lamb's book of life" (21:27 NASB).

Heaven's population is handpicked by God. In eternity (Eph. 1:4) He chose us before we decided for him (John 15:16). Our being selected had nothing to do with our social standings. Our earthly personality traits or supposed moral fitness contributed nothing in influencing God. The church is gathered in "accordance with his pleasure and will" (Eph. 1:5 NIV). And the exact number of the citizens is known long before they are assembled. The number 144,000 was only representative of a larger body (Rev. 7:4-11).

That salvation is God-initiated is seen in the signing of the names in the Book of Life (3:5; 13:8; 17:8; 21:27) and their being sealed (7:4). The signing of the Father's and Christ's name on our forehead, like a tattoo (3:12; 22:4) means we are marked by God as his property. Our being in heaven will not be self-scripted (2:17; 6:11; 13:10; 20:12). In other words, God personally chooses those who will be there, not on the basis of merit or worthiness, but on the basis of his purposes alone (Rom. 9:16).

Fill up the role of thine elect,
Then take thy power and reign.
HENRY ALFORD

Our enrollment in heaven is credited to Christ's registration of us. The reference to the high numbers (144,000 was a "ball park" figure) did not obscure the personal nature of Christ's choice of us. Nor did it assert that the opportunity was limited to a published list. Only God revealed the hidden stone of choice to whom God gave it (Rev. 2:17). It is plain from the two-fold emphasis of God's election and of the invitation to all to enter heaven through Christ that in the mind of John pre-destination and the free offer of the gospel are not contradic-tory. Divine election does not prohibit, nullify, or discourage the gospel invitation, which significantly is nearby the assertion of divine sovereignty.

Nothing impure will ever enter it, nor will anyone who does what is shameful or deceitful, but only those whose names are written in the Lamb's book of life (21:27 NIV).

Compare 21:27 and 22:17:

The Spirit and the bride say, "Come." And let the one who hears say, "Come." And let the one who is thirsty come; let the one who wishes to take the water of life without cost (22:17 NASB).

Who responds to the invitation? Who is open to coming? Who will be there? Persons confronted with few wrenching problems, whose world was secure, whose passage in life was serene, without the turbulence of ups and downs, are least likely to be among the redeemed or to experience the same degree of pleasure. Here may be an indirect allusion to the fact that those most likely to be enrolled by Christ will be those most afflicted on earth, those who have known many tears (21:4).

Life seems to bear out a pattern that the healthy rich are the ones least disposed to trust God and to cry for mercy. If Revelation 21:4 cannot be given that construction, at its very least it affirms that God's exaltation will turn sad faces into happy and smooth the ridges of anxiety into heavenly calmness and lasting peace.

> The light of heaven is Jesus' face,
> The joy of heaven is Jesus' presence,
> The harmony of heaven is Jesus' praise,
> The theme of heaven is Jesus' worth.[19]

John has aided us by giving an impressive visual aid. To help us grasp more of its meaning it would be useful to point out the two types of descriptions of the New Jerusalem. (1) There was the interpersonal and relational aspect (21:2b-7, 9). (2) There was the architectural, the dimensional part of the presentation (21:2a, 10-23). Somehow the statistical description of the city sticks. It was given to convey what interpersonal aspects can't convey. The structural aspects of the New Jerusalem are packed with theological meaning.

We must not allow drafting and blueprint details to obscure the equally emphasized personal aspects of heaven. To begin with, it should be noted, what descends is not of a physical mass, a mammoth structure, as if heaven were an elaborate gargantuan space station. But what descends are assembled believers, symbolized by a bride (21:2).

How are we to envision the descent? Are we to view it as God's bringing heaven into existence, so that bringing it down is equivalent to bringing it about (compare our discussion of the contrast between Dante's approach and the wording of 21:2)?[20] Or is the meaning simply that the people are the place, that the city is the bride (21:2)?[21] In this case the material aspects are beneath the personal aspects.

Both meanings belong to the passage. It fits the complexity

of heaven to have these two ideas working at the same time. Just as the fact that there would be no more sea (21:1) would not make the old earth when remade any less the earth, so the fact that the movement of heaven to John did not destroy the concept of the church on the new earth.

Admit a new earth and a new people (the church), and it is not inconceivable that heaven comes to the new earth. It is hard to imagine that God would recreate a new earth and then not have it used. The suggestion of Anthony Hoekema allows both for the city's being the bride and the new earth being used. He wrote:

> From [Rev. 21] verse 3 we learn that the dwelling place of God will no longer be away from the earth but on the earth. Since where God dwells, there heaven is, we conclude that in the life to come heaven and earth will no longer be separated, as they are now, but will be merged. Believers will therefore continue to be in heaven as they continue to live on the new earth.[22]

Christians have sometimes complimented themselves that they hold a biblical view of heaven when, by perpetuating the Intermediate Heaven into eternity, they have inadvertently succumbed to making heaven more like an intermission between acts of a great play. Others have fallen into reducing heaven to shining spires, fluffy clouds, of having everyone wear a halo. The most ludicrous image has to be of humans sheepishly flapping wings or methodically preening feathers. Such conceptions, however, are not taught in the Bible.

Only as we get the broader picture of redemptive history shall we be spared the absurd fantasies which have accumulated around a grand reality. When we take the Bible seriously, we accept the concreteness of the final heaven; yet we see it related to the perfection of what we already have, rather than regressing to simplistic materialism that implies subhuman characteristics. One truth stands clear: without a new earth, heaven becomes antiearth.

God originally created earth and declared it good. Through sin our planet has been spoiled. In the renovation of heaven and earth God will salvage what man spoiled. And it will be returned to the church for full use and enjoyment at a level that is hard to imagine (1 Cor. 2:9).

To restrict the ultimate deep heavenly life to a distant point ignores God's purposes for the other half of his original creation. Making heaven an idealized state runs the risk of holding a notion of heaven which is more pagan Greek than Christian.[23]

> [In Greek thought] Salvation consisted of the flight of the soul from the sphere of the transitory and ephemeral to the realm of eternal reality. However, biblical thought always places man on a redeemed earth, not in a heavenly realm removed from earthly existence.[24]

Objects reflect their makers. The universe, even after we compile its depletions and chart its decline, still mirrors God's almightiness, wisdom, and goodness. The heavens we traverse at thirty-two thousand feet have their own glory and show the imprint of God. The new heavens and the new earth will be co-occupied, co-owned, and co-operated by those redeemed to enter into them.

Nature is glorious now. It will be even more glorious when righteousness fills it after it is remade. We have yet to comprehend the complexity and completeness of the coming beauty and of the new agenda for the new earth. Paul anticipated the recapturing of all of nature for Christ's glory in new forms. He likened it to a new birth, which will begin with convulsions before the final emergence of changed nature (Rom. 8:22).

Once a new earth is taken seriously and seen as fact rather

than symbol, and once the theological position voiced earlier of the recovery and transformation of nature is on-target (anticipated by the prophets and apostles), then we are not out of place to ask about the possibilities regarding the plant and animal kingdoms. Edmund J. Fortman, S. J., asked:

> If plants and animals shared in man's fall, will He not want them to share in man's redemption and glory? If plants and animals were meant to be man's companions and joy in the past, why not in the future? What would planet earth be without them? Will they be corruptible as they are now? Or will they be incorruptible?[25]

There are no definite allusions to the restoration of nature in the details some would want. One possible exception could be Isaiah 11:6-9, which some have associated with a physical millennium. The passage from Isaiah 11 refers to the taming of the ferocity of wild animals, of how they are given a "personality" change, and of their being rendered harmless. This passage of animal illustrations applies appropriately to Christ changing the disposition, human contrariness, stubbornness, and viciousness. It relates as much to Christ's work now as to his work later. When Christ reigns, viciousness is replaced with kindness, cooperation is put where there was resistance, and approachableness characterizes us rather than orneriness. And wherever Christ reigns (now in the old earth or later in the new earth) abuse, destruction, and fear of others are banished.

Whatever the possibilities in the future, we look forward to heaven as a replacement and as restoration.

> There's no disappointment in heaven;
> No weariness, sorrow, or pain:
> No hearts that are bleeding and broken,
> No song with a minor refrain.
> The clouds of our earthly horizon
> Will never appear in the sky,

For all will be sunshine and gladness,
With never a sob nor a sigh.

We'll never pay rent for our mansion,
The taxes will never come due:
Our garments will never grow threadbare,
But always be fadeless and new.
We'll never be hungry nor thirsty,
Nor languish in poverty there,
For all the rich bounties of heaven
His sanctified children will share.

There'll never be crape on the door-knob,
No funeral train in the sky:
No graves on the hillsides of glory,
For there we shall never more die.
The old will be young there forever,
Transformed in a moment of time;
Immortal we'll stand in his likeness,
The stars and the sun to outshine.

I'm bound for that beautiful city
My Lord has prepared for His own:
Where all the redeemed of all ages
Sing "Glory" around the white throne;
Sometimes I grow homesick for heaven,
And the glories I there shall behold:
What a joy that will be when my Savior I see,
In that beautiful city of gold.

F. M. LEHMAN

6

Who
Will Be
in Heaven
?

*T*his question has bothered more people than they would care to admit. Those who feel rejected are predisposed to think they will not be there. Others who have no lack of self-confidence scarcely ponder the prospect that they may be self-deceived about their entrance.

To entertain this question—even as a passing thought—despite its speculative nature—will get us thinking about heaven as a reality and about whether we will be one of those who will be there.

Many people will not want to bother asking the question or wait for an answer, if there is no heaven to begin with. Skeptics were just as hard on John Bunyan (1628-1688) in his day. In his classic allegory *Pilgrim's Progress,* the central character, Pilgrim, who was a disguise for Bunyan himself, was absorbed in getting to the Celestial City. So driven was he to attain heaven that all other pursuits fell by the way. This made his closest friends consider him odd. Mr. Obstinate ventured the opinion that he was "brain sick." Others used the expression "crazy headed."

Attitudes now are little different than what they were then. Anyone who talks glowingly of heaven, who makes it his study, who seems preoccupied with it, is considered morbid, unrealistic, fanatical, and possibly maladjusted. Haven't we noticed on TV talk shows that when heaven is raised it rarely gets a serious, full, or sympathetic hearing? It is thought dull, weird, irrelevant, or too controversial. The audience, seen and unseen, may want to keep on the subject, but the irreligious host, for the most part, does everything in his power to switch to another conversational track.

Underlying this avoidance is the belief that attention to heaven is escapism, which is considered unhealthy.

The escapist charge is one frequently heard. The argument is that heaven has been invented and used to tranquilize the forlorn, to mesmerize the idealist, to mollify the intense, and to energize the moralist. Even Christian psychiatrist, the late Paul Tournier, admitted:

> Escaping into the future, constantly making plans, is another form of flight into dreams, another way of escaping from the imperfections of the present.[1]

Metaphysician Peter J. Kreeft hit the bull's eye when he commented:

> Otherworldliness is escapism only if there is no other world. If there is, it is worldliness that is escapism.[2]

Heaven *is* as real as earth. Realistically our destiny should draw our attention without increasing our dread. Perfection should rank highest. What is final should be first. "If heaven is our homeland, what else is earth but our place of exile?"[3]

Jesus, ironically, was more realistic than the rabbinic theology of his day. The rabbis had given up on the present. For them, the hope of God's kingdom was not in the present but in the future. In contrast Jesus taught that in his presence and words, God's kingdom had invaded time, history, and life.[4] For Jesus the future was not something to escape to, but that the future has impacted on the present.[5] Our acceptance of Christ's Word and works confirms our willingness to be confronted by the greatest reality of all.

The benefits of heaven's intrusion yield results, for "those who are the most strenuously bent on their education for heaven [are] at the same time the happiest upon earth."[6]

The importance of the quest for heaven goes much deeper than one might originally suspect. Indeed, to ignore the search or to disparage the seekers is far more damaging and disrespectful than some would imagine. "He who does not long for heaven estranges himself from God."[7]

Since heaven is a people-place, we should ask, "Who will be in heaven?"

God

In heaven the central personage is God, its Architect and Administrator. Without God there would be no heaven. God observes and involves himself from heaven. His command post (the Book of Revelation uses the word *throne* frequently)[8] is in heaven (Ps. 103:19; Isa. 66:1; Matt. 5:34; Acts 7:49).

> While God shares heaven with the angels and the heavenly host, He does not share His throne with anyone else.
> We are to think of the throne which God occupies in heaven, and occupying it, is exalted above heaven as He is above the earth. But the space of this throne, while it is also space, is the space which belongs to God alone.[9]

In Revelation God's seat, his throne, is the place from which he rules and reigns (4:2). And the Lamb shares the throne with the Father (5:6). While earth is where God operates, heaven is where he resides. This does not deny his presence elsewhere and everywhere.

Jesus (the Lamb who is also the Lion) is the focal point of the execution of the Father's will in the world. The four living creatures, which are angels, and the twenty-four elders, who are prominent leaders of the past, are engaged in the worship of Christ. It was only the Lamb who could have access to and open the secret book of destiny (5:2-5).

God's greatness is not confined to heaven. Heaven multiplied by heavens could not contain him. He is there but not only there. In terms of the final heaven, he is behind every perfection in it. He provided the basic and continuous illumination of heaven (21:23).

Angels

Angels were more God's entourage than heaven's inhabitants. His immensity is partly conveyed by the myriad attendants and angels at his beck. Angels carried out God's orders. Their function was to "do service in the wings."[10] Because their service was not frivolous, but vital, we are not to think of them as ethereal ornaments that hung around to look pretty. They wait on Jesus, not because he is helpless or unwilling to work, but to show his greatness and carry out his will.

Angels are frequently considered fictional figures. Their role in Scripture is viewed as similar to the created chorus in ancient Greek drama. Though they symbolize the Lord's justice in delivering it, they were presented as real beings. In Revelation God gives them specific responsibilities, and sends them on large-scale missions. Global and partial global duties are fulfilled by them. They gave John the visions (22:6). And when John got too impressed with the revealing angel, the angel disclaimed any greatness and exhorted the writer "Worship God!" (22:9).

Heaven teems with angels. John wrote, "Again I looked, and I heard angels, thousands and millions of them! They stood around the throne, the four living creatures, and the elders, and sang" praise to Christ (5:11 GNB). Our conversion was described in Hebrews 12:22 (NIV) as coming "to thousands upon thousands of angels in joyful assembly."

Yet we are not to expect or look for them on earth. We cannot identify, hear, or see them in life. In the language of worldly diplomacy, they remain *incognito* (unidentifiable) and *incommunicado* (unavailable). They are meant to serve God and assist those searching for him (Heb. 1:14).

They are intended to guard as much as to guide. Luke inserted the curious belief in the early church that we have angelic doubles, those who look like us. This conjecture was current in apostolic times (Acts 12:15).

If Peter had a guardian angel, Jesus had a guardian army. For a large section of angels assigned to our Lord Jesus were declined by him in the agony of his final ordeal, beginning with his arrest (Luke 22:43; Matt. 26:53). But, in his work of consummation and final justice, he will descend with the heavenly hosts he earlier declined (1 Thess. 4:16; Jude 14; Rev. 19:14). Christ will return "with His mighty angels" (2 Thess. 1:7).[11]

We wonder if the job configuration of the angels was altered as the result of Jesus' resurrection. Were their previous employments reduced and remanded directly to Jesus or were their activities enlarged and their territories expanded? We can't be sure to what degree, if any, Jesus' resurrection, had increased, maintained, or reduced the level and amount of angelic activity.

We know that prior to Jesus' ascension angels acted as celestial escorts for the pious to paradise (Luke 16:22). It is still widely held that angels work as escorts of the deceased. We think of the fond farewell to dead Hamlet: "Good night, sweet prince, and flights of angels sing thee to thy rest!" (*Hamlet*, Act

V, Sc. 2). Angelic attention for the deceased according to public opinion includes accident victims, illustrated in the modern TV commercial which shows a dying man approached by two angels to accompany him to heaven via swift jet.

Do angels retrieve the saints from the earth in death and at his second coming? When martyr Stephen died, he saw Jesus stand to receive him (Acts 7:56). He then prayed, "Lord Jesus, receive my spirit" (Acts 7:59). Jesus' earlier promise, to "receive you unto myself" (John 14:3 KJV) may mean that Jesus himself actually fetches, as well as greets, his dying saints, not only at his second coming, but also in their deaths.

Animals

Revelation pictures horses in heaven. Perhaps the most familiar figures in the *Apocalypse* are the four horsemen (*see* chapter 6). In chapter 9 a swarm of locusts (a symbol) were themselves compared to horses (9:7) which were followed by a killing group from the abyss, like mounted troops riding horses (9:17, 18). Jesus himself is pictured as riding a horse both in Revelation 6:2 and 19:11f. Horses were representations of conquest rather than literal creatures.

The image of a horse kicked up some dust in the mind of C. S. Lewis, who gave an amusing twist to saints riding horses with Christ.

> These small and perishable bodies we now have were given to us as ponies are given to schoolboys. We must learn to manage: not that we may some day be free of horses altogether but that some day we may ride bare-back, confident and rejoicing, those greater mounts, those winged, shining and world-shaking horses which perhaps even now expect us with impatience, pawing and snorting in the King's stables. Not that the gallop would be of any value unless it were a gallop with the King; but how else—since He has retained His own charger—should we accompany Him?[12]

People are serious about taking pets to heaven. Some cannot imagine that heaven is a place of comfort without their animal companions. So attached are they to their pets that they cannot envision a heavenly life without them.

This desire is not new. The ancient Egyptians felt an inseparableness with their domesticated animals. Egyptian kings made sure replicas of their favorite animals, such as dogs, birds, monkeys, gazelles, along with cats, were placed in their burial rooms. Ceramic pets decorated their tombs.

English philosopher F. H. Bradley (1846-1924), a representative of absolute idealism, rejected the notion of immortal life because so many people desired the state only because they could be reunited with their beagles.[13] Closer to our time, Pierre Berton, a Canadian broadcaster, reacted differently. He was turned off from heaven because he could not contemplate or desire an existence where animals were excluded. This soured him on the value of church attendance. "I was quite shaken by this revelation: an afterworld that deprived me of my dog seemed to me less than heaven."[14]

Some aversion for literal dogs is reflected in Revelation 22:15, which says of heaven "without are dogs and sorcerers (KJV)." But what about the new earth (Rev. 21:1) and the restoration of all things (Eph. 1:10)? John Bradford (1510-1555) argued that these final forms would necessarily imply the restoration of plants and animals.[15] Such thinking influenced John Wesley (1703-1791) to espouse animal immortality in his sixty-fifth sermon (titled "The Great Deliverance"). If animals belong to the new earth, they need not be animals as we know them now, but something new.

But how far can we seriously maintain the thought of animal immortality? Animal lovers would be quite happy to make the new earth a giant post-time game preserve. While the new earth may fulfill their wishes, the danger is, of course, that attachment to inarticulate pets competes with occupation with

Jesus Christ. It is best to set the resolution of this controversy on the back burner. We must wait. Clearly animals do not fit into the main purpose of heaven, which is the articulation of God's praise. Song birds praise God on earth, true, but the main song of heaven is sung by redeemed humans and is about the glories of Christ's redemption, even beyond the praising of God for his creation work (*see* Rev. 5).

Animals are invaluable aids on earth. They serve good purposes as guides for the blind, guards for the weak, and companion "go-fors" for the lonely, but we let our sentiments run wildly excessive when we picture heaven as the reuniting of man and beast.

One problem is in saying which animals "belong." Where is the line to be drawn? Should snakes be allowed? Those who contend it evil to destroy life must make room for mosquitoes. C. S. Lewis, who is usually pictured holding a pipe in his hand, not a pet in his lap, suggested something that would accommodate animal lovers and animal haters. He said God could conceive of a plan to accommodate those who wanted to save mosquitoes. "A heaven for mosquitoes and a hell for men could very easily be combined."[16]

What about animal companions in the final heaven? What about the faithful hound or the cuddly cat that we can't bear to be without? If they are in the Infinite (final) Heaven, are they in the Intermediate Heaven?

We must detach ourselves from selfish identification with our pets and consider the broader issues. Scripture nowhere says animals have immortal souls. As differently and less-endowed creatures God meant them to delight and serve man on earth, and supremely, to provide God continuous satisfaction. Some hold animals have souls, but their souls, unlike man, are mortal. Do we not miss the grandeur of heaven by requiring the perpetuation of what is incidental to life? Again, C. S. Lewis prods us: ". . . a future happiness connected with

the beast's present life simply as a compensation for suffering
. . . seems a clumsy assertion of Divine goodness. . . ."[17]

Humans

Revelation spoke of heaven, initially, in specific quantity. The
144,000, for instance, were those who were faithful to Christ,
the martyred followers (7:4). That number was quickly abandoned and admitted to be innumerable: ". . . an enormous
crowd—no one could count all the people! They were from every
race, tribe, nation, and language . . ." (7:9 GNB). (For more theological significance on the numbering, turn back to page 45.)

Generally, hymns give relatively low or modest figures on
heaven's total population. Most begin with the number *thousand*. For example:

> Adoring thousands at thy feet,
> In faith and love shall fall.
>
> Thousand, thousand saints attending,
> Swell the triumph of his train.

The point being made was that the few of each generation after
multithousands of generations come to be a vast number.

Most of us are less concerned about the largeness of the
actual figure than with the question of who do we know who
will be there. At various times we have indulged in the innocent
speculation of whether So-and-So would be in heaven. We have
wondered if favorite authors, childhood friends, distant rulers,
or deceased relatives would be there.

Of course time spent in such speculation is self-defeating
and possibly an infringement into God's business. Who is on
heaven's roll is not for us to know or to seek. Rather than
wondering about others, we should make sure we believe in
Christ for eternal life. Idle theorizing on the inhabitants of
heaven is meddlesome. Instead of drawing us closer to God,

time spent in speculation has to displease God and indirectly distances ourselves further from him, for we are less concerned to apply his Word to our own lives.

One form of curiosity, however, may work to our benefit. If we ask why Christ assured one of the dying thieves next to him on the cross why he would be in paradise, then we may be on the way ourselves. Asking how prostitutes Rahab and Mary Magdalene could be citizens of heaven may help us to uncover God's rules of acceptance. Does it not intrigue (and at the same time) trouble us that the polished and pious of Jesus' time were warned of damnation and that a one-time swindler and at another time a prostitute were given assurances from Jesus that they would be among the host of God's redeemed?

Everyone will not be in heaven. Revelation 7:9 says, not every race, tribe, and nation will be there, but persons "out of" or "from" every tongue, tribe, and nation. That distinction is not incidental. It agrees with the rest of the New Testament and fits in with the later description of heaven as a place for those declared perfect by Christ.

Heaven is a holy place. Polluted persons would present an emergency. The morally impure are tolerated on earth but they are intolerable in heaven. Scripture tells us that iniquity-laden are excluded and the filthy prohibited (Heb. 12:14; Rev. 21:8; 22:15).

Where does that put us? Since we are all sinners, of one kind or another, we can't get in the way we are and we can't get in on our own. A good word from our family will not help. A commendation from our friends will not do. The praises of our supervisors will carry no weight with God, for our imperfections, our moral pollution hangs on us—though hidden from others.

Jokesters place Peter in charge of the heavenly gate. There is nothing in the Bible about any man overseeing the pearly gates. It says twelve angels will be tending the twelve gates

(21:12). Peter or other human attendants will not be gate-keepers or ticket takers. There is nothing there about pass-words and payoffs. If a human being were to be in charge, he/she could be bribed, bargained with, or we could sneak in, bolt any barrier, or, with a push from our crowds of friends, barge in. But Revelation 5:9 says that the only way we get in is that we are chosen by God, that we are brought in, and that we receive the application of the Christ's cleansing blood. Of Jesus it was said:

> ". . . For you were killed, and by your
> sacrificial death you bought for God
> people from every tribe, language, nation, and race.
> You have made them a kingdom of
> priests to serve our God
> and they shall rule on earth" (Rev. 5:9, 10 GNB).

We get in because Christ paid the admission price. It is as simple as that. Pay attention to this when reading through the New Testament. God does not let us in because he is impressed with our generosity, sincerity, notoriety, or ingenuity. We get in because Christ repossessed us through his death. The devil has delighted himself in the gross theft of the human race and all our lifelong we are in his clutches until Christ frees us. The only way we are spared Satan's fiery fate is by the rescue mis-sion of Jesus Christ. To suppose that we can rectify ourselves, and by self-improvement recover ourselves draws attention away from Christ. We, thereby, underestimate our spiritual bondage in sin and put ourselves in the center where Christ belongs.

Credit is given to whom it is due. (Heaven honors that rule!) But, who was the only one found worthy to open the books in Revelation 5? Who is the one praised in heaven?

> . . . "Worthy is the Lamb who was slain, to receive power and wealth and wisdom and might and honor and glory and bless-ing! . . . To him who sits upon the throne and to the Lamb be

blessing and honor and glory and might for ever and ever!" (Rev. 5:12, 13 RSV).

The chorus repeats in Revelation 7. Redeemed Gentiles to-a-man cue up for one ascription and affirmation. Hear it. "Salvation belongs to our God who sits upon the throne and to the Lamb!" (7:10 RSV)

Nothing is plainer. Yet it is found in the supposedly too complicated source book, Revelation! When all glory belongs and goes to God, can we dare pat ourselves on the back? There is a unanimous consensus by all those in heaven. It is this: Self-righteousness did not accomplish it, but Christ's righteousness did. The theme of the godly fellowship of the prophets, of the noble army of the martyrs, of the holy church throughout the world and afterworld is the shout: "All praise to God's adorable, true, and only Son."

Who will be in heaven? The question needs to be turned inward, for a moment. Never mind about this or that person, of whether they will be there. Will *we* be there? No one else can address himself or herself to that question. When we relinquish, resign, and remand our salvation into Christ's hands, then we can be assured that we shall be part of the mammoth choir and sing with heartiness and honesty,

> Salvation to God who sits on the throne,
> Let all cry aloud,
>   And honor the Son!
>   CHARLES WESLEY (1600-1661)

In Samuel Rutherford's (1600-1661) words:

> The Lamb is all the glory of Emmanuel's land.

Can we identify with that? Are we moved by that? Do we find it the most compelling grounds for glorying in heaven?

7

Is Heaven Delayed at Death ?

I n this snap-to-it age delays are difficult to take. We get impatient with long lines, slow elevators, and stalled traffic. We like to rush through life and have instant gratification. Death, however, is the big stop. Does the abruptness of death mean that man starts off from that point a little slower? Is there a waiting period at death—a pause—a hiatus? Is man kept in a holding pattern before he "soars to worlds unknown"?

Purgatory is the concept of celestial pause. It is the view that the experience of heaven is delayed. Why the layover? According to this belief, especially common to Roman Catholicism but not confined to it, a person who is a member of the church, no matter how devout, must suffer temporal punishment for his sins. Life in the church is not enough to prepare one for heaven. A rare few ever have passed into the presence of God from earth perfect. There is no encouragement that one can avoid the layover in purgatory.

The really important objections to purgatory do not spring from American intolerance for delay. Indeed, a Reformation Protestant can pause endlessly before the arguments in favor of purgatory and not bite. The wait aspect conceals greater issues.

First, get a perspective on this option proposed by a large section of Christendom. Some preliminary questions need to be asked instead of falling back on pat answers. Are there, to begin with, any points of agreement between those who deny and those who affirm purgatory? Also, where is purgatory? Finally, don't our pathetic imperfections require purgatory?

Is there anything in common between the Roman Catholic position and the Reformation Protestant position? Historically, these positions have not blended. Surprisingly there are several points of contact. To better understand the problem and the proposed solutions we would do well to walk through and talk through the rationale.

Agreement exists between the two camps on the matter of the need for the cleansing of fallen, sinful humans before they can enter heaven. Both groups recognize that heaven is for those cleansed from moral impurities. The impure cannot enter or exist in heaven (Heb. 12:14; Rev. 22:14, 15).

Earlier we noted a difference between Dante's idea of his ascending to observe heaven and John's view of heaven coming to man (chapter 5). Dante echoed the view of the historic Protestant and the modern Catholic, when, in Canto 1 he wrote, "The human spirit must be cleansed before . . . rising up to heaven."[1] Scripture, of course, first took that position. The idea of previous purgation comes right out of the Bible. As a matter of fact it is a common element to both the Old and New Testaments.

Isaiah the prophet refers to God as "The Holy One of Israel." He used the expression thirty times, as compared to only five times elsewhere in the Old Testament. God's holiness is inseparable from his nature and basis for deciding and working. It is not a fringe feature, a pietistic frill that can be cut from the garment of faith without it substantially altering its style, appearance, or usefulness. It is the very fabric of God's nature that we are discussing.

The demand for purity is part of his pure nature. The principle is "Be ye holy; for I am holy" (1 Peter 1:16 KJV). The issue is not incidental. Readiness is the prime requirement for entrance into heaven and we are not ready for it until and unless we are cleansed throughout. This is the faith of the biblical writers and of faithful spokesmen in the church through the ages.

But unfortunately it is not the faith of modern man. The subject of purgatory is not suppressed, avoided, or considered off-limits. In fact, it gets a better hearing than hell. Nowadays people reject hell, but hold to "a mild sort of purgatory."[2] It is easier for people to discuss purgatory than hell. In a discussion of purgatory they are less likely to squirm. Purgatory is manageable.

The modern man does not believe he is wicked enough to deserve hell, but that he is sufficiently bad to require purgatory. Man is willing to spend some time in the neighborhood of hell, but unwilling to make hell his permanent residence. Purgatory gives man the option to suffer for his sins, but not eternally suffer for them. It appeals to his sense of modulation.

Acceptance of purgatory outside the circle of the church reflects the fact that the average person no longer believes in the separating and absolute punishing power of divine holiness. Modern man has a distaste for pain in any form, but he will accept a little if it leads to something better. But he holds both a definite dread and disdain for a brand of holiness which will exact eternal retribution. He would prefer to empty and board up hell for good and he hopes that God's holiness would lack the severity and strictness that would keep hell going.

Yet, ironically, the concept of purgatory first arose as one facet of those who believed in God's absolute disgust with sin and his determination to punish it. Purgatory arose to resolve a problem created by Catholic soteriology. It was meant to honor the holiness of God. Now the rationale for purgatory, in public views, is not because there is a strong commitment to God's holiness, but because people look for and want a place to atone for their sins and to have an opportunity to unlive the life they lived on earth.

Hence purgatory strikes a responsive chord. A person will believe in purgatory rather than hell, because he is not convinced of the need of eternal exaction against iniquity and he is not convinced he is "that wicked."

This approach, however, means man must reshape God. Whenever man is made the determiner of truth, he writes up what is proper and what is improper for God to do. Purgatory is allowable and appealing to the average person, because in the afterworld it introduces moderation and leniency. The excessiveness of hell's torment is what is too tough to accept. Hell is objectionable because endless languishing is perceived as patently unfair. Purgatory, however, is tolerable.

Again, however, when purgatory was first devised, the original intent was not to throw aside or to shave down the emphasis on the complete and unrelenting holiness of God. Clearly, the older adherents of purgatory and the modern advocates of purgatory differ on this point.

Increasingly we are faced with Protestants who are open to purgatory, not because they believe strongly in God's purity and of his right to judge wickedness, but because, as is frequently said, "Man is not so wicked as to deserve hell." But from the viewpoint of Scripture, heaven allows in the holy and excludes the impure. Given man's sinfulness in his present condition, he is excluded and barred from heaven. He is unready and unacceptable the way he is. Isn't purgatory, therefore, the solution of saving face for God's holiness and sparing God the image of allowing large numbers of humans to remain in a miserable state?

Purgation? Yes. Purgatory? No.

Purgation does not require purgatory. Another way of putting it is to say purgatory is required, but it is past. A vital distinction is expressed in these statements. It preserves the separation between the biblical method of purging and the postbiblical alternative to purging.

Before we can answer *why* purgatory *is not*, we must answer the question *where* purgatory *is*. By focusing on the place of purgation, we discover there is no need for purgatory. Purgation is something in the past. Purgatory is thought to be in the future.

There is no need for purgatory in the future because purgatory is past. This is a unique approach, but it is a forgotten old approach. Purgatory in the past? How can that be? The Bible tells us where purgatory *was*. The place was Calvary, where Jesus died for our sins. He became our purgatory and took our hell. Hebrews 1:3 (NEB) says:

> When he had brought about the purgation of sins, he took his seat at the right hand of Majesty on high. . . .

Several other texts say essentially the same thing (Titus 2:14; Rev. 1:5). The combined message of the New Testament is that all our sins were judged, exacted, and punished in Jesus Christ on the cross. He felt the banishment of a holy God in bearing away our sins. The conclusion of Scripture is that while purgatory was necessary for the sinner before he could enter heaven, Jesus Christ did the purging and completely absorbed the pain caused by all our iniquities.

Historically, the original Protestants took offense at a purgatory *ahead*, because Scripture said it was *behind*. Calvin wrote:

> [It] is a deadly fiction of Satan, which nullifies the cross of Christ. . . . If it is perfectly clear . . . that the blood of Christ is the sole satisfaction for the sins of believers, the sole expiation, the sole purgation, what remains but to say that purgatory is simply a dreadful blasphemy against Christ?[3]

Welshman John Owen (1616-1683) followed this approach when he wrote that purgatory after death is a "groundless fable; an invention set up in competition with the sanctification of the Spirit and the blood of Christ."[4] In our own time, Anglican J. A. Motyer has written: "On the ground that the saving work of Christ is *really* finished, purgatory must be denied."[5]

The classic Protestant objection to purgatory is that any addition to God's remedy is ultimately disrespectful, undercutting the fullness and freeness of Christ's purgation of sins. In Hebrews 1:3 (cited above) and elsewhere in Hebrews (9:12; 10:14) nothing could improve, fortify, or redo what Christ has already done. These and other passages deny legitimizing the view that we must do or can do something extra. To add anything to Christ's work is not to reinforce his work but acts as a pull-stitch of what he has done.

In today's climate of opinion Jesus is only one of many options. Both the necessity and sufficiency of Jesus Christ are no longer believed as they once were. People are more willing to suffer in themselves for their wrongdoing than to let someone else be their patsy. They don't want to shove off on anyone else the inconvenience or minimal pain they must endure for misdeeds. They are content with a purgatory *in time* or *after time* in which they can work through their own forms of self-salvation. Self-punishment allows for self-perfecting. Penance takes on that function in popular thinking. A mild form of hell will be assumed. This is the newest attitude toward purgatory.

Those who have difficulties with the dogma that surrounds Roman Catholic thought are more inclined to believe purgatory is in life. In this view life is seen as a training school, a series of soul sieves in which are screened out objectionable immoral particles. According to this approach man makes his own satisfaction for sin by his own suffering. I find it interesting that the rabbinical mindset with which Jesus had to deal had this as one of its elements of atonement. (We shall look at this more closely in chapter 11 "Is Heaven Earned?")

Is it a quibble to insist that Jesus' purgation was sufficient? Obviously any item of belief can be demeaned as a quibble and thereby discounted as a quirk of the narrow-minded and petty. If that argument is used, then one must conclude that the apostles were nitpickers and sticklers, too. Hebrews teaches that Jesus purged our sins once for all. In Hebrews 1:3, the tense of the Greek verb "purge" is aorist, which means it was one action and unrepeatable! His "sitting down" after the purgation reinforces that Jesus' atonement was completely finished and totally acceptable to the Father.

> Eternal life! Eternal light!
> How pure the soul must be,
> When placed within thy searching sight,
> It shrinks not, but with calm delight,
> Can live and look on Thee!
>
> O how shall I, whose native sphere
> Is dark, whose mind is dim,
> Before the ineffable appear,
> And on my naked spirit bear
> The uncreated beam?
>
> There is a way for man to rise
> To that sublime abode:
> An offering and a sacrifice,

A Holy Spirit's energies,
An advocate with God.

These, these prepare us for the sight
Of holiness above:
The sons of ignorance and night
May dwell in the eternal light,
Through the eternal love!

THOMAS BINNEY (1798-1874)

To insist on further suffering for sins is to dim and darken the glorious purgation of Christ. Purgatory has drawn attention to human corruption and that is good, but a future purgatory also draws us away from the Christ's success in his death and the completeness of his atonement. To say something else must be done to what Christ already did is to encourage people to think Christ was ineffective in his mission. When we realize through Christ that we are now fully accepted and that there is no delay in approaching him because of what Christ accomplished, our beings are flooded with the comforting light of God's truth.

Thus Dante's poem, however well phrased, is laced with sadness. For Dante one must climb the purgatory mountain that leads to the Garden of Eden. Scripture, however, says we stand, not at the base of the mountain, but at its summit! It is not striving for acceptance, but the arrival of acceptance which is celebrated in Hebrews 12:18, 22-24 (NIV):

> You have not come to a mountain that can be touched and that is burning with fire. . . . But you have come to Mount Zion, to the heavenly Jerusalem, the city of the living God. You have come to thousands upon thousands of angels in joyful assembly, to the church of the firstborn, whose names are written in heaven. You have come to God, the judge of all men, to the spirits of righteous men made perfect, to Jesus the mediator of

a new covenant, and to the sprinkled blood that speaks a better word than the blood of Abel.

There have been recent repackagings of purgatory by Roman Catholic writers that turn down or turn away from the suffering aspect of the traditional doctrine as it appears in the description in *The Council of Trent,* Session 6, Canon 30, of "temporal punishment."[6]

The apologetic freely admits that there is little in the Bible about it, but that it is in harmony with the Bible.[7] According to Roman Catholic presuppositions, of course, purgatory is required. Since they equate salvation with sanctification (purity of life), since they define justification before God as this sanctification, and since no one is fully sanctified in life, then some accommodation must be made for man to be prepared to finish the purifying process. Hence purgatory.

Toning down the torment element with which purgatory has been traditionally associated has been the next ploy. German Catholic theologian Michael Schmaus referred to purgatory as "a way of life after death wherein man has a particular relation to God"[8] American advocate for purgatory, Peter J. Kreeft, has softened the sharp corners of purgatory by saying (a) that purgatory is part of heaven; (b) that it is joyful, not gloomy; (c) that it is involved in spiritual reeducation, not a second-chance doctrine. He likened it to an incubator, not an incinerator; a place where one is warmed up, not burned up. Like an incubator, purgatory finishes what was started in the womb.[9]

It does no good, from the classical Protestant viewpoint, to make purgatory the final stage of sanctification, because some problems seem insoluble. Kreeft's contention that Protestant objections are resolvable if the subject would be looked at "as the saints do"[10] will *not* do it. Why? Initially, because the classical Protestant doesn't consult saints to find truth. Scripture, not other Christians, is the norm for determining truth. They are not opposed to listening to saints in writing (for in Catholic theology, that would be the only place where saints could be heard, since to be a saint one must have died), but they are unwilling to put credence in a position because of how sold saints are on it.

Serious theological hurdles have been ignored by Kreeft in his desire to commend belief in purgatory. There are four major reasons why purgatory doesn't wash with historic Protestants:

(1) The authority of Scripture stands over human opinions. First allegiance is to what the Bible says. If a case cannot be made from Scripture, then the case is lost. If purgatory were real and a justifiable theological extension of "moral realism", then one would expect to find some allusion to it in Revelation. But its absence in the book, which is concerned about people entering heaven pure, is significant.[11]

(2) The doctrine that has made purgatory necessary is that one cannot be sure of salvation in time before death. In the Catholic system, since salvation is only sanctification (a process) and not a declarative act by God (a crisis), then salvation-assurance is excluded. Central to the purgatory belief is that one can never be sure one is saved in life. Once one denies one can be sure he is saved, then the door is open to accept purgatory. Christ's righteousness alone as the ground of our acceptance by God is obscured and overridden in the teaching of purgatory. Recently, an Anglican has claimed that "the doctrine of purgatory is not in conflict with the doctrine of justification. It is rather an aspect of sanctification, a process recognized as far from instantaneous, even by the most committed believers of justification by faith. It is quite compatible with conviction that salvation is God's work alone to hold that it takes effect gradually through experience and growth in spirituality both this side of the

grave and beyond it. Moral realism dissuades us from supposing that instantaneous transformation from imperfection to perfection takes place at death any more than it does at conversion during one's earthly life."[12]

In reply it must be noted that salvation is never based on our compliance with God's law, but with the gift of righteousness. Perfection *is* ours when Christ's righteousness is given to us in life! Attitudinal conformity to Christ's image is the ongoing work of purgation *in this* life. The argument of Hebblethwaite that an instantaneous perfecting at the death-line is unlikely for God, imposes on God our view of time. But what may be a problem for us is not a problem for God. While his view gets rid of the odious, which some find in instantaneousness, it is replaced with a theological diminishing of justification and spiritual insecurity, which are far worse.

(3) Purgatory does not come alone. The belief in the value of prayers for the dead is objectionable. The need for such prayers detracts from Christ's merit applied to true believers. Prayers for the dead is a denial of salvation-assurance, which is an important correlative to the doctrine of justification by faith apart from the works of the law. Prayers for the dead follows a denial of salvation-assurance, just as purgatory follows a denial of salvation in time. To deny that one can realize and enter into the joy of salvation won by Christ and applied by the Holy Spirit in time is a delay which flies in the face of the ringing certitude promised to all believers in the New Testament.

(4) Classic Protestantism finds too much value is attached to human suffering. It disputes the power of other suffering to either make expiation for venial (nondamning) sins or to be necessary punishment for forgiven mortal

sins. The older and still authoritative formulations of purgatory, real human suffering was involved. Our suffering will not produce sanctification anymore than our suffering will produce repentance. Note that those in Revelation who experienced pain through hardship remained adamantly opposed to God (9:20, 21; 16:11, 21). In Roman Catholic theology purgatory provides the too-easy out for postponement of sanctification.

The apostle Paul expressed a triumphant note, resulting from Christ's redemption of us, when he referred to death as "absent from the body and present with the Lord" (*see* 2 Cor. 5:8). Despite this, a question nags: "Don't our pathetic imperfections still require purging?"

The purgatory of Calvary is the purgatory that counts. Scripture speaks of two other purgatories: (a) the purgation of earth, when the world as we know it is remade. (This matter was considered in chapter 3); (b) also, it mentions the purging of base desire and of dross (1 Peter 1:7; Heb. 12:14).

Our sins have been purged, removed, destroyed, forgotten by God once and forever. Scripture is emphatic on that point. Yet sinning defiles our attitudes and disrupts our fellowship. Sinning cannot sever our relationship with God, nor can it invalidate Christ's death on our behalf. That is why it was necessary once only.

Yet we are urged to confess our sins (1 John 1:9). How is this to be understood if our sins are purged? It may seem to be a backing down (if not a denial) of the previous position.

The reference to inward cleansing from sin is possible because of the death of Christ, not in addition to it. Where does confession fit? Confession of sins serves a secondary but an important role. It is not what causes our salvation, but what restores our fellowship with God and with each other. The believer not only grieves over his disobedience and neglect of God in his confession, but he also celebrates the basis for his forgiveness which is Christ's death. Our sins were taken away through Christ's offering of himself, yet we are to continue to rely and reflect upon his deed (Heb. 9:14; 10:14). We cannot improve on his purgation, but we need to be purged through prayer of our fascination with sin, of our admiration of sin, and of our attachment to sin.

The distinction is clear that there is purgation accomplished and purgation applied. The first insures the second. Application must follow accomplishment. Turning to God in prayer is a sign that sin's allurement has been broken. We misread the value of sin's confession if we think that a list of committed wrongs repeated to God cleanses the slate. The real cleansing is the restoration of a positive relationship and a renewed dedication to the Author of salvation. All our sins, past, present, and future, were taken away by Christ when he died. Through the Holy Spirit he is at work having us seek the continued forsaking of those sins, for which Christ suffered. First John 3:2, 3 (NASB) expands on this idea:

> . . . We know that, when He appears, we shall be like Him, because we shall see Him just as He is. And everyone who has this hope fixed on Him purifies himself, just as He is pure.

In this passage the point is made that looking to Jesus and the confession of sin are of a piece. The two go together. And they are not optional activities, but part and parcel of being Christian. Without them we are not Christians.

Giving up our sinful ways and living more for and with Christ come with the dawn of divine grace. Our path shines more clearly as we approach the day of Christ's final appearing. Paul put it this way:

> We, who with unveiled faces reflect the Lord's glory, are being transformed into his likeness with ever-increasing glory, which comes from the Lord, who is the Spirit (2 Cor. 3:18 NIV).

Truth is a prime-purging ingredient. It is used by the Holy Spirit to scrub us and take off the tarnish. Jesus said to his disciples, "You have already been cleansed by the word that I spoke to you" (John 15:3 NEB). A believer who absorbs God's Word lives more for God, reflects more of God, and resorts more to God. Trouble also is used by the Holy Spirit to burn out our fascination and commitment to earthly, selfish, God-dishonoring ideas and ways. Job's statement is true also of everyday experiences for Christians, "When He has tried me, I shall come forth as gold" (Job 23:10 NASB). Trials that purge are God disciplining us, not God punishing us. (That distinction will relieve many minds who wrongly think God is punishing them for their sins.) Herman Ridderbos, a Dutch exegete, properly differentiates between sufferings taken as prelude to hell and sufferings that are preparatory for a more heavenly life:

> Suffering, calamities, etc., are not only a prelude to God's eternal judgment: there is also a kind of suffering in which God is through Christ glorified in His grace, and which thus becomes an example and a prelude of eternal salvation.[13]

Therefore, there is a sense in which in time we go through the wringer to squeeze out waste and wrong. This is not a bad reflection on what Christ did, nor is it a supplement to what he did. Rather, it has to do with our attitudes toward our choices, our circumstance, and our reactions to people, events, and objects.

Our attitude is cleansed as we look at Christ as he is in Scripture. There is a transforming sight of Christ in time, before we pass on into the eternal presence of him with whom we have to do. In a real sense, the beatific vision has begun.[14]

> Changed from glory into glory,
> Till in heaven we take our place.
> CHARLES WESLEY (1707-1788)

We are not only purged, we press forward to be purged for God promotes that purgation in us. It is not a passive view by us, but we are given grace to look unto Christ for increase of faith and for perseverance in the cause of Christ. Our seeing God, through the eyes of faith, being still sinful, "requires that something be added to man's nature, an enrichment enabling him to behold true being."[15]

Ahead, therefore, we anticipate a final transformation. It is not a gloomy, grueling purgatory. Peter said we have awaiting us an "abundant entrance" (see 2 Peter 1:11) into heaven. There is not a breath of postdeath, anteroom suffering. Rather, we are promised an immediate, royal, and lavish welcome into the courts of the Lord.

We feel the final thrill awaiting us when we sing those stirring lines from "Guide me, O Thou Great Jehovah":

> When I tread the verge of Jordan
> Bid my anxious fears subside;
> Death of death, and Hell's destruction
> Land me safe on Canaan's side!
>
> WILLIAM WILLIAMS

Time
in Heaven
?

Got a minute? We need to ponder if time will fit into eternity. Why not? After all, doesn't eternity fit into time? Are time and eternity interchangeable?

Let's begin by considering the phenomenon of eternity in time. It will not give us a definitive answer to the question "Is Time in Heaven?" but it will get us started and possibly provide some clues. First, which heaven are we talking about when we ask "Is Time in Heaven?" Does it matter? Surprisingly it doesn't.

Although Scripture speaks of three heavens (Immediate, Intermediate, and Infinite) they are not totally different. They are parts making one whole. The earliest acquaintance humans have with Immediate Heaven provides a clue as to the nature of the other two heavens. There is a qualitative link between all three forms of heaven. For some purposes it may be better to speak of a heavenly state, rather than heavenly states.

"Eternal life" is the Immediate Heaven, the first heaven God wants us to participate in. It is the heaven which comes to man. It is God creating his life in humans born in trespasses and in sins. Heaven does not self-erupt or self-evolve as if it were a natural development. God must create his qualitative life in us by the Holy Spirit for us to catch a glimpse of the escalating fullness of the next stages of heaven. In chapter 11, "Is Heaven Earned?" we will look into the concept of "eternal life" at length. It is sufficient here to note that "eternal life" gives us a foretaste of the essence of heavenly life.

Indirectly, at least, in "eternal life" we meet the question of what we ask of the Infinite or final heaven: "Is Time in Heaven?" Without heaven beginning in our earthly existence, our appetite for its final form would considerably lessen. "Eternal life" in us now is God's way of building in his own advertisements and advance notices of its later fullness.

We first meet with the idea of God's presentness in "eternal life." Sequence loses its importance in "eternal life." What the person enjoys is God's nearness, that God is alive in us now. But can we be sure that this is what the Infinite heaven will be like?

The question, "Is Time in Heaven?" cannot be given an easy, quick, and unqualified yes or no answer. What do we mean by time? There are different senses of what time is. It would be of some help to know what meanings have been given to time before we can know what Scripture says about it.

A favorite assumption is that heaven is absolute timelessness. Eternity is conceived as vastly different from time. The word *eternity* is considered the opposite of time. People speak of heaven as timeless. But that term doesn't really bring us any closer to an understanding of whether or not time is in eternity.

Timelessness presents problems. Timelessness, for instance, does away with music. Music raises the question whether or not heaven is timelessness.

Music, of course, requires timing. Other recreations do, too. The games of tennis and golf, as well as other sports, cannot be played well without coordination, which requires timing. In music it is obvious that time and timing play vital roles. Music notes are timed eighth, sixteenth, quarter, and half notes. This presses us with an important and difficult, yet elementary question: "Is there time in heaven?"

There are three basic positions on this question:

1. Heaven is timeless.
2. Heaven is endless time.
3. Heaven is everlasting present.

Take a little time and run through these options to see which one best describes heaven.

Is Heaven Timeless?

Timelessness has several meanings. In Buddhism, for instance, timelessness means time is extinguished. Nirvana, their heaven, is the obliteration of time. In Buddhism, time is considered evil. But a Christian does not say time is evil, for God made time. Time is unaffected by sin. At worst it is neutral, but certainly not intrinsically evil. Without time could there be an eternity?

Poets are not concerned about ideological precision. That, more than any adoption of a Buddhist view of time, explains why J. M. Black in his 1921 hymn "When the Roll Is Called up Yonder" denied time in one line of stanza one and asserted time ("morning" assumes time) in the next:

> When the trumpet of the Lord shall sound,
> *And time shall be no more,*
> And *morning breaks* eternal bright and fair,
> When the saved of earth shall gather over on the other shore,
> And the roll is called up yonder, I'll be there (italics added).

Hymns such as John Newton's (1725-1807) "Amazing Grace," refers to heaven in terms of the extension of time:

When we've been there ten thousand *years*,
Bright shining as the sun,
We've no less *days* to sing God's praise,
Than when we first begun (italics added).

Revelation 22:2, which is indisputably connected with the Infinite Heaven by various schools, says the tree of life will bear twelve kinds of fruit "every month." Of all the things said to be eliminated from heaven, time is not one of them. Some may quibble that there is an inconsistency here, for with the removal of sun, moon, and night (21:23; 22:5), the method of keeping track of time is gone, therefore, time is gone. Yet there is the monthly yield of fruit (22:2)! One could also argue that with perpetual day, too, there must be time of some sort. Isaac Watts (1674-1748) wrote poetically of heaven: "infinite day excludes the night." And by the same token, infinite day includes time. Unlike the viper that Paul shook off into the fire after his shipwreck, this paradox stubbornly hangs on heaven to bedevil Christians.

It's the same kind of problem one faces in reading process theologian Nelson Pike's *God and Timelessness* in which he argued that without time divine *fore*knowledge is impossible. If there is not time, then, "Puff!"—there goes FOREknowledge.[1]

Timeless can be used in the sense of no limits to the extent of time. In this sense, heaven is looked on as glory going on and on without let up or conclusion. Endless time, however, is not strictly timelessness, so this definition cannot be used, although unending time needs to be looked at more closely.

Is Heaven Endless Time?

This concept has strong appeal. Time stretched to infinity assumes time continues indefinitely. In mathematics *infinity* occurs when the value of a number exceeds any preassigned finite number. There is no last number. Heaven would seem to have no last minute. But to have random time or time that just goes on and on and never stops, it may be argued, is hardly an improvement on what we know on earth. Indeed, if there is no goal to infinity, then it can be argued that time is a little less attractive. True, without goals disappointments and frustrations are eliminated. But how can one have satisfaction without goals? If nothing is sought, can anything be attained? If anticipation is deactivated because there are no goals, then isn't pleasure partly reduced if not entirely removed?

Stand-still or present-time, which we'll discuss next, is a better option. The problems connected with endless time seem to outweigh its appeal.

Albert Einstein's Theory of Absolute Speed Limits in the universe, which he developed after his famous Relativity Theory, held that when an object's mass increases to infinity, its length goes to zero and its time comes to a stand still. Measurements of time and space become relative, varying with the person making the observations. His general theory of relativity restores absolute time to the universe, but locally time and space are distorted by the gravitational fields.[2]

These matters have eschatological implications. They especially bear on how we are to perceive space and time. A stand-still quality of time, briefly mentioned above, is not a figment of theological speculation, but a respectable scientific theory. It seems to strengthen the case, from a Christian's viewpoint, that stand-still time is not an indefensible hypothesis. Paradox may well be an essential ingredient to reality without denying that separate, contradictory, and parallel factors are valid forms or hypotheses, which in their own way contribute either to the explanation of reality or are essential to reality's fabric.

Is Heaven Everlasting Present?

When some people refer to timelessness in heaven, they mean time that is stretched and kept. They perceive heaven to have no past time, no future time, just present time perfected.

This would be like frozen time, but without the connotation of chilling statuesqueness. C. S. Lewis wrote in reference to God. ". . . with Him, it is, so to speak, still 1920 and already 1960 . . . !"[3] Keep in mind Lewis wrote this *before* 1960!

Carl F. H. Henry said the "everlasting now" proposal attempts "to combine the conceptions of timelessness and unlimited duration."[4] P. T. Forsyth's phrase for it was "one infinite simultaneity."[5] Ulrich Simon altered the expression slightly calling heaven's time "a divine simultaneity."[6] Louis Berkhof referred to it as "one indivisible present."[7]

The popular biblical word *age* escapes the need to assign specific dates. *Aion* fits the bill for describing the eternal ages, the qualitative life of eternity.[8] Two other Greek words bear on the subject. *Kronos* is calendar time, reflected in our word *chronology*. And *kairos* which is opportune time, season, time for fulfillment.[9] *Kairos* time is final time, the spiritual moment which cannot be recorded numerically. Sheldon Van Auken referred to "'the still point of the turning world.' All our most lovely moments perhaps are timeless."[10]

The word *new*, which is used to describe the "new song" (Rev. 5:9) is close sounding to *kairos*, but kainos is definitely different. *Kainos* is the word *new*. We looked at it briefly in chapter 5. It is time to take a second look.

Kainos (used in new name—2:17; 3:12; new song—5:9; new Jerusalem—3:12; 21:2; new heaven and new earth—21:1; and all things new—21:5) relates to quality, not to how recent it is. *Kainos* is different from the other Greek word for "new"— *neos*. *Kainos* is new in kind. *Neos* is new in time. *Kainos* is "in the sense of something not previously present, unknown, strange, remarkable, also with the connotation of the marvelous and unheard of."[11]

Qualitative time, God-in-action makes the present-time special and significant or "new." Timelessness is not unscientific or impossible. Time can stop and still exist for the astrophysicist.

To be timeless along scientific lines one has to be present everywhere in that coordinate system. In absolute timelessness there is no motion—and get this!—no sound. So while time made permanent or present time standardized has the advantage of making boredom impossible and preserving the biblical message of God's grace in action, it has the disadvantage of making music meaningless. A "new" song in a timeless environment describes the music of heaven, yet it is paradoxical.

For present time to endure not only means the abandonment of calendars, but also the impossibility of measuring beats. Without the passage of time, music becomes impossible to play, to sing, or to hear. Sheldon Van Auken imagined his deceased wife playing an organ in heaven, a celestial organ "on which perhaps every note of a song can be heard at the same time."[12]

The paradoxical combination of music and stand-still time does not mean it is an impossibility anymore than the wavelength theory of light and the particle theory of light (because they are mutually exclusive) means one or the other is wrong. Physics experiments show that both traits are true of light. Both exist. Yet they are mutually exclusive. Scientists refer to this phenomenon as an "antinomy." Insoluble, yet real. That is probably the case with eternal present time and music in heaven. It certainly fits with the description of "new" song in a way theologians never originally imagined.

Kainos ("new") is a kind of newness which has yet to be marketed. It would be comparable to a model machine which has not yet been delivered to dealers, something like the prototype of the aircraft industry. Heaven's music is an unknown new. The music of heaven will be so new that it *does not require the lapse of time*! That's new! It is so completely new to have music without traditional measured time that it leaves one shaking one's head, instead of tapping one's foot. Take away the sensual beat and do you have music? The thought must be very disturbing, even to musicians who know music is more than beat.

The matter of music in heaven being "new" that is, totally new, new in kind, gives support to the recommended view of present-time in eternity. Sam Storms, in his discussion of the stand-still view of time, ended rejecting the strongly supported view of eternity being an eternal present. To him one could not postulate stand-still time and maintain that God knew a time Christ would return. He questioned whether God would be totally absorbed in present-time to the neglect of accepting past and future. He mentioned others who struggled with the same problem in reference to God's changelessness.[13] How could God be said not to change, if the traditional categories, past, present, and future, did not exist for God?

In explaining God we must speak of God as if he were man, as if he were locked into our realm of existence. Therefore, we use a time-conditioned vocabulary to describe God. But we must not insist that the manner of speaking is to be taken literally. Otherwise, we will insist eternity runs on time.

The traditional anthropomorphic language is to use words and ideas from our existence. It still seems the best way to proceed, but only if we don't think anthropomorphic references are absolute, that is, that God runs heaven and rules with time as past, present, and future.

Sam Storms objected to thinking of eternity as eternal present, for it would prohibit God from scheduling Christ's second coming or prohibit us from thinking God would schedule Christ's return. Instead, Storms proposed that "everlasting eternal" be applied to God.[14] It was his attempt to resolve what appeared to him to be a problem. His conclusion was to say God was without beginning and without end.

The weakness of his presentation, it seems, was twofold:

First, he had to fall back to an anthropomorphic way of referring to time in eternity by using unendingness, for unendingness assumes the time-conditioned ideas of past, present, and future. Secondly, because of that he never avoided the problems connected with retaining our time in eternity.

His alternative proposal has to be rejected as superficial and deficient. The problem is not with thinking of eternity as "eternal present." The real problem is a literalistic mindset which says "eternal present" makes nonsense out of God's foreordination and the scheduling of Christ's return to earth. Support for "eternal present" is indirectly found in *kainos* (new) applied to heaven's singing. "Eternal present" takes more seriously the radical newness in *kainos.*

But that alone does not exhaust the meaning of the "new song" in heaven ahead. Thus, heaven's music needs to be looked at in greater detail. We have devoted the next chapter to that subject. Music is probably the best-known activity associated with the Infinite Heaven and it deserves even closer attention beyond the technical aspects of what makes musical sound.

Before we leave this subject we should note, in conclusion, that modern physics has enhanced the concept of eternal present-time. The traditional understanding of time has been challenged by the new physics.

We tend to carry over a common sense approach of time into heaven. We believe time flows. We say time starts, it runs on, it runs out, it flies, it drags, it waits, it speeds, and it slows. Most nonscientific descriptions contend that motion, or at least movement, is an essential characteristic of time.

Modern science, however, questions whether time passes.[15] If it flows they ask "How fast?" To most people the clock not only tells us the time, it also uses time. But can we appeal to the operations of a clock to describe the essence of time?

We think a clock measures time. We say the clock records the passage of time. But the scientist cautions us here. He notes that the clock only measures the intervals of time; it does not tell us its speed. In other words, the concept of time's speed is not settled by appealing to what a clock "says." And, in turn, this raises the question of the alleged sequence in time. In 1915 Einstein proposed that "spacetime is elastic, so that it can be stretched, bent, twisted, and buckled."[16] Microphysics and the quantum theory help make "eternal life" in time, which biblical skeptics once dismissed as absurd, a credible concept. In addition, the emphasis on presentness in time does not necessarily mean that the distinctions of past and future are illusions, for the relationship of past and future events are measured every day in scientific laboratories. Measurements would appear to be thrown into a muddle if past and future, left and right, extensions and intervals, up and down would cease to exist.

Once the biblical views of the future in the present, the present in the past, and the past in the present were considered ridiculous and physically impossible. Now, in the new physics, a biblical approach to reality, which anticipated time's flexibility, should have a greater credibility beginning with scientists. (This is not to say, however, that there is anything of a mass movement of scientists to embrace Christianity!)

Perhaps what will force the average person to rethink his concept of the Infinite Heaven, however, will be how music, as we know it, will fit into a final dimension never dreamed possible.

The pictorial language of Revelation, admittedly, uses a time-conditioned vocabulary. But the actual experience of the heavens described in the Book of Revelation doesn't mean that it must conform to the dimensions we know here. It may be that John himself entered into dynamic spacetime in his Patmos vision. He was not occupied with a "Big Bang" in the past, but had an insight into the complex series of "bangs" throughout history culminating in the final "Big Bang," when God unilaterally inaugurates for us what he has always known. If, as some astronomers believe, the universe will eventually pull apart at the seams because of the limitless exertion of space-time forces, John saw, by the Holy Spirit, farther physically or further mentally (than any other human) into the causation of that catastrophe.

The average Christian who has neither training nor talent in science may be somewhat bewildered by the complexities of antinomies and other scientific explanations. What I have written is meant to produce further reading, reflection, and discussion.

My venture into this phase of heaven is intended to raise your curiosity so that you will delve more deeply into the subject. The value of this particular chapter will have been to introduce you to some of the key issues and major alternatives. Perhaps enough has been presented to edge skeptics of the Scriptures toward a greater openness to them. And, hopefully, Christians will be encouraged to value the eschatological perspectives of Scripture in a new way.

What Shall
We Do
in Heaven
?

*H*ow can one chapter adequately cover eternal events in heaven? Don't be scared off, thinking I will go on and on! And don't think I'm presumptuous or preposterous in trying to compress the activities of the eternal ages in a small space! Of course, heaven ahead is far too glorious for any one man or for any number of books to comprehend its magnitude, to condense its multifacetness, and to adequately commend its magnificence. We can't begin to mine all the scattered, scintillating nuances of the biblical information on heaven, let alone to list its agenda, to trace its variety, and to convey its grandeur. There is more in store than what poets have dreamed possible. And what is encountered will be far better than what I have been attempting to highlight here!

"What shall we do in heaven?" Surely, the final heaven must

provide an infinitude of functions, fulfilling activities that approximate its outward splendor.

Revelation gives only partial and periodic glimpses into the activities of the Intermediate State and of the Final Heavenly State. Heading them all is *singing.* It is probably the most interesting carryover from this life into the next. We cannot let it slide by as one activity among many. Music ranks as one of the creative activities of heaven. Because music employs the redeemed as individuals, as groups, as bodies, as thinking persons, and as emotional beings, we have decided to use it as a paradigm of other activities in heaven which we will not explore.

Music is symbolic of heaven itself. What is music? Dots on paper, decibel levels in the air? Yes, it is that and more. Of all pastimes music lends itself to mystical depths that words alone cannot reach. Thomas Carlyle (1795-1881) summed it up: "Music leads us to the verge of the infinite and lets us gaze on that."

But heaven's music *has* words, too. And it is the combination of words and music that expresses the best of both worlds! The music of Revelation is truth intoned, not the sounding of notes alone. The non-Christian could be attracted to heaven more if it were divorced from the message in the words. God-honoring words, lyrics that exalt Christ—not the melodies—would disturb the self-righteous.

Music illustrates heaven a second way. When words are sung they lose their regional sounds and individual accents. In singing one's distinctive pronunciation dissolves or becomes undetectable. The commonality of man comes through over and beyond our linguistic peculiarities. That is one reason why music has been called the universal language and the ultimate communication. Is this one reason why the ancient Greeks attributed the origin of music to the gods, not to men?

Music is also a mood, a state of mind. The activities of writing, playing, and singing music are a state of mind, in addition to art forms. Music sounds in the mind of the author one way, to the players in another, and it also comes across with yet other impressions to listeners.

Trained listeners pick out differences between average and extraordinary music. This is part of why the physical "I hear it" of music is not the same as the psychological "I feel it."

Probably the most familiar activity people associate with heaven is singing. Music is enormously popular with many people. Recorded music sales cover a broad spectrum of musical tastes. Music video is increasingly popular. One need not be a composer or performer to be able to appreciate variety in music.

But heaven is not just music, *it is a certain kind of music.* Mark Twain (1835-1910) poked fun at the fact that heaven is pictured as limited to hymn singing. Moreover, he found objectionable that it is "of one hymn alone."[1] If Twain had marked his Bible more carefully, he would have noted that several varieties of singing are referred to in Revelation.

People play music, but it is usually not hymns. The president of Rochester University, who also teaches philosophy courses, guessed that there was a reason why hymns don't strike a responsive chord with some people. He wrote:

> If the modern world seems particularly deaf to hymn singing, it may be because we are so convinced that the only story worth telling is self-scripted.[2]

Hell may be to have to listen to music one detests. Will hard-rockers and heavy-metal musicians be forced to listen to Beethoven's Ninth Symphony? Will snobbish non-Christian classical musicians, who never hide their contempt for "revival hymns," be required to beat time to "There Is Power in the

Blood?" On the other hand, to sit in silence may be sufficient torment to cause the grinding of teeth, which will hardly be music to their ears.

If the lyrics of heaven do not offend, the most likely instrument chosen to play the hymns may cause regrets. Admittedly the role of the trumpets in heaven was to announce the next events and to get attention rather than to accompany the singing. I've wondered how noninstrumentalist churches (where organs, guitars, and drums are barred) handle the biblical references to harps in use in heaven (Rev. 5:8; 14:2; 15:2).

No other modern country seems to have devoted national attention to the harp so much as Wales. The harp is the traditional musical instrument of Wales. The "Cymdeithias Cerdd Dant" (a society for the promotion of harp-playing and pennillion singing) finds stationary Grecian and Gothic pedal harps are becoming in short supply. Switching to hand-held harps may cause some diappointment to Welsh harp players who arrive in heaven fully practiced with the traditional stand-up models.

The trumpeters were the angels, but the harpists of Revelation were the twenty-four elders (5:8) and those who were loyal to Christ and lost their lives for it (the 144,000 martyrs) (15:2). Not everyone is pictured as playing a harp. Clearly special recognition went with God's handing one a harp, a "reward" for those who have laid down their lives, honor, and sacred fortune for Christ.

Any irritation over "harps of gold" or the use of a harp hardly compares to the aggravations of those who dislike any music. "The music which so sickened and fatigued them in time, will be all the entertainment they have to look for through eternity."[3]

Hell, not heaven, is to abound with tedium. The writer of Revelation seems to have anticipated the objection of alleged tedium of the redeemed when he noted the torments of the damned. George B. Caird wrote:

> In a grim parody of the worship of the heavenly choir (4:8) we are told that [the lost] have no respite day or night [in their torments].[4]

Get ready. Everybody in heaven seems to sing. Even the angels appear to sing. If "to say" in Rev. 5:9, 12, 13 is also viewed as song (5:9), then what seems to be simple chant in 4:8, 9, 11 is really singing by the angelic creatures, the living creatures.[5] Even now during the Intermediate Heaven two choral groups (the living creatures or angels, and the twenty-four redeemed representatives from the Old and New Testament periods) are busy singing (5:9, 12). They are joined by a larger chorus, all redeemed from all ages (v. 13). What is being sung is the worthiness of the Lamb, who has already come into history and disclosed God's love and purchased his church (v. 9). Three music makers have been noted so far: the angels, the elders, and the Intermediate State redeemed.

A fourth group appears in 7:9-17 and reappears two other times (14:3 and 15:2, 3). These are those martyred for Christ. What they sang in 15:3 were psalm portions (Pss. 96:1; 98:1; 144:9f) yet with a distinctly Christian flavor, for the Song of Moses anticipates the Song of the Lamb.[6] What God did for the Jews in the Exodus, Christ did in securing our deliverance from sin. It was a celebration of God's power, justice, holiness, and decrees.

A fifth choral assembly appears in 11:17, 18, again composed of the original combination of angelic beings and twenty-four elders. In their anthem they praised Christ's conquest of his enemies.

A similar anthem of praise to Christ for victory over his enemies occurs again in 19:6, which is a united hallelujah, following the hymns of praise in 19:1, 2, 3, 5. As noted earlier, it is more a chorus than a chant.[7]

Membership in the heavenly choral groups is determined more by nature, by spiritual function, and by common suffering, rather than by age, sex, musical training, or voice ranges. This unmusical way of describing the choirs reaffirms the supremacy of the lyrics over tunes, of truths expressed rather than moods sought. The absence of conductors, rehearsals, and training confirms that the central figure is Christ, not those who praise him.

Choral subgroups, which on earth sometimes react jealously against another, in heaven will have no rifts. It will be devoid of petty rivalry. The harmony of the choirs in heaven is the envy of all choir masters of earth. In heaven musicians are united, because they want all attention given to Christ. They are not concerned to be featured in solo roles. They are not hungering after recognition.

Revelation contains several hymn fragments.[8] The hymn form most common is the doxology. There is a two-fold doxology in 1:6 (glory and dominion); a three-fold doxology in 4:11 (glory, honor, and power); a four-fold doxology in 5:13 (blessing, honor, glory, dominion); and seven-fold doxologies in 5:11 and 7:12 (blessing, glory, wisdom, thanksgiving, honor, power, and might).

Doxology is what heaven is all about. It is one of the oldest hymn forms in existence. Some churches sing it at the beginning of the service; others sing it in the middle as part of the offering response; still others use it at the very conclusion of the service. The words are simple and express our deepest emotions about God in his goodness, mercy, and care.

The solidarity of the groups seen singing in heaven is one important characteristic to notice. Another is group satisfaction. There is no trace of boredom in what Revelation says about the musical program.

Traditionally, people have complained that heaven, as the Bible describes it, has to be boring. Mark Twain anticipated that the music of heaven would be monotonous. He wrote:

> This universal singing is not casual, not occasional, not relieved by intervals of quiet [wrong again: my insertion]; it goes on, all day long, and every day, during a stretch of twelve hours . . . . the singing is of hymns alone, nay, it is of one hymn alone [wrong again]. The words are always the same, in number they are only about a dozen, there is no rhyme, there is no poetry: "Hosannah, hosannah, hosannah, Lord God of Sabbaoth, Rah! Rah! Siss! Boom!—Ah!" [wrong again][9]

We have already seen that hell will be boring, but will heaven be boring? We have all thought of this question, for boredom is dreaded more than clammy weather. To be eternally bored is to make heaven hell. For heaven to be boring is the worst possible advertising. An image of heavenly boredom would discourage one from wanting to go there.

But heaven will not be boring, for four reasons:

1. Heaven will not be boring, for those there want to be there. Heaven takes away fatigue as well as pain. Boredom is one of the forms of pain that is no more.

   > My tongue shall never tire
   > Of chanting with the choir,
   > May Jesus Christ be praised.

2. Heaven will not be boring, because human selfishness, which contributes to boredom, will be removed. In heaven God is central and man is separated from his ear⟨⟩ habit of complaining about the most minor irrita⟨⟩

3. Heaven will not be boring for the human b⟨⟩ glorified form will not, as now, be vulnera⟨⟩ and body aches, weariness and drowsin⟨⟩

delivered from being bores as well as from being sinners. The biggest cause of boredom is often that the bored project their boredom.

4. ⟦Heaven will not be boring, because length will not be detected. If heaven is a place where "meetings don't break up," there will be no complaints, for heaven will be timeless, that is, stand-still time.⟧

Present time, the eternal present eliminates the possibility of boredom, for boredom requires or assumes time is not moving fast enough or that there is too much lag. As we saw in the preceding chapter, stand-still time requires a new kind of music. Yet it also renders the charge of boredom irrelevant.

Musically heaven will be the epitome of innovation. We have yet to grasp the radicalness of the heavenly music presently in the Intermediate State and in the coming Infinite heaven. Nevertheless, that newness has already impinged on the human spirit by creating a newness which opens man to praise God alone with abandon.

Revelation 5:9 says those redeemed in heaven sing a "new song." The newness of the new song of heaven, of course, relates to the message of salvation secured by Christ. The old gospel is vital to the new song, because the very song of eternity has entered our internal space and given us a revolutionized change of aptitude and attitude. A new life must produce the new song. The new life is individual redemption by Christ. It is

.t. The song is new because it
ible, and it is impossible not
: expression of God's grace,
ing is also the best song. In it
e.⟧

glorious thought!—
ie whole,
I bear it no more:
: Lord, O my soul.
SPAFFORD (1828-1888)

Be this the eternal song
Through all the ages long
May Jesus Christ be praised.

JOSEPH BARNBY (1838-1896)

The new song is sung in heaven, but it began on earth, where our redemption was actualized and accomplished by Christ. God guaranteed our appropriation of it by the Holy Spirit, who applies it to us and amplifies it for us. For such a new song to be sung, Jesus is not idly waiting in heaven. It is sung there by those who have finished with earth. But it was sung on earth as soon as they came to faith in Christ. Even now the risen and ascended Christ rescues the perishing. The Holy Spirit implants a hymn to Christ in the soul before it is vocalized. Through the Word of God, Christ draws people away from the devil's ditties to give us a song of thanksgiving of a complete salvation.

Music that is employed to push destructive and abusive life-styles is pathetically shallow, and essentially short-lived, even though plenty of customers are willing to perpetuate its philosophy by buying its production. In addition to often being devoid of good sound, it is frequently deficient in good sense. Moral values are attacked, mocked, belittled, ridiculed, and replaced by attitudes and practices which are dehumanizing and derogatory of both man and God.

Satan uses music as one means to seal the destruction of the unsuspecting and gullible, who are adrift in an amoral society. God's foe uses what God has created for man's enjoyment and improvement to solidify commitment in those who rebel against any authority figure. Regrettably, ruinous world views get daily plugs from industry indoctrinated disc jockeys.

A sizable number of non-Christians regard hymns as inferior music. These same individuals can be critical of pop music. Objections to the hymn form may reflect a hostility to the gospel or an undue emphasis on one form of singing (psalms). Anti-Christian commitment in composers is found in the lurid lyrics of heavy metal music and also, for instance in the lilting song of John Lennon, "Imagine."

From the ranks of rockers another sort of musician has come to write a new brand of song, truly "new" songs. Roger McGuinn was once the lead singer and guitarist of the "Byrds," which produced two 1960s classics, "Turn, Turn, Turn," and "Eight Miles High."

In 1977, after a third failed marriage, he crashed from his so-called "eight mile high." *People* magazine reported that when he hit bottom he turned "not to dope, acid . . . but to the Bible."[10] A year later, he decided "Jesus is the only way. I felt peace. My fear evaporated."[11]

The songs of sensualism, packed full of glittering promise, he found ultimately deceptive. They promised him great joy, but they delivered only emptiness and pain. They promised clear sailing, but provided only hidden reefs and death traps. It is true of other modern songs. They are so short on variety and interesting lyrics, and so heavy with man-centered thinking and living, that no longer can one regard the opinion of the great lexicographer Samuel Johnson (1709-1784) as having much wisdom, when he wrote of his time, that music was the only sensual pleasure without vice. Today many songs overflow with the vile. And former participants in the hard-rock industry, such as Roger McGuinn have acknowledged the emptiness and the destructiveness of them.

McGuinn now studies the Bible daily. He once lived with no thought of God. Now, however, amazingly, he prays about everything, even parking spaces.[12] Friends in the industry look on him as having lost his mind, but he says he has found it. The hard rock music he once delighted in and was proud of, he is now ashamed of. He described his old music as "decadent and superficial."[13]

We, too, can begin to sing Christ's glory before we near the final heaven. Christ supplies the reason why we sing to his glory and inspires us to sing along.

Jesus may be compared to a skilled piano tuner. Christ comes and finds us dreadfully out of tune and full of discord. Christ knows our loose wires. He can replace broken strings. He makes the right adjustments on our beings. He can, for he made us in the first place. He restores lost chords and creates a capacity to respond to the playing of the Holy Spirit. The only explanation of joy, where there were once sour notes, goes back to the fact that Christ has reached into our lives, gone behind our sounding board, and prepared us to make melody in our hearts to God. He tunes us to sing his praise. Harmony has come. Christ rearranges us so that we can sing the new song. We will join the heavenly choirs when God wills.

> There the song is never ended,
> There the praise will never cease;
> There the sorrows and afflictions
> Will be lost in tranquil peace;
> Never ceasing, we shall praise our God above.
>
> WILLIAM WILLIAMS (1717-1791)

10

Shall
We Rest
Eternally
in Heaven
?

When a person says, "Describe heaven to me so I'll want to go," I ask them, "Why do you want to go?"

Some are not ready to go; others are not willing to go. Still others don't know why *anyone* would want to go.

Those who don't want to go to heaven may not want to go because their expectations are low. They can't get excited about heaven because it may seem to be the extension of boredom. Who wants to be inactive for endless ages? Therefore reluctance to go may be due to heaven's bad image.

Why do we want to go to heaven? Do we have a strong desire to go to heaven because our attraction to earth is weak? Do we want to go to heaven because *there* we can retire without the crunch of aging and the medical costs that go along with it? Do we want to go to heaven because there we shall have greater opportunity to develop our talents? Is heaven the only place where one can waste "time" without being reprimanded? Do we want to go to heaven because we want to escape work and enjoy rest?

Let's be up-front about it: extended idleness without worry of vital services and security is very attractive to the modern worker, even though "rest" is the most passive form of activity.

Rest, of course, is a vital part of life on earth. Without it we cannot function at our best. We can't live without the cycle of rest and work. A person weary from holding down two jobs, or a person chained to one job—who works sixty hours a week instead of forty—both recognize they are behind in their rest. The volunteer staff in churches are often hard-pressed, overworked, and—sometimes—underappreciated. Their hours are long, beyond the time-consuming duties of raising a family and holding down a regular job. The emotionally burned-out don't want to suffer anymore. They desire heaven, because they are tired. A long rest is inviting.

In London, England, a gravestone epitaph, written by an obviously overworked mother, says:

> Weep not for me, friend,
> Though death do us sever.
> I am going to do nothing
> Forever and ever.

Jesus said, "In my Father's house are many *resting places*" [literal translation] (John 14:2). The Greek text is not "mansions," but "resting places." *Resting places* is the literal Greek. A close approximation is "rooms." Some modern translations reflect this finding. (*See* chapter 16, Growth in Heaven? in which an interpretation of the Early Church Fathers on this text is reviewed.) Despite the several merits of the King James Version, it is misleading, because "mansions" today means something totally different than what it did in the seventeenth century. Today it is ludicrous to insist "mansions" are inside the Father's house!

Because rest is associated with sleep, we need to ask afresh what "rest" means in the Bible. Was Rudyard Kipling right when he said, "We shall rest . . . lie down for an eon or two?" Does the Bible mean by rest what we mean? We may be in for a rude awakening to discover that "rest" can involve work.

On top of this, Scripture sense aside, quite honestly, rest does not appeal to everyone. If heaven is "luxurious lounge" or endless rows of hammocks, then many will *not* want to go.

If the active had a say as to what should occupy our "time" in heaven, they would probably want to do something that would relate to their favorite activity. But some people most interested in activity on earth are not seen jumping across tennis nets or jogging along the roadsides. They are sitting in wheelchairs!

We first heard of Joni Eareckson (then unmarried) at a roadside quick-service station in little Frannie, Wyoming, where we picked up a news magazine and read an article on her. We had stopped in our three-and-a-half-hour run to Billings, Montana, where I had made one of my routine hospital calls to a fellow Christian church member. (Pastors in the urban areas, who sit in slow city traffic when they make their rounds to hospitals, should think of the pastors in the West who sometimes chew up eight hours to make *one* hospital call!)

When we moved East in 1979, we were close enough to go hear Joni Eareckson in her "Night with Joni" at the Philadelphia Civic Center. As many know, Joni at age eighteen was paralyzed from the neck down as the result of a diving accident in shallow water in the Chesapeake Bay in Maryland.

Near the end of her testimony to the grace of God, she said something about heaven which greatly impressed me and seemed totally on target. She said that when she got to heaven, the first thing she wanted to do was to ask Jesus for a dance.

Then, from her wheelchair, she sang about this hope. It was a moving conclusion to her presentation.

Joni said she was not looking forward to rest in heaven. She had had plenty on earth. She was looking forward to nonstop activity, of using limbs that have been unresponsive for most of her life.

"Describe heaven to me so I'll want to go."

Heavenly rest, especially eternal rest, does not appeal to those who have been resting most of their lives on earth and don't like it, such as those who have lost limbs or whose arms and legs are useless.

Even those who have had full use of their bodies on earth can get tired of rest quickly. Sleeping wears thin after a while. Who hasn't found bed boring after several days? Mark Twain said to Captain Stormfield in his imaginary visit to heaven, "Why, Stormfield, a man like you, that had been active and stirring all his life, would go mad in six months in heaven where he hadn't anything to do!"[1]

Let's face it, activists would not like heaven if it were mostly or totally rest. Industrious persons are turned off by a heaven in which one sits on clouds and wastes "time." By elevating rest we make heaven a drag and drawback to activists.

If we like activity, heaven has it: "[They] serve [God] day and night in his temple" (Rev. 7:15 NIV). That describes what the *angels* are doing now. But while angels are ministering spirits for Christians on earth (Heb. 1:14) it doesn't mean that they are going to wait on us "hand and foot" in heaven. And just because we are passive and allow God to wipe away our tears (upon arrival, I presume) (Rev. 21:4), doesn't mean we lay back and watch God. Unlike other brides, the church will not have house chores, but that does not mean the redeemed will sit around, eternally primping and napping to look pretty for Christ.

Rest and activity are and will be in heaven—another biblical paradox. We should maintain both, for they are no more impossible than having both on earth. We shall look at these two aspects of heaven-life next.

Rest

Originally, Israel was a nomadic people. The word *Hebrew* reflects the migrant nature of their beginnings. Being constantly on the move, pulling up stakes and pitching their tents in new locations, was not a totally satisfying way of life. They were not a settled nation. And they were engaged in unending skirmishes with small nations bent on their annihilation. Israel lacked both rest from movement and rest from fighting.

The Hebrew concept of a future life centered on rest—entire rest—rest from harassments, rest from military conflicts, rest from business demands, rest from meal preparations and other daily duties.[2] Despite their relative and periodic calm, their story was of "failure to achieve *menuchah* (rest) in the promised land."[3] Ceaseless fighting for self-preservation (Heb. 4:8) made peace a community goal. To them, their King of Salem (peace) would bring wars to an end (7:2).

The Sabbath day was in anticipation of final rest. Christians found in Christ this longed-for rest. To them Jesus was the Prince of Peace beginning and bringing in that eternal Sabbath rest to the people of God (4:10, 11). Whereas Joshua never achieved rest, Jesus did, and we are to enter into the rest he won. Ironically, by his work in death he secured our rest. When our redemption was secured Jesus sat down at the right hand of the Father in heaven (1:3).

Christians are meant to enter their eternal rest long before they die. This distinguished Christian hope from Jewish hope. Our rest is ready to enjoy while we are alive. This rest begins when we rest from our works. When we cease trusting in our deeds, when we abandon trying to secure our own rest, then we will be open to entering into the spiritual rest Jesus secured. Entering the Christian rest means, primarily, resting from our works-righteousness (4:10, 11). We remain restless until and unless we rest in the Lord's doings.

Paul's heart went out to the fruitless efforts of his countrymen to achieve true peace by their self-promoting self-efforts. Of contemporary Jews, he wrote:

> For not knowing about God's righteousness, and seeking to establish their own, they did not subject themselves to the righteousness of God (Rom. 10:3 NASB).

We cannot mount the heights of heaven by piling high human "credits." God who requires righteousness has supplied it in Jesus Christ!

On earth, however, Christians have not abandoned hard work. Because of Christ the direction and dynamics of work has shifted away from trying to impress God to a willingness to step in to help others. Being freed from anxiety about our own future, we can concentrate more fully upon the plight of our fellow creatures on earth. That brings a new dimension to social action, which the person who does good to look good has not begun to appreciate and claim.

The work of the Christian, in one sense, doesn't truly begin until he has rested completely in Jesus Christ. Heaven is not going to be a haven for those who shirk work. But the once-struggling martyrs of Christ's family "will enjoy rest from their hard work, because the results of their service go with them" (Rev. 14:13 GNB). This particular promise forms the second of seven beatitudes in the Book of Revelation.[4]

The apostle Paul referred to the Intermediate State, the heaven believers enter at death, as asleep (1 Thess. 4:13-15). There is the initial rest we receive when we accept Jesus' saving as sufficient for us and following that, in death we enter rest as a sleep.

How is this description to be taken? Are we to think that our loved ones in Christ who pass on before us are in a suspended state, neither here nor there? If we would take the expression literally, then it would lead to the position known as "soul sleep," which is a state of unconsciousness for the deceased believer. But this is hardly possible.[5]

Paul carried over the term *sleep* from Jesus' usage. In Mark 5:22, 23, 39-41, Jesus contrasted death with sleep. He didn't mean that they were identical, for he denied that death was a final state for the girl. Her resurrection was assumed. But the sleep metaphor meant more than saying sleep is like death and death like sleep. The following ideas are carried by the expression:

1. Death is expected as sleep at the end of a day is expected. After labor, we must rest. It is inevitable. To fight it is foolish. Dying is part of life. Scripture does not imply the deceased take astral trips, for they have arrived. Traveling is done. They are in the arms of Jesus.

2. Physically, we sleep on our own, but we cannot awake from our sleep in death except at Christ's word, just as Jesus woke individuals from death (Mark 5:39; John 11:11). "Asleep in Jesus" means we wake when he calls. He gets us up from death on the day of our resurrection. It is not something we do on our own.

3. Sleep underlines the timelessness aspect of heaven. In heaven time is no more. In sleep time seems nonexistent or it moves at a clip. In a sound sleep time never drags. Sleep teaches us that we can benefit without time in time. A touch of eternity is in sleep, for time seems to have stopped or stretched. Has it absolutely disappeared or has it just disappeared to us? The expression, however, was not originally given to give us a complete statement on whether or not some form of time exists or ceases to exist in heaven. Check chapter 8 for time in eternity.

4. Sleep means death is reversible. We speak of death as inevitable if the condition is terminal. The final process of death is irreversible, but sleep is quickly reversible. That is what distinguishes sleep from coma. In a comatose state we don't wake up. When Paul likened a believer's death to sleep, the message was that we are not meant to stay dead. We believe that in the resurrection, we shall rise from death as readily and as quickly as we arise from a good sleep.

5. Sleep makes us renewed and ready to function at our best. When we sleep well, we rise better fitted to work. So the resurrection brings us to far greater effectiveness for God. We shall rise from death in resurrection with the same sense of refreshment that we do following a wonderful sleep. That is why resurrection is a form of an awaking (Ps. 17:15). In sleep we seem to lose much: our blood pressure decreases, our digestion slows, our breathing becomes shallow, and our body temperature drops. But, surprisingly, with this slowdown of nature, we arise with greater effectiveness. We are restored to a new level of performance.

> Sleep that knits up the ravel'd sleave of care,
> The death of each day's life, sore labor's bath,
> Balm of hurt minds, great nature's second course,
> Chief nourisher in life's feasts.
> SHAKESPEARE (MACBETH, ACT II, SEC. 2.1. 35-38)

In the Intermediate State, our consciousness is not slowed, but increased and heightened, contrary to what mortalists claim. We emerge as new persons, ready for the next assignment with our reaction time improved and our resources more responsive. Therefore, "through sleep and darkness safely brought," we are "restored to life and power and thought!"

Service

To an activist total rest is more like hell than heaven. To think we shall float on a fluffy cloud, twiddle thumbs, or pluck harp strings hardly seems admirable and useful. Idleness is irksome to those who enjoy work. Stress on rest in heaven is not an endorsement of sloth. There is something worth considering in the suggestion that one of the torments of hell is absolute idleness and isolation, two postures that go together.

Heaven is the ultimate work field. God does not need our labor, said Paul. God is not served by human hands (as if he needed anything) because he himself gives to all men life and breath, and everything (*see* Acts 17:25). Paul, of course, was speaking of God absolutely. We should have no problem in believing God's all powerfulness to think that he needs help from puny man.

Serving God in heaven does not mean God is incapable or indisposed to act. David Gregg (1846-1919) overspoke when, on the basis that angels on earth had rolled away a stone and unlocked a door, that therefore heaven work will be "just as secular as these."[6] Though heaven is said to have a river, there will be no grooming of its banks. Though the tree of life will bear fruit, it will not be because of our pruning.

Much of our work on earth is devoted to getting the bugs out of machinery and stopping burglars from breaking in to steal. A lot of jobs will be eliminated at Christ's second coming.

Occupations will be phased out. Spies, lobbyists, funeral directors, will be out of work. Physicians, dentists, waterworks employees, and the police will not be needed. Street repair will be unnecessary not because the traffic is light or because the gold is too soft to hold up, for "pure gold, clear as glass" (Rev. 21:18) suggests durability as well as clarity. Similarly, golden harps and crowns (halos are never mentioned) will never need buffing. And in the final garden of paradise (Rev. 22:2) no weeds will need to be pulled. Yet heaven will be a place of intense activity. It will mean that heaven will be one massive job retraining center.

Certainly, nonproductive activities will automatically cease. Gossiping and grumbling will not be permitted. Pastime freelancers in cruel cuts are among the defiling elements which won't be permitted in heaven. Opponents of ecumenicity based on truth will not be allowed to perpetuate scandal sheets and peddle their snap judgments. In heaven "there will be no plotting to strengthen our party, no deep designing against our brethren."[7]

But what about those restful activities of earth, such as painting? Painting for some is one activity that comes close to rest. Some imagine heaven will allow a person to dabble in paint; after all, the landscape will be more than enough to inspire duplication. Rudyard Kipling said in *L'Envoi* heaven's population will be happy

> They shall sit in a golden chair;
> They shall splash at a ten-league canvas
> with brushes of comets' hair:
> They shall find real saints to draw from—
> Magdalene, Peter, and Paul;
> They shall work for an age at a sitting
> And never be tired at all.

Sir Winston Churchill (1874-1965), who didn't try painting until past age forty, said, "When I get to heaven [I intend] to spend a considerable portion of my first million years in painting."[8]

C. S. Lewis commented on this idea:

> When you painted on earth . . . it was because you caught glimpses of Heaven in the earthly landscape. The success of your painting was that it enabled others to see the glimpses too.

> But here you are having the thing itself. It is from here that the
> messages came. There is no good *telling* us about this country,
> for we see it already. In fact we see it better than you.[9]

The argument Lewis made was that perfection implies that
everything is unimprovable. The same argument could be
made against music. Yet in heaven there is music. Whatever
the talents that may be preserved in heaven, they will not result
in God being sidetracked. The various occupations and our
love for whatever activities will not take the place of extolling
the Prime Mover and of worshiping the Lord. Yet how will personal development be possible without some skills being involved? Further questions on growth and use of talents in
heaven are addressed in chapter 16.

During our non-Christian days on earth we were mastered
by the will-to-sin, through Christ we are inspired with the will-
to-serve God, not only in our predeath days, but also in our
postdeath eternity. Even the martyrs who were both promised
and given rest in heaven (Rev. 14:13) were also pictured actively
serving God (Rev. 7:15). Every heavenly human resident, the
entire church, shall be devoted to God in service (Rev. 22:3).

> To serve God without intermission in every thought and act
> is the highest glory, and the ultimate goal of human nature.[10]

What will it mean to serve God? It will mean, primarily, to
worship him. As by "serving" John meant worship, so Jesus'
word "beholding" (John 17:24) did not mean mindless staring,
but active articulate adoration.

Martin Luther (1483-1546) at mealtime mused on this question in the presence of his student-friends. According to *Table
Talks*, he said, "No change, no work, no eating, no drinking,
nothing to do. I suppose there will be plenty to see." His successor, Philip Melanchthon (1497-1560) interjected, "Lord,
show us the Father and it sufficeth us." "Why, of course," responded Luther, "that sight will give us quite enough to do."[11]

Rest and Service

"Describe heaven to me so I'll want to go." Okay, but what is our preference? Rest or activity? Stillness or bustle? Ease or exertion?

Paradoxical screens are thrown up in Scripture when heaven is dealt with to remind us that we can't achieve that clarity of conception we would like to have. In heaven "all rest and work are identical; desire and fulfillment are one."[12] "Work without weariness, without rest . . . work which is rest and joy."[13] These are some of the complex images which remind us that whatever is done funnels back to and lends support to the primary purpose of heaven.

We should resist the desire to throw out these seeming opposites, for we can have rest *in* activity as well as rest *after* activity. We live with these ironies on earth with no trouble. Take, for instance, the posture of work. What is it? A person leaning on a rake is standing, but he is actually loafing, not working. But that is untypical in biblical pictures of those who stood to work. For instance, in the Old Testament, the Levite priests exhorted their countrymen to stand to worship. "The Levites said . . . 'Stand up and praise the LORD your God, who is from everlasting to everlasting'" (Neh. 9:5 NIV). It is pleasure, but work as well.

When we are seated we are resting. Right? Wrong, in some cases. Why? Many people sit to work. There are several Scripture references to judges being seated as they heard cases. Israel's local magistrates sat to hear cases at the city's gates where also was the execution of the penalty. Courts or tribunals, similarly, in New Testament times were raised platforms, in both public (John 19:13) and private (Acts 25:23) locations, where judges sat to hear cases.

Jewish judges traditionally heard accusations, charges, and testimony seated. USA justices, similarly, are seated to hear arguments, but unlike today's judge, the Jewish judge arose or *stood* to pronounce verdicts and to state sentences. This juridical posture is found in the prayers of Psalms where God as supreme judge is asked to "arise" and pronounce his judgment in favor of the oppressed (Ps. 76:9; 82:8; Isa. 3:13).[14]

The throne theme of Revelation continues God's role as Judge of all. Also, from his seat he rules or issues edicts, decrees, and laws (Rev. 4:9, 10; 5:1, 7, 13; 6:16; 14:15; 19:4; 20:11; 21:5).

Christ began execution of his sentence from his horse, the only place in the Bible where the back of a horse or saddle was considered a mobile throne (Rev. 6:2, 4, 5, 8; 19:11). From a cloud perch the angel of judgment dispensed judgments (Rev. 14:16). Christ is presented standing at the start of the Book of Revelation (1:13) in the evaluation and administration of his churches on earth, yet, elsewhere, he is pictured as seated in heaven (Rev. 3:21). That he is seated distantly does not diminish his involvement in history. Henry Swete's comments are still worth considering:

> When He sat down at the right hand of power, it was not for a brief cessation from warfare, but for an age-long conflict with the powers of evil. "Sitting" is not always the posture of rest. Some of the hardest work of life is done by the monarch seated in his cabinet, and the statesman at his desk; and the seated Christ, like the four living creatures round about him, rests not day nor night from the unintermitting energies of heaven.[15]

Working from one's seat was characteristic, too, of the Antichrist figure of Revelation, who was given the name Babylon and likened to a woman (Rev. 14:8; 16:19). Called "great" (but not morally great), the woman-whore ordered her evil actions like a monarch seated (17:1, 3, 9, 15, 18). To unseat her was, in effect, to undo her, to render her powerless. Apparently, the beast was also seated on a throne (13:2; 16:10), which was an appointment from Satan, not directly from God.

Lower level involvement of Christians in the administration of life is alluded to in those passages where it is said the saints judge (1 Cor. 6:2; Rev. 20:4). Paul saw it as a future-life activity (1 Cor. 6:2), and possibly John of Patmos (Rev. 20:4). But if one holds that Revelation 20 is a description of the life of the martyrs in the Intermediate State, how, then are rulership duties presently being executed? (*See* Appendix.) This would mean the enlargement of God's guardian program to include redeemed humanity in heaven and not just the unfallen, unredeemed angelic hosts.

The Marriage Supper of the Lamb (Rev. 19:7, 9) would involve table conversation seated, although being seated is not stated. The significance of being seated for the Marriage Supper of the Lamb is at least, twofold: (1) It indicates that it is time to rest and relax. The warfare is over. No one or thing has been able to annul or break up the closeness of Christ to his church. (2) Sitting down suggests the confidence that all other details of her being under Christ's upper roof will work out. The Bride is fully at home in heaven, forgiven, and justified forever.

Our table placement and posture are irrelevant. But the timing element (again we must lapse into time-conditioned words) deserves some comment. Notice, the Marriage Supper of the Lamb appears in chapter 19. What follows is the famous section on the millennium (chapter 20). Here we have another inference the writer leaves to the reader. The timing of the feast would throw it into the Intermediate State of heaven, if one follows a chronological interpretation of Revelation 19-22. My suggested resolution of this snag is found in chapter 13 ahead. If you care to pursue it now, *see* pp. 241-242.

The thrust of the Marriage Supper of the Lamb is to emphasize the glory of redemption consummated. Even if one follows the pattern of Hebrew marriage rites, that engagement is legal marriage (meaning that the church on earth was legally Christ's wife), and even though the Marriage Supper of the

Lamb in Revelation 19 is a dinner after the ceremony, not after the consummation (which is suggested later, 21:2), it still celebrates the finality of the union. Because Christ's bride, the church, is composed of the widest spectrum of humanity, the wedding meal celebrates the cosmopolitan, communal, universal nature, and completion of the church. The church on earth was no less Christ's Bride, but finally in heaven the Bride comes into the experience of full communion with Christ.

I defer to consider later two texts which bear on this subject (Matt. 8:11 and Luke 22:30). These will be examined in chapter 19, Recognition in Heaven?

"Describe heaven to me so I'll want to go!"

Although some are eager to learn about heaven, others are not. Still others want nothing to do with the Christ of the past, who will be the Christ of our futures. A large number of people do not want to be engaged, let alone married to Christ. To be yoked with Christ, whose burden is easy, is least wanted by the self-sufficient.

God intervenes in lives to reclaim the headstrong rebellious. Consider the case of John Newton (1725-1807), the author of the still popular hymn "Amazing Grace." At an early stage in his life John Newton did not want anything to do with Jesus. But God had his own means of turning Newton's desires toward him, even though Newton nearly drowned at sea in the process. Christ pulled him away from the strong currents of sinning and thereby saved him from being a total waste. In one of his letters, an indication of his life's change of direction stands out. He wrote regarding his anticipations of heaven:

> I hope one day to be all ear, all heart, all tongue; when I shall see the Redeemer as he is, I shall be like him. This will be heaven indeed, to behold his glory without a veil, to rejoice in his love without cloud, and to sing his praises without a jarring or wandering note, forever.[16]

We shall all share a similar encounter. The joys Newton described will not only belong to those who have been rescued from debauchery. Those spared the memory of gross public sins also know great joy in their deliverance from their guiltiness before God.

"Describe heaven to me so I'll want to go." How badly do we want to go? This can be answered by asking, "How badly do we need Christ?" We will avoid admitting our degree of need because of deep self-pride.

A great space may separate the difference between our *true* need and our *felt* need. Our deepest need may not be felt. That was Newton's problem. At one point, he saw nothing he needed in Christ. He was self-sufficient. That same contentment keeps people from discovering the glories of heaven today.

Do we want to go to heaven on *Christ's* terms or on *our* terms? This is the subject of the next chapter.

11

Is Heaven Earned ?

*O*ne of the veteran slogans in television advertising has been the plug of Smith Barney, an American investment firm, that they make money the old-fashioned way: "They earn it." Though they have changed presenters, they have retained the slogan.

If that doesn't inspire us to let Smith Barney handle our investments, at the very least, it should cause us to think about what it means to earn money.

How is money earned? And what is the old-fashioned way of earning it? Do we earn to invest or do we invest to earn? Do we earn when we buy in or when we punch in? Should earning be measured by perspiration beads or by percentage curves?

Some of us may see ourselves as earners, but not as investors. On the other hand, we all invest, whether or not we know it. All of us have investments.

We may not contact brokers for investment counsel. We may not have the capital to invest—but we *are* investors. Even the financially broke have investments. Our investments need not take the form of money put down. Big investments include our marriages, our children, our neighborhoods, our careers, our churches.

Every time we put an envelope in an offering plate, every time we play catch with our children in the backyard, every time we ski or sew, we are investing.

Despite a claim to the contrary, Smith Barney does *not* earn money the old-fashioned way. The old-fashioned way was personal hard work. The old-fashioned way was physical exertion, not buying stock.

Jesus worked hard as a carpenter. He earned money by providing a valuable service. He modeled industry. He patterned his life after the image of a son in Proverbs. Proverbs is a book which repeatedly scolds lazy workers. It comes down hard on those who refuse to start to work and those who delay in finishing the job. Laziness was to be avoided as much as stealing. And Jesus rebuked the dolts who refused to help those in distress (Matt. 23:4).

Our Lord praised those who wisely invested (*see* the parable on investments, Matt. 25:15-30). He felt resistance from those whose emotional investments were self-serving. A conflict came when Jesus distinguished between things we can earn and other things we cannot. He said some investments were wise and others were foolish.

"Is heaven earned?" Of all questions on heaven, this one is the most important, for to be wrong can mean that we miss heaven. This was the problem Jesus anticipated with those whose emotional capital was their good works. They bought heavily into themselves and not into Jesus. Recall the time Jesus discussed the surprised workers in the future judgment:

"When the Judgment Day comes, many will say to me, 'Lord, Lord! In your name we spoke God's message, by your name we drove out many demons, and performed many miracles!' Then I will say to them, 'I never knew you, get away from me, you wicked people'" (Matt. 7:22, 23 GNB; compare with Luke 13:26, 27)

Jesus said one could not be saved by good works. God alone saves. But in teaching that he drew criticism, for he had hit a major nerve in pious Jewish leadership. In so many words, Jesus said the stock of self-righteousness was worthless. They risked losing all in the future. What he said had an effect similar to overthrowing the tables of the money changers in the temple. In point of fact, however, he had overturned the tables of the merit mongers and piously proud.

Today, as then, society is conditioned to believe that each person earns his own way. The average person thinks his goodness is sufficient to save him. But to put our spiritual investments in the wrong portfolio will lead to our loss. By God's errorless accounting we are morally bankrupt and need Jesus' treasury of merit. Better to be upset now than later when the market is closed.

As mentioned earlier, investments cover most aspects of life, including our activities. Each time we go to church, support its budget, serve in an office, show up to greet, drive the bus, play the piano, conduct a meeting, paint the fence, cut the grass, we are making small increment investments. After a time, we say proudly, while pointing to the facility where we have spent hours, "That is *my* church!"

If a church is like a bank vault, then its pews are like safety deposit boxes. If we are a principal stockholder, we may get huffed that someone else with a smaller investment has equal or more influence or has more say. Subconsciously, his involvement is an investment in the church's future. He may even imagine that he is forwarding an advance to secure his seat in heaven.

Jesus' difficulty with the religious leaders went back to his questioning of the qualifications of those who thought their moral record counted for something before God.

People today are little different. Although we may not be as pretentious as the Pharisees were, we are just as prone to calculate our chances in the hereafter on the basis of achievements. How many times have we run across persons who feel their associations in a local church or working under the auspices of the tag CHRISTIAN in community affairs have secretly felt their sacrificial contributions of time and talent count for something before an impartial God, even to the point that they "deserve" heaven? Such may also become infuriated to think that God welcomes prostitutes before model citizens and loyal church-goers.

Traditional Americans hold that each man must earn his keep, pay his own bills, and look to his family's future. It is amazing how this philosophy has been imported wholesale into our thoughts on heaven.

In a public opinion poll by the *USA Weekend* supplement (Dec. 19-21, 1986, mentioned in chapter 3) the question "What are your chances of going to heaven?" was asked. The responses were not tabulated as to the percentage of those who gave positive or negative answers. A few respondents were cited: Harry Nelson of La Salle, Illinois, said: "50-50. The older I get the more I think my chances will improve." (Do senior citizens get a special break?)

To the question "What are your chances of going to heaven?" Mike Gallaghar, pictured in the poll article, who looks like he is in his early thirties, said "Eighty-five percent. I don't think the entrance exam will be that tough."[1] (Curiously, he put better odds on his entrance than the older-looking Harry Nelson.) His answer was nine percentage points higher than the *Newsweek* poll (Dec. 1988) in which 78 percent of those sampled thought they had a good or excellent chance of getting there.[2]

Sylvia Gibbs, of Hammond, Indiana, volunteered, "You have to be more than a nice person." She went further and added that to go to heaven "You have to be a good person, someone who is humble and doesn't just do good things to prove they're good." These were the answers selected by Jean Becker who wrote the article.[3]

What they all have in common is (1) that they lack the firm conviction that they will be going to heaven; and (2) they seem to predicate entrance into heaven on the basis of performance, competence, likableness. That amounts to a view of entrance that is based on what man does or is, rather than on the basis of who God is and what Christ has done for us.

We carry the American work ethic to the very gates of paradise. Man instinctively feels that unless he contributes, he cannot enter heaven. In fact the opposite is true. Only those who realize they cannot enter by their contribution will be the most likely ones to enter! Entering heaven is not like bringing home a paycheck. Heaven cannot be earned. It is a free gift. It is free, because Christ earned it. Man is reluctant to accept a gift, even when it is a token of concern. The jobless middle-income father of four may want to turn down an outright donation, even though his family is suffering from lack of food and he can't meet his mortgage payments. Consistent breadwinners have too much pride to look for handouts. But to refuse God's gift and determine to build one's future on one's self-efforts is to become the foolish man who built his house on sand, instead of welcoming the suggestions of constructing it on a rock (Matt. 7:24-27).

Grants and gifts come with "no strings attached." A wage is what we earn. A gift is what we cannot earn. A gift is free. The most marvelous message of all time is that heaven is a gift to the undeserving and an outright grant to the poor. Revelation 22:17 couldn't be plainer:

> ". . . Come, whoever is thirsty; accept the water of life as a gift, whoever wants it" (GNB).

What comes on the last page of the Bible is what one finds throughout the Bible—an open invitation to partake of a salvation secured by Christ. We get to heaven on the basis of God's mercy and Jesus' worth, not because of any professed worthiness in ourselves. John 1:13 and Romans 9:16 underscore the same position: that we have no grounds for demanding acceptance on the basis of our moral performance.

Sample other verses on the same theme:

> The wages of sin is death, but the free gift of God is eternal life through Jesus Christ our Lord (Rom. 6:23 RSV).
> By grace you have been saved through faith; and this is not your own doing, it is the gift of God—not because of works, lest any man should boast (Eph. 2:8, 9 RSV).

The Scriptures are clear: we cannot negotiate, demand, or pay for salvation. To attempt to pay our way is to bar ourselves from heaven.

We may think the news is too good to be true. Beside that, we are reluctant to accept anything we haven't earned, including heaven. The gospel is God's handing man the greatest gift— eternal life. But our instinctive reaction is to say we don't need help. The down-and-outers need it, the prostitutes need it, the drug-users need it, but we are persons respected by our fellow workers and neighbors. We have shouldered responsibilities, we have obeyed the laws, we have contributed to church, we say our prayers, we pay our bills, we give our share to charitable causes. The average person, deep down, is too proud to accept a salvation already achieved and given without consideration of intentions, reputation, performance, and human goodness.

The most prevalent and popular assumption about heaven is that only the good go there, that heaven is earned by the ethical and upright. People are literally banking on their prospect to get into heaven on the basis of their compliance with God's moral law, or on the basis of their best intentions. One way or another, we feel we deserve acceptance by God.

But the apostles taught otherwise. The Good News was that Christ alone could keep the law and his law keeping was given to us as a gift. Any appeal to our efforts and successes runs against the grain of the Bible. Paul said that boasting is excluded (Rom. 3:27; Eph. 2:9).

Where we bank is as important as *what* we bank. All investments aren't wise if placed in companies about to fold. The Bible gives us a glimpse into the condition of human stocks. Its unanimous conclusion is that to invest our futures in our own performance—mediocre at best—or in those of others is a very unwise investment. We can end losing more than our shirts— we can lose our souls!

Next time you read the gospels notice the negative feedback Jesus got from the sterling citizens, early Judaism's upper-crust. The run-of-the-mill sinners flocked to hear him, the down-in-the-mouth rejects trusted his words of absolution. But the long-worded, long-bearded, long-faced Pharisees, the men who were ultranice, without vice, and who had made too many investments in their bank of good works, were not about to withdraw their trust in themselves at Jesus' suggestion.

Similarly, getting people to withdraw from one account to invest in another, even for those who drive a hard bargain, is met with resistance. When our egos are firmly wrapped up in our own spiritual commodities, we are not going to sell low and buy high in Jesus' portfolio.

It is only through the miracle of divine grace that we place our destinies fully in Jesus' hands. To do so is the result of supernatural influence. The Holy Spirit must enter our psyche and give us a different attitude toward both ourselves and Christ. God himself must intervene. For us to see debt where once we saw only credit, for us to consider prospects dim where once we were wildly optimistic, and for us to withdraw our trust from self and put it in Christ is the result of the intervention of the Holy Spirit. The preparation of the heart to believe is God's doing. Our willingness to claim God's solution in Christ is due to his gracious gift of repentance. We turn to him because he has turned to us.

Jesus' position on the method of human salvation stood in opposition to what the rabbinic notions were at the time.

> Future salvation has to be earned by human achievement [in rabbinic theology]. In spite of God's mercy it depends on man's achievement, and the main function of God is simply to recompense the work of man. This Judaistic principle of human achievement leads logically to the dogma of merit and recompense. We see this everywhere in Judaism, with emphasis on the hereafter.[4]

This differs little from the way modern society thinks. We are saturated with the expectation that effort deserves pay. Cash awards are given at bowling tournaments. Merit badges are awarded in scouting. Stripes are presented for tours of duty. And we automatically expect God to operate according to the same rules. The universal consensus, outside Scripture, is that we deserve heaven.

We believe heaven is for moral achievers. Rabbinism taught the same concept. It was precisely what Jesus fought. Rabbinism taught that the Torah was given "for Israel to earn a reward from God by fulfilling the Torah."[5] In official, first-century Judaism "reward and correlated with it that of the meritoriousness of the fulfillment of the law"[6] was the way of salvation. Reward was "the dominant element of the Jewish doctrine of redemption."[7]

The belief is widespread, sometimes the strongest in churches, that salvation is reserved for the pious and denied the impious. Thomas Aquinas (1225-1274) wrote: "A reward means something bestowed by reason of merit, hence it would seem that a man may merit from God."[8] There is no substantial difference between his view and that of Pharisaism.[9]

Hans Küng, still a Catholic but denied the title of Catholic theologian by Rome, seemed to disagree with Aquinas when he wrote, "No achievement of ours can merit God's love."[10] He elaborated: "Man's salvation does not depend on any kind of prescribed works of the law, or devotional practices and moral efforts. It depends exclusively on trusting faith in Jesus Christ."[11]

We need to try to resolve these differing approaches in our own minds. We can see the sharpness of differences between the two views by seeing them in the context of Jesus' ministry and see what bearing his recorded messages had on the issue of how errant man is restored to a holy God.

What Jesus said was in conflict with what Pharisees taught. He "freed Himself radically from the Jewish concept of merit."[12] Interestingly, however, he did not refuse to use the word *reward*. There is ample evidence that Jesus and early Christianity "spoke freely of reward."[13]

Two opposing concepts were clearly meant. The important difference was that Jesus did not use the Pharisaic definition of rewards. Both Jesus and the Pharisees used the word *reward* but they used it differently. Jesus meant something different from his Jewish opponents, though they used the same word. Jesus' usage was in sharp contrast with his contemporary Sanhedrinists. He gave a totally opposite meaning. He transcended the traditional Jewish connotations to give his own. He *transcended* it.[14] It would be better to say he strikingly transvalued it, that is, he switched its meaning. The pivotal passage where Jesus' understanding and use of "reward" is seen to differ with the Pharisaic usage is found in Matthew 20:10-16, where Jesus reworked the word *reward*.

Jesus told a story. Some hired hands began in the early morning and agreed to give a full day's work for a specific amount. Other workers were added as the day progressed. They negotiated their terms and went for the offer stated by the farm manager. But just before quitting time some late comers were taken on. When the workers got paid at the end of the day, the first hired learned that the last hired got the same amount of money. In our day he would have gone straight to the National Labor Relations Board or filed a complaint with the EEOC (Equal Employment Opportunity Commission).

The first man hired was livid and furious. He thundered protest to the manager. The manager replied:

> . . . "Friend, I am doing you no wrong; did you not agree with me for a denarius? Take what is yours and go your way, but I wish to give to this last man the same as to you. Is it not lawful for me to do what I wish with what is my own? Or is your eye envious because I am [good KJV] *generous*" [The margin adds literally, "good"]? (Matt. 20:13-15 NASB; italics added).

The parable was told to show how Jesus meant "reward." The occasion which prompted Jesus to tell the parable in the first place was to clarify the difference between the way he saw "reward" and how it differed from the Pharisees' definition. The traditional rabbinic approach was to define "reward" as payment for work well done. Jesus, however, saw "reward" *not as payment but as donation*. "Reward" did not infer the recipient was deserving or merited it, but "reward" was given to the undeserving.

Admittedly, we are not accustomed to think the way Jesus spoke; but it is our responsibility to begin to think his way, else we are not fully following him. To Christ *reward* was a gratuitous donation.

Once we understand what Jesus meant by reward, we see that there is no contradiction between statements elsewhere in Scripture that heaven is a gift to us. Heaven is not earned, even though the word *reward* is used in describing heaven.

With this background, therefore, meritoriousness is extracted from receiving a reward. This is vitally important. Without grasping the starting point of the word as Jesus used it and as his apostles used it, we shall be confused and think Scripture is contradictory.

Therefore in Revelation, where rewards are mentioned for the redeemed who have suffered much in the cause of Christ, it is an acknowledgment by God for selfless service without the inference of merit. Compensation for hardships does not mean the person is inherently good. To think that way is to lose sight of the generosity of God and to lose sight of the meaning of "grace" as unmerited favor. Reward in heaven, unlike what we practice on the earth, is not *quid pro quo* (this for that) payment, but a generous compensation by God showing his goodness above all (Matt. 5:12; Luke 6:23).[15]

The overtone of merit still clings to reward with a greater tenacity than static cling. Our system of rewards and punishments in society fight against Jesus' way of talking. We are more influenced by what is around us in the world than what is before us in Jesus' Word!

The rabbis made personal merit the basis of reward, but for Jesus personal merit had *nothing* to do with rewards. Think again of the hired worker. He got a full day's wage, didn't he? Did he deserve it? No, not really. He got top dollar for minimal labor, not because he merited it. He got paid a full day's wage because of the generosity of the farm manager.

In God's opinion (following Scripture) we have demerits, not merits. Man does not deserve, earn, or merit heaven. Jesus took the word *reward* and turned it inside out. He emptied it of the self-congratulating element, and packed it with the proper meaning, which brought glory to the goodness of the Master. The danger with Bible reading is that we bring a contemporary meaning to a word and impose that on what is in the text. And we don't hear the meaning Jesus originally gave.

Consider what the late Herbert Preisker, a Professor in Halle, Germany, said on this:

> The one point that is made is that reward is not according to achievement. . . . The parable radically discards all thought of merit. Its core is the message of the generous love of God for highly imperfect man: *oti ego agathos eimi* ["because I am good"] (Matt. 20:15, RSV).[16]

Jesus reinforced this teaching in Luke 12:32, where he said, ". . . it is your Father's good pleasure to give you the kingdom" (KJV). George E. Ladd put it this way: "All reward is after all a matter of grace."[17] ("Grace" means undeserved favor.)

Many follow what contemporary thought says about the meaning of "reward" (which is identical with first-century rabbinism). Equal-pay-for-equal-work is a worldwide business principle. We are always pulled along by this strong current of opinion which runs through the middle of our social life. Following Jesus, therefore, is always rough.

Martin Luther (1483-1546) battled the same trend in his day. He wrote a book to show Desiderius Erasmus (1466-1536) that he had misread the Bible regarding reward. Luther said, "Merit is not proved from rewards."[18] Luther cited another verse from Jesus to show this. Matthew 25:34 (RSV) says, ". . . inherit the kingdom prepared for you from the foundation of the world." In the Latin version of *Bondage of the Will*, Luther translated Matthew 25:34 as "Come, ye blessed of my Father, *Receive* the kingdom prepared for you from the foundations of the world." Luther followed this up by asking: "How do they merit what is already theirs, and was prepared for them before they were in existence?"[19]

Somehow many have missed this teaching in the familiar Good Samaritan story (Luke 10:30-37). Jesus praised the mercy of the man who was low in the eyes of Jewish society. The Samaritan acted selflessly and spontaneously, without seeking or counting on reward from either man or from God.[20]

The first Protestant book of theology was written by John Calvin (1509-1564). It went through many editions. Some cannot buy the two-volume set, nor even check it out of a library. But what he wrote on reward is enormously clear, relevant, and still valuable. Therefore, let's cite him on this question:

> Man cannot without sacrilege claim for himself even a crumb of righteousness, for just as much is plucked and taken away from the glory of God's righteousness.

> [The concept of merit] can do nothing but obscure God's favor and imbue men with perverse haughtiness.

> The use of the term "reward" is no reason for us to suppose that our works are the cause of our salvation. First . . . the kingdom of heaven is not servants' wages, but sons' inheritance (Eph. 1:18].[21]

"Is heaven earned?" No, and we have given reasons why it is not earned. Build on it. It is nothing other than the solid rock, Jesus Christ. It will save us from sinking in the sands of personal achievements.

Relate this with the earlier subject of rebirth and we have further confirmation that the gospel is a revolutionary word. ". . . we do not do good to get into Heaven; we do good because Heaven has got already to us. . . ."[22]

> Let not conscience make you linger,
> Nor of fitness fondly dream;
> All the fitness he requires
> Is to feel your need of Him:
> This He gives you; this He gives you
> 'Tis the Spirit's rising beam.[23]

12

Can We Be Sure of Going to Heaven ?

What causes a top-level management person to drop out of his/her company, move to a quiet country spot, and take up a less lucrative career? Often it is not due to a career nosedive or to the flattening out of profits. He or she may be sick of contaminated air, frustrated with congested highways, and wornout from the pell-mell pace of city life. What once turned him/her on now turns him/her off. Other executives spin out from the fast track because they feel unfulfilled. In the corporate race they have lost their personal identity and the excitement of meeting new challenges. At the height of their careers, when great gains have bottomed out, they leave in search of themselves and of peace.

Searching for one's self is a contemporary repetition of the Ecclesiastes experience. Alas not all prescriptions of self-help schemes work. Many of the eight thousand ways to self-knowledge peddled in the seventies suffered the fate of early-rise, early-die.[1]

Interest in self-awareness, however, still seems to be a steady concern in contemporary society. People want not only to avoid preventable illnesses by watching their weights and diets, but they also want to feel better about themselves and about their futures. Across the age spectrum inner certainty remains a dominant drive.

Why has the quest for confidence building persisted? Why does it never end? Why do people fall for quick fixes in fad remedies? Is it because they have given up on old authorities, and abandoned outlets traditionally Christian? Is it not because outer certainties are fewer and more fragile? Is it due to the fact that material props destruct when leaned on?

Dreams of peace turn into nightmares of war when conflicts escalate. New environmental hazards madden and frustrate public health officials. Home buyers are leery about their areas being tainted by toxic wastes. Old confidence in physical appearances has been eroded. Joblessness has created a new poor. Family migrations are more common. Product popularity and company loyalties to its employees can no longer be counted on.

For yet others economic stability has not driven them to forsake materialism for simpler living. Not having reached the top, they still hold out for it as being the ultimate satisfaction. Consequently, heaven is the least concern of blue-collar workers.

Many fear that time is running out. "How long will single digit inflation stay?" "How soon will the national deficit reverse?" "When will big bonuses return?" An assembly-line employee may be overheard saying, "Forget being sure about going to heaven when I die. We can't be sure about going to work next month." It is this life, not the next, that is their chief worry.

Yet nothing turns our attention to a happier future than the miserableness of the present. Deep in our psyche there is a longing to enter heaven when we die. The insecurities of our temporal lives do not destroy or render irrelevant and unprofitable the question: "Can we be sure of going to heaven?"

The question is not farfetched. It is fundamental to human existence. When someone says, "I know I am going to heaven when I die and will be with Christ," inevitably someone raises the question, "Can we be sure?"

Ultimately, there are only two answers: yes or no. But there are interesting varieties in the answers. There is not just one kind of *no* or a single *yes*. Simple answers—*yes* or *no*—will not do. We must look into the body of these answers, for people give a yes or no for different reasons.

Several varieties need to be looked into:

The *No* of the Non-Christian Skeptic
The *Yes* of the Proud Moralist
The *No* of the Despondent Believer
The *Yes* of the Exultant Apostle

The *No* of the Non-Christian Skeptic

Talk of heaven, says an unbeliever of everything in Christianity, is meaningless. Moreover, in his utter rejection, he may say humanity has no future on earth. Beside that, in his estimation man has no future beyond the grave. A heavenly or hellish hereafter is so much bunk in his eyes. But not all unbelievers go that far. Some may grant a heaven ahead, if not a hell below, but they deny that anyone can possibly know or deserve not to be going there.

They say belief that one can know where one will land after death is an overrated and overwrought conviction. Such assurance, they claim, is a sign of colossal ignorance. They argue that certainty increases in direct proportion to ignorance. The less well-informed a person is, the more things he is sure of.

Add to that the known psychological finding that one's basic anxiety makes one dogmatic and Christian confidence is explained away. The oversure, say experts, are anxiety-ridden.

If these arguments fail, the final rapier lunge is this: the claim is egotistical. The spiritually cocksure are arrogant creatures. To be certain about going to heaven gives one a big head. Skeptics of sure knowledge ask, "Where is Christian humility? What happened to the virtue of modesty?"

Whenever Christian salvation-assurance gets voiced, these objections surface. How would you reply? The objections are serious and should be taken seriously.

Several statements must be made:

1. *First of all, we readily admit that some Christians have carried assurance too far.* They are too sure about everything, even into fringe matters and in gray areas. When everything is black and white, when there are no grays, then something is wrong. Part of Christian growth is the admission we don't know. Only as we discover our ignorance about many subjects, including many Christian subjects, are we maturing. How reluctant or ready are we to admit that we simply do not know enough to make a judgment?

2. *Because one shows remarkable conviction about one's spiritual life direction and destiny, does not, by itself, mean it is ill-conceived or baseless.* There are many "givens" we have to unlearn in our studies, but our trust in Christ, through more thorough examination, rethinking, and reworking of the biblical material, comes back to the same bedrock reality of the all-sufficiency and durability of Christ's righteousness given to us. The dual witnesses of the Holy Spirit through the Scriptures converge and reconfirm to us that Christ's saving benefits given to us are no less true or reliable than the certainty of our own existence. As William Adams Brown (1865-1943) once wrote, "To say that I am certain of a thing does not mean I know all about it, or even that I know what I know with exactness."[2]

3. Why does the skeptic want to rob the Christian of what the apostles desired for them? Strange but true, a person who vehemently denied that one can be sure of heaven is probably secretly envious, and subconsciously angry because of it. And the person who is so stoutly sure that the Christian is wrong in his assurance is expressing his own brand of assurance. If the Christian is guilty of arrogance, then by the same token the skeptic is guilty of arrogance too. How? On the premise that it requires the same degree of certitude to deny a statement as to make it.

The criticism cuts both ways. An *un*dogmatic Christianity is sought by the supersure, so that they can shape their own Christianity, rather than let the original Christianity shape them.

4. The nature of Christian salvation-assurance is not a personal boast, but an acclamation that Jesus' perfect righteousness is a free bestowal to the unworthy wicked. No one can toot his own horn in Christ's presence. The individual who says he is heaven-bound is not—if properly conformed to Christ's own word—making any self-claims. As a refresher, turn back to chapter 11 on rewards or think again of who gets all the praise in heaven.

Self-glory is taboo as much on earth as in heaven. To say one knows the Lord and knows he is going to heaven is not an assurance based on pious performance and human achievement. God has done it all, provided it all, supplied it all, accomplished it all. Our righteousnesses are as filthy rags, literally "menstruous cloth" (the Hebrew text of Isa. 64:6).

Christ's flawless righteousness is given to us. We are saved by God's unmerited love and favor. Augustine (354-430) put it well: "To be assured of our salvation is no arrogant presumption; it is God's praise. It is not pride; it is devotion. It is no presumption; it is God's promise."[3] Christian salvation-assurance is not going beyond the Scriptures or attempting an unwarranted leap of faith. It is held out as the normal Christian mind-set, encouraged and fed by the finality of Christ's victory over sin and death. Objections to salvation-assurance amount to broken whistles, blown in desperation by those offended by persons advancing in faith across the playing field of life. The Christian does not claim he is going to heaven because he has earned it, but because Christ has earned it and given it to him apart from any alleged worthiness.

The *Yes* of the Proud Moralist

Heaven has been likened to the harbor of the happy righteous. Some say they will reach it by self-propulsion. If hard rowing would do it, some little boats would beat large liners.

Occasionally we meet someone who has the audacity to say that on his own, in his right, he will reach heaven. Exuding of confidence in this instance varies significantly from the person who credits his salvation to Christ. This person points to his reputation and his record. He says he has done enough, that he is good enough. We may have felt that way one time or another—although we lacked the nerve to say it or admit to it. Self-righteousness fosters self-confidence.

"Can we know we are going to heaven?" This is so high-powered a matter to some that they would prefer to back off from Christianity entirely. But the question need not be intimidating or embarrassing. Rather it gives us an opportunity to explore a dominant dimension one finds on the pages of the New Testament.

We are wise not to be gullible in accepting all claims of knowing God as genuine. Jesus taught us to be skeptical of those whose confidence before God was self-generated. Some may find that surprising, but it is true. He told the parable of the publican and the Pharisee (Luke 18) on false claims. The Pharisee could pray loudly and long, making his devotional exercise a platform for self-praise. He patted himself on the back all the time he seemed to be worshiping God. He prayed to himself, rather than to God. If he had entered into God's presence, the piercing holiness of God would have shattered his prepared statement of personal greatness into a thousand pieces.

Our schedules get so crammed that we can only scan or skip through weekly news magazines. The great books go unread. For your convenience the following have been culled from John Calvin's *Institutes of the Christian Religion*—a classic—which is still Class One in quality thought and Grade A in contemporary clarity. What he wrote on fraudulent claims to self-righteousness is still powerful stuff:

> One can see how there are none who more confidently, and boisterously chatter over the righteousness of works than they who are monstruously plagued with manifest diseases, or creak with defects beneath the skin. That happens because they do not think about God's justice, which they would never hold in such derision, if they were affected even by the slightest feeling of it.[4]
>
> All ungodly men, and especially all hypocrites, are puffed up with this stupid assurance because, however much they recognize that their hearts teem with impurities, still they bring forth any well-seeming works, they think these worthy not to be despised by God. Hence arises the pernicious error that, convicted of a wicked and evil mind, they still cannot be compelled to confess themselves empty of righteousness, even when they acknowledge themselves unrighteous because they cannot deny it, they still claim for themselves some righteousness.[5]

Lack of contact with God in his holiness through his Word explains why sinfulness is concealed from people. It is only a low view of God that breeds a high view of self. But it is not always works they take pride in. Often it is the sincerity or apparent depth of their faith that fosters their feeling of goodness.

But we are never saved *by* faith, we are saved *through* faith.[6]

The difference between the two is that in the former instance faith is something one generates and uses, giving one the feeling of self-accomplishment. In the later sense, we recognize that what saves is not our receptivity to salvation, but the Giver of salvation. God saves, and we receive it as a gift through faith. The proud moralist, however, insists he has had a part, that he is saved by his faith exertion. The informed Christian, on the other hand, says he has been granted faith as a gift, as well as being the recipient and the object of salvation. Grace is the source of faith, and faith is the means of salvation. That is a crucial distinction, or else one can be justifiably proud of saving himself.

The *No* of the Despondent Believer

Salvation-assurance is the Christian's spiritual birthright. First John 5:12, 13 (GNB) puts it this way: "He who has the Son has this life. I am writing this to you that you may know that you have eternal life—you that believe in the Son of God."

In receiving Christ we receive salvation. And Christ does not enter our lives without bringing in confidence that we know him. Not only is there the realization that God's Word is trustworthy, but on taking possession of us we are supplied confidence before God and about God that we lacked.

The enemy of faith, Satan, is also the opponent of salvation-assurance. He specializes in criticizing Christians for their poor performance and lack of consistency. He also assaults them for their certitude. Since he cannot destroy the Christian's Savior (he cannot destroy Christ), he attacks the Christian's confidence about his relationship with Christ.

A Christian falls in with the skeptic when he says he cannot know he is going to heaven. Some believers get so low that they doubt the greatest reality in their lives! John wrote his first letter to hesitant, half-sure believers—not just in his time, but in ours, too, for we get down on ourselves as easily as the first Christians.

Heaven is ours in the future, because it is ours in the present. And heaven is ours in the present because Jesus laid to rest the problem of our legal guilt before God in the past and secured the forgiveness of our sins on a permanently just basis. The future we anticipate follows from the past and from the present.

We feel pardon from Christ, because the pardon is rooted in history and part of reality. God was not going to shut off any feedback in feeling for those who are declared righteous (justified) by himself. Some true believers, rather than enter into the glorious liberty of being sons of God, sell their salvation short by disclaiming what God has designed for them. Thus their fear and feebleness feed on each other, and they are too weak to stand tall and witness strongly to the grace of God.

Farming provides food for our tables. It also continues to be a source of illustrations in the Christian life. I once met a greenhouse farmer who had a small harvest under glass. One year his specialty, jumbo tomatoes, never developed into the plump giants they ordinarily became. The reason for their stunted growth was a root-disease germ that got into the enclosed space of the greenhouse. By infecting the roots, the large tomatoes failed to become large and juicy. The stems seemed strong, but the roots were infected.

The same is true in our Christian development. Our yield in joy, peace, godliness, and confidence is significantly reduced because our thinking is infected with erroneous Christ-dethroning, Christ-minimizing thoughts. Our ideas come from sources that can spoil the fruit by damaging the roots. We have stunted growth in Christians and shrunken harvests because of the insidious damaging ideas that attack the roots of our confidence.

Two specific thoughts do the Christian life harm:

We wrongly think salvation is only future. John's emphasis was on the presentness of salvation. He wrote, "That you may know that you *have* eternal life" (1 John 5:13, italics added). Note, that he did not write, "That you may know that you *shall have* eternal life." The tense of the verb in this verse is vital to his argument. He constantly referred to eternal life as a present reality. Eternal life is the life of God in time in us (compare with chapter 4). Heaven comes to us before we go to heaven. So the fact that heaven has begun means the claim to enter heaven later is not the first giant claim. The prior claim is just as big, even more basic. That claim is as startling, as special, and as strong as the other. Because salvation is a present reality we know it will be a future reality, for ". . . He who began a good work in you will perfect it until the day of Christ Jesus" (Phil. 1:6 NASB).

The second injurious thought is that no one can claim to be going to heaven because he is imperfect. We met this earlier in chapter 7, dealing with purgatory. The writer John was very conscious that Christians were imperfect (*see* 1 John 1:6-10). In his first chapter he held that human imperfections are a given, and he said it was a mark of being a true believer to acknowledge it. (By the same token, it is the non-Christian who resents mentioning of human sinfulness and need.)

John wrote to imperfect people, yet he wanted them to be sure of their salvation. Imperfection is no argument to exclude salvation-assurance. Salvation is not our doing. The reality of our forgiven state depends on Christ. Heaven begun in time is not calculated on whether we do enough good, but whether we have been made alive through Jesus Christ. "He who has the Son has life . . ." (1 John 5:12). Because it is God's life, it is not temporary. He will not let our faith in him die out. Eternal life is God's life and that is not a time-limited life. We don't itch after seven years to exchange it!

No deeds of mine are needed
To make Christ's merits more:
No frames of mind or feelings
Can add to His great store;
'Tis simply to receive Him,
The holy One and just;
'Tis only to believe Him—
It is not "try"—but "trust."

A safe rule of thumb in the spiritual life is this: whenever we introduce a human ingredient as securing or insuring our salvation, to that degree uncertainty is guaranteed. Another rule of thumb follows: every claim to salvation-assurance should include a strong disclaimer. We are in the picture in terms of benefits, but out of the picture when it comes to the matter of cause. Nevertheless some people regard full assurance of salvation in us as outlandish. The same people are likely to think not giving full honor to God is no outrageous offense.

The *Yes* of the Exultant Apostle

The ancient Greeks pictured heaven overarching the earth. But the apostle John, in Christ's coming again, presented heaven as overlapping history, intersecting time, and intervening in lives.

Perhaps John's most representative summary of the Christian life is the simple, but dynamic statement: "He who has the Son has life . . ." (5:12). Christ embodied all that was enduring and enriching. Separating the Christian life from Christ would mean the soul, source, and secret to spiritual vitality would disappear. The Son has us as much as we have him. There is a double possession, but also a predisposing initiated by God's prevenient grace. ". . . he first loved us" (1 John 4:19). Here is another crisp statement for which John is famous. The apostle-writer had his joy increased (1:4) as his readers entered into the realization of God's saving Son.

The writer John was exultant, triumphant in spirit, virtually shouting in print, when he wrote: "See how much the Father has loved us! His love is so great that we are called God's children—and so, in fact, we are . . ." (1 John 3:1 GNB). At various points, he warned, rebuked, cajoled, reviewed, calmed, and taught. But he also rejoiced, reveled, and soared with the blessed assurance that Jesus was his.

It was the same joy that made Bishop Ambrose of Milan (339-397) say:

> I will not glory because I am righteous, but because I am redeemed. I will not glory because I am void of sin, but because I am forgiven. I will not glory because I am profitable or because any one is profitable to me, but because Christ is my advocate with the Father and His blood was shed for me.[7]

Christ's eternal conquest of sin, making redemption secure through the ages, and the authentic application of his victory never gave a green flag for Christians to race ahead, following reckless lifestyles. Salvation-in-place meant salvation-in-progress. License to live independent of Christ's law, allowing the Christian to be a law unto himself, cannot be reconciled with the apostolic criteria of what makes a person Christian. When Christ masters us, we cannot live to satisfy our self-centered instinct. ". . . If you love the world, you do not love the Father" (1 John 2:15 GNB). Pushed to specifics, that would mean the worship of God has priority over private recreations. Again, ". . . Whoever knows God listens to us; whoever does not belong to God does not listen to us . . ." (4:6). One of the results of our linkage or union with Christ is that we have a new interest in learning God's Word and obeying it. And we evidence a teachable spirit (James 3:17).

The way we approach other Christians has a bearing on our claims of knowing God. We cannot claim to love Christ if we hate our Christian brother (1 John 2:9). Some would minimize their tactlessness, meddlesomeness, caustic comments, and verbal slashing, but 1 John 2:9 will not allow it. We cannot duck the incisive, laser-penetrating injunction to seek the welfare, improvement, and commitment of other Christians. To shrug off our duty to the corporate body of Christ in the name of individual salvation is to deny the love of Christ. Indeed, "We ought to give our lives for our brothers" (3:16 GNB).

Faith professions which produce contradictory behavior are false at heart. "Everybody talkin' about heaven, ain't going there." Spurious and superficial claims are shown by their failure to express saving faith in spiritual discipline and compliance to God's Word. First John makes conduct a criterion in judging whether confidence about salvation is true.

Christ makes us look differently on others. Special stress in the passage of 1 John 5, which discusses salvation-assurance, is the progress we promote in other Christians. We should be engaged in using every means to urge others to be more Christ-minded. Immediately following the text regarding salvation-assurance (5:13), the importance of praying for others is mentioned (5:14-16), especially those struggling with sins. First John 5:14-16 illustrates the eternal life of 1 John 5:13.

Legalistic browbeating is not the primary way of seeking others to live more for Christ but personal prayer is. "Prayer is the exercise and expression of eternal life."[8] Eternal life is not a possession that leads to self-satisfaction, producing an uncaring attitude about the state of others. Our words are not worthless when directed to God. It is sometimes more profitable to speak to God about men, than to limit our talk to men about God. Eternal life in us means that though we knock on closed doors on the earth, God has freely opened the entrance way to himself through Christ. And it may be that our only spiritual access to others is through Christ.

"Can we be sure of going to heaven?" Yes. We can be sure that our destiny is settled. Because we are given the confidence about our state, we are freed to work on behalf of others in sharing the gospel. The urge to let others in on the glorious Good News is a spontaneous overflow that wants others to be included in the good we have received.

We must get to asking these questions about the faith we don't show or of the profession of faith we make. Entering into self-examination should be a phase through which we make individual adjustments in our lives so that our profession does not ring hollow.

Midcourse Corrections
INFERENTIAL

13

Sex
in Heaven
?

Sex inevitably surfaces whenever life in heaven is introduced. Since sex occupies much of our thought, if not of our time, we are naturally curious as to its continuation in heaven.

Straightway, many Christians feel that even posing the question is out of place, out of character, and in poor taste. In their minds sex connotes sensualism, and sensualism is what Christians want to flee. As they see it, to devote a chapter to it in a book on heaven is outrageous. Other Christians are more ambivalent and less critical. Some readers, whose minds are not made up, may have turned to this chapter out of inquisitiveness. The question, despite objections and hesitations, is worth asking.

First we should ask why sex is important—why it is all-absorbing to some? Psychologists see in a preoccupation with sex a desire to avoid thinking about death. ". . . The clamor of sex all about us drowns out the ever-waiting presence of

death. . . . Repression of death equals obsession with sex."[1]
Those most interested in heaven may also be those most fearful
of dying. And those most interested in sex care least about
heaven. It is when people feel that sexual fulfillment is all-
sufficient that the matter of their eternal destinies is ignored.
An eternity of separation from God, however, should make any
sexual privations or dysfunctions trivial. Among the sexually
obsessed we should include those who crave its perpetuation in
the life of heaven ahead.

The question "Will there be sex in heaven?" however, is not
itself an obsession. We are not less Christian for asking it. In
fact we cannot read the Bible without facing it, for Jesus was
asked about it. We shall attempt to look at the question from
several sides, compile facts, pursue pieces of evidence, then let
each draw his own conclusion.

The question "Will there be sex in heaven?" cannot be answered until we first consider which "sex" is meant. *Sex* has
more than one meaning. Meanings range from male/female
organs, to sex as an act, to sex as gender, to sex as an attitude
(sexuality). The first question should be "Which *sex* is in
heaven?"

Jesus was confronted with the question of sex as activity
and institution. Some have argued that the Jewish apocalyptic
notion of marital life in an earthly millennial life was made a
polemical joke by the Sadducees' question about polyandry
(many husbands, one wife).[2] That would hardly embarrass
Jesus for his eschatology differed from Jewish apocalypticism.[3]
Several questions were involved in the one question, true, but
the intent was to ridicule Jesus more than apocalypticism.
They baited Jesus with the assumption that marriages on
earth are perpetuated in heaven.

Jesus answered the Sadducees: "When they rise from the
dead, they neither marry, nor are given in marriage, but are like

the angels in heaven" (Mark 12:25 NASB; compare with Matt. 22:30).

Does that mean gender will be no more, if marriage is no more? Or because Paul said that glorified Christians will conform to the image of Christ (Rom. 8:29), that every redeemed inhabitant in heaven will be male? Augustine (354-430) commented on this in his massive *The City of God*, where he noted that vice associated with gender will be removed but that nature will be preserved (Book 22; par. 17).

Anthony A. Hoekema explained:

> Jesus' teaching here does not necessarily imply that there will be no sex differences in the life to come. What we do learn, however, is that the institution of marriage will no longer be in existence, since there will be no need to bring new children into the world.[4]

The parallel Lukan passage has an added feature, not found in the other Gospels, that the dead are "like the angels" (*isangeloi*, Luke 20:36). This cannot mean that those in heaven are bodiless or pure spirit, for the point of comparison was not whether they had bodies or were bodiless, but whether they would be dead or alive in heaven. The preceding phase has "*neither can they die any more, for* they are like the angels." The sense is that the resurrected are "no longer subject to the natural conditions of earthly life, including marriage."[5]

The resurrected share in the final heavenly state. The Sadducees erroneously assumed that Jesus believed sexual union between husband and wife would continue in the resurrected state.

A few have wrongly concluded that because there is no copulation in heaven that sex is less than divine, ungodly, or closer to evil than to goodness. Some have gone so far as to identify original sin with sex. The passage, however, makes no such assertions nor intimations.

Equating sex with sin is where the initial error is made. Historically some Christians have drawn a fallacious inference between the sexual act and sinning. The founder of the Shaker sect, Ann Lee (1736-1784), for instance, regarded sex and marriage the root of all evil. To her sexual lust was "the cause of human depravity."[6] She went so far as to claim that no one who engaged in intercourse could reach God. Ann was married and practiced sexual abstinence. (Ann was obsessed with sex in a negative way.) Her husband, Abraham Stanley, however, was not entirely pleased with her commitment to abstinence and he took to drinking intoxicants at night. She claimed her sexual drives had died away in God's love. But the more she talked of "the exuberant bliss of Divine intercourse" the more he drank.[7] Roman Catholicism's understanding of evil comes close to this view, at least in practical application, reflected partly in the exaltation of virginity over marriage and in the statement by Pope John Paul II who said a married man, in lusting after his wife, committed a form of adultery in his heart.[8]

The Sadducees had tried to make resurrection look ridiculous by presenting Jesus with an absurd hypothetical case. Interestingly, on the very point of bodily resurrection, he said one of the most physical of physical actions would not be continued and wouldn't be needed in heaven. Jesus was insisting that in the eternal state the central concern was contact with God, not contact with former mates.

The nature of the resurrection body is a matter on which we have little information. And the biblical hints and clues are hardly enough to construct an exhaustive set of conclusions. The New Testament is silent on the functions of the resurrection body, yet what it does say is important. Of primary importance is the fact that the New Testament distinguishes between resurrection and immorality. Our chief source on Christian resurrection is 1 Corinthians 15. But how the resurrection body works is left "up in the air."

Two passages on the reality of Jesus' resurrected state are Luke 24:30, 31, 42, 43; John 21:12, 13. Only real hands could break real bread, and only real hands could prepare a real breakfast of fish. From 1 Corinthians 6:13 we learn that digestive functions in the life to come will no longer be necessary.

First Corinthians 6:13 needs closer consideration. The issue at the church at Corinth, which Paul wished to alleviate, if not finally answer, was the role of our bodies in the context of Christian freedom. Paul digressed from the subject of freedom, momentarily, to illustrate his point that full freedom is not strengthened by the permanency of the body in resurrection. In an incidental way, therefore, the nature of the resurrection body is introduced.

It appears Paul is borrowing a Corinthian slogan in 6:13a, apparently agreeing with it, yet going on from food and sex on earth to comment on the nature of the resurrection body in heaven.[9] He granted that food and the organ of digestion, the stomach, were meant only for our journey on earth. He disagreed with any use of the Corinthian slogan to include indiscriminate, unrestrained, and full use of ordinary functions including one's appetite for sexual gratification. Yet Paul agreed that the body is relevant for the resurrected state.[10]

The application of 1 Corinthians 6:13 for the role in Infinite Heaven against the Lukan passage, where it says Jesus ate broiled fish (24:42, 43; also indicated in John 21:13 and Acts 1:4, where the meaning of the verb is of disputed meaning, yet 10:41 adds support), is not easily resolved. Whereas Paul seemed to dismiss eating (while retaining the materiality of resurrection), Luke's narrative indicated Jesus engaged in eating following the resurrection. Some commentators chose to note Luke's penchant for literalism and realism, and of materializing the supernatural.[11] Others are content to note the value of the text to support the reality of Christ's resurrection body.[12] Robert H. Gundry ventured that there was a likelihood that Luke's and John's account of Christ's resurrection ". . . show that materiality and pneumatic, glorified corporeality need not have been incompatible . . ." and that Jesus' resurrected body was ". . . capable of partaking of food, perhaps even hungering for it (Luke 24:31, 39-43; John 20:11-29)."[13]

It is problematical, despite the instances of concrete consumption by Jesus, that our resurrected bodies will engage in any eating in heaven. The most, it seems, we should make of Jesus' resurrection eating, aside from His new corporeality, is that His new body was adaptive but not dependent on ingestion of food stuffs. Neither John nor Luke drew any inferences from these allusions to Jesus' eating after His resurrection. Paul's affirmed resurrection corporeality, yet he denied gullet gratification. First Corinthians 6:13 is best taken as normative of our anticipated resurrected form.

In the neither-marrying-nor-given-in-marriage passage (Mark 12:25), Jesus' point was not that the body is evil, but that the form of corporeality will change. "The resurrection does not mean a transformation into another nature, but rather the establishment of human nature in an imperishable state."[14] Our resurrected forms will be undying. The population of the eternal state will be stable and procreation will cease. Individual marriages will be passé. Elsewhere the New Testament teaches that marriage as a union terminates in death (Rom. 7:1-3; 1 Cor. 7:39).

But there are two other senses of "sex" which have yet to be considered: sex as gender and sex as sexuality. Sex as a gender is either male or female. Sex as sexuality would be the characteristics of the separate genders. Concern for understanding one's sexuality means a better grasp of gender traits. Myths are many on what comprises male/female sexuality. What distinguishes a male from a female and a female from a male in terms of attitudes, thinking, perspective, and objectives?

Before we turn to the sexuality issue, a few facts must be

shared on gender. In the first eight weeks of embryonic development in humans, we all have androgynous features, and therefore, distinguishing male from female would have been
difficult. However, we all had our gender predetermined at
fertilization because the gender-determining chromosome X or
Y in our father's sperm fused with our mother's oocyte (egg).
The sex of a child, however, is fixed at conception. Infants
emerge either male or female.

Humans are not like earthworms, although some have felt
that low. All earthworms are hermaphrodites, that is, they carry
both male and female reproductive systems in themselves. But
at birth our gender is either male or female. There is no such
thing as unisex in the Bible.

Jesus referred to several reasons for the absence of sexual
activity in males (Matt. 19:12). He may have alluded to the not
uncommon condition of cryptorchidism (undescended testis).
In addition, he mentioned forced castration and voluntary castration.

Eunuchs were included in Bible stories, but no unisex or
sexless persons. Generally a eunuch was a castrated male. Castration was either a punishment or a safety precaution by wary
rulers who wanted to insure there were no sexual scandals in
his absence from the palace. (One eunuch saved the life of
Jeremiah, and another was the Ethiopian treasurer whom
Philip led to Christ.) Jesus added another option to eunuchs,
that is, those who are voluntary eunuchs for the kingdom of
God (Matt. 19:12).

Gender is not an arbitrary description of humans. It is not a
distinction we have created, but it is part of reality. Gender is
genetically built into the nucleus of every single cell in our body.
Strictly speaking, gender is endemic to our cellular structure.

This is not to say, however, that gender identity is not
learned, partly acquired, reinforced or challenged. Therefore,
our sexuality is not a characteristic confined to isolated parts of

the body, but it involves the entire person—shape, psychological temperament, hormonal characteristics, such as amount of facial hair and voice range capabilities. Sexuality affects more than our reproductive organs, it affects the entire person. In addition our outside-person-factors, such as training, environment, and nurture, interact with our biological base, so that there is an integration of sexual identity that influences the total picture. Gender and sexuality, therefore, are more fundamental than the sexual act.

In view of the fact that some Christians downplay gender, we should emphasize that without gender we do not exist. There is no such being as a neuter person. Yes, a surgical procedure may radically alter one's gonadal sexual state. Surgical procedures, hormonal supplements, and shots may alter some sexual characteristics. Humans can be neutered, but there is no transformation into a new or third sex. There are only two sexes.

A quick review of gender would provide a helpful background to the discussion. Gender began in *Genesis*. The beginning of sex was at the original creation. Today gender of an unborn child is determined at the moment of fertilization. One's gender is determined by the father's sperm, not by the mother's egg. Less certain is to what degree sexuality is inborn.

Gender identification must be distinguished from gender identity. Influences may bend a person away from his or her individual sexual classification. But we cannot be authentically one gender or the other without the basic building blocks of biological structures and chemicals.

Gender traits increase through growth. Although chromosomal, gonadal, and hormonal capabilities are established at conception (our capacity for sexual development being genetically implanted), it is brought to completion in the teenage years. In philosophical terms, we say gender is ontological. That is, it has to do with our beings.

Gender is part of who we are. Surgically desexed individuals are alive enough to appear on various TV talk-show programs. But one wonders to what extent they can claim to be *fully* human unless they have a sexual identity. (God had no difficulty in creating the sexes, but we have trouble sometimes in distinguishing them.)

We need to relate gender facts to theological and psychological studies. A theology of gender is a neglected theme. We should ask, "Did God create sexual differences from what he was in himself? Were these sexual dissimilarities replicas of what he was in himself or were they specially created categories? When Scripture says man is made in God's image, does his image include one gender, no gender, or both genders?"

And what about the psychological significance? Why do men enjoy conquering a five-hundred-mile-road trip and get angry when their wives want to stop to shop? Why do women like to read a Harlequin romance novel and men prefer to read *Field and Stream* or a Louis L' Amour Western? Why do men consult a dictionary to find out what love is and women consult their feelings? These kinds of questions are more frequently asked than the theological ones. But these questions can have a detrimental affect in perpetuating false disjunctions regarding gender characteristics. Before we deal with the theological origin of gender and its implications, we need to address common misconceptions about gender.

Gender identities, feminists have complained, have been grossly stereotyped. Opinions vary between myths, true differences, and debatable conclusions.[15]

First the *myths:*

1. Girls are more social than boys.
2. Girls are more suggestible than boys.
3. Girls have a lower self-esteem than boys.
4. Girls lack motivation to achieve.

5. Girls are better at rote learning and simple repetitive tasks. Boys are better at high-level tasks that require them to inhibit previously learned responses.
6. Boys are more analytic than girls.
7. Girls are auditory, boys are visual.

Second, the *accepted differences:*

1. Males are more aggressive than females.
2. Girls have greater verbal ability than boys.
3. Boys excel in visual-spatial ability.
4. Boys excel in mathematical ability.

Third, the *controversial, debated contentions:*
The following areas are toss-ups, depending on the studies:

1. One sex is more competitive than the other.
2. One sex is more dominant than the other.
3. One sex is more compliant than the other.
4. One sex is more helpful (that is, nurturant) than the other.
5. Females are more passive than males.

The above summary from gender studies provides essential background information. When the dust of controversy has settled, statistical evidence supports the contention that men are more aggressive than women. Keep in mind, however, that is not the same as dominance, competitiveness, and overall activity levels.

The next question is whether or not the New Testament points to or establishes any gender continuation in the resurrection state. Are the eternally ageless sexless? Many of the church fathers, who lived monastically, and who considered celibacy the ideal state, projected nonsexuality into the Infinite Heaven.[16]

The body, in medieval thinking, was considered the chief factor in sinning. Some held that the human will and mind were neutral or uncontaminated by sin. Luke 20:36's phrase "like the angels" was taken out of context, and it was reasoned that man would be free of body in heaven. As we saw earlier no "angelic" neutering was intended.

Therefore, to believe what the fathers taught regarding checking our sexual thoughts at the pearly gates is to be rejected. We would do better to seek for biblical truth, rather than seek confirmation from the church fathers.

Probably the argument with the most wallop was the state of our Lord's resurrected body. The gender of Christ seemed retained from his preresurrection humanity. In the mist of Easter morning his form was mistaken as a groundskeeper. (Groundskeeping, then, was a male occupation.) His tone of voice was the same as before his crucifixion. Mary did not mistake the voice characteristics as being anyone but Jesus. He called out her name in his distinctive way (John 20:10-16).

On another occasion, Thomas saw the scars left from his crucifixion. Thomas exclaimed, "My Lord and my God!" (John 20:28). John's vision of Christ in heaven saw him as the restored Lamb showing marks of his being slaughtered (Rev. 5:6). By inference rather than by direct statement, it would appear that Jesus' maleness was also carried into his resurrection state. Donald G. Bloesch has added the observation that Elijah and Moses appeared as men on the Mount of Transfiguration. [17]

Some have gone on from this to conclude that other distinctions of earth carried over into the resurrected, glorified form. Jesus continued the teacher-student relationship in his resurrected body. He taught his disciples for forty days between his resurrection and ascension. Were other relationships continued? (We shall look briefly at the matter of race in the next chapter.) Jesus seemed to have dismissed the perpetuation in the heavenly state of the husband-wife relationship.

But what about brother/sister, mother/child, and father/ child relationships? Is there anything to Donald Bloesch's contention that on the basis of Matthew 22:30 and Luke 20:35, 36, "The man-wife relationship is now transformed into a brother-sister relationship in Christ?"[18] In those texts Jesus neither excluded gender, nor did he say there was a transformation to another type of earthly relationship. His answer returned attention to the central issue of the reality of resurrection (Luke 20:37, 38; Matt. 22:31, 32).

Gender differences are certainly mentioned in Revelation. Both women and men are used significantly in the book. Two wicked women stand out: Jezebel's spiritual lookalike (the only kind of replication Scripture will allow) may not be counted as a futuristic figure, for she is mentioned in the portion addressed to a specific church in Asia Minor (Rev. 2:20). The city of Babylon (Rome) is likened to a disgraceful whore (17:3-5). Prominent in the last chapter is the body of the elect, the pure bride of Christ (19:7, 9; 21:2; 22:17).

Revelation 12 uses the figure of a mother prominently. Who is the mother in 12:1, 2, 5, 6? Associating her with Mary, the mother of Jesus, is problematical, first because the subject is less Jesus' birth than his death, and second should Catholics concede that she had multiple births after Jesus (12:17)? The chief objection to Mary being the woman is her numerous offspring over a time period exceeding her probable lifespan. Long-term, mega years are intimated, for the hostility between the dragon and the woman is undying.

The woman is undoubtedly the believing community, spiritual Israel, the messianic people (12:1, 2, 5). Christ came out of (birth) the believing (mothering) side of old Israel. After God took the Son into heaven ("snatch" is used to describe his resurrection-ascension [12:5 GNB]), he protected the remnant of faith from destruction (12:6). Saints are alluded to in the mother figure. Believers or saints, contrary to the contention of some futurists, do appear elsewhere after the fourth chapter of Revelation (13:7, 10; 16:6; 17:6; 18:24).[19]

The persecution motif in chapter 12 of Revelation reappears throughout the book. These references are comments on the past, the present, and the future. To see chapter 12 as entirely future seals up the vision, rather than unlocking it. The action of Revelation pivots on otherworld beings given human characteristics. Personhood serves the purpose of making forces believable.

Social relationships in Revelation include harlot and lovers, bride and groom, king and subjects, mother and child. John Charles Ryle (1816-1900) represented a view of an idealized heaven in which all social distinctions, both arbitrary ones and those fixed by nature, are done away, so that "there will be perfect equality, perfect fraternity, and perfect freedom."[20] If all distinctions are dissolved in heaven, then don't degrees of reward reintroduce distinctions? (This is the subject of the next chapter.) Are all distinctions, including gender, avoidable in heaven? Abraham Kuyper (1837-1920) seemed to have thrown up his hands in despair on this matter. He confessed, "We find it extremely difficult to form any idea of the social state in heaven."[21]

Gender is as much how we *think* and *feel* as how we *look*. It is pervasive to our personhood, that is, it is part of the human essence. An acceptance of the perpetuation of gender in the final heaven is predicated on the basis that gender is not an accidental characteristic but is inborn. But to argue that gender continues because we were born that way doesn't hold water with many people. After all, suppose a person is born blind or suppose someone never knew a time they were not handicapped. If they have always thought like a handicapped person (and no other way) would that handicap them in heaven? Their argument is that perfection, conceivably, may be the elimination of individual body characteristics. Birth reality cannot be completely convincing. A lot of Christians are not eager to grant that birth factors continue into the heavenly state.

Still other arguments are advanced to see gender preserved in heaven. Since satiation, conquest, and allurement make contacts between the sexes interesting communications, one argument for accepting gender in heaven is that without it interest in each other would wane. Fixed differences in gender have functional value.[22] But many hold that gender differences will be superfluous in heaven. Need there be gender for *agape* love to be shown?

Another question is "Does lack of gender guarantee dullness?" If it is true that dullards find dullness and bores experience boredom, then do different genders by themselves insure that the heaven life will be exciting? We may lean toward accepting gender as an eternal state when we ask what is left. When gender goes, then are we robbed as to how we conceived of ourselves on earth? The option of egalitarianism is the elimination of sexes. But egalitarianism seems a poor substitute for gender. Some women's liberationists think sexual distinctions should be erased and gender should be viewed as a cultural conditioning.

Gender, however, is endemic to human, not something extra, added on by society and culture. "Egalitarianism is clung to at the price of denying not only biological differences . . . but emotional differences."[23]

Are we to be divested of gender? The Bible refrains from direct statements that gender is eternal. It only gives us intimations. As long as *eros* is extracted or extinguished, then gender, like body, is essential to who we are. It is as hard to conceive of our personalities without our gender as it is to conceive of a resurrected body without our physiology. More and more Christians are asking these kinds of questions—yet they go to the very core of resurrection life.

Two famous New Testament "sex texts" cannot be used to justify the eradication of gender in the hereafter. When Paul wrote "neither male nor female," he was not venting a repressed barrage against gender (Gal. 3:28). He was saying that neither sex predisposes us to seek the Lord or qualifies us for acceptance in Christ.[24] He wasn't saying that both were excluded from heaven and that we would be indistinguishable or that our sexual identities would cease.

Similarly the prohibition that "flesh and blood cannot inherit the kingdom of God" (1 Cor. 15:50) cannot be used to dispute the tangibility of the resurrected bodies of the redeemed.[25]

While individual marriages are outlawed and former marital relationships null and void in heaven, this does not mean "marriage" in a broader sense is excluded. Although marriage as an institution is impossible in heaven, marriage as a metaphor and state of mind is not. After all, the marriage between Christ and his church is a major topic in Revelation.

Before we deal with that matter, we need to think more on the possibility of sexuality in heaven. Sexuality, the fourth usage of sex, is an outgrowth of gender's permanency. Posit gender in heaven and sexuality follows. C. S. Lewis (1898-1963) was a Christian apologist, whose writings are well known. In his apologetical work, *Miracles* (1947) he argued for the retention of both gender and sexuality in heaven.

> In denying the sexual life [in heaven] . . . it is not of course necessary to suppose that the distinction of sexes will disappear. What is no longer needed for biological purposes may be expected to survive for splendour. Sexuality is the instrument both of virginity and conjugal virtue; neither men nor women will be asked to throw away weapons they have used victoriously. It is the beaten and the fugitives who throw away their swords. The conquerors sheathe theirs and retain them. "Trans-sexual" would be a better word than "sexless" for the heavenly life.[26]

"Trans-sexual" is not to be confused with *bisexual*. *Bisexual* refers to sexual activity with male and female; *trans-sexual* refers to male and female sexual polarities being interchangeable. But *trans-sexual*, while seemingly overcoming the onus of sexuality, only makes it less identifiable and less desirable for most humans. It would seem that retention of distinctive male and female sexuality better illustrates the relationship of Christ, the groom, and the church, his bride. Although Lewis liked the idea of gender continuing in the heavenly realms, it was Karl Barth (1886-1968) who made a strong case for both genders being in God.[27]

Donald G. Bloesch bought into the view that masculine and feminine are both part of God's image. We may still wonder that if sexuality is *from* God is it *in* God? Sexuality would exist for us in heaven if it existed for God who precedes us. Barth argued that sexuality differences existed before God made humans. This would make sexuality a live option for the redeemed in heaven.

A Roman Catholic philosophy professor, who was once a Protestant, in a rare (not raw) essay on the present subject, came to the same conclusion of Barth, perhaps independently of Barth:

> God is a sexual being, the most sexual of all beings. . . . Sexuality is "the image of God" according to Scripture (*Genesis* 1:27), and for B to be an image of A, A must have all the qualities imaged by B. God therefore is a sexual being.[28]

Will humans be desexed? How can the image of God in man be restored without gender being retained and without sexuality perfected? It requires us to think more deeply on the character of God.

> God includes masculinity and femininity within himself, though not human sexuality; yet the God of the Bible is not

androgynous, half male and half female. He includes masculinity and femininity as movements within himself indicating initiative and power on the one hand (the masculine), and receptivity and loving obedience on the other (the female). In one respect he appears to be altogether masculine, and in another predominantly feminine. The *masculine* and *feminine* are ontological categories which are not absolutely transcended in God, but which arise out of God. God as the initiator and determiner is the ground of the masculine, and God as the receiver and implementer is the ground of the feminine.[29]

Of course time is well spent in looking up in Scripture male and female images applied to both generic man and God. Does God combine both genders in himself? Or is he neither? Barth says God is both genders and that explains how humans are made in his image. Bloesch says that God "encompasses" masculinity and femininity.[30] When pressed, however, he says maleness is prior:

> Femininity is grounded in masculinity and not vice versa. . . . The masculine is the foundation of the feminine, so the feminine is the flower and fruit of the masculine, the glory of the masculine (1 Cor. 11:7).[31]

Some feminists may see red when Bloesch contends that the predominate figure used to describe God is masculine. He argued that even though James 1:17, 18, refers to God giving birth to his people, that the Agent is the Father, not Mother.[32] But Bloesch has not said enough on James 1:18.

James 1:18 is a unique usage of the birth analogy, which lends exegetical weight to the contention that both genders reside in God. The word for birth in this passage is *apokuein* from *tiktō*, which "in the New Testament is used exclusively of the women."[33]

James makes the point that God is like a woman. She gives

birth to us. Whereas in the Gospel of John the new birth is said to take place in us, James 1:18 says the new birth takes place in God. This is a startling analogy to some Christian males. But the figure has special value and spiritual force, for unlike the conception aspects emphasized in John 3, this usage underscores the fact that God, like a mother, carried us to full term. God is the one from whom we have derived our form. In the depths of his being we were remade. From the depths of his nature we have been given birth. Lest one try to build a case for exclusive use of feminine for God, Bloesch cited Susan T. Foh's comment that all adjectives, verb forms, and pronouns in the Old Testament referring to God are masculine.[34] On the other hand, Jesus did not feel it demeaning to refer to himself as a solicitous hen trying to gather errant chicks (Matt. 23:37). It should be stressed here, of course, that Jesus was not trying to force a hidden message on gender. The two main points were Christ's desire and their rejection of his advances.

Femaleness comes to the fore in the Bible's description of the church.[35] Revelation refers to the "marriage of the Lamb" (Rev. 19:7) and the "marriage supper of the Lamb" (19:9). Though some Christians would like to forget their own gender, God designates a gender for his church. The female gender of the church is consistently stressed in the New Testament.

Comparing the church to a bride, however, goes one step further than gender. The figure seems not to be confined to the static legal relationship of husband and wife, but includes the psychology of lovemaking between Christ and Christians. It is well known that absolute intimacy is part of the sexual act. The Hebrew word for "knowing" one's wife and of God's "knowing" the way of righteous is the same word.[36]

Rollo May has summarized the emotions of lovemaking as intimacy and withdrawal, union and distance, separating ourselves and giving ourselves in full union. He sees elements of this even in acquaintanceships.[37] Therefore, while intercourse between male and female is not part of the Infinite Heaven, there is a true spiritual union between Christ and his church.

In Peter J. Kreeft's essay, referred to earlier, on the union of Christ, the bridegroom, and the church, his bride, he contended, ". . . we are more, not less, sexual in heaven. . . ."[38] Some may feel that as atonement types passed away with Christ's atoning death, so the institution of marriage would be archaic after we are eternally with Christ. This overlooks, however, the perpetuity of Christ's atonement throughout eternity. By the same token our union with Christ will be both real and unending.

It is hard to argue that there is not a spiritual union between Christ and his church in heaven without assuming that gender traits will be there as well.

Vernard Eller has argued similarly. The image of God in us "is to be feminine in respect to his [God's] masculinity"[39] (Eller also follows Barth.) The parallels have a spiritual message:

> God has revealed himself to us as "masculine" precisely in order to invoke our (humanity's) "feminine" response. . . . God equals "masculinity" plus "deity"—and those two are not the same thing. As masculine, he is *Father* (to us as *children*) and *Wooer-husband* (to us as *beloved-bride*). But as divine, he is also *Deity* (to our *humanity*), *Lord* (to our *liege*), and *Creator* (to our *creature*).[40]

Feminine style receptivity is an illustration of openness to Christ. Sometimes the New Testament links the church with the purity and chasteness associated with virginity. At other times it is the church's submission and attractiveness associated with femininity! (No inference should be drawn that maleness characterizes rejection of the Word of God.)

We must be careful how far to draw this comparison. If the fault of some Christians has been to brutalize women by insisting on total submission, on the opposite end of the spectrum

has been the fault of those who eulogize the female temperament so that an erroneous theological conclusion is attributed
to female sexuality.

We cannot biblically justify an attribution to women of a
natural predisposition to understand, believe, and reflect the
gospel because they are women. The father of theological liberalism, Friedrich Schleiermacher (1768-1834), from a sexist
viewpoint, eulogized the eternal feminine. He claimed they got
to the heart of Christmas because they were more concerned
with feelings.[41] To devalue propositional statements and words
because women seem incapable of handling the ineffable is an
indirect slur against a woman's sexuality. It was more Schleiermacher's intuition, rather than scriptural inference, which
made him claim women better understood the Christmas event
than men because of their "quiet and gracious nature."

The female gender describes the attitude of the purified
bride of Christ in heaven. There is only one marriage in
heaven: that is, our marriage to Christ. Submission will not be
to each other but to him. Therefore there is a segment of sexuality in heaven, but it has to do not with our bodies but with
our spirits.

If receptivity describes the eternal attitude of the redeemed,
what does it say about Christians still in the world? And how
far should the attitudes of submission, surrender, and compliance get stressed?

These questions bring us back to earth to consider the styles
of sanctification, which reflect female sexuality. Female sexuality,
of course, cannot be made the basis for justifying the tyrannical
methods of some modern disciplining, in which another Christian slavishly adheres to the advice of his spiritual guide/guru.
Nor can it be used to buttress a claim that quietism's (*see* Glossary) approach to sanctification had it right all along.

Submission is a definite mark of a learner. "The first mark"
of a rabbinic disciple was submission.[42] Receptivity to the

Word of God is the main mark of a believer. Jesus said, "He who belongs to God hears what God says . . ." (John 8:47 NIV).

> Interpretation of the Word of God can take place only through man's subordination; this subordination now comes concretely to mean that we have to subordinate ourselves to the Word of the prophets and apostles.[43]

Translating the general principle into practice is where excesses appear. Quietism is an aberration of the female role. Madame Guyon (1648-1717), a French Catholic, represents the position of quietism. Her view of the Christian life was "absolutely passive receptivity." She held that the soul which is empty is the soul which is filled.[44] Very close to her position was that of Hannah Whitall Smith (1832-1911), an American Quaker, who wrote of absolute surrender to Christ.[45]

Three major dangers grow out of this emphasis: (1) Perfection is said to be attainable on earth. (2) The submissive Christian loses self-identity. Like many other forms of mysticism the subject becomes absorbed in God even to the point of becoming God. (3) This approach to Christian living is passiveness to the point of abdication and immobilization.

Richard Lovelace has raised a caution:

> [The doctrine of biblical sanctification] must be dissociated from quietism, which can manifest itself in two forms: one which assumes that major problems of sin are easily conquered by a simple moment of believing prayer and do not involve hard work in mortifying sin; and another which suspects that all efforts of the will against sin are "fleshly striving" and must not be undertaken until the Spirit gives inspiration in response to faith.[46]

Similar objections were raised by James I. Packer:

> Passivity, which quietists think liberates the Spirit, actually resists and quenches him. Souls that cultivate passivity do not

thrive, but waste away. The Christian's motto should not be "Let go and let God" but "trust God and get going!"[47]

The tension between submission and assertion is part of female sexuality. Scripture, contrary to some, does not demand from wives an absolute submission to their husbands, but the recognition of the husband/masculine priority in a leadership role.

Subordination is not an absolute requirement in one gender over another. Each is equal before God. Therefore, submission to each other because of God takes submission out of the realm of sexuality and makes it theological (Eph. 5:21). One partner is not superior to the other; each has a different role to fulfill.[48] Fulfilled as women, happy wives exercise a healthy assertiveness in the context of submissiveness. Subordination of function does not deny or diminish equality of natures.

These motifs (submission and participation) seem to appear in Revelation 19:7, 8 (NIV):

> . . . his bride has made herself ready.
> Fine linen, bright and clean,
> was given her to wear.
> (Fine linen stands for the righteous acts of the saints.)

In biblical passages elsewhere Christ's righteousness is pictured as clothing. Two possibilities exist on the identity of the righteous acts of the saints: (1) The "righteous acts" are those compliances with Christ's words, which are a result of having been "set aside" for Christ's use, or the deeds of the redeemed in gratitude to Christ's love. Or (2) The righteous deeds of the martyred Christians will be something supplied and shown off by the entire church, reflecting the glory of Christ. What in secular society was once regarded as immoderate loyalty and mindless obsessiveness, in eternity will appear as appropriate, reasonable, and deserving adornment. At any rate, we see combined both the activity of the bride in getting herself ready and her passivity in accepting what is given to her. Female sexuality in its give and take turns out to be a corrective to the present-day excesses of manipulative discipleship techniques and of shrink-back quietistic interpretations of the Christian life. In Revelation female traits of submissiveness and aggressiveness are maintained.

Because the first reference (19:7) and second reference (21:2) to the marriage of the church to Christ are separated by chapter 20, some have inferred that either two wedding celebrations take place or that there is a tremendous wait for the wedding day of Revelation 21:2. This view is taken because one has followed a chronological view of the book to the end.

But chronology only complicates the message of these chapters. If Revelation 19:7 were the engagement announcement (in first-century Judaism, the engagement was legally marriage) and 21:2 were the actual wedding, then it would mean that there would be a one-thousand-year engagement! (In the biblical analogy of marriage, the church before Christ's return is engaged to be married, in anticipation of the final event of full marriage at Christ's second coming).

John may have had in mind aspects of a major event separated by a millennium: (1) the engagement which was legally binding; (2) the wedding itself. Jesus did not believe in long engagements, even though he never married on earth. Chapters 19 and 21 both refer to Christ's second coming, but from slightly different perspectives. The two texts refer to the same event.

A linear assumption of the progression from Revelation 19 to Revelation 21 requires that there be such a lag. But chapters 19, 20, and 21 are contrapuntal in arrangement. Chapter 19 is about the return of Christ. Chapter 20 backs up and describes the success of the preaching of the gospel before Christ's return. Chapter 21 is also about the second coming of Christ, but from two different camera angles.

Those who say the millennium of Chapter 20 is *after* Christ's return, rather than as a result of his first coming:

> . . . assume that the thousand years will follow the Lord's coming in Revelation 19, and such a delay of the marriage does not fit the context. If the millennial age, however, is a recapitulation of this present period between the first and second advents, then the problem vanishes. The wedding announced at the close of this age (Rev. 19) will take place a short time later at the dawning of the age to come (Rev. 21).[49]

Therefore, the same marriage event is being described in both chapters 19 and 21. Chapter 19 refers to its commencement; chapter 21 to its consummation.

We have attempted to show how the Bible is realistic in addressing the multifaceted humanity issue. Sexual scruples are sometimes superimposed by Christians, and in rare instances some would berate the questioner for his or her thoughts. Our exploration of the subject has not produced answers that have the same degree of finality that we find in Scripture on the matter of how God saves man. But there is enough in Scripture to open up our eyes to the possibilities that await us in the final heaven.

Occasionally, one will hear Christians say that, as far as they are concerned, the omission of sex in heaven will be no loss, but a plus. This response has the appearance of personal projection and may hide a failure to enjoy and appreciate all aspects of sex as a gift of God. We have argued that this type of answer puts our heads in the sand regarding scientific and biblical evidence about human nature.

Individuality and sexuality were bonded in us before birth. Each has participated in the other all through earthly life. To hold that redeemed persons will be without gender (and the sexuality that goes with it) would mean, in the final heaven, that individuality as we know it will be no more.

But separating the human psyche from its sexual connectedness seems as problematical and as unlikely as trying to unscramble an egg. To achieve that separation would create at least two obstacles. (1) Our identity would be significantly altered and reduced, rather than the perfection of what we have known. (2) It would seem to suggest that gender is part of iniquity.

Another form of denial of gender and sexuality is the view that in the final heaven sex will be absolutely sublimated. To speak of sublimation in heaven would be anachronistic, laced with asceticism, and, therefore, unacceptable. Sublimation would seem to retain gender and sexuality, but, at the same time, it would exalt sublimation rather than fulfillment, and it would suggest that human passion even in heaven is not under control. The final heaven, however much it retains of earth, cannot be a simple extension of this life, for it would fail to factor in the yet unknown, but assured, components of ultimate dedication to God, the redeemed state, and glorified forms in an environment where procreation and physical fulfillment detached from spiritual values are no longer necessary.

A glorified relationship with Christ will eclipse every earthly pleasure in such a way that the former capacity will not be reduced to an evil or inferior status. Thus, sex, in its purest form will persist in Infinite Heaven. Indeed, heaven ahead will be the only place where there is absolutely safe sex. It will be perfect communion without the divesting of our individuality. It will be the ultimately satisfying interpersonal relationship principally with Christ. Left unknown is how male or female gender will measurably influence the form, style, and energy of worship in heaven. How our distinctiveness, along with our gender will add to Christ's glory and heaven's enjoyments, are two ponderous questions, among many, for which we do not have answers.

The experience of the multi-dimensional aspects of sex on

earth and its illustrative use regarding the Infinite Heaven ahead are worthy of continued reflection. After all, in Revelation the marriage figure seems to loom larger than the management aspects of heaven. As we probe further into the depths of what it means to love Christ, ourselves, and each other we will come closer to a greater appreciation of what it means to love and to be loved by God.[50]

14

Humor in Heaven ?

*I*t's no joke: laughter is like sex. How can that be? From the Department of Health, from the Surgeon General, from mental health professionals down to the local pastor, we are told of the seriousness of sex. And those who have contracted AIDS don't think casual sex is a laughing matter, either.

Laughter is like sex in its general popularity. Nearly everyone enjoys a good laugh and nearly everyone enjoys intimacy. In addition, serious lovemaking is not without playfulness. And like laughter some people approach sex as a diversion. Is it not a willingness to laugh which breaks the stranglehold of boredom? Is it not therapeutic to be loved passionately, unconditionally, and physically?

Nevertheless, there may be fewer objections to having humor in heaven than to having sex in heaven. Of all the activities humans would like perpetuated in heaven, laughter is high on their list. In the *Newsweek* poll of 1988, 74 percent of those sampled thought there would be humor in heaven.[1] But what were *their* reasons? As you will see, *we* have our own.

The vocal minority of 26 percent felt strongly enough to put their foot down on hilarity in heaven. Assuming they voted against humor in heaven not merely to get attention, what did they have against the idea? We'd be more likely to know *who* would object to humor in heaven than *what* actual reasons they would have against it. Those persons who would object to laughter in heaven would probably be the same ones who would look disdainfully on those who laugh in church.

The late Grady Wilson, associate evangelist with Billy Graham and his long-time friend, loved to hear people laugh. Once he was reprimanded for being humorous in a sermon. (Joy was a trait he found unavoidable.) A woman stopped him afterward to tell him, "I just don't think it right to disgrace the pulpit by telling a joke."[2] She would have been pleased to know that the Methodist evangelist E. Stanley Jones (1884-1973) would have partly agreed with her, for he wrote in his auto-biography, "The bane of the American pulpit and platform is the telling of 'corny' jokes."[3]

Overuse, humor in poor taste, alleged sacrilegiousness, or even constitutional sternness may explain why some would like light-heartedness outlawed in chancels. There is plenty to be said, however, in favor of enjoying laughter in church.[4] Effective humor is not something taught, but it is worthwhile for ministers to look into the subject more closely than in studying the history of weak verbs.

Many people may be willing to tolerate a chuckle in church, but would they want to go to heaven if there were more punch lines than lunch lines? After awhile even laughter gets tiresome and jokes become jejune. Some people could be annoyed at humor in heaven. Others are horrified at the thought. Before we attempt to quiet these objections, perhaps the best approach should be to consider why people laugh.

What will be the basis for humor in heaven? On earth much of humor revolves around *faux pas*—mistakes, muffs, and malapropisms. But in heaven there will be no mistakes, no misuse of language. The riddles of earth will be made plain and the ridiculousness of life will be ironed out. Nervous, nefarious, and nasty laughter will not be heard in heaven.

Humor on earth is used to break up awkward moments, release tension, and soften tough spots, but in heaven everyone is at ease at home. Humor on earth is used against pomposity and pretentiousness, but in heaven all are equal even though distinguishing traits of individuality are retained. If all jesting on earth is considered in poor taste, doesn't that imply that joking, which uses jests, will be hushed in heaven? Proverbs 17:22 reminds us that a merry heart acts like a tonic for the weary, a medicine for the depressed. But once we are cured of all depression in heaven, will humor be needed?

For these reasons, one may suppose that humor in heaven is least needed, even less appropriate, for only on the plains of sadness is laughter useful to raise spirits. Since much of comedy depends on human failure (failure to succeed, failure to understand, failure to appreciate) does that mean humor doesn't belong in heaven? It is not a silly question.

Yet few have taken it seriously enough to address it. Check out any book on heaven from a library. If indexed, you are *not* likely to find humor listed. Few scholars consider humor in heaven. I found only one reference to a writer, in the recent collection of views on heaven (*Heaven* by McDannell and Lang), who thought of heaven as a place where laughter will be heard. French theologian, Francois Arnoux (c. 1600) in his book *Marvels of the Otherworld* (1614) opined of life in heaven, ". . . people talk of nothing but pastimes . . . laughter never ceases."[5]

Artwork on heaven is revealing. If writings on heaven are barren of references to humor in heaven, what about artists who are often less likely to be ideologically fixed? But, again, we are disappointed. Pictures of the angels are shown in various poses. Often given human forms, they are seen reaching out to console, standing at attention to perform duties, or with heads slightly bent in adoration, but no one has pictured them doubled up in laughter!

A look at specific depictions of heaven bears this interpretation out. For instance, the central portal of Notre Dame Cathedral, Paris, photographed for readers in the McDannell/Lang volume, show the redeemed in heaven holding hands.[6] Of the ten shown, four have ever so slight smiles, but these are not facing toward Christ as the other six.

Regrettably, from medieval times on, drawings of the blessed redeemed beholding the Savior and the holy family in heaven haven't dared to give them beaming faces, let alone little grins. In the fifteenth-century painting of paradise by Dieric Bouts, duplicated in the McDannell/Lang volume, I notice a slight smirk (or was it wistful anticipation?) on the face of a nude woman.[7] The nearest thing to fun in heaven (in the history of paintings) is the cherubic infant with a bow and arrow. Unfortunately, however, this figure was not introduced to produce a laugh. The end result of overserious expressions is to make the decent mirth-loving individual laugh at heaven.

Plenty of writers on heaven speak of the joys of heaven, but dare not venture that laughter is one way the joy is expressed. If heaven is social, not just solitary, how can genuine, satisfying conversation take place without humor? If all heavenly conversation is devoid of humor, then the impression will be that heaven is a pretty dull place.

Have the longest residents of heaven been humorless? No. The humorless are on earth. The truly miserable sinners are the conceited self-righteous on earth. They want, even demand, acceptance by God because they have *never* told off-color jokes. Look back on Jesus' life. His critics were deadly serious. Proud people today find it hard to confess their sins and laugh at their pretentiousness. God's grace gifts us to see that the greater one's commitment to rebellion against God, the less likelihood there is that we can laugh.

Demons, Satan's clones, are sad sacks and celestial sourpusses. His dupes are dullards, slavishly and stupidly following orders of their infernal leader. Loaded down with schemes, they don't know what it is to smile when the enslaved are freed. They don't know what it is to smile when the dead are raised. They grin with glee only when man is kept captive to sin. To them Jesus' resurrection wasn't funny. Easter, however, was to be God's ultimate satirical barb that has stuck in Satan's memory to be an eternal irritant.

> Once in Eden and later on Golgotha, the demons thought they had made the whole plight of man one of never-ending seriousness. The monster death was allowed to close its jaws and then, suddenly, it burst asunder, teeth, jaws, and all, with a party-balloon bang. To witness that man can be free from sin, the devil, and the world, what could be more appropriate than to laugh.[8]

Joy fills and overflows heaven now. Jesus said that laughter replaces tears in heaven. He contrasted the sadness of time with the joy of eternity (Luke 6:21). Joy bubbled up when Christ threw down Satan in his first coming (Rev. 12:12; John 12:31), and rejoicing erupts over each sinner whose life is changed (Luke 15:5-7, 9, 10, 32).

John F. MacArthur, Jr., has contended that *Luke* 15:10 "does not actually say the angels were joyful. Whose joy is this? It is the joy of the triune God, existing in the presence of the holy angels. Of course, the angels share in the celebration, but the emphasis in both parables [that is, in the parables of the lost sheep and of the lost coin] is on God's joy."[9] It must not be overlooked that the woman who found the coin had called in her friends and neighbors (15:9). Because 15:10 begins, *"In the same way,* I tell you, there is joy in the presence of the angels . . ."* it *does* actually say the angels were joyful! The point of the passage is that the joy of heaven is a shared experience. As God does not keep his happiness to himself now, so we can be sure that he will include the expanded population of heaven later. The laughter of heaven will involve everyone.

What type of joy will be in heaven? Humor in our time depends on incongruities, contrasts, and surprise answers. Heaven's humor is going to be better than earth's. Since music in heaven will be new, will not humor have a new wrinkle, an added dimension, a rejuvenated form? One likely place for humor in heaven will be those initial "moments" when we begin the rounds of meeting heaven's interesting inhabitants.

The laughter Jesus referred to in the hereafter (Luke 6:21) will undoubtedly include innocent banter in identifying famous figures in heaven. Personal introductions will surely be one occasion when humor in heaven will happen. Suppose the original Abraham spoke to us. If his first words in heaven to us are, "I'm Abraham and who are you?" We may be tempted to say (as a pastor's wife whose ancestors were from the Netherlands once said), "Get him to laugh by asking, 'Abraham Lincoln or Abraham Kuyper?'" Perhaps we would hear Sarah laugh *before* Abraham, since Sarah was noted for her laughter on earth. Will those noted for their laughter on earth, like Sarah, continue with this characteristic into eternity?

Some may be shocked as to how funny heaven will be. Expect grumps to be transformed into wits and grouches changed into masters of the repartee. Heaven will surely be a place where soreheads will be healed, where people will no longer groan at puns, where light farce will replace heavy satire, where the tickle will no longer be fiendish. It will be heaven indeed when sourpusses easily smile (and like it). In heaven ahead all wet blankets will be eternally dried out and hilarity will be made holy. The humor of heaven will be vastly improved over earth, made infinite both in variety, use, and amount. There humor will not be hollow, harsh, or dirty. There put-down jokes will not be directed against others, but directed against the devil. There joy will not shun to use the sign of laughter.

Fortunately, humorists will be at home in heaven. Wags without wickedness will be welcomed. Some earthlings are now so starched with religiosity that they equate their somberness with sanctity. God has originated all good things, including good humor. He has always had a sense of humor. His creation is proof of it. He would prefer to hear "Ha ha" than "Ho hum" when we view it.

Although John's vision of heaven showed the heavenly city in the shape of a square (Rev. 21:16), it doesn't mean only "squares" will dwell there. Since the heavenly city will have walls, "off the wall" humor will be in place. Since the better humor results from comic self-discovery (when we laugh at ourselves), considering the too-serious-approach we had in life; for some more than others, there will be an endless number of things to laugh about in heaven that we couldn't laugh about on earth.

Heaven ahead will be the continuation of the humiliation God handed the devil on Christ's resurrection day. Jesus' enemies thought he was finished in the crucifixion. God turned the tables on Satan. In reference to the unsuccessful attempt to permanently destroy Jesus, Psalm 2:4 says God scornfully laughed at the foiled designs to destroy Jesus. Elaborate precautions to prevent his emergence from the tomb failed. The tomb seal was broken, not from the outside in, but from the inside out. In the resurrection of Christ the devil was shown to be a cosmic fool. Jesus roared with delight all the way to the right hand of the Father on his Ascension Day. And we can laugh with him and because of him. Revelation 18:20 is the Christian's continuation of God's scornful laugh in Psalm 2:4.

The spirit of celebration belongs with Christ's victory over sin, death, and Satan. In early Christian Greek tradition, Easter Monday was a "day of joy and laughter" and called "Bright Monday." In early Latin Christian tradition the clergy cracked jokes to awaken the people to the realities of joyous resurrection and to draw out the *risus Paschalis* or "Easter smile." Kudos to the Fellowship of Merry Christians, who sponsor April as "Holy Humor Month.[10] They have anticipated heaven.

We may not be given the talents of a comedian in heaven, but it is hard to believe that we will not acquire or be given a greater appreciation of the comic elements in cosmic events. With perfect memories in heaven, if jokes are told, the punchline will never be forgotten, which means we won't be laughing at our friends for messing up a good joke. If we go to heaven expecting to experience *trance,* only to discover that God's idea of celebration is *dance* (because part of the happiness of heaven is mixing with others of like mind), then some may not have the strength to suppress a snicker.

The humor of heaven, however, will be less related to the trivialities of life and will deal more with the big issues of time and eternity. None will miss the ironies which emerge from and within the history of redemption. To see pomposity shrink like a slowly deflating balloon and to watch the authors of tomes deleting all their slurs against Christ will strike the persecuted believers in heaven as very funny.

This raises another question: "In a perfect state would we laugh at those whose eternity is endless suffering? Will we be allowed to laugh at others in heaven when we are taught that it is impolite to make light of another's embarrassment, loss, and bitterness?" Some could as well argue that laughter of the vengeful kind will be universal in hell. If humans haughtily laughed in God's face when they were on earth, it is not inconceivable that they would still try to poke fun at the supposed illogic of God in showing mercy to sinners.

When people are the target of laughter, it is not pleasant, especially when it is relentless. It would seem unChristlike to think anyone's dreadful fate could elicit a chuckle in heaven.

It raises a more basic question: "Does perfection require the absence of a drive to punish? Will God, the author of our perfection, invite his redeemed to indulge in humor that hurts? Must the martyrs be scolded in heaven for rejoicing in the affliction of their former tormentors?" Of all the questions on the hereafter, perhaps this one can become the most heated.

It is ironic (a form of fun) that scornful laughter can raise the most profound theological questions. We should begin by saying that what we find funny can reveal a side of our nature which other characteristics would not. In our lifetime we have seen those occasions when dislike for a person makes it easier to rejoice in his downfall. Even on earth, the rule for Christians is to rejoice with those who rejoice, not to rejoice over those who fall. Satan delights when Christians stumble, but cries in despair when Christians kneel. The Christian is in the business of healing hurts, not on a campaign of making others targets of abuse. We are encouraged to avoid put-down humor and to engage in humor which pulls up. The Christian doesn't need put-down humor to laugh and know joy.

Other Scriptures, such as the Book of Revelation 6:10, where martyrs are pictured as praying for the overthrow of their persecutors on earth, must be put on the other side of the balance. Assuming their presence in heaven meant their perfection, how could the prayer of Rev. 6:10 escape their lips? Is it that imprecations must be totally squelched even if the horrendousness of the perpetrators is unquestioned? And what do critics of scornful laughter do with Revelation 18:20)? It says, regarding the overthrow of "the great city, Babylon, the strong city" (18:10 NASB), "Rejoice over her, O heaven, and you saints and apostles and prophets, because God has pronounced judgment for you against her" (18:20 NASB). In a sense, it is another form of the old question, was it right for God to order the execution of Israel's vile and vicious neighbors? And was it right to rejoice in their victims?

We are at a point in our discussion when everyone is becoming deadly serious. There may be no way anyone is going to be totally convinced one way or the other, given our state of present imperfection. Perhaps a step toward the resolution of this problem would be to go back to the question of how God could be completely holy and scornfully laugh at the wicked (Ps. 2:4). In reply, some may argue that God laughs only at evil in progress and that he would not laugh at the hurtful consequences they produced. On the other hand, is there not a built-in assumption that God's laughter at evil's conception and its continuance was predicated on the basis that he anticipated the end of this evil, that he looks ahead to the "time" when he will have the last laugh?

Heaven is laughing *with* God. It may therefore, involve laughing at God's enemies. The main persons we shall laugh at in heaven are ourselves. We are not among God's enemies but we have made him look bad at times. Since final redemption is the capping of self-discovery and since healthy humor is the capacity to laugh at ourselves, then not only will the vault of heaven ring with choruses of praise, but also the halls of heaven will reverberate with both individual and united laughter. Proof that heaven is not dull will be that earth's cranks will want to crack jokes and enjoy laughter. Sure, the Bible says there will be no more tears in heaven (Rev. 7:17; 21:4). It doesn't say there will be no more giggles. The Bible says sin, but not necessarily silliness, is excluded from heaven. Heaven will be a serious, but not a joyless place.

Onions may be scratched from the vegetable list of the new earth, for it is one vegetable of old earth which makes people cry. (And in heaven there are to be no more tears.) Perhaps God will introduce us to vegetables in heaven that will make us laugh, such as the gnarled yam!

As we have seen, however, we shall laugh in heaven not because of gags, not because of comical props, not because of slap-stick routines, but because of the essence of pure joy that will pervade the place. "The joy of the Lord" will be ours to a degree we never thought possible.

We should look forward to the endless happiness that heaven will bring. One part of that will be the jubilant and exciting heavenly reunions. Laughter will be inseparable from the reception we await from loved ones who have gone before, the subject of chapter 19.

Satirical laughter in heaven, as we have seen, has multiple cutting edges. Laughter itself is in danger of being cut from the activity list of heaven. Can believers in the Intermediate State, that is departed spirits, laugh since they have no larynx, lungs, and body-locus? Isn't it a misuse of language to attribute laughter to bodiless spirits?

We wish we could laugh the question off, but we can't. One explanation is that the activities in the Intermediate State are put anthropomorphically, that is, in words with which we can relate. As God's sight does not require that he has actual eyes, so the souls of the redeemed are said to worship, sing, and even laugh without having bodies.

Second Corinthians 5:1-8, however, would seem to suggest that in the Intermediate Heaven we are given bodies. The claim is that Paul says it is impossible for a Christian to be bodiless between his death and Christ's second coming. Indeed, the passage would seem to support the view that we get our resurrection bodies at death! Most commentators, however, say that Paul was merely saying that the Intermediate Heaven would be cozy, like being in a house. The passage, however, goes along the following lines: that for Paul a Christian would not be disembodied at death, that it would be an individual body, and that he would receive it immediately (that is, without a time lag). The argument hinges on the consistent usage of "house" referring to body. F. F. Bruce, one of those who maintains this viewpoint, referred to it as ". . . the immediate investiture with the new body. . . ." In addition, the wording of 5:4 (NIV), of being "swallowed up by life," is strongly reminiscent of Paul's language of resurrection in 1 Corinthians 15:53.

W. D. Davies found reinforcement in this interpretation in the fact that later Paul does not speak of deceased Christians' resurrection, but of their revelation (Rom. 8:19; Col. 3:4), which would have meant he already assumed their resurrections!

One must read the arguments on both sides of the issue.[11] But if Paul's position was that a Christian is given resurrection at death, then it would fit the eschatology of the Book of Revelation, where, as we have argued in the Appendix, the meaning of "the first resurrection" (chapter 20) was the Christian's death.

Second Corinthians 5:1-10 is pertinent to the question of how laughter could be part of heavenly activity now. If we have resurrection bodies, in the Intermediate Heaven, then laughter from bodiless spirits is an objection laid to rest.

Laughter will surely be in heaven for Jesus, who has brought joy to the world (that is, to people of every clime and time) is there. One of the most serious, yet one of the most humorous preachers in any age, Charles Haddon Spurgeon (1834-1892) gave a reply to those who have argued that the Gospels never said Jesus laughed. He wrote in a letter (October 22, 1861):

> To me a smile is no sin, and a laugh is no crime. The Saviour, the man of sorrows, is our example of morality, but not of misery, for He bore our griefs that we might not bear them.[12]

Surely, laughter will be in the Infinite Heaven for it is part of the joy Christ brings when he enters our lives on earth.

15

Equality in Heaven

?

*I*n a previous chapter, Sex in Heaven?, we explored the idea of being different but equal in heaven. (In a sense we anticipate heaven by respecting differences yet affirming our own individuality. That's part of wholeness. Affirming others' uniqueness is preparation for heaven.)

The principle of equal-though-different bears on other aspects of life in heaven. If body identity continues and "equal though different" persists, then it would appear that racial identity is not lost either, for that is as much endemic as gender. Suppose racial, national, tribal identities are removed before or on entrance into heaven, how then is Christ to be extolled by those from every tongue, tribe, and nation? Does Revelation 5:9 require that these distinctions continue in heaven?

National identities, of course, are not necessarily racial identities. Orientals, for instance, cover a variety of nations. Would continuation of racial identities also mean continuation of national identities?

There is one place in the Infinite Heaven where nations are mentioned. Revelation 21:24 (NIV) has special bearing here. It says, "The nations will walk by its light, and the kings of the earth will bring their splendor into it" (NIV). Does this mean specific nations will persist into eternity? In heaven will we lose our ethnic identity? Will we also lose our national identity?

From one viewpoint, if we took Revelation 21:24 literally, then countries without kings wouldn't be there. The USA, for instance, would not be there, for we have only had presidents. It would be hard to argue that all kings of all countries would be there. Surely some rulers, especially the demonic tyrants, will be in hell, for they gave people hell when they once ruled and ruined their countries.

Some people can see this fulfilled even with the dissolution of nationalities, since saved individuals would be unofficial representatives. The cleansed church would be cosmopolitan in complexion. The redeemed from a complete national spectrum would participate in the praise of Christ. This does not mean that secular governments and their leaders will be registered rooters, for they were among those who opposed Christ.

The point of Revelation 21:24 is learned from earlier references. An influx of nations into Jerusalem was anticipated (Isa. 2:3; 60:3-11). The expansion of the city of Jerusalem was emblematic of the enlargement of God's following. As Revelation 5:9 and 7:9 spoke of the variety of recipients of grace, so 15:4 said that the triumph of God was to be universal in scope.

Usage of the word *nations* in the New Testament means Gentiles, rather than specific countries and their unique forms of government.[1] Historically, the earliest believers, Jews, were reluctant to admit the Gentiles into the churches.

But this prejudice was abandoned by the apostles. Revelation reinforced the theme of the Gospel of John that Christ came, not for one part of the world, but for all the world. Satan's hold on the Gentile nations was broken by the Christ of history (Rev. 11:1, 2; 18:23; 19:15). The church would be allowed to penetrate countless frontiers. Matthew 4:14 (NASB) says, "And this gospel of the kingdom shall be preached in the whole world for a witness to all the nations, and then shall the end come."

In Revelation 21:24 literal nations are not pictured as pouring into the New Jerusalem to enhance its glory. Homage was to the Lamb.

One of the less obvious ironies of the Book of Revelation is that Israel's sourcebook, the Old Testament, is often alluded to though not directly quoted.[2] Its symbolic numbers and figures are woven into the fabric of the visions, yet, at the same time, the writer distances himself from Zionist convictions. Recall how he used the expression "synagogue" in a pejorative sense (2:9; 3:9), of how the old Jerusalem was likened to Sodom (11:8), and of how heaven will be rid of temple (21:22). Notice, too, the significant omission in Revelation 20, the only passage in the book on the millennium, of Old Testament images regarding Jewish millennial expectations. Bruce Waltke thought it significant that none of the millennium verses in Revelation 20 "link it with the OT kingdom promises, a remarkable absence in the NT book that shows more links with the OT than any other book."[3]

Less obvious criticisms of first-century Judaism are found in Revelation. One such place is Revelation 11:2, which if the inner sanctuary is the church preserved, then "the outer court is perhaps the rejected Synagogue."[4] The point of the passage is that Israel, symbolized by the outer court, "is given up to the Gentiles in punishment for its sins."[5] Swiss theologian, Mathias Rissi wrote, "There is scarcely a sharper disparagement or condemnation of Jewish unbelief in the entire New

Testament than here in the Revelation of John."[6] The two gospel witnesses (11:3) would be rejected in the capital city (11:7) and be the cause of world wide celebration (11:9).

Revelation is recognized as more anti-Roman, than anti-Jewish.[7] But that does not mean the book does not contain judgment passages regarding anti-Christ Jews. Preterit (fulfilled-in-past) interpreter, J. Stewart Russell (1816-1895) argued that the expression *ga*, which some translate "earth," should be translated as "land."[8] He held that Revelation 6:10 and 8:7, for instance, referred to the land of Judea. Hence, the judgments were not describing global repercussions, but regional troubles.[9] But if one adopts the hermeneutical principle that initial local fulfillments project a later, further fulfillment (leading to consummation), then a global dimension is not completely ruled out.

Even if Russell's interpretation is rejected, there is not the slightest hint, despite the extensive borrowing of Old Testament imagery, that Israel is the localization of the kingdom of God. One land and to one people is not in Revelation. The older Jewish hope for Israel being the focal point of conflict and victory is not in Revelation. A territorial realization of an earthly Jewish triumph is significantly missing, because the gospel witness and spiritual conquest Christ aimed at was global, not regional.

Even the multinational character of the inhabitants of the final heaven was indirectly critical of the eulogization of Israel over other nations. It may seem to some that the numbering of the twelve gates after the twelve tribes (21:12) meant that Israel's superiority was being recommended—but such was not the case.

The writer showed that the twelve tribes were to be mystically, rather than literally, taken. By mixing the traditional order of the Jewish tribe names and an omission, a "new mythical twelvefold Israel" is introduced "to be companies gathered round the Apostles, than as the actual descendants of Reuben, Simeon, Levi, and the rest."[10] (John's description of the twelve gates differed from Ezekiel's [compare 48:31-34], who saw the tribal gates for individual tribal use.)

John had detribed the heavenly city though he retained the number of tribes in honor of their former roles. Rather than elevating Israel, the gates stress that God *used* Israel as a vehicle for his purposes. It was grace, not race that Revelation emphasizes. The new Israel, or the fully spiritual Israel, has replaced the old Israel. Moreover, the fact that the gates were never closed in all directions of the compass underscored the New Jerusalem as a city of the new humanity formed from numerous nations streaming through its gates.[11] We don't find in Revelation putting Israel on a pedestal. The closest kind of eulogizing of believing Israel occurs in 12:1-17, where the largely messianic people are presented positively. Even here there is no nationalistic emphasis.

Failure to emphasize the spiritual heritage of Israel, which was only carried forward by a remnant, or failure to accept "Israel" as a spiritual entity, some futurists interpret the New Testament in the light of the Old Testament, instead of the Old in light of the New. Consequently, the New Testament inadvertently becomes "subservient to the Old Testament."[12] And Augustine's famous maxim: "the New is in the Old concealed and the Old is in the New revealed"—becomes through premillennialism, accurately: "the New is by the Old restricted and the Old is on the New inflicted."[13]

Jesus deliberately chided a Zionistic trend within his own group of disciples when he said he was the "true vine" (John 15:1), that is that he was the true Israel. The Gospel of John, because of Christ and through Christ, calls for missionary inclusivism (not to be confused with soteriological universalism) to replace Jewish exclusivism. Thus evangelism should be denationalized.

Since Christ's coming Israel has receded of itself into the ranks of the other peoples and is included in the missionary charge to "all nations." . . . The history of the promise recedes behind the anti-thesis of "law and gospel." Israel is then, through the gospel of the justification of the sinner, demoted to the ranks of the nations and made "profane." Its history loses its special quality, becoming a matter of indifference: all men, whether Jews or Gentiles, are sinners and fall short of the glory of God. The justifying gospel is therefore directed towards all men, Jews and Gentiles alike. No special existence in the history of salvation can be ascribed to Israel any longer, because the Christian faith is not interested in world history, but only in the individual history of the justified sinner.[14]

The one sacrifice of Christ on the cross, the churches' missionary mandate, was not to anticipate a return to Old Testament patterns, but was to be a dedication to the enlargement of the spiritual kingdom through the message of Christ's all-sufficient atonement. The goal of the church is not back to Jerusalem, but from Jerusalem into all the world.[15]

We are left with a question that doesn't go away. Did John anticipate the dissolution of biological and racial differences? Since world history has been replete with racial conflicts, wouldn't race be removed along with hunger and thirst, sun, moon, artificial lights, tears, sea, death, sorrow, pain, temples, sin, and the curse on the ground?

Heaven consummates and celebrates the original unity of humanity, which racial conflicts have obscured. Scripture asserts our common origin. "Beneath the fact of racial sin lies the fact of racial unity."[16] Heaven elevates the unity of mankind under God never realized on earth.

If gender continues, does race? Peter Kreeft has legitimately argued, ". . . sexuality, like race and unlike clothes, is an essential aspect of our identity, spiritual as well as physical. . . ."[17] This contention involves still other facets of human life, such as languages.

Languages may go along with the continuation of race. In heaven we wonder which language(s) will be used for communication. Some Christians are accustomed to think that heaven will be like pre-Babel earth, when there was only one language in the world. Will heaven's new song be sung in a new language? Some hold language will be new, not in the sense of recent, but in the sense of qualitatively better. How new? So new that to some it will require the elimination of known language structures. Peter Kreeft, for instance, referred to a cosmic language:

> . . . In Heaven the fragments of the broken mirror will be melted into a great, multifaceted lens to prismatically reflect the white light of the single eternal Word into the many-colored words of our heavenly language.[18]

The earthly distinction of night will be no more in heaven (Rev. 22:5). In that case whatever language is used, adapted, or created, it may mean words for all the missing factors, one of which was "night," would be dropped.

Linguistic skills in heaven will reach new levels of attainment. If talents begun on earth will not be eliminated, but sharpened, developed, expanded (which would probably include languages), then we wonder which ones would be allowed to continue?

Which languages would go? Which languages will remain? Would any "dead" languages be resurrected? On top of these questions how would those who had a marvelous talent on earth with words apply their talent? Would Shakespeare and authors of his caliber need to pick up a new language? Would the gifted and talented have to start with a new language? If so, how could that talent be genuinely developed and perfected in praise of God, if one had to begin with a different language?

If there is a new language all must learn, we will not struggle with mastering it the way, for instance, we may have stumbled in learning a foreign language. Nor will a new language be required because the languages of the earth have been necessarily evil. Since people and their actions are evil and not their disciplines, then what prohibits the possibility of diversity of languages?

There is no need to seek uniformity of language, in one sense, if national and racial identities are retained. The only differences will be that each person will understand other persons perfectly, and there won't be the rivalries and enmities which have existed between racial groups such as Jews and Arabs, Saxons and Normans, Iraqis and Iranians, Serbs and Albanians, Sikhs and Indians, Flemish and Walloons.

Heaven is heaven because of its permanent unity, tranquillity, and harmony. The kind of unity heaven will preserve and enhance will be the kind in which diversities are allowed, recognized, matured, perfected, and cleansed of jealousies, of bitterness, and of pride. "The unity is perfect; these differences are not done away. Quite the contrary," wrote Klaas Schilder, "each person's individuality will come to full expression, and not one will find his own special pathways of life insignificant."[19]

Is there equality in heaven? Originally equality on earth was confined to mathematics. Equations are an important part of everyday life. There is something beautiful about a circle and about an equation. But what about equality on the social level?

Inequality yields variety and helps banish dullness. A long-distance driver, before whom the road is flat, fights tedium. An even road can be boring. Universal equality can be supremely dull.

Does racial equality mean we cease being black or Caucasian, or Chinese? Equal opportunity is the base for competition in the American dream. In heaven ahead, it seems, spiritual equality would override racial differences.

Justice systems are meant to punish those who mistreat

equals unequally. Congress doesn't legislate uniformity. Our courts don't penalize nonconformity. Their purpose is to make sure that differences are not made a pretext for favoritism. Class solidarity results from common equality, and legal complaints arise when one sex or one age is given preferential treatment, despite equality of qualifications. Inequalities, arising from abuse of minority groups, are instances of injustice. In heaven injustices will be no more. Jesus will reign in righteousness. Crimes against individuals and groups will be nonexistent.

Can equality and inequality coexist without conflict, without infringement and injustices? Need one or the other be extracted to produce or preserve heaven? Must inequalities be removed from heaven? Does perfection require total equality?

What did Jesus teach on equality which would have some connection with the hereafter? Is there a continuity from one location of the spirit world to another? A brief review of Jesus' statements on status issues would provide a basis for thinking ahead to the afterlife.

To Christ and his apostles, all are equally sinners, equally lost, and equally in need of God's grace. Not everyone who heard this from him was willing to agree to it. In a sense Jesus approached everyone as a potential believer. He felt no restrictions. The social taboos of his day did not prohibit him from mixing with those of low or no rank. He threatened the caste system of his day when he confronted and condemned the practices of the social upper crust. He violated relational rules which maintained inflexible restrictions regarding companionships, eating habits, and hospitality patterns. He befriended outcasts, such as the 'am ha'aretz, the unlearned country folk who were socially "at the bottom of the scale."[20] The wealthy classes became targets for his preaching. He declared that riches created a barrier to accepting him and the forgiveness of sins (Matt. 19:24).

Jesus declassed himself by going into the homes of collab-orationist tax collectors. The bottom line of his outreach was "offer the message to all." Consequently Christianity has had a strong emphasis on the value of the individual, despite the stigma society has attached to one's background, origin, or occupation. Artisans were as welcomed as aristocrats. In Christ plebeians were on equal standing with patricians. The uneducated had an equal share with the learned in the spiritual inheritance Christ secured. Second Peter began by emphasizing that his exiled readers had a faith "equal in honor" (1:1).[21]

The gospel has been revolutionary wherever caste thinking is a cultural force. The Brahmans in India, for instance, still have a locked-in superior feeling over so-called lesser castes.[22] Those listed in the *U.S. Social Register* or in the British *Debrett's Peerage and Baronage* may feel automatically better qualified for preferential treatment by God. As soon as baby rattles go into the mouths of infant members of the rich and powerful, their tiny feet are booted to begin their rise from the bottom rung of the social ladder.

Rank figured significantly in the thinking of Jesus' disciples (Matt. 18:1 NIV) when they asked, "Who is the greatest in the kingdom?" This desire was shared among their relatives as well. Jesus received a request for special favors by a mother for her two sons. She wanted Jesus to make sure one sat on his left hand and the other on his right hand in the kingdom (Matt. 20:20-28). Places of honor would be prestigious in her mind. Jesus said, however, that heaven did not operate by the same rules of struggling for rank and status. Special privileges were unworthy goals for those heaven-bound. Where one sat in heaven was less important than what one did. Jesus awarded duties in heaven not on the basis of physical closeness or to a parent's pull, but on the basis of faithfulness and loyalty to him on earth. Christ encouraged the faithful that they would be made rulers over many things, because they wisely handled few things on earth (Matt. 25:21, 23).

Near the end of his ministry Jesus told the parables of the talents (Matt. 25:14-20) and the parable of the ten minas (Luke 19:12-37). Both bore on the matter of rewards. Faithfulness, not endowment, was the point of the parable of the talents. Any gain was due to the investment of the benefactors, not because of the status of the possession.

Selfish interests and proud ambitions would spoil heaven. Our prime interest for recognition should be from God. All are to honor him ceaselessly. In the courts of heaven "the first will be last, and the last first." (Mark 10:31 NIV). But the reversal of roles did not mean the elimination of higher and lower responsibilities, for on several occasions Jesus spoke of those "least" in the heavenly kingdom (Matt. 5:19; 11:11).

The point of the streets of gold was its concentration, its value, its stability (not its durability), and its abundance. It may have been a sign of contempt to have the gold as something walked over, but more certainly the idea was that the gold belonged to everyone (Rev. 21:21). None will be deprived there. Elitist social groupings dissolve. Similarly, the jewels were jointly owned. The gems enhance the total city, not any individual inhabitants (21:11, 19-21). Those made joint heirs with Christ on earth will have entered into full enjoyment of riches without hindrance or threat of devaluation.

We have reviewed Jesus' stress on equality on earth and of the equality promised in the eternal state, but what about the matter of rewards? "If all is of grace and there is no merit whatsoever in believing, how can there be status symbols in a Christian heaven?"[23]

We are confronted with eschatological paradoxes that defy reconciliation. If all, finally, are conformed to Christ's image, do we lose our individual differences? Does being "like him" (1 John 3:2) mean the obliteration of self? We can't become

Jesus though we will resemble Jesus. We shall be equally saved, equally honored, equally purified, equally perfected, yet retaining our individualities. Jesus' parable of the talents seems to suggest that nonuse leads to loss, whereas receptiveness results in cultivation and wise investments produce measurable dividends. The dividends are partly received beyond the death line on the principle that ample sowing of seed yields a bountiful harvest (2 Cor. 9:6). And, adding to the irony, the most gifted excel because they are more receptive, resilient, and resourceful. Latent talents are expressed in overt action.

Whenever there are differences in heaven, they will not develop into strife and divisions. Heaven is a place of sharp contrasts. It would seem that the absolute melting pot is hell, not heaven.

Is status in heaven pictured in Revelation? Though the theme of disintegration may be part of the concept of hell's destruction, personal identity must be retained to guarantee individualizing suffering. Those who will have preceded us to heaven, the twenty-four elders, are pictured as *sitting* on thrones (11:16), whereas the four living creatures are said to *stand* around the throne of God (4:6). From this, Klaas Schilder concluded that the four living creatures, the cherubim, who are angels, were given less honor than the elders who are probably humans, thus man is superior to the angels.[24]

All humans recovered by Christ enter as part of the kingdom of priests (1:6). Every citizen has equal access to the twelve mammoth gates (21:25 [Isa. 60:11]). There is freedom of movement facilitating socializing. Any individual characteristics carried over into heaven are incapable of becoming a cause for jealousy and strife.

Differing glories will exist in the ranking of the redeemed, just as heavenly bodies vary in size and in the degree of their celestial shine (Dan. 12:3; 1 Cor. 15:40, 41).[25] The expression "hosts of heaven" (*see* Glossary) assumes that each star is unique. Any transformations, improvements, advancements exclude the change of being. ⟩

Many still wonder whether humans are transformed into angels in heaven. In chapter 3 we surveyed the extensiveness of the belief that deceased believers became angels. Are there any biblical grounds for thinking that people become angels after death? A careful reading of Revelation shows no hints or direct statements that humans ever have that opinion or outcome. Humans in heaven are redeemed. Angels in heaven are unfallen and unredeemed. It would be no advancement to go from being redeemed to being unredeemed. No song in heaven, anticipated and recorded by John, has as one of its themes thanksgiving for being made angels! The idea of persons, whether infants or adults, becoming angels is traceable to mystic writings, fairy tales, and sentimental poems. It is not found in or founded on Scripture.

Without our ego-orientations retained, how can our egos remain? This will be true of the saved as well as of the lost. That is the significance of Revelation 22:11 (niv): "Let him who does wrong continue to do wrong; let him who is vile continue to be vile; let him who does right continue to do right; and let him who is holy continue to be holy."

Revelation 22:11 means that hell must be perceived differently from what many assume. I believe that God doesn't send unwilling people to hell. They prefer it to heaven. Their actions reflect their attitudes. God's judgment is his "validation" of their decision. And it is, at the same time, a vindication of his own justice, for obstinate rejection receives appropriate measured response. The rich and the powerful, slave and free, male and female, courtiers and common citizens, "small and great" will stand before the great white throne for judgment (20:12). Interestingly, the same phrase "small and great" describes the redeemed in heaven, too (Rev. 11:18; 19:5). The comparison of small and great is a sociological expression, not a physical description of size. The intention, however, is not to suggest that God continues to allow earthly ranking to continue, but for descriptive purposes the lowly are no less privileged than those formerly treated among the great. The ultimate value of our solidarity with the rest of the redeemed would be that the apostles will be as approachable in glory as a near relative. The point of heaven is that God is equally near us and we are equally near each other.

Housing has a way of emphasizing social class. We know enormous differences between the poor sheds in the Deep South and the expensive mansions of millionaire-stars on the West Coast. A lot of jokes have been told about heavenly entrants who discover that the mansion they expected to live in in heaven was occupied with earth's homeless and that emergency housing on the outskirts is theirs. Jesus talked about his going away to prepare a place for his disciples (John 14:2). This Scripture has helped inspire such hymns as "Ivory Palaces." It has also been used as a springboard for interminable speculations about "mansion" life.

Modern speech translations of John 14:2 wisely abandon the word *mansion*. The Greek text clearly states "in my Father's house are many *rooms*." Some church fathers thought Jesus was suggesting stages of development here, that all in heaven would pass from one room to another.[26] But the significance of the word[27] is that of a permanent dwelling. In addition, what he was stressing was not opulence, not privacy, but diversity and security.

Before we deal with the reward allusions in Revelation, which bring equality in heaven into question, we need first to deal with the arguments from the Gospels, which might seem to argue against degrees of glory.

Matthew 20:1-16 is a case in point. This passage says everyone got the same wage, despite the fact that some began earlier

(20:10). Jesus was not thereby suggesting, however, that distinctions will be excluded from heaven, for Jesus told the parable in the first place to teach the meaning of "grace"—how that reward in any case is due to the goodness of the owner, rather than to the performances of the workers.[28]

Jesus did not exclude degrees of glory if we look again at the answer he gave to the mother who wanted special privileges for her sons. Jesus allowed the option of the Father to seat whomever wherever (Matt. 20:23). Paul seems to have advocated degrees of recognition in his Corinthian correspondence (1 Cor. 3:12-14; 15:41; 2 Cor. 9:6).

Abraham Kuyper (1837-1920) wrote:

> The heavenly state . . . is not based upon the principles of the French Revolution; on the contrary, in the assembly of just men made perfect we shall never ascend to the rank of apostle or prophet, probably not even to that of martyr. Nevertheless there is in heaven no saint whose sanctification is incomplete. In this respect all are alike.[29]

The ground of rewards was looked at extensively in chapter 11, Is Heaven Earned? One further comment is in order. We have yet to deal with those Christians especially mentioned for recognition in heaven in Revelation. What we discover is that Christians scarred in Christ's service, who received their wounds for adherence to Christ's despised Word (1:9; 2:2, 3; 14:12; 19:10), will be recognized for their troubles. But unlike Iranian martyr-soldiers, death is not a ticket to paradise. Those Christians who become martyrs for their loyalty to Christ are not rewarded because of their self-sacrifice. They did not seek martyrdom to earn their salvation. Salvation was already secured for them by Christ.

Also, we must not think of heavenly acknowledgment calculated according to the faulty standards of success on earth. Modern Christians are too enamored with newness, quantities, size, and statistics. Their basis for judging who has best served Christ is too much influenced by secular counterparts. We may think rewards for Christians will be based on church size or public notoriety. Heaven holds a lot of surprises then, because rewards will be calculated more on the basis of fidelity and suffering rather than on successful ventures, big budgets, and achievements.

Unflinching, loyal application of Jesus' teachings was promised to produce trials for Jesus' followers, and the "reward" the world gladly pays without restraint would attempt to discourage conformity to Christ and, at the same time, reasserts its contempt for Christ (Matt. 5:11, 12). Recognizing that any reward is the result of God's goodness, the next important emphasis is that reward is presented as a compensation for earthly suffering, not a testimonial to meritorious service. A common misunderstanding of rewards, when the full range of Scripture is not heard, is that it is a payment for a good performance, rather than God's honoring those whom the world has mistreated.

Revelation was written to console those headed for martyrdom. Those who arrived in heaven earliest were the twenty-four elders, who probably represented twelve patriarchs from the Old Testament and the Twelve, of whom John was one, who would be crowned for their ordeals, but who would refuse to wear them, since they wanted to exalt Christ who sent and sustained them (4:4, 10). Later in the book, Christ is pictured as wearing multiple crowns of royalty (14:14; 19:12).

Heaven has particular relevance for those facing death. John's first readers were to join the martyrs of old. Revelation 6:9-11 relates the fate of two representative martyrs, who, as a punishment, were denied an honorable burial. The expression "until" (6:11) indicated that other Christian heralds would be objects of the same injustices inflicted against the two witnesses.[30]

In heaven the martyred freely acknowledge the perils they

passed through, but they have no interest in rubbing in their exploits and endurance with the other redeemed. "The only reward which Christ's confessors really want, namely, God himself in the company of all who love him"[31] is the final sign that human conceit is not part of the sanctified.

Samuel Rutherford (1600-1661), who was imprisoned for teaching that the Law is king, not the King law, in his famous hymn "The Sands of Time Are Sinking" wrote:

> I will not gaze at glory,
> But on my King of grace,
> Not at the crown he gifteth
> But on his pierced hand.

Those lines could just as well be applied to the martyrs in Revelation. For them, just being with Christ in glory will be reward enough. Notice how the rewarding is put in terms of what they were deprived of:

Eating of the tree of life (2:7)

Not being hurt by the second death (2:11)

Eating of the hidden manna (2:17)

Given a white stone (2:17)—whereas in real life the black stone was the decision to have them executed!

Clad in white robes (3:4; 6:11)—the symbol of victory, whereas on earth their ignominious exits were cast in the form of seeming defeat!

The significance of the rewards was that they were described in terms of what the murdered witness-bearers lost or were deprived of in their tour of duty. Their rewards were not described as consolation prizes for those who met premature death, but were a celestial recovery of lost benefits. The life-maintenance aspect of the rewards prohibits considering the rewards as display items. Another feature, often overlooked, is what the martyrs brought to God, not what they received from God.

Revelation 14:13 (NIV) was addressed to and about martyrs. It reads, "Blessed are the dead who die in the Lord," what they have accomplished goes with them. The good works, it must be emphasized, go with them and are not sent ahead of them, lest readers think he was referring to advance merit. The works which accompany them are probably those of individuals who through their witness believed in Christ.[32]

The number of victimized Christians would grow (6:11, 12), until they would become 144,000 (7:9; 14:3).[33] Those who suffered for Christ were likened to be a percentage of the twelve tribes. Twelve tribes had a representative percentage from each making up the total. It was like a census of twelve battalions. Here the tribal aspect had less to do with the original twelve tribes and more to do with the totality of the believing group.[34] To maintain that the 144,000 were Jews or Christianized Jews misses the intentions of the author.

Disagreements proliferate in the interpretation of Revelation when the apocalyptic genre is treated as straight prose. It is especially true in references to Israel. Apocalyptic genre requires a consistent symbolic interpretation. In reference to the 144,000 John had not lapsed into a plug for Zionism. The point was not Jewish loyalist particularism. It was rather the apocalyptic technique of emphasizing a sizable number known and numbered by God from every conceivable origin within the visible organization which he used as his revelatory vehicle. John did not add a further group (an addition), but quickly abandoned and discouraged any figure fixation (a midcourse adjustment), for he wanted the readers to realize he shouldn't be kept to 144,000 (7:9). The main point was total support. Tribal origin would not get a person in, but the Father's choice would (14:1).

However large or small the body of faithful Christians, the

entire church would share in the protection of God. God's seal of safety was their guarantee of surviving the worst ordeal that Satan could concoct and inflict. Heaven is a place where earthly wrongs are righted and injustices exacted. That is the final equalizing and balancing of the moral tally sheets to which every Christian who suffers for his faith can look forward.

Momentarily the "overcomers" (2:7, 17, 26; 3:5, 12, 21; 11:11; 12:6-11; 14:3-5; 15:2) were overcome (11:7-10). The beleaguered troops of Christ (described in the section on seals) would be vindicated (described in the section on trumpets). Initially their sufferings were described as coming from unbelievers (chapters 4-11), but on closer examination their tormentors were inspired, fueled and driven by Satan and his representatives (chapters 12-19). The overthrow of evil, however, in all forms and force would come through Christ. Evil organizers, evil perpetrators, evil masterminds, evil agents, and evil originators are finally done away and righteousness triumphs.

Victory is the theme of Revelation. And accompanying the victory is vindication. Part of the vindication is expressed through vengeance, but it does not stop there. It goes on to celebrate the rewarding of those who have passed through tribulation for voicing the testimony of Jesus. The victimized share in Christ's vindication.

Near the end of the Revelation is a warning to those tempted to deny Christ in the face of opposition. Those first cast into the lake of fire were cowards (21:8).

> He sees *cowards* leading the cavalcade of the reprobate. However highly we value courage, we are not accustomed to think of cowardice as one of the deadly sins, let alone the first of them.[35]

In the foregoing we have investigated the place, problems, and potentiality of equality in the New Testament, with particular attention to Revelation. We have briefly examined how the early church was taught to view status. And we went on, using biblical principles, to speculate on the working out of equality against the background of development in matters, such as race, national identity, language, and literary gifts. The role of rewards, which initially seemed a denial of equality, in the context of specific texts in Revelation, was shown not to conflict with the gift character of salvation. Resounding praise of God takes priority over recognition of others.

Indeed a recognition of what individual Christians endured for Christ was always placed under the ordeal and victory of Christ. In the reserved references to rewards, therefore, we detect a design to brake the tendency to think of heaven as a place for human eulogies, testimonials to human toughness, and excessive self-interest.

Adopting that perspective one is faced with an assessment of what is being sung on earth about heaven. Some hymns have inadvertently fanned self-interest or they have been misleading. One such is Charles H. Gabriel's (1856-1932) 1928 stirring hymn, "O That Will Be Glory." The enthusiastic refrain goes, "O that will be glory for me, glory for me, glory for me." Such words should be sung with the balancing thought that Christ's glory is what matters most. While elements of the hymn exalt Christ and the glory of being "near the dear Lord I adore," the impression sometimes left is that the wording is too self-centered. The main desire of those in heaven is Christ's exaltation. Personal participation in heaven may have been the only intention of Charles Gabriel. Nevertheless we sing the refrain with mixed embarrassment and excitement. It may have been an innocent emphasis, but one needs to be aware of its self-centered sound.

One style of unity is to erase diversities. Intimations of heaven are, however, that "unity appears (in God) in the communion of existing diversities, and human plurality is maintained."[36] One cannot, however, proceed from this to maintain that dialectic thought is necessarily divine or that opposition to dialectic thinking is ultimately denounced by the maintenance of differences in heaven, for staring at us eternally are the two great opposites, heaven and hell, one side of which is desirable, the other is not.

When timelessness takes over, heaven's equality will eclipse earth's in the thoroughness and endurance of its application. Heaven's equality will combine distinctions without divisions, differences without disagreements, variations without vanity, individuality without jealousy, classes without clashes and unity without absorption. Whenever these elements are found on earth, we are experiencing a foretaste of heaven ahead!

16

Growth in Heaven ?

Should we anticipate growth in heaven? Will the redeemed pick up where they left off on earth? Will we progress in sanctification or receive it in fullness immediately on entrance? Will those deprived of physical, mental, and emotional development on earth be granted full growth instantaneously or will they be engaged in Spirit-guided and generated maturation? Will infants become instant adults or will there be a kindergarten section in the eternal ages? And, if ageless, is growth automatically excluded?

These questions have been asked numerous times. Although we cannot arrive at or supply final answers to many of them, there are some points, however, which can and should be made. We need to explore them as far as we can, yet realize that our responses are only provisional, and subject to a greater degree of error than those questions on which Scripture has more to say.[1] Affecting all responses will be the question of whether or not "space/time" questions have relevance in a state of timelessness.

Growth is a time-conditioned word. In heaven time is no more. We anticipate drastic changes for the better in heaven, of course, but since perfection is required both for entrance and for maintenance of its state, we can hardly conceive of perfection which needs growth.

Since in stand-still time there is no progression,[2] *development* is a word which cannot reflect a reality. If heaven is absolute timelessness, then growth is impossible as we know it. Growth implies imperfection, because the goal is still unreached. Conversely, perfection excludes growth.

Perfection precludes advancement in spiritual attainment. John Calvin (1509-1564) was the leader in this viewpoint in his first published work. He wrote:

> [Salvation] is nothing else than that union with God by which they are fully in God, are filled by God, in their turn cleave to God, completely possess God—in short, are "one with God." For thus, while they are in the fountain of all fulness, they reach the ultimate goal of righteousness, wisdom, and glory, these being the blessings in which the kingdom of glory consists.[3]

Similarly, John Owen (1616-1683) considered entrance into heaven as immediate perfection, denying the need for progress. He said that in heaven there was "the constant, immediate, uninterrupted enjoyment of God and the Lamb supplieth all."[4]

Older Roman Catholic theology took the same position. Englebert Krebs (1881-1950), professor of dogmatic theology at the University of Freiburg, Germany, was representative of standard Catholicism. In a 1917 treatise (frequently republished), he wrote that the departed soul who enters heaven enjoys an "instant imprint of the divine essence."[5] The rationale for this approach is supplied by Jesuit Edmund Fortman:

> As mobility, mutability, imperfection characterized pilgrim
> men, so immobility, immutability, perfection would charac-
> terize glorified men eternally.[6]

If Catholicism did not take this position, then it would appear that purgatory was a failure and a farce, for there is where
progress is to be made. One wonders whether the greater pressure to subscribe to this position came from Scripture or from
the need for dogmatic consistency.

Another view is that perfection should be followed by perfection. Paradoxical as this may seem, an American sports mentality practices this attitude at least every spring. The
expectation of today's demanding baseball fan, for instance, is
that umpires be perfect on opening day and then get better as
the season goes on.

One second-century Christian believed spiritual fine-tuning
continued in heaven. Origen (185-254) said Scripture saw
heaven as a place for spiritual advancement. John 14:2, 3, he
argued, supported this notion. "In my Father's house are many
rooms [*monai*]. . . ." Origen didn't use the King James Version,
but he came up with an idea similar to those who take
"mansions" as the only allowable phrase for the Greek word
monai [singular, *mone*]. *Monaie* is really resting places, stations, or halting places on the way to God.[7]

This seems to fit the agenda Paul saw of the Christian advancing from glory to glory (2 Cor. 3:18). J. C. Ryle noted that
holiness means the believer's "sense of sin is becoming deeper,
his faith stronger, his hope brighter, his love more extensive,
and his spiritual mindedness more marked."[8]

Progress in Christ-like graces is the goal of believers on
earth, but is it necessary in heaven? God's purpose for us is
"nothing less than the full stature of Christ" (Eph. 4:13c NEB).
But once we arrive in heaven in the intermediate state or enter
on the life of the eternal state, having been purified (1 John

3:2, 3), what need is there for further cleansing, growth, or improvement? The matter is debatable.

Clement of Alexandria (150-220), similar to Origen, took John 14:2 as an indication that saints in heaven would go through progressive moral stages. But the Johannine text cannot support that view, for *mone* means permanent dwelling place, not temporary stations on a journey.[9] What Jesus referred to was not continuous development, but "the bliss and permanence of heaven."[10] Moral development in heaven cannot be established from John 14:2.

Timelessness, despite its seeming limitations (chapter 8), supplies us with an early "out" if not an "easy" answer. Nevertheless, one of the paradoxes of heaven, as Scripture unfolds it, is that heaven is described in language that encourages us to think of development there. The New Testament words for "perfection" (*teleios* and *teleiosis*)[11] equate it with maturation. The word which most epitomizes the life of heaven suggests growth.[12] The Greek words for "perfection" seem to require a time lapse in a timeless state. This is one of the fundamental paradoxes facing any inquiry into the life of heaven.

Without the potential of development individualism in heaven would be fixed, halted, standardized, and made permanent. But to have everyone always on the same level would seem to leave heaven life without challenge, variety, and interest. Many anticipate that heaven will provide opportunity to see our gifts, powers, and talents raised to a new level of expression and employment. If there will be no capacity for creative change in ourselves, wouldn't that mean that those totally disabled in life would never experience the joy of advancement from what they knew on earth?

Furthermore, "Will there not be the possibility for development of talents cut short by a premature death or by unwanted early disabilities?" Joni Eareckson Tada, the quadraplegic, has written and sung about dancing with Jesus in heaven. Will she be disappointed about that recreational activity as well as other more physically productive movements?

The question may sound foolish or disrespectful, but everyone wonders. "How can there be redeemed individuals without differences?" To expect change, growth, and continuing improvements in heaven has respected backers. Abraham Kuyper, referred to earlier, wrote in his massive *The Work of the Holy Spirit:*

> [In heaven] there will be room for development. The complete sanctification of my personality, body and soul, does not imply that my holy disposition is now in actual contact with all the fulness of the divine holiness. On the contrary as I ascend from glory to glory, I shall find in the infinite depths of the divine Being the eternal object of richest delight in ever-increasing measure. In this respect the redeemed in heaven are like Adam and Eve in Paradise, who, though perfectly holy, were destined to enter more fully into the life of the divine love by endless development. . . . at the moment of their entering heaven the sanctification of the redeemed lacks nothing. Nevertheless their sanctification will receive the fullest completion when, risen from grace . . . they enter the Kingdom of Glory.[13]

Henry B. Swete (1835-1917), whose exegetical works still endure as valuable, recognized that "duration" in a timeless state seems—in street speech—to be "done in." Clocks and calendars will not be in heaven. Yet, he thought:

> There will be succession there, age following age, though no age, as it passes, takes from the total sum of that deathless life. Certainly this is assumed everywhere in the Bible, where the next world is called "the ages of the ages," (Phil. 4:20) and even once by S. Paul "all the generations of the age of ages" (Eph. 3:21). As the ages roll by, only that other ages may succeed them, the happy saints will find themselves nearer to God and to Christ, not raised as on earth by a cross, but drawn towards

the Throne by growing love and fellowship—of which there is no limit and no end.[14]

Can anyone describe stand-still time without using time? This is one frustration. The same frustration occurs in reference to the similar concept of agelessness. But can one delimit agelessness without timelessness? C. S. Lewis approached the subject in one of his shortest allegorical writings. He wrote,

> . . . no one in that company struck me as being of any particular age. One gets glimpses, even in our country, of that which is ageless—heavy thought in the face of an infant, and frolic childhood in that of a very old man. . . .[15]

Raymond Moody's description of heavenly agelessness is "the perfect age that includes all ages."[16] Peter Kreeft said, "The heavenly age is no age and all ages."[17] C. S. Lewis thought that perhaps age roles would be reversed or that characteristics of one age would be adopted by another, but that age was no longer an issue.

That may not be particularly reassuring or consoling; but the thought that the limitations known on earth are removed, corrected, disposed, and replaced may put more fire in our desire to reach heaven.

> Those now prevented because of mental illness or illness of soul will be there, healed by the great Shepherd of the sheep; those who are now too young will be there, fully matured, all worthy partakers. Children will not be seen there. For a child is in the state of becoming, and in heaven there is no immaturity and no marriage or birth or growth. For this reason parents cannot expect to "recognize" their own children there, though they will *know* them and sit at table with them.[18]

Someone speculated that children who go to be with Christ during the Intermediate State are enrolled "at school with the angels for his tutors."[19] Swedish mystic Emanuel Swedenborg

(1688-1772) wrote, "In heaven children advance in age only to early manhood, and remain in this to eternity."[20]

At this point, again, we are brought back to the initial question, "What is our source for this knowledge?" To accept Swedenborg here means we should ask our justification for accepting him later. If we accept the opinion of Swedenborg on the matter of how children appear, are we to accept his other postulations, such as his estimation that heaven is a collection of cities, with avenues, streets, and squares, where angels live in houses with courtyards, gardens, and lawns?[21]

We should *re*-ask ourselves: Can anyone know and has not God deprived us from knowing the ultimate state of heaven? John of the early church confessed, ". . . it has not appeared as yet what we shall be . . ." (1 John 3:2 NASB). Nevertheless, even evangelicals with the most impeccable credentials continue to speculate. When Jonathan Edwards (1703-1758) was forty-four he thought "the heavenly inhabitants . . . remain in eternal youth."[22] This stands in contrast to Klass Schilder who looked forward to being surrounded by mature adults. Edwards, however, did not specify what he meant by eternal youth. The 1988 *Newsweek* poll found that 32 percent of those sampled thought they will be the same age in heaven as when they die on earth.[23] Several writers have speculated from Jesus' resurrection at age thirty-three that our resurrection would mean we would be made youthful, like Christ, more specifically that we would appear "thirty-three eternalized."[24] In the three resurrections reported in the Gospels, each one was apparently restored to where they left off chronologically. But it has been argued that these were not resurrections in the fullest sense, but resuscitations (Luke 7:11-17; 8:49-56; John 11:1-44).[25]

As it is hard to imagine an orange without color, a cut diamond without sparkle, a square without sides, or a rose without smell, so it is difficult to imagine our continuation into heaven without personal self-identity and growth potential that go with perfection. It may be that in out-of-the body experiences, in which the person dying makes initial contact with beyond-life, which have been described in similar symbols (city, and so forth) such as are found in Revelation 21 and 22, that the person has been preconditioned to these figures either by the Scriptures themselves or by conceiving of them in dying in order to feel some relatedness.[26]

It seems that the areas in which we seek most development in heaven are those in which we are deprived on earth. Those without limbs, without hearing or sight, or those who lack total mobility, sensation, and independence look forward to shedding their disabilities, deformities, and disadvantages in heaven.

I suspect earth's intellectually lazy on earth would look forward to heaven if learning was no more—a thing of the past. In the Gallup poll published in 1982, although 33 percent believed they would grow spiritually in heaven, only 18 percent thought that they would grow intellectually.[27] This low figure may hide the belief that a lot of people may think they arrive smart, or what is equally likely, 82 percent of those polled thought heaven would not be boring because mental development was not part of heaven's activity.

The expressions "the kings of the earth will bring their splendor into it" and "the glory and honor of the nations will be brought into it" (Rev. 21:24, 26 NIV) may mean importations of sanctified culture and intelligence into heaven. Some disagree, however, arguing that earthly treasures are not transferred or transferrable.[28] The Greek word for "new" *(kainos)* means something made over, rejuvenated; not new *from* the old, but new *upon* the old.[29] In some cases it would have to involve new *replacing* old on the assumption that "nothing unclean" (Rev. 21:27) will be allowed into heaven, including unclean thoughts. But grant that the new earth is populated by the redeemed, then a residue of the glory of the old creation, rejuvenated, is allowable.

The Infinite Heaven apparently will include new objects (with a trace of the transcendent glory of God in former times) requiring new perception. Older writers stressed the new perception. Stephen Charnock (1628-1680) reasoned that heavenly knowledge will "consist not so much in knowing new objects as in knowing with an inexpressible clearness God and Christ, whom we know but in a glass."[30]

> There are depths of love that I cannot know
> Till I cross the narrow sea;
> There are heights of joy that I may not reach,
> Till I rest in peace with Thee.
>
> ISAAC WATTS

God's interest in education never flags. He himself is beyond learning, for he knows all. Yet his capacity for communication is unrivaled and unimprovable. It is likely, therefore, that heaven will be a school without bells, recess, and the tedium of boring instructors. Learning is part of heaven if progress is an element of its dynamic. Edwards said, "God is a spiritual being and he is beheld with the understanding."[31] We can identify with Richard Baxter (1615-1691) in his thirsting for this knowledge when he wrote in *The Saints' Everlasting Rest* (1650):

> If "the queen of Sheba came from the utmost parts of the earth to hear the wisdom of Solomon," and see his glory: how cheerfully should I pass from earth to heaven, to see the glory of the Eternal Majesty, and attain the height of wisdom, compared with which the most learned on earth are but fools and idiots?[32]

Learning will suit our condition and attitude. We shall be prepared to learn what by nature and disposition we were prohibited from learning. On earth our minds are the very basis of heavenly pleasure and development. If mind is inseparable from person, then heaven must have a place for the use of our minds.

Joseph Butler (1692-1752), considered the greatest Anglican theologian of the eighteenth century, commented on intellection as being foundational to heavenly perception. To him it was very likely that the new song and the New Jerusalem meant new minds. He wrote,

> As our capacities of perception improve, we shall have, perhaps *by some faculty entirely new* [italics mine], a perception of God's presence with us, in a nearer and stricter way; since it is certain he is more intimately present with us than anything else can be.[33]

Development of skills requires development of mind. Enjoyment and satisfaction is a function of intellect. States and conditions appeal primarily to the mind. To grasp even the heavenly state and condition minds must work. Moral maturation is not accompanied without mental maturation. If everything is known all at once, the joy of learning is destroyed. And as in all learning, the higher, deeper, holier knowledge will lead to higher, deeper, holier joy. H. R. Mackintosh (1870-1936) calculated that mental progress will be constantly going on in heaven, but at different paces. He wrote:

> Some will advance more rapidly than others in exploring the wide continents of the Divine love; some will push out more boldly than others into the infinite oceans of truth; some will assimilate more than others of the Christlike power to serve and wait. That will mean divergence. Variety of acquisition is a thing inseparable from progress, where progress is real.[34]

Of course, we must not think that there will be slow learners in heaven. Everyone excels there. Abraham Kuyper cautioned, "He who is least mentally endowed can enjoy the nearness of his God as richly as the most talented."[35] To have it otherwise would mean humans would have to pass an intelligence test for entrance. That would mean heaven was only for the so-called smart. "But God has chosen the foolish things of the world to shame the wise . . ." (1 Cor. 1:27 NASB). Our desire for knowing God will be strong and we shall not be discouraged in what we discover. We shall arrive at a knowledge of God, which will outshine anything we have known before, and what we learn will generate total glorifying and praising of God.

Static perfection would be as much a problem as no perfection. Just because there is no apparent growth in the angels,[36] that does not mean the saints will stop growing in knowledge. Our knowledge of God will never be so full that we have exhausted the inexhaustible wisdom of God. We will probably not be stuck with the ages we had when we left earth, but in heaven we will all be babes in knowledge—ready, eager, and able to learn as never before. The infinite wisdom of God will be shared on the particularly painful and puzzling experiences of life. Heaven will be a place where the mysteries of life are made plain, where complex truths are perceived quickly, and where lost opportunities are reopened.

> Not now but in the coming years,
> It will be in the better land,
> We'll read the meaning of our tears,
> And there sometime we'll understand.
>
> We'll catch the broken threads again,
> And finish what we here began;
> Heaven will its mysteries explain,
> Ah then, Ah then, we'll understand.
>
> MAXWELL N. CORNELIUS

"Will what we have 'learned' on earth be lost?" We have already indicated, in answering the questions of gender and equality, that there is a likelihood of abandoning some knowledge, and of the possibility of grasping, broadening, and building select earthly information. Paul said, ". . . Then I shall know fully just as I also have been fully known" (1 Cor. 13:12 NASB). Previous talents will be retained rather than replaced, improved and refined rather than ditched.

A God-centered, God-generated improvement of what is, is foreign to modern evolutionary-based anthropology. A man-generated eschatology, for instance, waits for the final development of the ideal man. Perfection of man *by* man is the goal of secular humanism. Herbert Spencer's (1820-1903) sociological scheme for the future of man in his social and cultural dimension was for the arrival of heaven at his own hands. A Christian rejects any form of perfection claiming to be humanly produced.

Yet theists, such as Pierre Teilhard de Chardin (1881-1955),[37] famous for his cosmological evolutionary theory, elevated the "within" factors and said they are the indispensable ingredient for the vision of God's reign.

One of the more interesting wrinkles in contemporary Christianity has been the eschatology which seeks to retain earthly events into eternity without the perpetuation of selfhood. Known as "process theology," it accommodates secular psychology, which says there is no soul, yet retains what self has gone through on earth in a Christian "forever." Alfred North Whitehead (1861-1947) fathered the view that there is no survival of persons, because there are no persons. "There can be no survival of anything like a substantive person, because a substantive person never existed."[38] Because self has never actually existed, self cannot continue into heaven. Charles Hartshorne (1897-   ), also one of the early leaders in the movement, insisted that while persons exist, substantial soul does not. They argued that while human biographies are remembered, they are remembered not individually, but remembered collectively in Cosmic Consciousness or a recording agent called God.[39]

The process theology movement, which is largely American in origin, emphasizes development as the key to heaven more than do classical or contemporary Christian conservatives. Since process theology is hailed as the most ecumenical theology and a school of thought that has become a major movement, it would be in the interests of a better informed Christian public to see how process theologians speak of development in the hereafter.

While Schubert Ogden dismissed the continued subjective existence after death,[40] others make the God-in-all theory (pan*en*theism—*see* Glossary) extending into the hereafter as the retention and refinement of matter and man. The ultimate goal is to reach a one-world religion in time before eternity becomes everything. In process theology "Each religion . . . mediates authentic subconscious prehensions [this means "feelings"] of the progressive reality that is God."[41] As one modern proponent writes, heaven "interpenetrates all things, is present in all things, bearing the secret of the potential and inwardness and unfolding of all things."[42]

In process theology heaven is where antecedent thrusts, drives, and aims produce a new synthesis called "concrescense." Norman L. Geisler described "concrescense" as follows:

> Once an actual entity has become objectively immortal, it can act as an efficient cause for other actual entities that is in the process of "concrescence" or coming to be.[43]

While individual earthly experiences are lost, in the cosmological memory the successes are preserved in a cumulative, processive advance.[44] Heaven becomes a grand energy-event within the person. In process theology, all participate in a happy future. But that does not mean that heaven is pushed ahead or made more distant. The following quote has a semi-conservative ring to it. Wink sounds evangelical in parts. What he wrote must be read carefully:

> If heaven is not some other reality but the inner essence of present reality in its fullest potentiality, then the mystical "ascent" is not out of the body and into a wholly incorporeal spiritual realm, but *into the body's very own essence as the temple of the Holy Spirit within us* [his underline].

Wink stresses that spiritual development assumes corporeal continuance:

> What seems to be qualitatively different from normal body experience is indeed qualitatively different, but not because it escapes the body. On the contrary, it appears to be so different precisely because the inner essence of bodily existence has for once been actually apprehended. The beatific vision does not involve renunciation of the stuff of humanity, but the recognition that our human stuff can itself become translucent, incandescent with the fire of the divine which indwells us.[45]

Therefore, process theology begins by motivating each person to win for justice by justice, to seek gains for those victimized by corporate sin and conglomerate structures, which Wink and others equate with the biblical "principalities and powers." At the same time, they look forward to the cosmic setting-free of creation.

> For heaven is not simply the "within" of all present reality: it is also the womb of the future, that toward which God entices us by offering us in each moment new ways of being more real, more vital, more united with that which tends toward the good of the whole.[46]

The Scriptures stress individual process. The process, initially, occurs on earth and concerns, unfortunately, man's "advancement" in sin. Process theologians, however, ignore this aspect, for it militates against universalism.

Jesus spoke of the process of externalizing the internal, of evil hearts producing and participating in evil acts (Mark 7:21; Matt 7:17). Paul said, ". . . charlatans will make progress from bad to worse . . ." (2 Tim. 3:13 NEB). "When Scripture speaks of a 'process,' it does so in reference to this transition from man's corrupt heart to his own sinful activity."[47] The Bible's emphasis on process, therefore, is not what process theologians consider valid, for to them human sinfulness is not real. As with pantheism, so with panentheism, there is a superficial understanding of human depravity and, in some cases, the denial of endemic sinful natures.

Both cosmic and cumulative development are capitalized in process thought. Their eschatology is the salvaging of what is good so that nothing is lost. The perishing subject becomes the immortal object. Unlike Alfred N. Whitehead, considered the founder of the movement, and like his chief disciple Charles Hartshorne, John B. Cobb, Jr. (1925-   ) views God as a living Person, but a God who is discovered in experience rather than through cognition, and who preserves *our* individual beings in the divine future. Norman Pittenger (1905-   ) is content to view the future life as the retention of all achieved values of a man's life in the divine memory.[48]

In chapters 13 and 15 we discussed whether or not gender and gifts are preserved in the Infinite Heaven. On the matter of preservation and improvement of the God-initiated conditions, gifts, attainments of earth, there is some similarity between the present study and process thought.

> The notion of the retention of past values in the divine memory, as it has been developed in process theology, is certainly not to be rejected in its entirety. It may well play a part in our eventual statement of a contemporary eschatology, both in respect of the past values of particular human lives and in respect of the

many temporary values of natural beauty, including animal life, and cultural artifacts, which we can hardly suppose to be transferable, in their present actuality, to a resurrection world.[49]

While Hebblethwaite's approach fits into a new heaven/new earth eschatology (*see* chapter 3), one must realize that process theologians do not mean that the God of classical theism is the God they are talking about. In process theology one part of God changes constantly. God is bipolar: (1) He has a timeless side or transcendent nature; and (2) he has an immanent nature that is part of cosmic processes. For them the God of the Bible is the God of relativity. The biblical God, however, is not the God of process theologians.

To them the Infinite Heaven is not considered an ultimate think tank, because prehension (feeling) replaces comprehension (intellection) as the basis for knowing. As they see it heaven is feeling-oriented rather than fact-rooted. For them "Revelation is monolithically defined as lived experience, . . . [which] takes little account of the validity and centrality of objective special revelation."[50]

Nothing is inherently wrong, evil, or erroneous in process theology. Each contributes to the whole. Hence, it accepts differences not as evils to be shed, but as differences to be assimilated, refined, affirmed, and preserved. "Salvation becomes the fulfillment of human potential rather than deliverance from sin and death."[51]

Advocates of this position are at the controls of a hovercraft theology, that is, they are sure not to touch down on any one position. For process theology devotees, relativism is not a naughty word to shun or to skedaddle. It appeals to those who have judged religious truths on the basis of feelings, rather than on the basis of the Bible. It attracts those precommitted to universalism (the belief that none can perish). It suits an anti-intellectual age and pluralistic atmosphere. Its characteristics make it ideally suited to lead the way for a one-world religion, which, in the view of many Christian futurists, will be the religion of the final Antichrist personage.

Revelation abounds with verbal images. In some places it uses architectural splendor, in other places agricultural success. Heaven's outward signs of opulence suggest, at the same time, a wealth of opportunities in personal dimensions. We should not limit the Infinite Heaven to displays of material prosperity. Further dimensions of interpersonal pleasure and inner-personal growth should also be included.

We have presented the opinion that the finalization of heaven has no limits either in the capacity to excel in depth and degree of understanding. The knowledge of God, especially, will take priority over any other disciplines continued. Unlike the acquisition of the knowledge of God on earth, it will not be subject to erosion, exaggeration, and error. Because of a fuller and more accurate insight into the character of God, all other activities, occupations, and duties will reach the ideals cut short by sin in the Garden of Eden.

Answers as to what the Intermediate and Infinite States of heaven bring, in this point in time, are estimated rather than established. What the final product is or will be is known only to God and those to whom the Lord has already called into his eternal presence.

What we say is always a poor approximation of what God has decided. Therefore, in the final analysis, heaven will be the fulfillment of *God's* expectations first—before and above our own expectations. This perspective of growth underlines any understanding of growth in heaven ahead.

17

Ownership
in Heaven

?

Modern views of marriage throw out ownership as both honest and humane. Even mutual ownership is sometimes scorned. The saying is "People are not property." The Hebrew culture, however, had no hesitations in viewing the property aspects of marriage. We think almost exclusively of marriage as a partnership; they thought of it in terms of ownership. While we may be critical of the Hebrew comparison, we cannot avoid the concept of ownership entirely, for we use the possessive pronoun "my" as in "my husband," in "my wife," or "my marriage."

Certainly, we consider marriage a legal contract. Marriage is a binding relationship in the eyes of courts. Property settlements, divorcing couples painfully discover, are part of the termination of the relationship.

To the Hebrews, also, "Property was like people." They felt wedded to the land. Ironically, one word we associate with

295

heaven comes out of the marriage analogy. In *Isaiah* 62:4, "Beulah" (a woman's name) is used with three other women's names to describe the land of their inheritance. "Beulah" meant "newly married." The many inhabitants of the land would be her possessors.[1] The word occurs once in the Old Testament:

> It will no longer be said to you, "Forsaken,"
> Nor to your land will it any longer be said, "Desolate";
> But you will be called, "My delight is in her,"
> And your land, "Married";
> For the LORD delights in you,
> And to Him your land will be married.
>
> (Isa. 62:4 NASB)

Here are four Hebrew women's names, translated for us in the New American Standard Bible as "Forsaken," "Desolate," "My delight is in her," and "Married." "Beulah" is the word *married*, the passive participle of *ba' al*, which conveyed the ideas of both physical intimacy and joy.[2] The LXX (Septuagint) puts *oikoumene*, or "be called inhabited" for "married." Both the Hebrew and the Greek substitution call attention to owning or possessing.[3] The concern of God for Israel was asserted here in human, relational terms. Israel would not be abandoned, but provided care and protection which came through her marriage.

Two hymns to my acquaintance on heaven employ "Beulah land" as a figure. C. Austin Miles' "Dwelling in Beulah Land" and Edgar Page's "Beulah Land" employ the figure of "Beulah" for heaven.

Each hymn expresses different moods. The mood of Miles' hymn is rousing:

> Let the stormy breezes blow, their cry cannot alarm me;
> I am safely sheltered here, protected by God's hand;
> Here the sun is always shining; here there's naught can harm me,
> I am safe forever in Beulah Land!

The feeling conveyed in Page's hymn is consoling:

> O Beulah Land, sweet Beulah Land,
> As on thy highest mount I stand,
> I look away across the sea,
> Where mansions are prepared for me,
> And view the shining glory-shore,
> My Heaven, my home forever more.

The latter hymn may show the influence of *Pilgrim's Progress*, Part 1, where John Bunyan (1628-1688) describes the midpoint phase between life and death as Beulah land, a kind of para-eschatological state. Physicians refer to a terminal patient as entering the comatose stage, a deep coma, from which the person does not return. It was this idea expressed in *Pilgrim's Progress* and carried over into Page's hymn "Beulah Land." Bunyan wrote of Beulah land as follows:

> The country of Beulah, whose air was very sweet and pleasant; the way lying directly through it, they solaced themselves there for a season. Yea, here they heard continually the singing of birds, and saw every day the flowers appear in the earth, and heard the voice of the turtle in the land. In this country the sun shineth night and day: wherefore this was beyond the Valley of the Shadow of Death, and also out of the reach of Giant Despair; neither could they from this place so much as see Doubting Castle. Here they were within sight of the City they were going to: also here met them some of the inhabitants thereof; for in this land the Shining Ones commonly walked, because it was upon the borders of heaven. In this land, also, the contract between the Bride and the Bridegroom was renewed.[4]

(Sounds a little like a Protestant purgatory without the painful purgation part found in Catholic views.)

Edgar Page carried on the theme of possession from the Beulah land reference in Isaiah 62:4. The first stanza: "I've reached the land of corn and wine, and all its riches freely mine." In 1911, when he wrote this hymn, people were apparently less critical of possessions than we are.

Today we would prefer to be less possessive looking in our hymns, for we associate it with selfishness. With some, renunciation of ownership is more godly than gleeful ownership. Yet we expect Lotto winners to *claim* their prizes, and to celebrate a little after they get their first check!

"Living for things" should sicken Christians. Extravagance among the ruling classes, who seemed to own everything, may have been what inspired Thomas More (1478-1535) in his *Utopia* (1506), when he wrote of the ideal state without private ownership. To him the perfect communal life required forced relocation or voluntary moves every ten years. By such means an equalization of existence could be achieved. "It is clear that, according to More, ownership is the source of misery."[5]

Abundance desensitizes us. The famous French author, Simone de Beauvoir found this true. She said, "The possession of an object takes away its newness."[6] In our own country, social scientist Christopher Lasch observed that the cycle of immediate gratification leads to a perpetual unsatisfied desire.[7]

An alternative lifestyle that reacts to materalism is renunciation, self-denial, leading occasionally to forms of monasticism. Anyone who lives in a Christian commune could be very disturbed to discover on his arrival in heaven that the possessiveness he denounced on earth permeates the place. Would monks claim anything as theirs in the hereafter?

And should we admire their practice of owning nothing? An on-paper ownership document does not mean that we have escaped psychic ownership. Refusal to actually possess an object does not necessarily mean we escape materialism. Frenchman Jacques Ellul said, "The use, manipulation, and approval of the things of this world is no less dangerous than owning them."[8]

Are we more occupied with consumption than possession? Or is our drive more to possess to consume? Our greater problem appears to be consumption (not the lung disease, but the gullet addiction). Consumption is a step beyond the web of consumerism. A Christian should be one freed from being over-occupied with transitory things (Matt. 6:21). Overvalued possessions can possess the owner.

Realistically, we cannot totally avoid attachment to things. To gain a perspective on ownership, we need to ask what Scripture says. Before we consider what the Bible says about possessions in heaven, we need to take a look at what it says about possessions on earth.

Ownership was assumed and incorporated into the Ten Commandments. Behind the misuse of God's honor (in his name), the wasting of another's life, the taking of what does not belong to us, and the coveting of what others have is the principle of individual ownership (Exod. 20:15, 17; Deut. 5:19, 21; 27:17; Prov. 22:28).

In Old Testament terms "inheritance" meant "possessions." Israel was God's own possession (Ps. 2:8; Isa. 19:25), as later believers were said to be God's property (Eph. 1:18; 1 Peter 2:9). God was the possession of his people (Ps. 16:5, 6; Josh. 13:33). God's ownership of the land put Israel's possession of it on a secondary level (Lev. 25:16, 23).

The priority of God's claim was frequently recited in Israel's worship. His ownership was the central presupposition of biblical economics.[9]

> The earth is the LORD's and everything in it;
> The world, and all who live in it (Ps. 24:1 NIV).

The New Testament continues the theme of God's absolute ownership. Christ was included as co-owner of heaven and earth (Heb. 1:2). And we were joint-heirs with Christ (Rom. 8:17; Heb. 1:2). Ownership for the Christian was primarily of intangibles, the blessings of forgiveness, righteousness, acceptance, reconciliation from God. Ownership was in our vertical relationship with God. We are Christ's sheep (John 10:14). We were given to Christ by the Father (10:29). The church is sanctified, which meant it was his body, claimed as his possession: "to purify for himself a people that are his very own . . ." (Titus 2:14 NIV). Our bodies are more God's than ours (1 Cor. 6:19, 20). We are Christ's slave-servants (Rom. 6:18, 19) and "Christ Jesus has made me his own," wrote Paul (Phil. 3:14). We live as strangers and pilgrims in this world (Heb. 11:13), journeying toward heaven where our true citizenship is (Phil. 3:20). Even though we may lose our earthly belongings through robbery, we rejoice that our heavenly inheritance is safe (Heb. 10:34). Of all the New Testament books, Hebrews stresses what "we have" in and through Christ (4:14; 8:1; 10:19, 23; 13:10, 14) "in such a way as to promote a future-oriented, historical faithfulness."[10]

Earth is the sphere where the blessings of the coming age begin to be realized and can be relied on. Already here for enrichment and enjoyment are the ultimate blessings. We are already seated with Christ (Eph. 2:6). We have already arrived at the Zion above (Heb. 12:22). Our possessions in Christ are secure. Unlike the claimed prizes of earth, our heavenly inheritance is "imperishable and undefiled, and will not fade away, reserved in heaven for you" (1 Peter 1:4 NASB).

Revelation describes heaven in more detail than any other New Testament book. And it is there that we are confronted with the topic of ownership. As in the other New Testament books, so in Revelation, we have reaffirmations of God's final, ultimate, and inclusive ownership.

Revelation pictures Christ in charge of his chosen clergy (1:16, Christ holding the seven stars or pastors in his right hand). Christ only had the right to open the secret book of destiny (5:1-10). What belonged to Christ was also praise, glory, honor, wisdom, and power, for he alone authored and finished salvation (7:10; 12:10; 19:1). What belongs is also what is owned. Christ has exclusive right, deed, and certification to our final salvation.

While on earth, Christians are marked as belonging to Christ (3:12; 7:3; 22:4, 5) permanently and prominently (the forehead). The theme of Revelation 7 is that believers are Christ's property and he will not abandon us in our conflicts with errorists and the punishments they devise. "[It] . . . re-assures the faithful that the awful events of the eschatological tribulations are not a sign of eternal doom, but of hope for those who are faithful to God."[11] The same confidence builder is used in chapter 11 where the heavenly city is measured (11:1). The measurement was a technique to illustrate God's record keeping. He would not neglect his more essential prop-erty, the prophets who represented Him (11:11).[12] Those as-saulted, assailed, and beaten for the testimony of Christ were repeatedly assured in Revelation of God's faithfulness to them in their faithfulness. Repayment for losses came in the giving of white clothing, crowns, and complete access to all of heaven (21:3, 7). The dispossessed will become the heavenly re-possessed. (For a discussion of the meaning of rewards to the martyrs, turn to chapter 15).

In brief, that is some of what Revelation says on the posses-sions theme. Next, we should inquire how these principles work out in application.

At the start, it is assumed in the above passages that *what-ever we have in heaven we did not take with us.* That is why there are no luggage racks on hearses. We come into this world naked and leave it naked. Advance shipments to the other side are tacitly impossible and taboo.

Second, *heaven stresses corporate ownership.* We are not given deeds to heavenly real estate. It is jointly owned. The wealth of heaven belongs equally to everyone. Whereas commu-nal living develops rivalries of one type or another (sometimes we can be jealous of space), envy will be eliminated in heaven.

Finally, *to deny private property inevitably ends in denying privacy.* And that could lead to a concept of corporate personality which is a denial of individuality. As entrance into heaven is on an individual basis, for we enter as one person, not several, so that individuality continues throughout the eternal state. Recognition of the martyrs will be on an individual basis, even though there will be a single classification of martyrs. Our unique roles on earth will be both recognized and celebrated. To take that away is to take us out of heaven!

Mystics say they will eventually blend into the total One, the absorption of the individual into the corporate whole, so that individuality disappears. The late medieval German mystical work, *Theologia Germanica* says,

> In Heaven there is no ownership. If any there took upon him to call anything his own, he would straightway be thrust out into hell and become an evil spirit. [13]

Peter Kreeft cited this quote approvingly and added an expansion:

> . . . To *have* truth is to be dogmatic; to *have* goodness is to be proud; to *have* beauty is to be vain; to *have* joy is to be miserable with the fear of losing it. God . . . is the only Haver. . . . [14]

I submit, however, that that position necessarily leads to the typical mystical obliteration of selfhood. Kreeft maintains the retention of selfhood—"the ultimate possession."[15] At the same time, he maintains personal ownership of virtues is out. The problem, however, is that there is no realistic, credible way of showing how selfhood is retained given those conditions. Selfhood is known through individual traits. To remove the traits is to remove the self. Self-detachment leads to self-destruction.

Another conclusion is more likely. Throughout our discussions on sexuality, equality, and growth, we have maintained that individuality persists and is affirmed by God. In a perfected state, what is impossible on earth is possible and actual there. We can have our differences, but these differences are welcomed, affirmed, maintained, and developed. All contribute to the praise of Christ, and Christ's praise is furthered by the individual's maximum maturation.

> The only bond of unity between our present and future bodies is that they will be "owned" successively by the same personality.[16]

Kreeft's position flirts with the denouement of personhood in heaven. The new heavens and the new earth will be a revision of terrestrial and celestial matter, but in a better form. The resurrected Christ is our only model of what *we* shall be in heaven. Unlike Christ, however, our ego will need transformation. Our self will be retained but revised. In our spiritual resurrection bodies we shall be identified, somehow, by what we were on earth.

C. S. Lewis argued similarly:

> [Citing *Rev.* 2:17] . . . "To him that overcometh I will give a white stone, and in the stone a new name written, which no man knoweth saving he that receiveth it." What can be more a man's own than this new name which even in eternity remains a secret between God and him? And what shall we take this secrecy to mean? Surely, that each of the redeemed shall forever know and praise some one aspect of the divine beauty better than any other creature can. Why else were individuals created, but that God, loving all infinitely, should love each differently? . . .[17]

Our view of heavenly ownership, then, recognizes the rights of God over all, who is the source and sustainer of all benefits, temporal and eternal. He is the Giver and Gift combined, our ultimate Benefactor and Benefit. Without him all possessions cease. He can give and he can take away as seems good in his sight.

Flowing from God to us through Christ is the sterling gift of righteousness. Without that given and relied on garment none may enter heaven. The initial and eternally lasting possession both on earth and into eternity is the freely donated covering of Christ's perfect righteousness. None in heaven is without it.

The essence of salvation both on earth and in heaven is the wholeness of the individual. Wholeness, however, can be eroded by the diminution of personality. Individual development and recognition in heaven are also realities of the Infinite Heaven, which find their fulfillment in the praise of Christ alone as the Author and Finisher of faith, the Alpha and Omega of our understanding of faith. Selfhood is a gift from God. He will continue, and mature of self under his power and grace. Spiritual possessions, and the rewards of the martyrs, are not denounced, but applauded in the final heaven. We will celebrate the Lord as the Giver and Provider.

Perfection of ownership does not mean we lose it, but that we view spiritual advances and attainments differently. Whatever we are and whatever we become belongs to God, although we are vehicles through which his greatness is shown.

18

Memory
in Heaven

?

Memory and immortality have a long association. The best pre-Christian comfort human philosophers could propose was the perpetuation of the deceased in thought. The ancient Greeks, such as Homer (est. from 850 to 1200 B.C.), held that when a person's soul separated from the body at death, he continued in the minds and memories of his survivors.

Plato (427(?)-347 B.C.) went further. He held that immortality was more than the spirit of the departed living in the memories of those left. In his *Phaedo* we have Plato's version of immortality. In one of his dialogues he shows Socrates, his teacher, extracting from an uneducated slave the proof of Euclid's 29th theorem (the theorem of Pythagoras) that the square on the hypotenuse of a right-angled triangle equals the sum of the squares on the other two sides. The slave had never been to school, much less have read, yet he knew the answer. Plato argued from this that knowledge is remembrance. And from remembrance he argued that man pre-existed. An *a priori* (beforehand) element is buried in humans, and learning is drawing out what is originally there. The closest humans ever get to heaven, which for him was the realm of Idea World, was (1) to draw from within timeless universals capable of being recalled from memory; (2) to realize that this unusual knowledge was due to a pre-existent state.

Ironically, within organized Christianity today concepts have arisen which are neo-Platonic. These theories are advanced by those who have rejected the traditional concept of a spiritual bodily resurrection. By biblical standards the position of David L. Edwards is hardly Christian. He held that men live on in God's memory.[1] H. H. Price (b. 1899) advocated the view that life's collective memories continue in an "image world" beyond death, that the disembodied mind lives on in a telepathic relationship with others.[2]

Telepathy is a form of spiritualism. The claim is made that thought, feeling, and desires are communicated with other people at a distance. Contact with the dead by the living is the ultimate expression of telepathic powers. Shirley MacLaine refers to her telepathic contacts (counselors) as human telephones.[3]

A telepathic concept of heaven seems to be compatible with Plato's Idea World. But instead of the person's drawing from what is past, there is contact claimed for persons who have gone into the future.

Telepathy is irreconcilable with the Christian Scriptures for several reasons: First, it usually begins with and is based on a denial of the Bible's teaching on resurrection. Paul Badham argued, unsuccessfully in our opinion, that Jesus used telepathy.[4] The evangelists, but especially John, showed Jesus having advanced knowledge of others' thoughts, but he also showed awareness of nonmental things. His knowledge as God incarnate raised his awareness outside the human plane.

Three other objections show telepathy to be counterproductive to confidence building and comfort regarding the hereafter. Foremost development in the hereafter is automatically excluded if heaven is only feeding on good memories. It is hard to look forward to the hereafter where the self is unreal, and heaven is but an image. Telepathy, a nonentity, assumes personhood. Our individuality is reduced to thoughts only. This conflicts with the idea of individuality presented in Scripture. In the Bible "the name is the person."[5] Our names are linked with the reality of our individuality.

Another neo-Platonic theory, which so reinterprets resurrection as to deny it, is the view of John Hick of Birmingham, England. Hick's hypothesis was that another "us"—a replica of our earthly body—exists. He maintained that somewhere God has provided for a duplicate but better "us" in a different space, subject however to similar physical laws. Our so-called replica possesses both memory and self-awareness of our prior selves.[6] Hick substituted replication for resurrection. He says a resurrection is a replica of us. He wrote:

> It is . . . an intelligible hypothesis that after my death, I shall continue to exist as a consciousness. I shall remember both having died and some at least of my state of consciousness both before and after death.[7]

Paul Badham, who rejected Hick's theory but was attracted to it momentarily, thought resurrection of our dead selves would be a recreation "on another planet on another galaxy."[8] From a biblical perspective, these views are deficient, and rather than being postulated by persons who have established they came from God, the theories are projections of individuals who are uncomfortable with the traditional Christian understanding of self and of the hereafter. More so with Hick, but to a degree with Badham, their views create an identity crisis. With Hick,. this is because the living replica would also of necessity die, since the mortality of replication would be intrinsic to the predeath replication. With Badham the identity crisis is less obvious. He does not escape the criticism that to hold on to replication in another sphere erodes the oneness of individuality in Scripture.

Replication is little more than an ingenious dodge of biblical Christianity. It is Platonism warmed over, the Hollywood "stand-in" approach projected into heaven, an instant replay of spirits where each person has a celestial lookalike.

Plato's concept of preexistence did not go so far as modern theories of reincarnation. With him it was preexistence in the World of Ideas, but with reincarnationists preexistence is confined to lives in other "spent" lives.

Modern reincarnatists reduce heaven entirely to memories of former lives. Probably the most widely read advocate of heaven as remembrance is the actress-dancer Shirley MacLaine, whose autobiographies *Out on a Limb* (1983), *Dancing in the Light* (1985), *It's All in the Playing* (1987) and *Going Within: A Guide to Inner Transformation* (1989) describe the evolution of her thinking on reincarnation, remembrances of former lives, and soft-sell propagandizing for New Age thought. In *It's All in the Playing*, she wrote,

> Since we have all lived so many lifetimes over so much of the planet's experience, it is very emotional when you finally remember something that you know belongs to your experience, but which you have been unable to integrate before.[9]

Every autobiography will dredge the memory, but one feature of MacLaine's works, beginning with *Out on a Limb*, has been the belief that she should explore memory in other existences.

Memories of former states, she contended, puts us in touch with what we already know.[10] We know the answer before the question is asked.[11] She considered each person in possession of a "higher unlimited superconsciousness."

> The soul that has been through incarnation after incarnation and knows all there is to know about you because it *is* you. It is the repository of your experience. It is the totality of your soul memory and your soul energy. It is also the energy that interfaces with the energy which we refer to as God. It knows and resonates to God because it is a part of God. As in the mind of man there are many thoughts, so in the mind of God there are many souls.[12]

Memory becomes valuable baggage which we checkout with and checkin with in our next incarnation. "We carry the memory into each incarnation and those memories need to be resolved and cleared if we are to go on to a higher enlightenment."[13] She also believed that memory is cellular or in the muscles of the body.[14] In *Going Within* she said memory is in the body's DNA.[15] Her view of memory suffers from the same defects found in the view of H. H. Price and of reincarnationists generally. We shall deal with these in detail in the final chapter.

Shirley MacLaine is confident of having been other people in other places. But she appeared not to be completely satisfied with the questions of why she had lived before.[16] It seems dissatisfaction was built into her theory, for she has yet to find all her former selves. Her search goes on for "a missing dimension in myself."[17] That hardly commends her approach as having achieved wholeness. Apparently, her view of self is not only scattered, it is also shattered, for she cannot tolerate either in her present form or in previous existences the notion that she was evil.

Her Russian male lover gave her fits on this aspect of her philosophy. Her momentary dissatisfaction with having found all of herself found solace in her audacious awareness that she is God. This claim is peppered throughout *Dancing in the Light*.[18] It continued in *It's All in the Playing*. She wrote,

> . . . My higher self was the all-knowing me, possessed of all knowledge, which puts this aspect of me now Shirley through loops of learning.[19]

Her claim to deity was no slip-of-the-pen. The theme is deliberate and sustained. Ironically, her belief in herself as God has an affinity, if not an indirect derivation from Greek pre-Christian philosophy, for the Greeks held that the soul was immortal independent of God, that the human spirit was a piece of the godhead, "able to guarantee immortal being to itself."[20]

Sadhu Sundar Singh (1889-   ), an Indian Christian evangelist, commented on the fact that belief in reincarnation could not console him in the loss of his mother and his elder brother within a few short months of each other. He wrote:

> The loss of these dear ones was a great shock to me; especially did the thought that I should never see them again cast me into despondency and despair, because I could never know into what form they had been re-born, nor could I ever even guess what I was likely to be in my next re-births. In the Hindu religion, the only consolation for a broken heart like mine was that I should submit to my Fate, and bow down to the inexorable law of Karma.[21]

From a Christian viewpoint, Shirley MacLaine is more to be pitied than admired. She needs our prayers more than our praise. Americans, however, are falling for her slick propagandizing in autobiographical dress, whereas the apostle Paul said,

> If only for this life we have hope in Christ, we are to be pitied more than all men (1 Cor. 15:19 NIV).

A merry-go-round of reincarnations is a poor substitute for Christian resurrection in heaven.

Christians should dismiss memory of so-called former lives,

since they are nonexistent. Once we are occupied by our Maker and Redeemer, Jesus Christ, our true persons have been found, and there is no desire to keep up the search. Christ finds us, and in finding us we find ourselves. While not denying that some Christians have yet to explore with Christ how their egos have retained the bends and bruises of their prior years, it is the non-Christian who, apart from Christ, seeks to find his or her lost soul. Seeking to be repossessed by "former selves" may end, for the non-Christian, in being possessed by "other selves," that is, demons.

What, if anything, does Scripture say about the perpetuation of memory in heaven? Will heaven be the place where we wax nostalgic? Will we sigh for "the good old days?" Will our memories be more complete in heaven or restored to a sharpness that we failed to utilize on earth? Will we have all earthly memories erased or only the bad memories taken and removed? If Alzheimer's disorder is a low-grade disease, and since all diseases are banished from heaven, will not memory loss be banished? A resident at Judson Village Retirement Home in Cincinnati recently said to me, "I'm glad memory will be in heaven, for I don't have it here!" Bliss Carman's anticipation is shared by many Christians. She wrote:

> . . . .
> Where the days pass one by one
> Not too fast and not too slow,
> Looking backward as they go
> At the beauties left behind
> To transport the pensive mind.[22]

Now we hanker for a heaven lost. Heaven ahead will be the restoration and regaining of the prefall state of the Garden of Eden. Humans carry about an implicit nostalgia for Eden. Is this behind the surfer's search for the perfect wave, the textile worker's goal of the perfect weave, and the photographer's hope for the perfect exposure? When dissatisfied with what we are, are we longing for our original state, that time before sin disturbed the way we were?

> Our nostalgia for Eden is not just for another time, but for another kind of time. Time in Eden was the pool in which we swam. Time is now the river that sweeps us away. . . . We long in both directions; we feel both nostalgia and hope, fallen from the heights and on the upward road, exiles from Eden and apprentices to heaven.[23]

Through God's goodness and grace, earth has became the scene of golden times of heavenly visitation. The Christian takes with him the greatest experience of his life, contact with Christ. What Christ has done for him and in him will never be forgotten, for it affects the fabric of his nature and his fate. It will not be a memory only, but an ongoing reality. The sweetest memory will be the discovery of saving faith in Christ and determination to follow through on the decision to accept Christ. A Christian doesn't outgrow the moment when the Lord gave his life a new direction, for the alteration of his being is an eternal wonder.

Mysteriously, consciousness accompanies the departed though separated from the body. Do non-Christians have good memories following death?

The most relevant passage on this question is Luke 16:22-31. "It contains the most vivid and colourful account of the afterlife that is to be found in the gospels."[24] It is the famous story of the Rich Man and Lazarus, which traditionally has been tied with the Intermediate State.

Some are convinced this passage is more than parable, because the poor man has his personal name used, and because all other parables are about *this* life, not the *after*life.

> The parable would be utterly pointless if there is not in actual fact a difference between the lot of the godly and that of the

ungodly after death. The point of the parable turns on the future misery of the rich man and the future comfort of Lazarus.[25]

Those who take the parable as eschatological-ethical should exercise some cautions. Otherwise, we draw inferences which have no other support. Four inferences are suspect: (1) That the departed had bodies in the interim state, just because the "finger" and "tongue" are mentioned (16:24);[26] (2) that Lazarus was physically elevated above the rich man because of the descriptive phrase regarding the unnamed rich man "lifting up his eyes" (16:23); (3) that hell is for the rich and heaven is for the poor. Although there was probably some sarcasm for the rich in the story, Jesus never meant to make it an absolute law that the rich could never rest with Abraham. Indeed the warning element presupposed that one need not suffer the fate of the rich man; (4) that Jesus was giving a lashing to Jewish interest in ancestors in having Lazarus go to be with Abraham, rather than with his relatives. Abraham, here, was selected as a firm example as one who made it to paradise, rather than having chosen a relative whose arrival in paradise would be more likely to be doubted. Of course Jesus did not believe the main interest in heaven was reacquaintance with relatives. Paradise was more a venture for faith's completion.

The purpose of the passage was to warn against living for material gain on earth. Yet some inferences have had broad acceptance.

1. Dead people do not go out of existence (16:22, 23)
2. That separate destinies are irreversible and these divisions at death are final (16:26)
3. The departed dead have a memory, even to the name of the person who begged at his gate (16:24)
4. The final insight of the insufficiency of a totally secular life in the tormented rich man (16:27)

5. The understanding of the continued apathy to the things of God in his five brothers (16:28)
6. The erroneous belief that the disembodied poor Lazarus could be the messenger of the rich man to his five brothers (16:27), a possibility that was denied (16:31)
7. The misapprehension of the departed rich man that a miracle would cause repentance easily in his brothers back on earth (16:30)
8. Abraham's awareness of who followed him in time: Moses and the writing prophets (16:31)

These inferences should be tested by other Scriptures. Inference 8, for instance, seems to conflict with Isaiah 63:16. However, in that text the only thing being denied for Abraham and Isaac is involvement like God's with those alive on the earth. If the departed have any insight to what is transpiring on earth, it is not a controlling insight, as Luke 16:22-31 shows.

Puritan John Owen (1616-1683) argued from the awareness of those having gone to the Intermediate Heaven, that deceased believers are aware of developments on earth. He wrote:

> To suppose the church above, which has passed through its course of faith and obedience in afflictions, tribulations, and persecutions, to be ignorant of the state of the church here below in general, and unconcerned about it,—to be without desires of its success, deliverance, and prosperity, unto the glory of Christ,—is to lay them asleep in a senseless state, without the exercise of any grace, or any interest in the glory of God. And if they cry for vengeance on the obdurate persecuting world, Rev. 6:10, shall we suppose they have no consideration nor knowledge of the state of the church suffering the same things which they did themselves? And, to put it out of question, they are minded of it in the next verse by Christ himself (6:11).[27]

Christ's keeping the martyrs informed of the state of affairs on earth (Rev. 6:11) is backed up with the angels' knowledge of repenting sinners (Luke 15:10), as the prophets, saints, and martyrs are conscious of and rejoice in the defeat of Satan in stages (Rev. 12:10; 18:20).

How did the memory of the deceased in Luke 16 differ with Shirley MacLaine's refusal to dwell on wrongs committed in her present life and in alleged prior lives? The rich man of Luke 16 had bitter memories of having lived for the wrong purposes, whereas Shirley MacLaine has no guilt or regret over what she does and has done.[28] But like Shirley MacLaine, the rich man in Hades thought there could be communication between the dead and the living. His request that Lazarus be a courier to his brothers on earth was declared impossible (16:28-31).

Strong memories of the dead may include hearing the voice of loved ones who have died. Hearing lifelong mates years after separation by death is not uncommon, even to Christians. But that is a far cry from actual communication with the dead. What we sense of those gone ahead of us to heaven is more the bubbling up of long and strong associations, rather than the deceased telepathically contacting us. "It has been possible to produce evidence of wishful thinking, unconscious delusion, and even deliberate deception in spiritualistic experiments more often than in parapsychology."[29]

The moral punch of the parable under discussion is that regrets make hell hell. Not only are we after death what we are on the earth (our identities remain), but the essence of hell is the memory of what we missed or could have had, if we had only anticipated the possible anguish in hell or awe in heaven. There is no second-chance eschatology in Luke 16:19-31.

Memories will continue into the Infinite Heaven as well. The ground rules seem to be the following: (1) God's final judgment of persons will involve memory. But this is not to suppose that God need eternally retain matters not worth remembering throughout eternity. To whatever degree the saints are involved in judging, it would necessarily involve the saints in sharing

God's memory while retaining their own. (2) Of course, since God knows all without flaw and since heaven is eternal present, God's "memory" (an anthropomorphic expression) is talking of God as if he were man, of heaven as if it were earth, and of eternity as if it were time. (3) In the life of the resurrected righteous, it appears our memories of God's grace on earth will continue, revive, sharpen, and be part of the impetus behind praising God.

We should consider the Scriptures that impinge on and apply to this topic. (All citations will be from the New American Standard Bible).

Memory for Judgment

Matthew 12:36: Every careless word that men shall speak, they shall render account for it in the day of judgment.

Matthew 25:44: They themselves also will answer, saying, "LORD, when did we see You hungry, or thirsty, or a stranger, or naked, or sick, or in prison, and did not take care of You?"

Revelation 13:8: . . . everyone whose name has not been written from the foundation of the world in the book of life of the Lamb who has been slain.

Revelation 18:5: For her sins have piled up as high as heaven, and God has remembered her iniquities.

Revelation 20:12: And I saw the dead, the great and the small, standing before the throne, and books were opened, which is the book of life; and the dead were judged from the things which were written in the books, according to their deeds.

To protect our egos we will unconsciously be motivated to push from our memories, into our subconscious, what evil we have done. Psychologists tell us that this defense mechanism is one of the ingredients in temporary amnesia. The denial mech-anism is frequently used when one is faced with unpleasant news. Our mental stability depends on not remembering the horrible.

Shirley MacLaine shouted at her Russian lover, "There is no such thing as evil. Evil is fear and uncertainty. Evil is what you *think* it is." "There is no evil, only a lack of knowledge."[30] To buttress this belief, she convinced herself that "the God energy is no judge of persons. In fact, there is no judgment involved with life."[31] How convenient! The only admission to wrong by Ms. MacLaine, who picked various lovers along life's road, was that she was wronged by others. She noted with some pride that she has responded positively to those who have used or abused her.[32] She would probably feel wronged to hear Christ's condemnation in Scripture of her self-flattery and sexual flings.

> The individual will undoubtedly have his memory sharpened in the Day of Judgment. It has been the experience of individu-als at time of danger that their lives stand out in bold relief in a few minutes of time. This will be intensified at the time of judg-ment. The conscience then will be fully awakened. It will not be dull or dead. Forgotten sins will come vividly to mind.[33]

But according to Revelation 18:5 and 20:12, God is not going to trust individual memories, nor the memories of our friends. (We conveniently forget what is distasteful and tawdry.) When the Lord judges in unerring justice there will be no mem-ory gaps, no missing minutes of tape, no erasures of vented feelings, no sudden forgetfulness and no shredding of hateful thoughts. We shall see our deeds as God has seen them. The day of coverup will be over. The masks will come off. The righ-teous Lord will pierce pious facades, show up hypocritical pre-tentiousness, expose the self-deceived, and bring into sharp focus the plots people were party to in their efforts to stop the spread of the gospel and the increase of new converts. What was denied on earth will be affirmed in heaven.

Those, however, who wear the robe of Christ's righteousness in heaven, the redeemed, will have beautiful memories. For what they have admitted to on earth by the power of the Holy Spirit will have vanished from their consciousness. One of the ways the New Testament describes forgiveness is to say God has forgotten. It does not mean that God has a bad memory, but that his act of forgetting is a positive disposing of our sins. Conversely, when God remembers sins, it is not a passive recall, but an active taking of action.[34] This is implied in Isaiah 65:17 (NASB):

> "I create new heavens and a new
> earth;
> And the former things shall not
> be remembered or come to mind."

Dante could only lose the memory of sin and sinning by drinking from the mythical river of Lethe, but the believer will not lose his memory of sins by drinking any potent. It will be the recollection of Jesus' death and resurrection that is the basis of his forgiveness.

One characteristic of the saints in heaven is that they had no memories of serving Christ by helping others (Matt. 25:37-39). A minimal anticipation in heaven will be total recall of those times when God's goodness had been special. Our heavenly deliverance from earth's limitations will certainly include this. But if we recount God's goodness in sparing us from a devastating flood, be sure to remember that Noah will be in our audience.

The mental transformation of the Infinite Heaven will include, (but not be confined to) keen memories of the grace of God operating in our lives. The great evangelist of the eighteenth century, George Whitefield (1714-1770), was doubtlessly right when he said, "One part of our entertainment in heaven will be to count the steps of the ladder, by which God brought us there."[35] In the final heaven reliance on memory will be a thing of the past. Faith shall expand to sight. "The knowledge of sin in heaven will be insight rather than recollection."[36] But we cannot have insight without recollection!

> In the Great Supper the meaning of history becomes clear. Faith gives way to sight—we shall see that which we have already gratefully accepted by faith. In that other supper [that is, of the lost, referred to in Rev. 19:17ff] the judgment supper, the meaning of history also becomes clear, but there it is the rejection that is clarified.[37]

Our resurrected bodies will insure that we shall "receive new powers and fresh energy."[38] Paul intimated that our mental state will pass from dimness to clear depth, from weak understanding to tenacious comprehension, from partial knowledge to full knowledge. He wrote, "Then shall I know fully just as I also have been fully known" (1 Cor. 13:12 NASB).

Some have incorrectly taken 1 Corinthians 13:8 that knowledge will pass away to mean ignorance will be bliss in heaven. Our mental capacities in heaven will not shrink and shrivel, nor will our interest in learning wane, because if anything "faith abides" in the form of full knowledge (13:13).

The knowledge that will go is foul, false, flawed, all imperfect knowledge—not *all* knowledge. Knowledge of divine love, of God's love of us, will not diminish but expand. Knowlege of divine sovereignty will not vanish, but will increase with precision and pleasure. Paul gave no comfort to those who hate knowledge. Heaven is not going to be the cessation of school. If anything it will be graduate school for everyone, including those who were the learning disabled on earth!

> [We shall] know all at once, not in part, not darkly, not through a glass, but as a whole, in manifestations, face to face, not this now, and that thing anon, but all at once, without succession of time.[39]

One writer claims that the believer in a perfected state will acquire paranormal mental powers, including telepathic powers, clairvoyant powers, retrocognitive powers, psychokinetic powers, and projective powers.[40] While Scripture does not use these terms, some of what Paul was driving at would probably include them, so long as our anticipated heavenly perceptions are not considered on a par with God's complete knowledge.

The superiority of Christianity over Buddhism, for instance, is that heaven is not a big puff in which ego is blown out like a candle, in which memory ceases because we cease. Their Nirvana requires the dissolving of self and the destruction of memory. But the Christian Scriptures, however, make a significant contribution in the recognition of the imperishableness of the human self, not because it contains indestructibleness apart from God, but because man is made in God's image, and our continuation in life as well as after death is due to the willing of the heavenly Father.

As in the matters of sex, equality, growth, and ownership, so in memory and recognition, the reality of individuality is retained in the heavenly state. Both in the Intermediate as well as in the Infinite Heaven, we will still be the same persons. We will not forget who we are!

Scripture teaches man as man, and renewed man as renewed man, goes into eternity. To limit his preservation to memory is a truncated immortality not traceable in the Word of God.

> Being retained in memory is something quite different from being in living relation to some presently actual being. This is why we cannot suppose that being held in the divine memory, however vividly, is an adequate way of understanding our eternal life. Only if creatures, by an act of new creation, are made imperishable, can *they* participate in God's eternal life.[41]

In the earlier half of this chapter we examined a number of theories of memory in the afterlife, from Plato to the present time, but, ironically, all these theories, which cling to memory as their only ray of hope, have little worth remembering. Ironically, also, those memory theories of the hereafter ignore the accountability issue. Thinking themselves part of the universal world soul and not holding to a personal God who is Judge and will bring into judgment, there is no reason, considering their premises, to have a place for divine judgment and for individual immortality.

The Christian view of memory in heaven honors both our individuality and God's, and keeps the two separate. The faultiness of the earthly memory will be recognized; and God's flawless memory will bring back evidence and exhibits for the final judgment. God's forgetting of our sins (on the just basis of Christ having substituted himself for us) was an active, positive, and eternal act. It will prohibit condemnation of believers, for their absolute acquittal was pronounced on earth (Rom. 8:1). Our recollection of God's mercies in time will prompt us to ceaselessly renew the presentation of ourselves to him for continued service throughout all eternity in the perfect new heavens and earth.

19

Recognition in Heaven

*O*n the psychological level, recognition is a vital ingredient to one's well-being. It reinforces self-worth, feeds our need for acceptance, and inflates sagging egos. It makes us feel desired and desirable.

Neither age, nor wealth, nor success totally frees us from the need for and pleasure of peer recognition. Though we may deny it, in various degrees we look for the pat on the head, the slap on the back, the plaque for the wall, the reference letter for the dossier, the hand extended in welcome, the arms stretched in embrace, the door opened in courtesy. In our entrances and exits we thrive on signals of being considered valuable, popular, and important.

Apart from our workplaces, we value recognition most at home, among family. Parents look for recognition from children, children thrive on recognition by parents, husbands and wives grow in love to the degree that positive recognition is

322

mutually shared. Appreciation and affection are two important phases of recognition in the home. When either of these is withheld or withdrawn, in revenge or in punishment, then relationships are weakened, mutual commitments wane, self suffers, and family stability is threatened.

The strength of this need is borne out when frustrated persons, who have been snubbed, belittled, and neglected, have abused others and retaliated by maim or murder because recognition has been withheld. Notoriety, whether sought through antisocial behavior or whether gained by legitimate means, is a quest for wide-scale recognition.

Who we *know* is another dimension of nurturing who we *are*. We seek recognition, unknowingly, by our associations. Indirectly our importance is tied with the importance of others. Hero identification intensifies to the degree we have not achieved recognition directly. If personal self-worth is absent, sometimes we cease being ourselves and become the idol object. Such an intense and complete identification is a substitute recognition. It hides the resentment the person feels who has not achieved, gained, or received praise on his own.

But *what* we know is an equally powerful factor in life as *who* we know or wish we were. It is the failure to recognize *what* is truth, *what* is right, *what* is enduring, and *what* contributes to our good, that has given rise to destructive pastimes and Christless thought systems.

People are attracted to pop movements for their *what*, especially if the *what* pumps their egos and provides the justification for pursuing self-recognition all-out. When we place being recognized *with* someone, *by* someone, and *as* someone as the highest good, then we have allowed self to be the focal point of judgment, the standard by which we judge between the multiple *whats* being peddled in society.

The burden of this book has been to sharpen the reader's discernment between spiritual *whats*. Recognition of ideas, seeing concepts in their historical roots, is vital to distinguishing between nutritious theology and junk theology. Unless we become confession conscious, our awareness will be so shaky that we will be vulnerable to ideological entrapment. In the 1970s the Hare Krishnas were pulling in idealistic youth. By the 1980s and into the 1990s, yuppies and groupies alike, though in different social hemispheres, have in common the desire to develop personal opinions apart from any organized religion.

The New Age movement camouflages its theosophic beliefs. Dig deeper and we find New Age is skeletal Hinduism, but without the dedication to poverty and pain, without gurus, orange gowns, oriental sandals, and looking Eastern. George Orwell is famous for his *1984*. Most people know it as a warning about oppressive government. It is less known for the insight that "concern for self . . . . all you are about is yourself" runs through the book as well. Those wary of Big Brother are wallowers in Bigger Self.

New Age celebrates self with enthusiasm. The Maypole around which New Age people dance has self as the narrow axis. No wonder, therefore, that the children of the parents who followed Ayn Rand, est, and Psychocybernetics in the 50s, 60s, and 70s have shifted into New Age writings. The New Age approach is to let you seek past incarnations and press for better reincarnations without having to cut out chicken livers, to bathe in dirty rivers, to shun Big Macs, to read palms, to gaze into crystal balls. Instead, in the confines of one's family room, one can play with mystic numerology, talk to one's "higher self," say an occasional mantra, practice some yoga exercises, try to cleanse the so-called seven chakracenters and indulge in symbolic word games. The New Age both retains and retrains a suburbanite, hard-driving, upper-class all-American image.

How has this revolution come about? Why has it taken off with all the seats taken and standing room only? Two major factors have contributed to the easy transfer from nominal Christian to enthusiastic New Age.

First, society is moving away from institutional religion in droves. Links with the synagogues and churches are shorter and more tenuous. Lodges show consistent yearly losses, company picnics are declining and disappearing, church-camp enrollments have dropped steadily, and group gatherings have shrunk and hold limited appeal. Society is going more individualistic. VCR machines are now standard home equipment and video rentals have skyrocketed. People shop by means of television. Individualism is everything. And New Age promoters have tapped into that market trend.

In addition to the social factor there is a key spiritual reason why New Age is the new rage. The second reason for the swing to New Age—why it has gained momentum and infiltrated our institutions and businesses so deeply, even to the highest levels—is that our Christian roots have been cut, withered, and discarded. Outside organized Christianity, among the millions who have abandoned religious connections, the New Age movement has emerged as the substitute belief system that feeds the ego as nothing has done in a long time.

We have drawn attention to the New Age movement not because we believe it is really "new" in the sense of "refreshing," nor have we highlighted its presence among us because it is comparable with the new age Christ brought. In fact, the New Age is neither new, nor is it truly new age. It is a new expression of Antichrist teaching. New Age says, "Trust yourself"; the Bible says, "Trust Jesus!" The Bible says, "Today, if you hear His voice, do not harden your hearts . . ." (Heb. 3:7, 8 NASB). "Reincarnation declares, 'You have plenty of time to hear your inner voice and save yourself.'"[1]

Once we familiarize ourselves with Eastern religions, such as Hinduism and Buddhism, we see not only a similarity, but kinship of thought between them and the New Age movement.

New Age representatives, however, such as Shirley MacLaine, project that their governing beliefs are original, otherworldly, and come to them in flashes of divine inspiration.

MacLaine in particular seems genuinely convinced that her ideas arise from herself. She has avoided acknowledging her indebtedness and her heavy dependence on mystical religions in the past. To a degree she has, when she has acknowledged being guided by various spiritual guides into the thought patterns she now propagates with the enthusiasm of a new convert. But in the shadows, undetected by the modern readership, is substantial dependence upon ancient panentheism and an old reincarnationist approach. The frequent use of the words *karma* (which is presented as a law of consequences), *avatars*, and *mantra* should tip off the public that what is being reported as new is really very, very old.

The New Age movement of the 1980s, in a real sense, was parented by the narcissism of the 1970s and the new consciousness of the 1960s. In the 1960s the West began to turn East in a big way. Then the general populace associated reincarnation with rebellious long-haired youth. Today, movers and shakers in white-collar management at all levels are openly using and promoting New Age methods to better employee performance. The 1990s will, doubtless, show some restlessness with previous humanistic expressions. Variation is inevitable in an orientation inherently characterized by flux. But whatever forms, labels, and movements emerge in the decades at the end of the twentieth century, a pantheistic, panentheistic, and secular humanistic core will persist.

For people to put recognition of others before, above, and in place of thought recognition is symptomatic that occupation with the social aspects of salvation-future has greater priority than occupation with salvation-future beliefs. The concern to know if we will know each other in heaven is a legitimate concern. But it should be farther down our list of questions needing to be answered. That is one reason it comes up as chapter 19 rather than chapter 1.

When you read Shirley MacLaine's autobiographies, you are invited both into the privacy of her mind as well as into the privacy of her bedroom. (She is not out to mess with our morals so much as to mess with our minds). What is our reaction? Do we see a difference? Do we sense a danger?

My concern in tackling heaven questions is to remedy the widespread neglect of traditional Christian doctrines, especially the incapacitation of man by sin and the complete salvation Christ has won, secured, and applied. The key to avoid falling for New Age hype and hoopla is in belief recognitions. That is why significant space has been given to address the replacement and reduction of Christian beliefs. At the heart of our vulnerability is a predisposition to favor individualism. Church members place too much emphasis on meeting their needs, even at the expense of ignoring God's Word. We have placed so much stress on relationships that we have let up on the reliability of stated ideas. In other words, we have been overly protective of earthly associations to the point that we push analysis of belief systems to the side. And, in the process, we set ourselves up to be potential high-risk spiritual suckers.

The record and scenario of New Age growth have been fed by the secular public's preoccupation with recognition. Recognition is big in new Age thought. As in onion peeling, there will be a stinging sensation, but let me briefly pull back three layers of the New Age.

1. *Self-preservation.* Big in New Age propaganda is that determined willing can extend years, improve life, even eliminate aging and death. Self-reprogramming is advocated.

Linda Goodman has urged, "If you are eighteen, you must learn how to prevent aging. . . . If you are eighty, you must learn how to reverse aging." We die, she contends, only because we think death. "All deaths are suicides" only because we believe death is inevitable.[2]

2. *Self-recognition.* Shirley MacLaine's autobiographies in 1982, 1985, 1987, and 1989 contain the stories of her search for herself in the present and in alleged past existences. The heaven quest, to which she invites and encourages her readers, is the ultimate in privatized religion. Her ambition is to encounter her past self (or is it selves?) and to uncover her true self. She is not clear whether she is one person or many. Recognition by others is pushed back in her list of priorities. What is true of Shirley MacLaine is true of the entire New Age movement. From the simpler *deja vu* to the more advanced trance channeling, a person cannot be part of the New Age without a self search.

3. *Self-exaltation:* Enormous powers are attributed to self. Self is God. Shirley MacLaine utters her mantras, "I am God in stamina. . . . I am God in coolness. . . . I am God in strength," in the privacy of her room. And she advocates that each person see himself as God: "You are God." Rather than taking credit for creating reality, for turning reality into illusion, she should weigh the probability of herself entertaining delusions. The human will in New Age can do anything God can do, for man is God.[3]

A frequently asked question in Christian circles is "Will we recognize each other in heaven?" Of all the questions on heaven, it seems the one on which most every one agrees. Whether in the Intermediate or Infinite State, we expect recognition by and of others. More people question the continuation of gender in heaven compared to the matter of recognition of loved ones in heaven. But how easily or accurately can recognition take place if a person is desexed? Acceptance of recognition, also, assumes the presence of mind and the perfection of memory.

One of the inferences from laughter in heaven (Luke 6:21) is that it is the result of heavenly reunion. Jesus said those who are sad at partings due to death shall find their sorrow replaced with laughter. Laughter, happiness, and joy are the emotions of reunion. Reunions on earth produce laughter and joy. We see this in others as well for ourselves when, for instance, we pick up a returning son or a visiting mother at the airport. We grin and we chuckle as we exchange greetings.

The transfiguration scene of the Gospels when Christ was on the (traditional) Mount Tabor with Moses, Elijah, Peter, James, and John illustrated something of future heavenly reunions. Peter said, "Lord, it is good for us to be here . . ." (Matt. 17:4 NASB). His happiness is partly indicated in the fact that the inconvenience and effort of constructing shelters outweighed the benefits of more time together with two Old Testament favorite men. Similarly, we shall know exhilaration when we will be reunited with those with whom we have shared a lifetime.

Probably the most frequently recurring theme in hymns on heaven is reunion, and with it, recognition.[4] Henry Alford [1810-1871] was better known as a hymn writer than as a Greek scholar, although he excelled more in the latter. When he was minister of the Anglican parish in Wymeswold, England, he wrote the famous harvest home hymn.[5] Each thanksgiving season we sing,

> Oh, then what raptured greetings
> On Canaan's happy shore,
> What knitting severed friendships up
> Where partings are no more:
> Then eyes with joy shall sparkle
> That brimmed with tears of late;

> Orphans no longer fatherless,
> Nor widows desolate.

Charles H. Gabriel (1856-1932), born on a farm in Iowa and eventually settling in California, was one of the few gospel hymn composers who sometimes wrote under a female *nom de plume* (Charlotte G. Homer). In one of his hymns mentioned earlier, "O that will be Glory," a stanza reads—

> Friends will be there we have loved long ago;
> Joy like a river around me will flow.

A little-known hymn writer, Virgil P. Brock, was guest at the Winona Lake, Indiana, Rainbow Point home of Homer Rodeheaver, evangelist Billy Sunday's choir director (1909-1931). While there Mr. Brock was inspired, after seeing several beautiful sunsets, to write the hymn "Beyond the Sunset" (1936).[6]

> Beyond the sunset, O glad reunion,
> With our dear loved ones who've gone before;
> In that fair homeland, we'll know no parting.
> Beyond the sunset for evermore.

Before the invention of the airplane, Augustus M. Toplady (1740-1778) referred to going to heaven as flight. In "Rock of Ages" he wrote, "When we shall soar to worlds unknown." Toplady, in true Protestant fashion, believed it was a direct, non-stop flight. Roman Catholics have traditionally opted for a layover (purgatory) in their flight to heaven.

We may not like to think of the destination of heaven as an airport "terminal," but the analogy has some value. If we would wish to continue thinking along this line, heaven will be the only "terminal" that has no baggage-claim area, for as we brought nothing into life, so we shall take nothing out.

Popular professor of pastoral theology at Yale Divinity, Henri Nouwen, took off with this thought when he said,

Heaven will be like returning from a trip on an airplane and as you enter the terminal you will see all those faces staring at you, trying to recognize you and God will be there, and he will recognize you. He will say, "Hi Henri! Welcome home! How was your trip? Let me see your slides."[7]

William Barclay (1907-1978), who produced a popular New Testament commentary set, expressed the conviction that reunion and recognition would happen in heaven. But he added a curious twist to the heavenly meeting. He wrote in his spiritual autobiography:

I have never been able to see in this only the joy of meeting again those whom we have loved and lost awhile. We shall have to meet again those whom we have wronged; those to whom we have been disloyal; those whom we have hurt; those whom we have deceived. There will be no doubt the reuniting of love, but there will also be confrontation with truth. The one thing that haunted Paul long after he had become an apostle was that he had been a persecutor (Gal. 1:13; 1 Cor. 5:9; 1 Tim. 1:13). "When they were put to death," he said of the Christians, "I cast my vote against them" (Acts 26:10). F. W. H. Myers makes Paul think of this in his poem "Saint Paul," as he remembers the deaths of the saints for which he was responsible:

> Saint, did I say? with your remembered faces,
> Dear men and women whom I sought and
> slew!
> Ah, when we mingle in the heavenly places
> How will I weep to Stephen and to you![8]

The recognition factor in eternity has been carried over from the Old Testament. Before there were leanings toward the concept of resurrection in the late Old Testament period, there was the early belief that in death one went to where one's relatives were. Death was to be assembled with one's ancestors as far back as patriarchal times. *See* Genesis 15:15; 25:8; 35:29;

47:30; 49:29, 33; Num. 20:24, 26; 27:13; 31:2; Deut. 32:50; 1 Kings 1:21; 2:10; 11:21, and so forth. Here it seems the bare survival of the soul in some kind of immortality was less the point than the communal relations of the whole person.

The chief New Testament passage on heavenly reunion is Matthew 8:11. Jesus said:

> And I say to you, that many shall come from east and west, and recline at the table with Abraham, and Isaac, and Jacob, in the kingdom of heaven (NASB).

Some have seen in this saying a rebuke of popular Jewish deceased kinsman veneration. Our Lord wanted interest in meeting others in the hereafter to center on matters of faith, not matters of family. Those with whom we shall be gathered in eternity, Jesus said here, will not be close relatives, but distant peoples and religious heroes.[9] There is no mention of family network: fathers, mothers, wives, children. Colleen McDannell and Bernhard Lang, in their heaven anthology, went so far as to suggest that we should see this passage, therefore, as a rebuke of excessive focus on the family. Jesus had an anti-familial bias to utter this.[10] "Family relationships with their petty loyalties meant little to him."[11] An element of truth is here, for Jesus showed detachment from family agenda, which tended to perpetuate regional values. But his functional distance, however, cannot be construed to conclude he intentionally built a wall between himself and his family. Their hypothesis of Jesus' alleged family hang-ups would make Jesus seem mean-spirited, unappreciative, distant, and scornful. Two pieces of Gospel history should make their conclusion suspect. First, Jesus used the father image in describing the nature of God in the parable of the prodigal son. It was likely that the ideal loving Father in the parable of the prodigal son (Luke 15) was suggested by the high regard he held for his foster father, Joseph. Secondly, tender feelings and familial love were evident in Jesus' third word from the cross (John 19:27).

The gathering to which Jesus alluded was not the millen-nium, but of the eternal state of the new heavens and new earth. In Matthew "kingdom of heaven" was equivalent to "kingdom of God." The subject was heaven. The centurion who was seeking the healing of his son, got that, and heaven too!

But fellowship in heaven contrasted with those who were excluded from the table. Jesus continued:

> But the sons of the kingdom shall be cast out into the outer darkness; in that place there shall be weeping and gnashing of teeth (Matt. 8:12, NASB).

While heaven will be international in flavor (the meaning intended by "east and west"), Jews were not to presume that they were guaranteed a seat. Though they were ostensibly "sons of the kingdom," they were not guaranteed their place in heaven. "What Jesus is attacking here is that possessiveness, that sense of exclusiveness which disfigures every religious community too sure of itself."[12]

As a game is not over until it's over, so regarding heaven, we're not in until we're in. Thus, Jesus added a warning to his comfort. We dare not presume that we shall feast in heaven. Genealogical, racial, or religious ties cannot assure us that we shall meet the spiritual "heavies" of former times, let alone get-ting reacquainted with deceased believing relatives.

Prior to this meeting of the centurion and Jesus, and Jesus' comments about feasting in eternity, was the transfiguration (Matt. 17:1-8). One inference which can be validly drawn from that episode is that:

> . . . there is no substantial or structural continuity from the old to the new existence. On the other hand, however, the trans-figuration will occur to the same earthly body that we are here: something different will not be produced in its place, but there is a historical continuity in the sense of continuous transition in the consummation of the transformation itself.[13]

In other words, the transfiguration reality and recognitions were a prototype of our future resurrection identities' being retained. Also, this is assumed in what Jesus said about feasting with the Old Testament patriarchs.

Will we sit down with Abraham, Isaac, and Jacob and not recognize them? Recognition, in this instance, of course, would not be based on prior acquaintance. (Artists' pictures of the patriarchs are only guesstimates what they could have looked like, not what they actually looked like.) Lack of personal acquaintance, however, was not a problem on Mount Tabor for Peter, James, and John, although they had never seen Moses and Elijah.

Would beards help or hinder in heavenly recognition? Facial hair may only compound the task of recognition. On the other hand, agelessness does not require baldness. According to the old saw, baldness is like heaven because "there is no parting there."

Agelessness will not make recognition easier. It would seem that agelessness, though eliminating shaving and shampooing, would have the problem of overcoming sameness. This would probably make identification harder. We have serious doubts about whether hair will be there and whether hairstyles will be genuinely permanent. We can be more sure that humor will be in heaven than that hair will be in heaven. If hair is not there, humor surely will be. We will be close to everyone in heaven—close enough to be moved by other's laughter, close enough to converse. In heaven there will be a sense of closeness without the feeling of being crowded.

Technology has rendered Rudyard Kipling's pretelevision lines, "East is East and West is West, And ne'er the twain shall meet" obsolete. One of the advantages of the present age over former centuries is that distant places have come near. East and West are culturally as well as geographically close, celebrated in the East-West Center of Honolulu, Hawaii (1777 East West Road).

Some representatives of the Christian afterlife have so emphasized the beatific vision of God and the contemplative life that interpersonal relationships, the social dimension, are absent, if not denied. This has not just been an oversight, but, in essence, amounts to an outrageous obfuscation, if not obliteration, of the permanence of personality in heaven. A community chuckling will be part of the communion of saints.

> The vision of God cannot be isolated from the communion of saints and the kingdom of God; for if God is Love, the object of our contemplation is the pattern and inspiration of all interpersonal relationship and union. . . . In the perfected consummation individual life and experience are not lost but transcended in corporate experience and interpersonal solidarity. . . . The reason why the notions of the beatific vision and the communion of saints are inseparable in the Christian doctrine of heaven is that God himself, in whom we shall find our true being and destiny is the trinitarian relational God of love given and love received.[14]

Real people engaged in real communication will be a vital part of the life of heaven. Without it, isolation is the alternative. Fellowship in churches on earth, around Christ, is a foretaste of fellowship in heaven. In one sense, communication in our glorification will not be a new feature of heaven that always has been. Heaven has always had instant communication. There communication is immediate. (Also, we may presume from Christ's rapid resurrection movement—from Galilee to Judea—that travel in heaven will be swift.) For a long time on our globe international distances have prevented informational flow and better relationships between nations. Although we have more technical means at our disposal, our time lags, space barriers, and rusty communication skills prevent us from thinking that this world is heaven.

Heaven's perfection will be communications deluxe. Jesus is not only the "only Mediator," he is also the only truly "Great

Communicator." Through him God has sent his message to man and through him we can communicate with God (John 1:51). We have no space to develop the hypothesis here, but hell is the ultimate breakdown of communication as well as the absence of comic elements.

Good conversation will be one of the trademarks of the Infinite Heaven. The best illustration of this was the mealtime Jesus used. Table fellowship was a favorite way to describe heaven in the Gospels.[15] It didn't cause offense to mention the mealtime beverage. Jesus referred to drinking wine "new" in heaven (Mark 14:25). Here we have an instance where Jesus resorted to a playful pun. There is new wine on earth, but there is a *new* or newer wine in eternity. In his anticipation of the heavenly feast and the serving of wine, Jesus was not attempting to insult the standards of the Women's Temperance League, which from its founding has promoted abstinence from wine drinking. Literal wine cannot be meant, for wine takes time to produce—not because the Bible is against drinking wine[16]—but because of the long process involved in fermentation. It takes time and the right climatic conditions to make excellent wine.

Wine with a meal in first-century Israel promoted convivial conversation, the sense of commonality, increased closeness, the free exchange of ideas, and the sense of fellow feeling. Christ used the sharing and sipping of wine to convey unity, harmony, spiritual perception, fraternal enjoyment, and perfect peace away from the din and discord of time.

At the banquet marriage table of the Lamb we shall gain new insights on history. For those once occupied with the happenings in their private spheres, their comprehension of history's inner workings shall broaden. Knowledge of the wheel in the middle of the wheel shall be shared (Ezek. 1:15-20). Doctrinal agreement will be achieved, which on earth was difficult if not impossible.

O then, what a blessed society will the family of heaven be, and those peaceful inhabitants of the new Jerusalem, where there is no division, no differing judgments, no disaffection, nor strangeness, no deceitful friendship, no, not one unkind expression, nor an angry look or thought; but all are one in Christ, who is one with the Father, and all alive in the love of Him who is love itself![17]

The modern Christian needs to be stimulated in the art of recognition of others. Reaching out to others means we must fight against natural reserve. Others may be too shy to approach us. We must approach them.

Someone asked George MacDonald (1824-1905) if he thought there was going to be heavenly recognition. He replied "Shall we be greater fools in Paradise than we are here?" Another story has circulated that one Sunday a Boston minister gave a sermon on the subject "Shall We Know Each Other in Heaven?" He presented what he thought Scripture said on the subject. A few days later he received a letter from a visitor that Sunday. It read: "Dear Sir: I wonder if you will preach next Sunday on the subject: 'Do We Know Each Other on Earth?' I have been attending your church for nearly a year and to date nobody has taken any notice of me whatever."

We show ourselves having the atmosphere of heaven on earth when we assert ourselves by welcoming strangers into our places of worship. One of the marks of the Christ is his unconditional love and his willingness to cross boundaries to make others feel accepted (John 13:34).

We have seen how recognition has provided an elemental psychological dynamics in spiritual quests. In the non-Christian a protective ego need makes self-recognition seek self-support. Belief systems such as the New Age movement feed and fortify the feeling of personal power and self-importance. The outrageous ego claims of New Age teaching, including the so-called ability to create reality, and to delay and destroy death, by itself has not been sufficient to startle shoppers in the truth market that New Age philosophy is patently false, progressively snobbish, and dangerous to our futures.

Christians who are oriented toward Christ and his Word should be aware from Scripture that amassing, assessing, and organizing truths around the center of self is derogatory of Christ, for the elevation of self through feelings, intuitions, and experiences, results in attempts at Christ's demotion and displacement. Unless we recognize the error of self-salvation that is so strong in the New Age thought, we can forget about recognizing each other in heaven, for on the basis of human goodness, we will not be there. Recognition of others and by others in heaven comes as a byproduct of God's love for us and Christ's righteousness given to us, rather than something we achieve through concentration, determination, and "willpower."

Recognition follows from our God-created uniqueness and from a God-implanted desire to know, in new ways, our loved ones and friends.

> We certainly shall not know less there than here. If we know our friends here, we shall know them there. And as we know our friends here, we shall know them there. Love to Christ here draws us nearer to each other, so there we shall love friends, not less but more, because of our greater nearness to Christ.[18]

20

Is Heaven Reincarnation

?

*T*he 1988 *Newsweek* poll showed 24 percent of Americans believing in reincarnation.[1] In the minds of many of those polled reincarnation is compatible with the Bible's view of heaven. They probably see no difference between what reincarnationists say and what Scripture says. A clue that this is the case was given when Shirley MacLaine, well-known actress-writer, appeared on the "Phil Donahue Show" promoting her book *Dancing in the Light.* She was amazed that except for one woman who accused her of dabbling in witchcraft, "*not one person* said 'This stuff is crazy' or anything even resembling such a point of view."[2] When she propagated her New Age views among the film crew producing the television miniseries *Out on a Limb,* she found ". . . most had come to the conclusion that they themselves were essentially spiritual beings who had not recognized the power within themselves to bring about whatever they desired in their lives."[3]

Some audiences are passive toward reincarnation. Vigorous protests are often wanting. Rebuttals are rare. How do we explain the absence of revolt against the view of ourselves reappearing in other lives? Is it because of commitment to fair play, the popularity of pluralism, and practicing the right guaranteed by the First Amendment? Or does it involve and reflect an underlying skepticism that truth is unattainable? The underlying belief that produces this question is the further question: Who has a right to criticize another belief?

Part of the problem, it seems, stems from the belief that only opinions, not facts, characterize religion; that reliable external authority is nonexistent when dealing with questions of spirit; and that tolerance is the only response when there are no established truths.

Unfortunately people are content to retain as valid incompatible and conflicting views. In dialectic thinking one amasses contradictory claims without attempting to resolve them. It is acceptable today to have a Bible on one's coffee table, requiring weekly dusting, and on the same table, underscored copies of Shirley MacLaine's last four autobiographical installments— and see nothing prohibitive or problematical in shuffling their contents like a deck of cards.

One tactic of the New Age movement, which presents an alternative approach to heaven, is to cite the Bible. This is one major reason why many see no problem in holding to belief in reincarnation and think it Christian. Shirley MacLaine, found in talking with actor John Heard, that if his friend was typical, many assume that the Bible taught reincarnation.[4]

Before we take another look at the alleged support for reincarnation in the Bible, we need to recognize that traditional Christian views of heaven have gone past erosion to the stage of replacement by New Age ideas.

New Age is a subculture movement with a large following. It is probably the leading American pop theology outside of organized Christianity.[5] Within denominational seminaries process theology is being taught. It is just a matter of time before it filters down to the local church. It is not inconceivable that since process theology and New Age thought are equally panentheistic (see Glossary) in perspective that they may cooperate in advancing or supporting a shared world leadership in the person of the final Antichrist, who will be thoroughly humanistic, yet theistic.

The New Age movement is a hodgepodge of pre-Christian, sub-Christian, post-Christian, and anti-Christian ideas regarding man, his origin, his will, and his destiny. It is a hybrid Hinduism with a jumble-lie eschatology. The proponents of the New Age thought will use terms that sound biblical, such as "rebirthing," "the higher self," "cell regeneration," "higher heaven dimension," "the power of choice," "personal transformation," "mind science," "spiritual beings," "meditation," "God in you," "alignment with the God-force," "mirror image," "at-one-ment," "immortals," and "New Age recognition." New Age reps also talk of earth as Eden Heaven.[6] They refer to the movement as "the Easter altar of these children of the New Age."[7]

The public has been drawn unsuspectingly into the New Age net by their clever marketing tactics. One method is avoidance of the old words of spiritualism. Instead of referring to "seances," they speak of channeling, which is an abbreviation of transchanneling, which, in turn, is an abbreviation of trance channeling. Another technique is to downplay mediums, although MacLaine has been up-front in acknowledging her indebtedness to "spiritual guides" (the word she prefers).[8] She has admitted that there are fake psychics and even warned against consulting transmediums, for they are generally unreliable on dates and mathematical figuring.[9]

New Age stresses the priority of self, not just the preexistence and solidarity of self. Plato's idea of preexisting knowledge has come back to haunt us in the writings of Shirley MacLaine who contends that we are "each in possession of the total truth at all times if we *wanted* to recognize it. . . ."[10] Whereas old spiritualism put contact with the "other side" in the hands of an intermediary, New Age puts the responsibility on the inquirer. MacLaine wrote:

> . . . the giant truth [is] that one individual is his or her own best teacher, and that no other idol or false image should be worshipped or adored because the God we are all seeking lies inside one's self, not outside.[11]

Going Within (A Guide for Inner Transformation), which appeared in the Spring of 1989, has less to do with Shirley MacLaine's travels and more to do with her travails in practicing self-mastery. References to her personal struggles in achieving harmony serves as a subtle apologetic, for the impression left by her earlier autobiographies was that she was arrogant. In a few places she tried to address the criticism of her apparent conceit.[12] Her motivation in writing *Going Within* was said to provide practical help to others who desire self-mastery. What motivated her, said the book jacket, was to provide a kind of inner road map for those confused on how to achieve self-control.

In *Going Within* MacLaine has gone out of her way to project modesty,[13] and to confess to her need for communal and collegial sharing.[14] Nevertheless, she did not abandon her earlier contention of self not needing saving, rather self is the vehicle of saving. In *Going Within* she continued the rhetoric of her previous three books. Consider the following claims from *Going Within*.

". . . higher power in himself. . . ."[15]

". . . Higher Self. . . ."[16]

". . . the Higher Self, the soul, is our personalized reflection of the Divine Spark. . . ."[17]

". . . the God energy of our Higher Selves within us. . . ."[18]

". . . we are each Godlike . . . . we are each part of God. . . ."[19]

Along with these self-gratulating titles, she attributed power to self to change and to create.[20]

A distrust for other sources of information about oneself, God, and the hereafter is one mark of the New Age movement.

> Each soul is its own God. You must never worship anyone or anything other than self. For *you* are God. To love self is to love God.[21]
>
> ". . . Each religion thinks it has a hot line to God. When the truth might well be that we are *all* attached to God. We are all part of God.[22]

Instead of doubting her blanket acceptance of all thoughts arising from her so-called "higher self," she complained that she was wrongly influenced by "societal conditioning" which suggested going by feelings was unwise.[23]

New Age belief goes beyond the teaching of self-reliance and proposes self-creation. Toward the end of *Dancing in the Light* she ventured the daring thought: "*we are our own creators.*"[24] This claim received more emphasis in *It's All in the Playing.* Traditionally, what Christians have attributed to God, she claims for human beings. "Each of us creates his own reality. . . ."[25]

Too many have passed off such comments as another form of thought control. As mentioned earlier, one New Age writer, Linda Goodman, believes that mind can by thinking avoid dying, and by sheer concentration prevent and reverse aging (which in itself shows the ludicrous side of the aging New Agers).[26] Even Shirley MacLaine, in her earlier *Out on a Limb,* voiced a similar upbeat proposition:

> . . . every second of each of our days we are creating and dictating the terms of our futures by our own positive and negative actions.[27]

In *Out on a Limb,* creative powers of the human psyche are loosely conceived or limited to shaping reality rather than starting reality. But Shirley MacLaine has gone one step further. She was not advocating simple mind control, but she made the claim she has created reality. We haven't taken her seriously if we dismiss her views as a variety of positive thinking or possibility thinking. She has gone beyond emphasizing that positive thoughts contribute to spiritual victory over depression, failure, and a low self-image.

She made the claim that the person does what God does. We predestinate our futures, she claimed.[28] We make it all happen, good and bad.[29] Beyond that she claims she created everything! Astonishing in one sense, but it is the logical outgrowth of her initial premise that self was God. People have been admitted to the psychiatric ward of a hospital for making the following claim, but she has indulged in what seems to be a form of paranoia yet she is considered totally normal:

> . . . if we each create our own reality, then of course we are every thing that exists within it. Our reality is a reflection of us. . . . I could legitimately say that I created the Statue of Liberty, chocolate chip cookies, the Beatles, terrorism, and the Vietnam War. . . . I knew I had created the reality of the evening news at night. . . .[30]

Our society, in the irony of life as we know it, permits such a crazy notion to be published as nonfiction, whereas we lock others up who have illusions of grandeur. Shirley MacLaine has espoused the philosophy of solipsism, which holds that self is the only reality. She wrote:

> If I created my own reality, then . . . I had created everything I saw, heard, touched, smelled, tasted; everything I loved, hated, revered, abhorred; everything I responded to or that responded to me. Then, I created everything I knew. . . . If that was true, then I *was* everything.[31]

Solipsism is a little heard word, because solipsists are few and in the history of philosophy it is rarely followed. It represents one of the smallest branches of the limb of idealism. A famous solipsist statement, attributed to an anonymous Oxford don, is "Anything I know not is not knowledge."

Shirley MacLaine is more out on the branch of solipsism than out on the limb of idealism. Herman Bavinck (1854-1921) described her views as though he had read advance copies of her books.

> The thoroughgoing idealists . . . regard the entire world as a product of the human mind, and man not merely as the orderer, but also as the creator of the world. . . . [But] most idealists, however, draw back from this phenomenalism, which would seem bound to issue in solipsism.[32]

Through the backdoor of spiritualism, Shirley MacLaine entered into the dining room of panentheism, in which the contention is that everyone contains God. But she did not stop there. Her next move in the house of her idealism was to the infrequently used door leading to the closet of solipsism, which has no windows to look out on the world and is the absolute dead-end of her philosophy. Shirley MacLaine has entered the abbreviated space of self. Don't applaud. Be appalled, for she has forsaken the reality of the God who has revealed himself solely in Jesus Christ. She is drawing nourishment from her own brain, which is as destructive as a crazed she-bear feeding on her own breasts.

Of all the outrageous claims strewn through her ongoing personal odyssey, the one which should show her readers the ludicrousness of her concepts is her solipsism. Even Johann G. Fichte (1762-1814), who claimed that the world had no independent self-existence, an early idealist, did not regard himself as the only existent being. To the majority of individuals Shirley MacLaine's solipsism is absurd, for reality *precedes* human reasoning, and has an independent existence. That is why "solipsism, although the inevitable outcome of idealism, is in itself an impossible theory."[33]

Reenacting the past is no problem if one is capable of creating the future. To have the power to create and control reality, reincarnation is a cinch. Some of the internal inconsistencies of the claim to deity include:

If self is God, then:

Why would one need new incarnations?

Why would one need to find previous existences?

Why need one emulate God if one is God?

Why would one need to consult transmediums if one possesses all knowledge?

Why would one need to subject oneself to gimmicks such as sound therapy, color therapy, word games?

Why would one need to fight back with "mental gravity"?

Why would one need to concern oneself with consequences or karmic actions?

How could all reality be perceived as illusion when originally it was made real?

If one grants almightiness to the designation God, Shirley MacLaine is not God. Any admission to being dependent, confined, vulnerable, defeated, restricted, unable to fathom oneself in all manifestations, and limited is not a description of omnipotence, omniscience, and omnipresence! Her claim of being a God in the traditional sense is absurd.

Sadhu Singh, mentioned previously, fled Hindu belief, almost identical to MacLaine's, when he thought through the humiliating consequent for their god (Brahma). He wrote:

> If Maya [illusion] is possible in Brahma [God], then Brahma
> is no longer Brahma, for he has been subordinated to Maya.

Hence, Maya is stronger than Brahma himself, and Maya will then not be Maya (illusion) but will be a reality that has overcome Brahma, and we shall have to think of Brahma himself as Maya, and this is blasphemy.[34]

Shirley MacLaine's god will wash away like her mascara. Her claims will be shown to be outrageously and patently delusive. She will discover how dangerous they were when she dies, if not before then.

In the next section we shall look into reincarnation. Then we shall explore the principle which makes it work: *karma*. Following that we shall examine the claim that the Bible teaches reincarnation.

Reincarnation in the writings of Shirley MacLaine is adaptive reincarnation, rather than classical reincarnation. She has developed her own brand. It is her own free-lanced variety. She differs with classical reincarnation at several points. First, Buddhist reincarnationists hold that at least one *avatar* is in each age. In Tibet, for instance, the Dalai Lama is believed to be the fourteenth reincarnation of Avalkiteshvare, the patron saint of Tibet. The followers of Dalai Lama number nearly six million. But Shirley MacLaine is not among them. She is concerned about finding herself.

She differs with classical reincarnationism in a second way. She has not precommitted herself to the Hindu *Law of Manu* which warns that a pupil who answers his teacher, though justly, will be reborn an ass, while one who falsely defames his teacher will become a dog.

A third way in which she differs from classical reincarnationism is in her view of *karma* (*see* Glossary). She presents a muted form of the ancient view of karma. Though she refers to karmic action and the belief that we are answerable for our actions and suffer the consequences (karma) for them, she has not spelled out how karma works. For instance, in classical karmic doctrine, karmic debt must be worked out through good works in the future. And there is no guarantee that a previous incarnation was in another human. In classical karma teachings if one is good enough in life, like the Brahmans, one can escape karma (the consequence) and thereby be exempt from reincarnations. Does she withhold this idea from American readers, because she knows it would not go over, because it smacks too much of Hinduism?

Karmic rewards and karmic retributions, in the New Age, await everyone. Shirley MacLaine has written,

> . . . Karmic justice is the extension of cause and effect, so that the seeds we sow in one lifetime may not be reaped until a much later lifetime. . . .[35]

The seemingly neutral law has a negative, cruel effect. It is more like a sword hanging over one's head, than a way of deliverance from an endless cycle. To talk about "dictating the terms of our futures by our own positive and relentless actions"[36] puts hope of happy hereafter out of the reach of the morally bankrupt. The only hope offered is in the next life, where one can work off the effects of the former life and try to go higher in life's ladder in the next.

New Age advocates hold out a problematic, pathetic form of hope. David H. C. Read, long-time pastor of Madison Avenue Presbyterian Church in New York City, spoke for many when he wrote,

> I am not at all helped by the thought that I may now be expiating some sin of a previous incarnation or enjoying the reward of an exemplary life as a horse in ancient Greece. If, like most of us, I have no knowledge whatever of my past incarnations, how can I derive any benefit from such experiences? If God is in this process, would he not let me know?[37]

Karma is a relentless law from which few escape. To accept the karmic action as the way of salvation means one is willing to agree that life goes on in other forms, but that man has no final destiny. It also means that it has no power to make one good. It only rewards good. Thus one cannot look to karma for help. It lacks the ability, desire, and incentive to intervene. It is a relentless and impersonal law.

The Christian Scriptures, however, show that a personal, all-powerful God has entered history to save man from himself. God has taken the plight of man into consideration. He has set his love on a sinner who cannot keep the law (Rom. 8:3, 4).

A major defect of karma law is that mercy is silenced. The supreme obstacle in reincarnation is karma, which makes salvation entirely man's responsibility. The spiritual foundation of the church and the basis for entrance into the heaven, according to the Scriptures, is God's boundless mercy and amazing grace. Hopeless sinners are not given the brush-off, but the come-on. God extends his invitation and welcome to those who have fallen short of the glory of God (Rom. 3:23) through the saving merit of Jesus Christ given to our account (vv. 24-26). Küng asked the question which goes to the heart of karmic catastrophe: ". . . instead of the pitiless law of causality of karma, why not the God of mercy?"[38]

Reincarnation and karma cater to one's pride. But there is no solution to moral guilt, no admission to guilt, only the recognition of consequences. In reincarnation the problem of evil is not admitted to, nor resolved, for the law of karma only postpones and protracts seeming solutions. Karma is not a net to catch those who falter and fall off the limb, for those who are out on it, but it acts like a hungry shark below waiting for those who lose their balance and fall headlong; whereas in the Bible God's saving grace and his everlasting love have caught us and rescued us from the jaws of hell.

In New Age thought, a person is never truly saved. The picture of heaven in Revelation shows multitudes as far as the eye can see, thousands upon thousands, from every corner of the world. These were sinners who were delivered from the chains of their sins, who were emancipated by the saving power of Christ in his death, burial, and resurrection.

New Age makes the higher incarnations the rewards for the achievers. In terms of volume it is self-presented awards for the few elite, rather than divinely given rewards for the bungling masses. In the Christian faith, however, all are offered the opportunity of entering through Christ to eternal life. One hundred forty-four thousand was the lowest count. It will go to the point which brings counters to the end of their ability to count (Rev. 8, 9). Another contrast between New Age "reincarnated" and messianic age saved is that the New Agers have only a sense of recruitment to their views, not a genuine compassion for the destitute. I sense little concern for losers in the writings of New Age representatives.

Satan is behind the blinding of those who refuse the gospel (2 Cor. 4:4-6). He has a firm grip on those who promote his style of religion, a religion in which a person feels pride, which to him is the epitome of virtue. How different is the faith of the apostles and the message of the Bible! In the Bible we do not look to self for salvation. When we look at self, we see only a helpless sinner. That is why Isaiah 45:22 comes as refreshment to those unsatisfied at the functionless fountain of self.

Turn to me and be saved,
all you ends of the earth;
for I am God, and there is no other (45:22 NIV).

In the Bible we cannot be the solution to our imperfections. We are the problem. That is precisely why Christ came to us.

Reincarnationists say we are all working our way back to God; Christianity says that we are running away from God, but that He has pursued us in Jesus Christ.[39]

Self-improvement schemes do not change us. We do not expect a better life in a next incarnation because we have behaved. Rather, in the removal of our sins from us in Christ, we are enabled to walk free of misdeeds and walk tall from the courtroom of God's justice, realizing that our liberty and new life are the result of God's acquittal based on his Son's payment of our debt. Whereas once we were spiritually dead in trespasses and sins, we are now alive forevermore in Christ (Eph. 2:1).

Reincarnation is only part of a total package. Behind that concept is the view of self. And both ideas—reincarnation and godhood for man—"lie at the heart of New Age teachings."[40] It is not just a different way of looking at ourselves. It involves views on the nature of self, the needs of self, what constitutes evil, what is the way out of evil, what comprises heaven, and how is heaven achieved.

To the New Age mind evil does not exist as legal guilt or as a moral disorder. If one would consult all forms of pantheism and panentheism, one would notice that the matter of evil is the Achilles' heel of their approaches. Since everyone is God, evil is eliminated. One interesting feature of Shirley MacLaine's autobiographies is that she is unable to absolve herself of dismissing evil. In *Out on a Limb* evil was fear. If one could overcome fear, one could get rid of hate.[41] In *Dancing in the Light* she made a valiant attempt to deal with the problem through the character Vassey, who from his Russian Orthodox background, gave Shirley a hard time on how she explained evil. To her evil was a ridiculous concept. At one point she could only say evil is what one says is evil.[42] At another point she said "there is no evil—only the lack of knowledge."[43] "Good" and "bad" were only positive or negative consequences of one's karmic actions. "Evil" is illumination, "evil" is ignorance.[44] Because sin is only in rhetoric, not in reality, there is no need for atonement. To MacLaine and to other New Agers Jesus is not the Savior but the exhorter. In New Age belief Jesus does not rescue, redeem, or restore man to God. At best he only instructs, advises, and encourages.

The New Agers, however, find it difficult to abandon the concept of sin entirely, for they cannot resist pointing out the failure of Christianity. Shirley MacLaine wrote disparagingly of "a particularly destructive form of fundamentalism . . . intolerantly believing *their* God was the only one."[45] Linda Goodman, another New Age voice, chided anyone from thinking that using the words "I accept Jesus as my Savior and God as my King" as unable to deliver a person from his karmic responsibility. On the same page she went on to say, "The 'Jesus saves' mantra often sounds less like a blessing than an unspoken threat."[46]

Salvation in the New Age has nothing to do with deliverance from moral guilt before God. At best it involves (1) alignment with one's energy source; and (2) deliverance from karmic consequences. Reincarnation is the result of one's actions.

New Age thinking sees the Christian heaven as an invention which humiliates man and reduces him to a dependent creature. As we are, says New Age belief, we need inspiration, not intervention. According to Shirley MacLaine, salvation is alignment with God, an alignment with God that does not postulate any sin. It is an alignment with our energy source, not an alignment required by moral deficiency. Salvation is an alignment with God-self as an energy source.[47] As if a goal not reached, she saw salvation as aligning with the Divine intentions of the universe.[48] Yet, in a moment of inconsistency, she stated that "each human being . . . [was] never separated from the God-force. . . ."[49]

The bottom line of the New Age movement is that self is not the problem source, but the solution source. It says that the way to see our conditions improve is not to implore a God outside us, but to look to the God inside us. In their eyes each is capable of devising his own future, of engineering his own improvement.

In New Age thought we carve our own futures. We need to be

stimulated to right thinking, not rescued from eternal destruction. The New Testament teaching of salvation solely because of Christ's substitutionary/propitiatory death is totally rejected, totally absent.

The only other sense of salvation in the New Age would be deliverance from suffering a bad reincarnation due to our prior karmic behavior. Goodman took the familiar story of the believing thief on the cross next to Christ's and turned it into a works-righteousness event. Of the dying thief's faith in Christ she wrote:

> The very act of faith . . . was an act of faith so powerful, so pulsating with conviction and innocence in the face of all contrary evidence, that it balanced the man's karmic scales, allowing that particular physical body to die totally free of the chains of Karma (until and unless in a future incarnation he created new Karma for himself).[50]

The underlying cause of meeting oneself in a past life form or of being freed from the bad consequences of karma, according to New Age thought, is the ability of man to save himself.

The success of New Age views in capturing the public imagination goes back to the need of natural man to feel he can secure his own destiny. Apart from the grace of God, man:

> . . . will always be the one who wants to carry everything. . . . Under no circumstances will he let himself be carried. Therefore, finally, and at the deepest level, he will always be an enemy of grace and a hater and denier of his real neediness.[51]

Thus far we have seen a variety of factors that indicate that New Age thought is incompatible with biblical Christianity. It is a religious belief system that puts man in total charge. Man becomes the absolute measure, for man is the expression of God. The controlling premise of the whole system is the primary one of the identification of God with man. New Age denies man's moral guiltiness before the one true God, that man has been distanced or disadvantaged by an inborn evil nature, that hell exists,[52] and that the human will is impotent to save himself. All together, these denials show that New Age views are at odds with classical Christianity.

The Christian should determine truth not on the basis of what side-effects or what euphoria it creates in the enthusiastic advocate. We should not judge a system by the claims to joyous feelings in the adoptee. If we were, then some credibility would be granted to the New Age movement. One should not, therefore, be convinced of the rightness of the New Age movement on the basis of testimonials, such as given by Shirley MacLaine:

> . . . When you finally begin to scratch the surface of who you are, it is overwhelming. You are never the same, nor do you want to be—and you are, whether you realize it or not, on the path of self-discovery, self-knowledge, and self-revelation.[53]

The New Age movement attracts some interest because they argue that reincarnation was a belief shared by Christ and found in the Bible. It is in the use and misuse of the Scriptures that we shall look next. Reincarnation has been easily confused with Christian beliefs when New Age merchants appeal to the Bible as one of the corroborating sources.

Does the Bible say our experience of heaven began before we were born? Did we have a prior existence as we shall have a future existence? Is our self immortal because it reemerges under different names in other locations at other times? Are we in the process of becoming? Is our purgatory to live out the results of our deeds today in the lives of unknown individuals in our tomorrows? What are we willing to admit as hard evidence for or against the theory of reincarnation? These are key questions New Agers force us to settle rather than sit out.

In New Age the Bible is not cited because it is a final source. They don't need the Bible. Indications are that they both oppose and hate the Bible.[54] And they don't bother to treat it as offering superior wisdom to self and to transchanneled voices. Yet they will throw out a verse and appeal to Jesus to make the unsuspecting public think that Jesus' teachings tend to agree with the New Age ideas.

In those places where they cite the Bible, New Age representatives show an abysmal ignorance both of the Old Testament and the New Testament. Verses are taken out of context,[55] Bible stories which teach salvation by grace (favor) are turned around to teach "reincarnation" by works.[56]

Even biblical history is rewritten to make Jesus out to be a prototype New Ager. In her latest installment of her spiritual pilgrimage, *Going Within*, Shirley MacLaine did this, first, by a pitiful attempt at drawing a parallel between Essene beliefs and the teaching of reincarnation.[57] (Readers ought to smell fraud in her blanket statement, that "traces of Essene teachings appear in almost every culture and religion of the world.)"[58]

MacLaine has taken her alleged capacity to create in the direction of rewriting history. Her next suggestion should make every student of Essene theology cringe when she made the outrageous claim that "Jesus was a student and master of Essene beliefs and techniques."[59] Unfortunately, some unsuspecting readers may be taken in by her sweeping statement. Her psuedo-scholarship and ideological trickery are two matters she has been unsuccessful in purging from her self.

Of course, she designed to prepare the reader for accepting her third great contention by preparing the way with two preparatory propositions in order to soften the readers to accept the notion which knowledgeable Christians should consider blasphemous. She said Jesus was ". . . very much like metaphysical seekers in the New Age today. . . ."[60] That comparison both distorts history and demeans Jesus!

In Shirley MacLaine's first published attempts to justify reincarnation, in *Out on a Limb*, she argued that early-on in the Christian history the church councils edited reincarnation out of the Bible.[61] But in her subsequent autobiographies she dropped that argument. Now she uses the Bible to make reincarnation appear Christian. Whether by deliberate deception or to make good copy, Shirley MacLaine related how she came across two Bible verses that reinforced reincarnation. She had heard from a friend of a friend that the Bible supported reincarnation. Then she said:

> I hadn't a clue where to look. So I did an experiment with myself. I went into a quick silent meditation, got in touch with my higher self, and said, "Where can I find a reference by Christ to reincarnation in the Bible?"
>
> The answer came back: "Most of the references have been discarded, but several still remain. You will find it in the book of Matthew."
>
> I heard the answer in clear English, and it was so definitive I was startled. I went to my bookshelf and pulled out a Gideon Bible.[62]

She found and cited two passages. Quite coincidentally, she would like her readers to know, she fell upon two "golden" confirmations of her belief in reincarnation. The two texts were Matthew 16:13, 14 and 17:12.

To appeal to these two passages in an attempt to justify reincarnation as biblically acceptable is to misuse the Bible.[63] The subject of neither was reincarnation, nor do the descriptions of John the Baptist and of Elijah allow a wedge for reincarnation.

The contention that John's audience, his Jewish contemporaries, were open to reincarnation is a misrepresentation. Old Testament thought did not entertain reincarnation even as a possibility. The fact that they entertained the reappearance of Elijah was not based on the belief that reincarnation was a live option. Strictly speaking, the Hebrews did not equate reappearance with reincarnation. This distinction and historical context of the two passages was ignored by Shirley MacLaine in her discussion of reincarnation.

Elijah had not died (2 Kings 2:11). Therefore, John's contemporaries perceived that a reappearance was possible. A reappearance was entertained in the minds of some of John's audiences. But the popular opinions of the Jewish masses were wide of the truth of what official Old Testament prophecy predicted.

John the Baptist was not Elijah's reincarnation, but a type of Elijah. This was made clear even before John was born. The angel's announcement to John's father, Zechariah, said that John would be going before Jesus "in the spirit and power of Elijah" (Luke 1:17 NIV), not that he would *be* Elijah. Moreover, at the point of John's prophet-forerunner functioning, he reinforced his prebirth-announced role. John the Baptist forcefully and flatly denied that he was the real Elijah revisited (or reincarnated) (John 1:19-23).

What should alert the modern reader to New Age twisting of the Scriptures is the degree to which they go in ignoring the historical context of biblical statements. One of the repeated Old Testament phrases that has been used by several New Age writers in supposed support of reincarnation is "an eye for an eye and tooth for tooth" (Exod. 21:24; Lev. 24:20). MacLaine and Goodman claim that was a karmic statement.[64] What the statement is, however, is not an endorsement of reincarnation, but the prohibition against *excessive* reprisal. The tendency in the exaction of justice had been to go beyond the injuries received. The injunction was to make clear that outrage should not be allowed to escalate to devastating retaliation and annihilation. What is typical in New Age publications is the apparent insignificance of source citing, the giving of book, chapter, and verse. This shuts the reader off from consulting the source material for himself.

Another passage which they have advanced as a reincarnation motif in the New Testament was Jesus' statement to Nicodemus that no one can enter the kingdom of heaven unless he is "born again" (John 3:3). The heavenly rebirth, however, has nothing to do with the cycles of reincarnation. In reincarnation there is no one rebirth, but an unending series of rebirths. The plurality of reincarnations, aside from the context of the passage, should make the modern reader see that the passage has been twisted by New Age. The second point to note is that what Jesus talked of was something to be experienced *before* death, not something resulting at death. Third, the meaning of the expression is explained by the more probable rendering of the Greek word *anothen*, which means "from above." What was being urged was not another form of life, but the life of God entering the dead soul of man, so that he would experience God's life in time.[65]

A credible defense of reincarnation cannot be mounted from the Bible.[66] Not only do their presentations fail as reliable interpretations of specific texts, but they miss seeing how their appeal to karma and self-works fly in the face of the unanimous teaching of Scripture that salvation is a gift from God. Using their own definition of evil as ignorance, one could apply sinfulness to their presentations because they have demonstrated their ignorance both of interpretation methods and of the teaching of Scripture that salvation is the result of God's grace alone, rather than the production of ambitious humans.

The New Age spokespersons have yet to include and face Hebrews 9:27 (NIV), which refers to the fact that "man is destined to die once, and after that to face judgment." The biblical principle is one man, one death, once before God to answer for one life.

Another aspect of their ignorance of Scripture is their having missed the consistent New Testament teaching on the resurrection of the redeemed to heaven and the resurrection of the lost to hell. In attempting to sell her readers that Christianity and reincarnation are compatible, Shirley MacLaine completely avoids the dominating, dynamic doctrine of Christianity of resurrection. Of course the underlying concept of resurrection is the perpetuation of our individuality and its inherent Teflon characteristic—that is, that no additional life forms can stick to it. To mention resurrection is an immediate challenge to reincarnation. The concepts cannot coexist.

The Christian's hope is not a shaky reincarnation but a sure resurrection. There is a world of difference between the two. It would be gross ignorance to confuse them. The resurrection principle (in contrast to reincarnation) is one body only as mortal for one person, and one immortal body for the one redeemed.

Resurrection through Christ begins with being made alive spiritually before death. A person's conversion to Christ is likened to resurrection (Eph. 2:1; John 5:25). What began as the gift of life in regeneration (the biblical concept of "born again") progresses and culminates in the total glorification of the redeemed in a resurrected body like Christ's, the resurrection prototype. Our resurrection will be the culmination and maximization of all that we are individually. It will not be another us, but the continuation but perfected version of who we are.[67]

Throughout her autobiographies Shirley MacLaine has stressed the responsibility of the person.[68] But consistent with her contentions that she is God and that life is illusion, insistence on responsibility lacks a defensible philosophical basis, for one is only responsible for realities, not for illusions; and second, how can one insist at the same time one is responsible, yet insist one is God? If God can be held responsible, then someone is greater than God. Responsibility is a word which is attributed to the creature, not to the Creator. She has shown no awareness of this inconsistency. Sometimes she has anticipated objections to her philosophy, but on this point she offers no defense.

Part of her inability to anticipate this major objection on responsibility is the fact that she has confused accountability and ability. Her recurring emphasis on so-called karmic actions and the importance of seizing responsibility is an old self-salvationist note that man's will is uninfected by evil, and not rendered impotent to achieve perfection.

In *It's All in the Playing* she pulled back the curtain on some tendencies (hardly wrongs) she was willing to share with her readers, such as smoking, her consciousness of an occasional protruding abdomen, and some scary fits of anger.[69] But she has not admitted to her most glaring defects: the hopelessness of her view of the human species. Instead, she made claims that are in agreement with the founder of Protestant liberalism, Friedrich Schleiermacher. One such assertion is: "each individual is a co-creator with God."[70] Another Schleiermachian-sounding sentence of hers was this: ". . . the ultimate enlightenment was to touch the 'Christ' consciousness in themselves and trust it. . . ."[71] But the claim is bogus. The ability is imagined, not real.

In addition the concept that ability is the measure of responsibility has no guarantee to remain true, for as ability wanes or as performance fails, then by the same token responsibility diminishes. Less and less responsibility results, therefore, as one's capacity in moral performance drops. When taken to its final logical conclusion, on the basis of alleged moral ability, moral responsibility can cease entirely. "The wholly evil man thus ends up having no responsibility."[72] Therefore, on philosophical grounds her insistence on responsibility is a chimera, a camouflage for the egotistic claim that she is able on her own to achieve salvation.

Gauged by the enormous sales of her books,[73] Shirley MacLaine is probably a millionaire. But her philosophy of life is bankrupt. She comes up short in providing a credible, compelling outlook on life, on the future, and on herself. In ignoring the Bible, in distorting the Bible where she mentions it, she has concocted a self-destructive philosophy. Her responsibility, which is genuine before the only God, and because he is truly God separate from men and women, will bring her before God's court to answer for the harm her views have inflicted on an unsuspecting, gullible public.

Shirley MacLaine, as part of the New Age, has proposed totally destructive views of her personhood, of God, and of other real people. She is *Out on a Limb* with no net below. Instead of *Dancing in the Light*, she is blind and dancing with her back to the Light of the World. And instead of finding that her views are confirmed *(It's All in the Playing)*, when she exits this stage for the next, she will discover, too late, that she will not be playing someone else. And she will not be acting when she confesses Jesus Christ is Lord to the glory of God. Her best hope is to give up her script and take up Scripture, for there she will learn that her salvation does not result from the way she lived, but in the way Jesus lived, died, and rose again.

Instead of providing practical guidance for achieving spiritual clarity and inner improvements, *Going Within* is but another chapter in her on-going quest of self-salvation. She would urge her readers to get involved in cleansing seven concentration points which allegedly reside in each of us. Along with self-cleansing, she suggests our (alleged) chakra system can be balanced by the use of crystals and colors, body exercises, sound therapy, and labored meditation.[74]

Shirley MacLaine was right in recognizing that self needs cleansing, but the cleansing the human ego needs cannot be accomplished by us. Only the purging power of God Himself can achieve that. In Jesus Christ we are assured Christ's death purged us from our accumulated guilt and from self-centered living (Rom. 3:23-25; Heb. 9:44; 1 Peter 3:18).

Apart from God's grace man cannot get in touch with that part of his ego which is infected with sin. Instead of trying to get hold of one's inner self to scrub it, seekers after a new life should get hold of Christ as He has revealed Himself in the Scriptures. Salvation is not achieved by seeking harmony with self, but in being brought into harmony with God through Jesus Christ. *God* must go within us and bring to the surface through Scripture and Spirit what we don't want to see. And what we see of our true selves, in the light of God's holiness, we need in the Spirit's strength to turn to Christ for cleansing, forgiveness, and restoration.

Appendix:

Is the Millennium Heaven
?

Books on heaven are usually published separately from books on the millennium. First it is more practical to focus on the future life one phase at a time than to try to cover two major topics in one volume. To thoroughly cover both subjects at once would be too demanding, too costly. For this reason, some may question the wisdom of raising the matter of millennium here. What is attempted here, however, is not to deal with the millennium in any exhaustive way, but to show as concisely and cogently as possible, that Revelation 20:1-6 is about life in heaven now, not about life on earth later.

These two subjects are often published separately because they are considered two distinctly different matters. Premillennialists believe heaven is not the millennium and that the millennium is not heaven. This view is based on the assumption that the millennium is a literal one thousand years of peace on the earth. Hal Lindsey is probably the best known representative of this usage of millennium. His books have contributed to the resurgence of millennialism.

As I see it, the Intermediate State of heaven and the millennium are inseparable. According to Revelation 20:1, Christ's reign began with the limiting of Satan and continues in heaven with those who are with him. It is not a literal one thousand years, but the span of the messianic age. In view of the fact that I see the millennium as part of heaven now, I would be remiss not to give the reasons in taking this position, hence this Appendix.

The two concepts (millennium and the Intermediate Heavenly State) are interchangeable. Revelation 20:1-6 is the Intermediate State, or heaven between the first and second coming of Christ. That this view has any basis in the text is dismissed by a large number of Christians. To seriously maintain the view that Revelation 20:1-6 is about a condition now is regarded as an interpretation to be hooted at, if not considered heretical, so deeply are people convinced that the millennium could not be heaven by any stretch of the imagination.

Chiliasm (another name for millennialism) has been around for a long time. In addition to orthodox Fathers Justin Martyr (100-165) and Irenaeus (last quarter of the second century), the physical millennium advocates have also included suspect leaders of the first and second centuries: Cerinthus, Montanus, and Tertullian. The idea that the earth would be ruled by Christ for one thousand literal years began with some early church fathers is pushed less than the contention that it went as far back as Isaiah, or as far back as John of Patmos. But the Fathers were largely infants in interpretive skills. And, as will be shown, Revelation never taught a geophysical millennium in which Israel figures prominently.

The motivation behind chiliasm or millennialism has been sincere and reflects a biblically justifiable concern that God is not done with the earth, that God will not finally abandon the globe to corruption, chemical and moral. All this is good. But millennialism was fostered partly by the confusion between references to new earth and one-thousand-year reign of Christ. Even today this confusion continues.

Is it to go contrary to what Scripture teaches to deny a physical, literal one thousand-year reign on the earth? Millennialists should step back from their emphasis to wonder whether they are not harping on the wrong note. After all the Bible does teach that God through Christ is going to remake, reclaim, and repopulate the old earth in its new state and that the heavenly population above will be inhabiters of the new earth below for eternity and not a measly one thousand years. This oversight was what struck John Calvin as regrettable. He wrote in his *Institutes* (III. 25:5): "Those who assign only a thousand years to the children of God to enjoy the inheritance of future life, observe not how great an insult they offer to Christ and his kingdom" (Henry Beveridge translation).

I am fully aware that this explanation of the millennium may never discourage or weaken the tenacious loyalty of long-time millennialists. Their commitment to the system is partly related to the modern mentality and to the modern methodology of how people form beliefs. The perpetuation of belief in the literal one thousand years of peace on the earth is fed by at least two factors: foremost is a literalistic mind-set. This, above all, holds them back from dealing with Revelation 4-21 in a way that honors its apocalyptic style. The second ingredient that fosters millennialism is presentations that deplore rather than deploy other options.

On top of that, premillennial paperbacks are everywhere. Often radio and TV preachers parrot premillennial catchwords as if the issues are settled. Influential evangelical schools of theology have adopted a pretribulational, premillennial eschatology as a touchstone of orthodoxy. Some millennial representatives and advocates have gone as far to both directly state or indirectly suggest that if one believes the Bible, then one has no other option but to hold to the millennium as an earthly paradise in which peace prevails.

Thankfully, however, here and there probing evangelicals are more demanding of eschatological spokespersons. The new learner wants to be presented with a choice, and not to be force-fed. He is no longer satisfied with cliches, party lines, and demands for conformity. He is seeing through smokescreens and turning from literalism in eschatology. The popularity of books that sympathetically explore several options continues. A new openness to examine the opposite side has contributed to a fresh atmosphere. Those who are asking the right questions are unhappy until they find more substantive answers. Church classes contribute to the airing of views and to the value of further study. Study Bibles that offer readers a variety of eschatological solutions (rather than just one eschatological slant) are making gains over those which present a tailored system. The curious of both sexes and those perpetually young of mind are eager to know what lies behind alternative viewpoints. Christians are reading more widely. They are out for second opinions. They are thinking for themselves.

Before we dive into the question: "Is heaven the millennium?" several statements need to be said up front. First, *that there is a millennium.* But the millennium of popular consumption is not the millennium of Revelation 20. The true millennium is the messianic age and the Intermediate State. I believe the evidence from Revelation 12 and 20 (through reduplication) point that way.

It will be shown that premillennialism is misguided. In exercising the principle of literalism in the interpretation of apocalypse, it misuses the Book of Revelation that it seeks to honor.

This task is not an easy one; premillennialists have a built-in advantage with those who have a strong Eden nostalgia. Seekers of utopian ideals are ready-made millennial adherents.

They think of the millennium as the golden age when purity pervades society. The average Christian associates the millennium with a sinless earthly society. But *the millennium of true-blue, informed millennarians is not a millennium without evil.*

Finally, it appears that presentations about the glories of a physical millennial period have relied mostly on parroting a tradition rather than on hard evidence. It is not that millennialists take the Bible too seriously, but that they don't take the Bible seriously enough.

To achieve these aims two topics will be presented: first, to show how premillennialism has insurmountable problems. The theory is pretty, but the probability is remote. Second, the presentation of the teachings of the brief passage—the only passage where a thousand-year reign appears—Revelation 20:1-6.

The Problems with Premillennialism

Three major obstacles prohibit advocates of a physical millennialism in making a credible case: (1) the effect of Christ's second coming; (2) the problem of evil in the millennium; (3) the separation of resurrections. Look at these now.

1. *The effect of Christ's second coming.* According to millennialism Christ returns to the earth a second time. For many, it is not rapture (considered the first phase of his second coming, according to popular premillennialism), but Revelation, the second phase of Christ's second coming.

When does Christ return the second time? Postmillennialists say *after* the millennium. (In this they agree with amillennialists.) But while historic premillennialists say there is no rapture (only one second coming, the revelation), they say with the dispensational premillennialists that Christ comes *before* the millennium. Both historic premillennialism and dispensational premillennialism say that the final destruction of the wicked take place *after* the literal one-thousand-year reign on the earth.

Perhaps if we used a pugilistic analogy the differences could be seen more easily. Dispensational premillennialists see in Christ's contest in the historical ring a one-two punch landing on the chin of the wicked. For them the first hit is at his second coming, when Christ initiates the millennium. During the millennium round (indeed a record round—one thousand years!) Christ beats up on Satan's supporters who enter the ring from the stands. Then at the end of the millennium, *POW*—Christ wallops all the wicked and Satan in one final blow.

Premillennialists contend that the wicked are not destroyed or called to judgment at the church's rapture. (Historic premillennialists say the dispensationalists distort the Scriptures by saying there is a secret rapture before the final revelation of Christ.) For both the historical premil and the dispensational premil viewpoints Christ's return is not *pow,* and the fight is over, but *pow* (the first *pow* is the revelation-second coming) and a thousand-years' round before the final blows are given (prior to the Great White Throne Judgment). According to premillennialism only *after* the millennium does Christ land the last punch. Then only is the fight over and Christ declared the winner, according to premillennialism. Then only will Christ flatten Satan and the wicked nations which will be followed by the White Throne Judgment and the inauguration of the eternal state.

Ironically, in *neither* the rapture *nor* the revelation of Christ (in both branches of premillennialism) is there a decisive and final knockout! The wicked are not completely destroyed when Jesus comes in the revelation, according to historic premillennialism. That's incredible! If the earth is where the millennium takes place and where Christ reigns, and the reign ends in a mass revolt, it would seem to be a reign that was failing and failed.

When reading the New Testament passages dealing specifically with Christ's second coming, one sees no such separation in the text. It simply does not read that way. To reduce the second coming to a series of staggering blows, but no conclusive KO when Christ returns to render judgment is bending the Bible to fit a preconceived idea, and renders premillennial rapture a hypothesis without biblical backing.

Scripture says the wicked are destroyed at Christ's second coming (Matt. 13:40-42; 24:39; 25:31, 32; 2 Thess. 1:8-10; 2:8; 2 Peter 3:9, 10, Rev. 19:17-21). One of the favorite passages used regarding the rapture as a separate phase of the second coming is 1 Thessalonians 4:14-18. What is passed over is the continuation of Christ's descent into chapter 5:1, 2 and following. Resurrected believers ascend to meet Christ to accompany him down to the earth, escorting him to the place of judgment (such is the sense of eis apantesis). The day of the Lord (5:2) is part of the second coming descent of Christ. There is no gap in the text. (Chapter divisions were not Paul's!) When Christ comes and is greeted by the saints, he proceeds immediately to judgment (1 Thess. 5:1-11).

Sinners will not survive the second coming of Christ. Christ's enemies are defeated never to recover. Then all fates are finalized. The "last day" of John 6:39, 40 allows for no interim. The final judgment occurs. The above passages indicate that judgment of the wicked takes place at the same time of Christ's return. Hell proper is inaugurated at Christ's revelation. Following Christ's second coming the old earth and heavens are remade.

At Christ's return, Psalm 2:9 will be fulfilled. He will smash the wicked as if they were clay pots. The phrase is borrowed several times in Revelation (2:26, 27; 19:15) to describe the second coming. "Rule" (used in Revelation) was carried over from the Septuagint (LXX—Greek Translation of Old Testament) version of the passage. John used LXX Psalm 2:9, "rule" rather than the Hebrew, "break." "Break" (in the Hebrew text) assumed strong resistance. The ruling with a rod of iron alluded to a climactic event, an initial breaking, *not* a continuous ruling (Arthur Lewis, *The Dark Side of the Millennium*, pp. 30, 31). He referred to Christ's return as the one event of punishment of the wicked, rather than an ongoing "beat-'em-down" rule for one thousand literal years.

2. *The presence of evil in the millennium.* Hal Lindsey and premillennialists admit that evil men will occupy the earth during the literal one-thousand-year reign of Christ (Hal Lindsey, *The Rapture,* pp. 65, 143; earlier, W. Boyd Carpenter, *C. J. Ellicott Bible Commentary* (London: Cassell and Co., Ltd., 1908), vol. 8:625: "The millennial reign is clearly, therefore, not a period in which the rule of Christ is universally and sincerely accepted. There are powers at work which compete for human affections and interests; but the general acceptance of Christian principles keeps the evil forces in abeyance; and the gracious strength of God limits the power of the arch enemy."

The premillennialists admit to unbelieving offspring. (Compare their interpretation of Zech. 14:17-19). A massive revolt against Christ, organized by a recently released Satan from the abyss, would be impossible without the persistence of evil in humans (Rev. 20:7, 8). The earthly millennium has sinners revolting and ready to join a united action against Christ at the end of that period. Consequently Christ's ruling with an iron rod is hardly "happy days." It is more like a legalistic armed camp, a punitive house arrest for the wicked.

Millennium mesmerizes people. The fifth column in the millennium is little stressed. It is rarely mentioned by some. The majority let slide the presence of evil in the millennium, even though beaten down by Christ. They choose to minimize it or not pay any attention to it. Some imagine that the millennium will be without sin, but such is not the view of the trained millennialists (although admittedly they don't dwell on this aspect of the millennium because it is somewhat embarrassing).

The argument that a millennium period cannot be now, because of evil in the world, cannot be conscientiously used or used without a red face against the amillennialists or inaugurated millennialists. After all, according to the premillennial viewpoint, evil exists in the millennium, though controlled under Christ's rule. Their system requires a strange restriction on Christ's second coming: he will come, they contend, but sinners will not be brought to a final halt. Traditionally, however, Christians have seen the Scriptures saying that it is impossible to have the second coming of Christ and not have sinners gone.

Premillennialists cannot grant that sinners will be destroyed at Christ's second coming, for if they are destroyed, then they cannot live a thousand years. Premillennialists cannot have and eat their cake. With Christ back, sinners are automatically gone. Arthur Lewis's comments are to the point: "It is undeniable that there is no biblical support for the idea that evil men or wicked nations will manage to slip by the judgments set at the end of the age" (*The Dark Side of the Millennium*, p. 25).

3. *The separation of resurrections.* Regarding the timetable of the resurrection of sinners and saints, there may be some difference of opinion among premillennialists and dispensationalists but they agree that the resurrection of the saints is kept separate from the resurrection of the wicked, and in conjunction with this, dispensationalists hold that the judgment of Christians and non-Christians are held at different times. The denial of a general resurrection and of a general judgment, however, goes counter to Matthew 25:31-46, John 5:28, 29, and Acts 24:15. Earlier we noted that to have a simultaneous judgment was not unusual, for every time the gospel is preached judgment takes place. Those who are judged believers and those who confirm their position of rejection or unbelief

individually respond negatively or positively each time the Word is preached. The concluding position of Revelation 20 does not support their distinction. It is straining Revelation 20:11-15 to argue that it refers exclusively to the resurrection of the non-believer. The language of the passage would be meaningless if it meant only the non-Christian, for it says, "If any one's name was not found in the book of life . . ." implying that there were those whose names *were* in the Book of Life. We shall reserve our comments on the significance of the phrase "first resurrection" when we deal with the meaning of the central millennial passage, Revelation 20:1-6.

The Message of Revelation 20:1-6

Two key interpretative principles enable a person to work through this section and come out feeling that it is not total enigma. These two principles, when ignored, produce a physical, earthly millennialism. First, when only lip service is given to the fact that Revelation is apocalypse, when the symbolic character of the book is used only when convenient, it is no wonder that physical millennialism gains momentum. The second principle is that of reduplication or repetition. It is this that shows that Revelation 20 is what is going on now in heaven for those who are in the Intermediate State.

To interpret apocalypse literally is to violate its structure, intention, and message. Premillennialists are premillennialists because they are literalists. They allow literalism to be their hermeneutical tool in prying open the meaning of the text. But in apocalyptic writing this leads to both absurdities and aberrations. If literalism is the way to interpret Revelation 20:1-6, then why is it not used in 6:14 where the heavens are said to be removed, yet in what follows the heavens remain? Or, how can the extinction of the third part of the day in 8:12 be due to the extinction of a third part of the sun, moon, and stars? Doubtless they would recognize the symbolisms in these places, but they shift from recognizing the symbolisms earlier to deny symbolism in 20:1-6. It raises the question whether they treat the book as consistently apocalyptic or whether they make it selectively (and conveniently) apocalyptic. The Christian public ought to question whether they have adopted a legitimate interpretive procedure. When that is done, then their last word on the millennium will not appear accurate, attractive, and absolute.

Another place where selective symbolism is used by pretribulational, premillenialists is in the meaning of the various numbers of Revelation. The apocalyptic nature of the book should mean that *all* numbers are symbolic, even in those instances when the numbers have a basis in history. For instance, the on-target number of the 7 churches, the 7 kings, and the 7 hills of Rome are the only places where, coincidentally, there appear symbolisms in the actual numbers. But most commentators recognize that it is a major mistake to take 1,000 years as a literal 1,000 years. The fact that 1,000 years is used six times (20:2, 3, 4, 5, 6, 7) does not warrant the conclusion that it is 1,000 *literal* years. Bruce K. Waltke commented, "If 'key,' 'chain,' 'dragon,' 'abyss,' etc., are symbolic, why should the number 1,000 be literal, especially when numbers are notoriously symbolic in apocalyptic literature? The potential danger of interpreting numbers in apocalyptic literature literalistically can be seen in the aberrant eschatology of Seventh-Day Adventists and Jehovah's Witnesses, who derive their theology in part by applying that method to Dan. 8:14 and Rev. 14:1-4" ("Kingdom Promises as Spiritual," *Continuity and Discontinuity*, Essays in Honor of S. Lewis Johnson, Jr., edited by John S. Feinberg [Westchester, IL: Crossway Books, 1988], p. 273).

One thousand is a large number, but it is meant to represent both a long and limited period, a symmetric completion of what God has decreed. God gives the church on earth a limited time to spread the gospel to the nations (Matt. 24:14). He will complete the body of Christ within the length of time he sets, and Satan will be let out for his full-scale counteroffensive and Christ's final bashing and banishing of Satan.

The second interpretive guide we need to use in interpreting Revelation is reduplication. Millennium occurs earlier in the book, but without the use of the expression "a thousand years." The deceased martyrs of 20:4 are mentioned in 6:9-11 and 8:3-5. The "home free" state of the redeemed in the Intermediate State of heaven occurs also in 12:14. In the same way, Armageddon (16:16), cannibalistic feast (19:17-19), and Gog and Magog (20:7-9) deal with the same final confrontation of Christ's forces and Satan's. At the same time, caution must be maintained, for it appears that the use of the Abyss is not to be confused with the lake of fire, for while Satan is held in chains in the abyss (20:1), it will not be until later that he will be cast into the lake of fire (20:10).

Once we keep in the forefront of our thinking these two principles, we will be less likely to draw outrageous conclusions from 20:1-6. In the light of these governing factors, several observations arise.

Apocalypse requires that differing symbolisms be maintained. For instance, it says of heaven that there is a temple (7:15), and it says the temple is no more (21:22). In 8:7 all is said to be destroyed, but in 9:4 the grass is unhurt. In 16:1 all the bowls are poured out on the earth, but in 16:8, 17 one is poured on the sun, another on the air. Similarly, in 12:9 Satan is hurled down and in 20:2 Satan is bound. (The functioning of the two beasts in chapter 13 shows that the binding of Satan was real, but didn't stop all evil.)

A positive, total-book understanding of Revelation 20:1-6 is that it is *pro*millennial. But the millennium is the extended time between the first and second comings of Christ and focuses on the bliss of the redeemed in the Intermediate State.

Arrival at this conclusion is the result of taking two hermeneutical principles to heart (1) apocalyptic genre and (2) reduplication. These principles significantly contribute to making sense of two vital factors in the text: (a) the meaning of the binding of Satan; and (b) the meaning of the first resurrection. On these two matters rests the weight of our understanding of what type of millennial reign of Christ was in mind. We need next to look at these items in some detail.

The Binding of Satan: (20:1, 2)

In Matthew 12:29 the same verb (binding) occurs as in Revelation 20:2 *(deo)*. The binding of Satan in Revelation 20:2 is done by an angel. Here we see a rare imagery used in the context of high Christology. Christ is compared to an angel, but while it is untypical, we must understand that it is within the medium of apocalypse. The reduplication principle again gives us our first clue regarding the identity of the angel in 20:1. Revelation 12 is a commentary on Revelation 20.

Revelation 12:7-9 pictures the archangel Michael as having cast down the dragon (Satan) who was too weak for him. In the Old Testament the archangel Michael was another name for Messiah (Dan. 12:1 refers to the messianic figure as the archangel; for argumentation *see* E. W. Hengstenberg, *Christology of the Old Testament* (Grand Rapids: Kregel Publications, 1956), vol. IV:266-268; strangely James A. Borland, *Christ in the Old Testament* (Moody Press, 1978) did not deal with this text.

Milton S. Terry (1840-1914) properly understood Revelation 12:7, 8. He wrote: "Having appeared in 10:1, as the strong covenant angel of light, he now appears as Michael the archangel, the great leader of the hosts of heaven against the prince of hell" (p. 386, *Biblical Apocalyptics* [Grand Rapids: Baker Book House, 1898, 1988]). As only the wounded Lamb was worthy to open the book of God's decrees, so the mighty

Michael-figure-Christ was the only one powerful enough to thump down the dragon.

The contention that Christ was viewed as an angel is not based solely on an Old Testament apocalyptic source, for in the Old Testament, according to the writer of Hebrews, the angel of Jehovah was Jesus (Hebrews 6:13, in citing Genesis 22:16, identifies Jesus with the angel of Jehovah; in addition, the great angel of the covenant [Genesis 22:11, 12] is, according to Hebrews 12:25, Jesus. The one speaking is not Moses but Jesus, the second Person of the Trinity (*see* 12:26. John Owen argues cogently on these texts from Hebrews). A strong case can be made that the angel reference in Revelation 10:1 is to Christ.

It is likely, also, that Malachi 3:1 alluded to the angel of the covenant as the Lord, Christ (compare Karl Barth, *Church Dogmatics* I/1, p. 323; earlier Carl Friedrich Keil [1807-1888], *Commentary on the Minor Prophets* 2:456-459; E. W. Hengstenberg (1802-1869), *Christology of the Old Testament*, 4:162-171, especially 168; R. T. France's objection *Jesus in the Old Testament* [Baker Book House, 1982, p. 91 n31] is answered in Hengstenberg: similarity of essence does not overthrow logical-historical order of appearance.) The angel of the covenant was Christ.

In the New Testament one may deduce from First Thessalonians 4:16 and John 5:25-29 that the voice of the archangel is actually the voice of the Son of God (Hengstenberg; similarly J. Stewart Russell, *The Parousia*, (1878), p. 419; and G. G. Findlay, *The Epistles to the Thessalonians* [Cambridge, 1891], p. 100).

It should be noted that in Revelation 20:1, the angel was not given the key, but that he possessed the key already. It was rabbinic teaching that only God had the prerogative of having immediate access to the spirit world. Jesus said in 1:18, "I hold the keys of death and Hades."

Certainly, the attribution of Christ having, holding, possessing, using, and retaining the keys to spirit-world compartments was stated in Revelation 1:5, 18; 3:7. Revelation 20:1, therefore, would best apply to Christ.

In the light of the foregoing, therefore, Leon Morris's claim that "Christ is never called an angel in this book" has to be set aside (Leon Morris, *Revelation*, Tyndale New Testament Commentary [Grand Rapids: Wm. B. Eerdmans Publishing Co., 1983], p. 137).

We are accustomed to think that "angel" (which occurs over sixty times in the book) was used only one way in Revelation. But such was not the case. There is a good reason to take "angel" in the introduction to the seven letters to the seven churches, for instance, as applying to the local pastor (2:1, 8, 12, 18; 3:1, 7, 14). J. B. Lightfoot (*Philippians* [London: Macmillan Co., 1869], p. 198) argued against this. But Theodore Zahn (*Introduction to the New Testament* [Grand Rapids: Kregel Publications, 1909, 1953], pp. 414, 415, 422, 423) answered his objections. George E. Ladd's objection that to think of the "angels" as pastors "violates the New Testament usage" of angel (*The Revelation of John*, p. 35) fails to note in James 2:25 the word "angels" (Greek text here, elsewhere they were called "spies") spoke to Rahab about the glories of the Lord. Although considered an improbable reading, the Greek text at Revelation 2:20 has "*your* wife" in some significant manuscripts (found in the Uncial Alexandrinus, Uncial #046, and 8 minuscules, as well as the Peshitta, and in the early fathers Cyprian [A.D. 258], Andrew of Caesarea [A.D. 614], and Arethas [A.D. 914]). It would mean that the spiritual "Jezebel" in the church was the pastor's wife!

In the light of the foregoing documentation, we should be more flexible in listing the meanings of "angel" in Revelation. The meaning of "angel" as pastor is a particularly hard one to swallow. In view of the fact that many churches regard their pastors as hired employees, it probably goes against the grain of many present-day church boards to think of their ministers as "angels." It may be of some comfort to the boards that the word "angel" does not designate personality, but office (p. 60, R. C. Trench, *Commentary on the Epistles of the Seven Churches in Asia* 6th ed. [Minneapolis, MN: Klock and Klock, 1897, 1978]).

The binding of Satan means that Satan is denied full control of the destiny of human history and of the nations within history. From Christ's incarnation onward he has been prevented from giving full vent to an anti-Christian thrust in governmental actions. In comparison, the Christian gospel has been allowed to expand worldwide because Satan's previous hold on the nations was reduced though not removed. Christ bound Satan in his coming to earth (compare John 12:31; Matt. 12:29). Surely, the powers of evil are described as working in the world and that the world represents the satanic slant (Rev. 13:1f; 1 John 5:19). But "throughout the gospel age in which we now live the influence of Satan, though certainly not annihilated, is so curtailed that he cannot prevent the spread of the gospel to the nations of the world" (Anthony A. Hoekema, *The Bible and the Future*, p. 229).

Christians placed under ban and arrest, and subjected to horrendous death are said to be praying for the vindication of their losses in the place where they have found peace (6:9-11), to be nurtured in safety in heaven (12:13-17), and to rest from their labors in satisfaction (14:13). These descriptions are passive in nature.

Revelation 20:4, 5 refer to martyred saints and departed Christians presently reigning in heaven. The one thousand years, therefore, refers not to an earthly paradise, but to the reign of redeemed saints from and in heaven. They are participants in the execution of God's justice: "judgment was given unto them" (20:4 KJV). Revelation 20: 4, 5 makes the claim that the martyrs and deceased Christians are not "out of it" though they are dead. But this is not the only place where the reigning of the saints is mentioned in Revelation.

The reduplication principle of Revelation enlarges, clarifies, and specifies what this reigning entails. By itself, the reigning reference would seem to suggest that in the Intermediate State of heaven saints in heaven are engaged in some kind of judicial function. Does this involve collection of evidence (judicial process in biblical terms included the hearing, collecting, and recording of evidence) and possibly making lower-court judgments subject to review by the final judge?

At this point the earlier reference in Revelation to "reigning" illuminates how their judicial function was perceived. Consider, first, that an intimation of Christians' reigning powers appear *before* they die and go to be with Christ. Revelation 11:5, 6 say that a degree of judicial authority belongs to Christ's witnesses before they die, for their preaching, reminiscent of Moses and Elijah powers, is able to reduce proud thoughts to rubble.

Richard Lenski pointed out that the expression "fire comes from their mouths and devours their enemies" is a reference to the fact that it is the Bible on their lips that acts as a word of judgment on the world, similar to Jeremiah 5:14 (Lenski, *Revelation*) pp. 337, 584. Clearly, the prophetic function (11:3) is their bringing to bear the Scriptures on society. When the Word is preached we exercise our reigning power and God's judging takes effect in the spoken word.

But the portion which casts further light on the nature of the reigning is Revelation 8:3-5. This follows the sixth seal (6:12-16), which describes the cataclysm accompanying Christ's second coming. Revelation 7:1-17 is an interlude— anticipation of the glories of the final heaven. Revelation 8:1-5 covers, in recap fashion, the parallel period *before* the return of Christ or the same time frame as 20:1-6.

In 8:3-5 we learn that the judicial function of the saints in glory is through liturgical means. By their prayers the saints rule, for their prayers effect God's judgment on the world (8:5). In the Intermediate State in heaven, prayer, it appears, does not cease. "The prayers of the saints play an essential part in bringing the judgment of God upon the earth and its inhabitants" (Robert H. Mounce, *The Book of Revelation*, p. 182).

Surely, if the prayers of departed saints affect the course of history, our prayers bring about changes now. James Ramsey [1814-1871] in his partial commentary on Revelation (Edinburgh: The Banner of Truth, 1873, 1977) expanded on this function: "The rulers of the earth . . . ignore the prayers of the saints as having any influence on the course of political events, the safety or the ruin of parties, or of commonwealths. . . . These prayers . . . are none the less effective in secretly shaping the influences that sweep before them all human affairs" (p. 362). There is a sense today in which Christians reign through their prayers. We have a foretaste of our further reigning the more we engage in prayer on earth. The sense of triumph is unavoidable when one not only approaches the throne of grace, but also when from our knees we turn from the throne to see answers to our prayers. "Through God we shall do valiantly. And it is He who will tread down our adversaries" (Ps. 60:12 NASB).

Therefore, reigning in heaven not only produces vindication of Christ's cause, it also means the prayers of the saints are coordinated with the execution of God's decrees. Milton S. Terry thought perhaps the church was constituted as a jury or that individual Christians were considered associate justices (p. 451, *Biblical Apocalyptics*). To introduce a jury, however, into a heavenly justice system that never had a jury is improbble (in the courts of the Lord, the Lord is judge, jury, and executioner). Christ cojudges with the Father. In the final eschatological state it is doubtful that even perfected believers will do anything more than expedite the justice of God. Glorified saints will probably have less to do with the arbitration of cases and more to do with the implementation of God's will.

We should not push the church's inherent reign rights ahead to the point that they are totally confined to the eternal state. This has been a fault, I believe, in evangelical eschatology. Several biblical texts suggest that our involvement in reigning *precedes* the last judgment. This aspect of believer involvement in events has not received sufficient attention.

In Revelation Christians are active participants in the history of the world. The prayers of the saints focus, not only on the expansion of Christ's mission work and the coming to faith of new people chosen by God, but they also hone in on the frustration, consternation, and curtailment of the work of Satan in society. Christian prayers implement God's decrees in maintaining and strengthening of Christ's limitation of Satan's activity. In this way the prayers of believers, both living and dead, unite in a wraparound effect of the chain that holds Satan in check. The prayers of believers reflect part of the binding of Satan. Although praise of Christ by the heavenly dwellers is a major occupation of those in the Intermediate State (compare Revelation 5), present participation in earthly events seems to be a signficant role as well. And central in their prayers is the galling, diverting, and defeat of Satan by the reversal and routing of Satan's understudies by the multiplication of converts and the subtraction of divisions in the visible church.

Just prior to his arrest, Jesus foretold his disciples: "Truly, truly, I say to you, he who believes in Me, the works that I do shall he do also; and greater works than these shall he do; because I go to the Father" (John 14:12 NASB) This promise was not just for the disciples, later apostles, but for ordinary believers today ("whoever believes"—a participle). What he had in mind were not works of greater quality, but ones of greater quantity, which would result from his ascension, from the presence of the Holy Spirit, and from the prayers of believers. "The 'greater works,'" wrote Beasley-Murray, "are the actualization of the realities to which the works of Jesus point, the bestowal of the blessings and powers of the kingdom of God upon men and women which the death and resurrection of Jesus are to let loose in the world" (*Commentary on John*, p. 255).

The extension of Christ's presence through the witness of the church has produced ongoing changes in human lives from Pentecost onward. *The Acts of the Apostles* is a sample history of the mighty works Jesus predicted. The church at prayer was the church exercising its reigning rights. And, since then, testimonies of the transforming grace of God down the centuries are reminders of the living monuments of Christ's power in the world. The fact that Jesus' exhortation to prayer immediately follows (John 14:13, 14) indicated that the risen Lord responds in strength to the feeblest, faintest request to him for intervention and involvement. Jesus predicted that he would do greater things through them and along with that, predicted that they would ask for greater things. There is a sense, therefore, that the true church desires, expresses, exerts, implements, and experiences a reigning authority before being finally gathered in heaven.

In Roman Catholic theology prayer is a powerful instrument for good. In that view the living can pray dead people out of purgatory and the dead in heaven (usually saints) can pray for the living. As they see it, the Virgin Mary and the saints should be asked to pray for persons on earth. Though their theological practice includes the unceasing activity of the deceased saints, the saints in heaven are not appealed to the way the deceased are sought by spiritualists.

In spiritualism the dead do not return to life, but they influence life by renewing contact with the living. In spiritualism "the dead serve as the source of spontaneous inspiration, intuitive moral guidance, and scientific achievement. The dead, moreover, have more power than the Catholic saints who can only ask God or Christ to help their devotees" (pp. 297, 298, Colleen McDannell, Bernhard Lang, *Heaven: A History*).

Scripture is against prayers *for* the dead. It is also against prayers *to* the dead. But, apparently, it is not against prayers *of* the dead. Those "asleep in Jesus" (1 Thess. 4:13-15) are not unconscious, but engage in praying for us. This is not a lapse into spiritualism's intrusion of the dead into history, for God through the Spirit executes his will as believers participate in willing his will. Nor do the prayers of departed believers become a substitute for our need to pray. Nor do the prayers of departed believers mean the prayers of those in heaven are more readily heard than ours. We do not need to pray to the dead for them to pray for us. They pray for us without our asking.

What I have suggested regarding the prayers of deceased believers and the influence they have on history is neither a eulogization of believers in heaven as expounded in Catholicism, nor the eerie contact of the dead with the living as expressed in the teachings of spiritualism. My understanding of this phase of "realized eschatology" neither relinquishes prayers to the dead, nor does it propose the dead influence history on their own or at our pleadings.

Scriptural conformity means texts on the deceased be taken more seriously. In the past evangelical eschatology has had two enormous gaps: (1) Not much is said about what the deceased believers do in the Intermediate State; and (2) not much is said about what happens with the new earth. Part of this void is due, of course, to the fact that Scripture doesn't say as much on it as on other aspects of eschatology. But that may have less bearing on the meager amount of commentary on this subject than the cultural fear that what is suggested may smack too much of Catholicism or of spiritualism.

Amillennialists should have more to say on this subject than others, because it is part and parcel of their position that the saints are presently reigning. Because the millennium is the messianic age, it is proper to expect evidences of his rule. I have suggested how his rule works out in our time as well as in the eternal ages to come. Another area in which amillennialism can make a positive contribution relates to the function and activities of the new earth. There has been a tendency to back away from this subject and make it an eschatological no-man's land.

We have looked at the significance of the binding of Satan. We have yet to look at the crucial phrase "first resurrection" in Revelation 20.

The Meaning of the "First Resurrection"

Those who espouse millennialism rest their case very heavily on the meaning of the first reference to resurrection in the passage (20:5). The late George Eldon Ladd, who has been critical of dispensational premillennialism, based his acceptance of a physical millennium on the assumption that in 20:4 nothing less than a physical resurrection was intended.

The case for or against physical millennialism largely rests on this issue. Did John use "resurrection" in any sense other than physical? Ladd and others have argued that resurrection always and without exception has the sense of physical resurrection. But the root *(zaō)* is used in Revelation in several places (3:1; 4:9, 10; 7:2; 15:7) in the sense of being alive, not in the sense of bodily resurrection.

The apocalyptic genre does not lend support to a literal interpretation of "resurrection" in the phrase "first resurrection" (20:4, 5). Henry B. Swete has noted this: "To infer . . . that the *ezesan* of v. 4 must be understood of bodily resuscitation is to interpret apocalyptic prophecy by methods of exegesis which are proper to ordinary narrative" (*Commentary on Revelation* [Grand Rapids: Kregel Publications, 1977 (1911)], p. 263). Being alive is the sense of first resurrection, for 20:5 a and b is parenthetical (*see* Swete, Ibid.). In other words, the writer's sense of "first resurrection" is caught when we read the fourth and fifth verses together: "They came to life and reigned with Christ a thousand years. . . . This is the first resurrection" (NIV).

Meredith G. Kline, more recently, has pointed out that the use of "first" has less to do with the temporal sequence and more to do with the form of resurrection in the history of redemption, that is, *first* was used in the sense of "new" or as an initial expression of the final form. (*See* his article "First Resurrection," *Westminster Theological Journal*, vol. 37 [1975]: 366-375). Thus, the expression means to emphasize, in a continuation of Jesus' emphasis in Luke 20:35-37, that our going up to heaven is like a resurrection in the same sense as our getting up out of grave is characteristic of our second resurrection. Kline states it well: "Just as the resurrection of the unjust is paradoxically identified as 'the second death' so the death of the Christian is paradoxically identified as 'the first resurrection'" (Ibid., p. 371).

Traditional premillennialism regards the expression "first resurrection" to mean Christians, and that the expression implied "second resurrection" applies to *non*-Christians. (John F. Walvoord says this in his revised, enlarged edition of *The Rapture Question* [Grand Rapids: Zondervan Publishing House, 1979], p. 208.) To them it is inconceivable that there is a second resurrection for Christians. Therefore, premillennialists dismiss "first resurrection" as being a beginning stage for to them the "first resurrection" is the final product.

But the true meaning becomes clear when we realize that what is being contrasted are *not* two different groups of people in separate phrases, but two stages of the same people. This is as true of "first resurrection" as with "second death." Those who experience the second death are the lost. Those who are said to be resurrected first are the saved. As the Christians would experience a "second resurrection," that is, their physical resurrection, so the non-Christian had experienced a "first death," (by inference) that is, their spiritual death in sin.

The meaning of "resurrection," therefore, is deliberately contrasted with, yet similar to, the meaning of "death." The contrasts are immediately understandable, but not the similarities. How are they similar? They are similar only in the sense that they carry the modifiers/qualifiers "first" and "second." But the modifiers/qualifiers are intended to suggest the meaning of the nouns "resurrection" and "death."

Revelation 20:6 hinges on paradox to supply the meaning to both expressions. Some would deny that there is any paradox here. The phrases are used seriously by John, they contend. Unfortunately, they miss the subtle touch of humor involved in the paradoxes of the passage.

The paradoxes stand out when we think through what is meant by "second death," and "first resurrection." How can there be a second death? In the real world there isn't, for when a person is dead, he is dead. (Understand, this was before our present time when we draw fine lines between "brain dead" and "body dead.") Similarly, how can there be a "first resurrection," as if there will be a second, for when one is resurrected, it is absurd to think there can be another, an addition, an improvement.

The combinations of "first" with "resurrection" and "second" with "death" should be the first matter which signals paradox. A second clue to paradox should be triggered in the mind of the reader: "first" and "second" as they stand out as numbers. Concentration on the elementary, lower numbers "one" and "two" expressed in the words "first" and "second:" first resurrection and second death. Since Meredith Kline's suggestion of "new" is the intention behind "first," what would "second" imply? If "first" means "new" would "second" mean "old"? Because of this problem Kline's interpreting "first" as "new" is not fully satisfactory.

Rather, the significance of sequence is the key to meaning of the words "first resurrection," and "second resurrection."

But how is one to determine whether it is "first" in a series for the same persons involved or first in contrast with different persons? The answer to this question is found when one addresses it to the expression "second death," if it does not immediately occur to us in the expression "first resurrection." "Second death" for the persons described does not imply a "third" death, for the second death, which has no power over the Christian (Rev. 20:6), is described as the end of a short series: the second death is final (the lake of fire is not the second death for the two beasts (19:20), but only the second death for humans (20:14; 21:8). But the first resurrection implies a second resurrection. But, by implication, the second resurrection is the final resurrection. Yet it is not "second" in terms of correction of the first, as the second Adam's (Christ) obedience corrected the first Adam disobedience (Rom. 5:12-15). Rather, the second resurrection is completion/continuation of the life of God for the Christian.

The two expressions ("first resurrection," and "second death") are two sets of enigmas at the end of Revelation, pivotal pieces in the interpretation of the meaning of the millennium. They swirl in the millennium controversy, not like marbles in soup, but like neutrons around an atom. They are key phrases, vital parts to the meaning of the millennium.

The two phrases, inherently paradoxical, are a specific kind of paradox. The expressions are but oxymorons (*see* Glossary). An "oxymoron" is a verbal paradoxical combination of words which seem incongruous and contradictory, such as "terribly pretty," "awfully good," "immensely slight," or "severe mercy." Thomas Jefferson (in his retirement) described the USA presidency as "a splendid misery." The apostle Paul slipped into referring to our dedication to Christ as a "living sacrifice" (Rom. 12:1). Even the expression "born again" (John 3:3) could be considered another example of an oxymoron.

Not only are the expressions "first resurrection" and "second death" paradoxical, each contain a double paradox. There is the *paradox of sequence,* to which we have alluded. The more important paradox is the *paradox of consequence.* Death is a fact for Christian martyrs, but unknown to their tormentors their death is resurrection. Nonbelievers (in their totality) go to the lake of fire in a form of life in which they rejected the Lord. They are with resurrected bodies, but that is hardly a consolation. Second death entails resurrected bodies. Accordingly, we could compare the consequential contrasts in the following form:

"First Resurrection"
   (The paradox is that death is resurrection.)
"Second Death"
   (The paradox is that resurrection is death.)

It is because Christians have missed the paradoxical sense in these phrases that premillennialism has not died! Only after death can there be a glorious resurrection. Only by being sensitive to the inherent paradoxical sense of these key phrases will Revelation 20:1-15 finally come to life.

Apocalypse allows for an elastic interpretation of resurrection. Some may feel troubled in allowing a believer's glorification in death to be a resurrection. But in view of the foregoing evidence and argumentation we should dispel such fears. We should not fear following new ways of thinking, for we are dealing with apocalypse, a style which continues to baffle those who are used to one-way thinking. It is not that we have not taken the Bible seriously. The question is not whether or not we have taken the Bible seriously, but that we dare not force the Bible into a historical mold in an apocalyptic setting. Thus we have seen some cause for saying 20:4, 5 refers to the entrance of departed Christians into heaven for the Intermediate State.

Further support for this thinking is found when one compares what John wrote from Patmos and what Luke recorded of Jesus. We need next to examine the often overlooked, primary significance of *zaō*, the root of *anazaō* (20:5). As we do so, we shall discover that it was not untypical, even in the straight prose of Jesus' teaching, to find the emphasis to be first on life and that life after death was part of the total resurrection picture.

We catch this in Luke 20:37, 38, from which Jesus argued for resurrection, in the face of Sadduceean opposition. The Sadducees opposed belief in the existence of individuals, and with it, the resurrection of the dead.

After citing Exodus 3:6, which quotes God, saying, "I am the God of Abraham, of Isaac, and of Jacob" Jesus added, "He is not the God of the dead, but of the living . . . [*zaō*]. . . ." Jesus was not saying that Abraham, Isaac, and Jacob were resurrected. Certainly, Jesus did not try to argue that the resurrection as an event for Abraham, Isaac, and Jacob was over, but he said, from the voice at the burning bush, "Moses showed that the dead rise. . . ." (Luke 20:37 NIV). The argument Jesus used was that the kernel of resurrection was being alive. Man alive is the first step of man about. Therefore, the living states of Abraham, Isaac, and Jacob were the first phase of resurrection. The bodily finalization of resurrection was guaranteed by the living state of the three patriarchs. To grant the living state insured the other. The Sadducees admitted as such, for to grant that a dead person was first alive opened up the gate to resurrection. But they were not about to grant that dead men were alive.

Life was the real issue in resurrection. That was why Jesus

could apply the expression *resurrection* to people coming to life in faith (John 5:25).

John of Patmos used the expression "first resurrection," therefore, as a repetition of Jesus' earlier reply to the persisting, residual Sadduceean polemic that you can't have resurrection without life in a bodiless state. Thus death is a graduation, an ascension, an exaltation, a glorification, and in these features it partakes of resurrection, enough to be considered first-phase resurrection.

This usage is confirmed in Revelation 20 where the first part of verse 5 is parenthetical. With omission of that portion the text reads: "They came to life and reigned with Christ a thousand years. This is the first resurrection." Thus understood, "'the first resurrection' is expressly shown in the context to be a LIVING AND REIGNING WITH CHRIST" (Milton S. Terry, *Biblical Apocalyptics*, p. 452).

It seems to me that a wooden approach to "resurrection" requires premillennialists to reconcile their position with other uses of resurrection in the New Testament. Would those deny the use of the word *resurrection* to a Christian's death in view of the fact that Jesus viewed his death as an enthronement (the theme of the *Gospel of John*)? Would the dispensational premillennialist cease referring to Israel's restoration to their homeland as a resurrection, if resurrection always had to be physical (compare Ezek. 37:1-10)? Didn't Paul include death as part of the Christian's glorification in Romans 8:30, 38? Wasn't it large-scale Jewish conversions compared to resurrection by Paul in Romans 11:15? Certainly, in the apocalyptic genre there is more flexibility to warrant a broader use of resurrection than in nonapocalyptic writings.

A careful comparison of Revelation 20:1-6 with premillennial propaganda shows that so many ideas, which are not in the text, have been unfairly assumed and imported. Notice what has been hung on the concept of millennium, but none of them appear in Revelation 20. These include:

1. No mention of Jews in Revelation 20
2. No mention of the real city of Jerusalem
3. No mention of animals and their being tamed
4. No mention of peaceful dwelling on the earth

(Some would argue that the vision does mention both Jerusalem and the earthly scene in 20:9. But "the beloved city" is not the real Jerusalem, but the people of God, collected in compact as a unified city, identified together for Satan's final assault on their base.)

There is a sound contextual reason for taking this view. In the preceding verse the recorder, John of Patmos, used two Old Testament figures, not in a literal, but in a literary way. The original geographical-political relationship used by Ezekiel (38:2, 5; 39:1) was not used in Revelation 20:8. The localization factor of "Gog, of the land of Magog" was shortened and re-shaped to "Gog and Magog," so that the name of the ruler (Gog) and his land (Magog) lost their original identities. Thus, they became symbolical rather than factual; rhetorical rather than reportorial. Similarly "beloved city" meant the godly heritage of Jerusalem rather than the cit~ ~s a geographic site. Isbon Beckwith's conclusion is close   ~ificance of 20:9: "Unquestionably [20:9 is] actual historical city, unsuite and long since destroyed" (T/ 746). The location of earth is the scene where peace reign:

A premillennialist (Tracy I Goldsworthy's book, *The L(* *Evangelical Theological S* p. 222) tried to argue tha apocalyptic substance in the New Testament because with various limits assigned it was found in Jewish apocalyptic writings. That argument, however, is to confuse apocalyptic substance with apocalyptic style, and does not establish that temporal kingdom must be carried over into Christian apocalypse. Such reasoning attempts to turn a distinctly Christian approach to the future in Revelation into a rehash of Jewish nationalistic expectations.

Despite the hesitation of some to recognize the weaknesses of premillennialism and its failure to find verses that establish a geopolitical future for Israel in Revelation, it should become clear, on closer examination, that millennialists have forced unfounded conclusions on limited and highly symbolic verses. Anthony A. Hoekema offered the opinion: "According to dispensational teaching, the restoration of Israel is the *central purpose* of the millennium! It is therefore all the more significant that nothing of this alleged central purpose is mentioned in the only biblical passage which deals directly with Christ's millennial reign, Revelation 20:4-6" (*The Bible and the Future,* p. 222).

In view of the above information and argumentation, we can say again, that a physical millennium on earth for a literal 1,000 years is *not* what Revelation 20 is about and that the premillennial position is not a fair deduction from the biblical text. Enough data from 20:1-6 strongly suggests that the Intermediate Heaven is the millennium Christ established prior to the Infinite Heaven.

A growing number of evangelical scholars are challenging the dogmatism of millennialists and doubting their hermeutical assumptions. Listen to the Britisher Donald : "That a spiritual interpretation of the millennium is a literal interpretation becomes clear when note is egetical difficulties which a literal interpretation faces. Especially is this true of those who are obliged to postulate two stages for the *parousia* (a second coming at the 'rapture,' and a public coming after the tribulation), and various resurrections and judgments. The intention is no doubt to clarify, but in point of fact the result tends to be not only more confusing, but more difficult to support from other NT statements" (p. 871, *New Testament Theology*).

("Is the millennium heaven?" While some may not be willing to say it has the same degree of certainty of *yes* in answer to the questions, "Is the Pope Catholic?" or "Is the White House in Washington, D.C.?" nevertheless, Revelation 20 points more toward a millennium of spiritual dimensions, rather than a millennium of physical dimensions.

Each Christian who enters heaven through death should look forward to the millennium, for with Christ he or she shall reign!)

Notes

Introduction

1. For a survey of hymns on heaven up to 1874, *see* Henry C. Fish's *Heaven in Song*, 742 pages (New York: Sheldon and Co., Publishers, 1874). Wilbur M. Smith reviewed some hymns on heaven, pages 265-282, in his *The Biblical Doctrine on Heaven* (Chicago: Moody Press, 1968). For the role of music in heaven, *see* chapter 9, of the present study. For some insightful pages on hymns in heaven, *see* McDannell and Lang, *Heaven: A History* (New Haven, CT: Yale University Press, 1988) pp. 288-89.

2. Hans Küng, *Eternal Life?: Life after Death as a Medical, Philosophical, and Theological Problem*, translated by Edward Quinn (Garden City, NY: Doubleday & Co., Inc., 1984), p. 143.

3. For a collection of conceptions, both verbal and visual, on heaven, ranging from the willfully abstract to the comically precise, from medieval visionaries, through Reformation scholars, through Renaissance humanists, through Enlightenment spiritualists, through seventeenth-century Puritanism, through eighteeenth-century revivalists, through modern sentimentalism consult the provocative, carefully researched, and encyclopedic-in-scope study: *Heaven: A History* (New Haven, CT: Yale University Press, 1988) by Colleen McDannell and Bernhard Lang. The two historians intended the work to be descriptive, rather than normative. They wrote as historians, rather than as theologians. Yet they could not avoid evaluating the reliability of the New Testament documents. *See* Note 14 below. Given their approach (compiling views), their conclusion that "the concept of [heaven's] 'describability' must be dropped from the list of the characteristics of eternal life" is understandable, indeed, inevitable (p. 350).

4. Compare with Raymond A. Moody, Jr., M.D., *Life After Life* (1975) and his *Reflections on Life after Life* (1977).

5. Küng, *Eternal Life?* p. 19.

6. Ibid.

7. Whereas R. A. Moody, Jr., M.D., gave little space to Scripture and exaggerated the scarcity of Scripture on the hereafter in *Life After Life* (New York: Bantam, 1976), p. 111, Maurice Rawlings, M.D., used a significant amount of Scripture in his book, *Beyond Death's Door* (New York: Bantam, 1979). On the self-deceptions of the resuscitated, *see* Ibid., pp. 69, 70.

8. McDannell and Lang, *Heaven* pp. 352, 397 (Note 70).

9. Reinhold Niebuhr, *The Nature and Destiny of Man* (New York: Charles Scribner's Sons, 1943), vol. 2: 294 (the complete statement): "It is unwise for Christians to claim any knowledge of either the furniture of heaven or the temperature of hell; or to be too certain about any details of the Kingdom of God." It is rare in the late 1980s to attend standard brand liberalized Protestant churches to hear sermons on heaven. We are reaping what has been sown. Scholarly Protestant spokesmen, such as John Sutherland Bonnell (1893-   ) adopted a wait-and-see attitude, which has virtually shut down sermons on heaven. Rather than encouraging caution Bonnell's comments have had the result of making inconclusiveness smart and discouraged those who once thought truth attainable from seeking it. Bonnell wrote, "While we recognize the necessity of employing symbols in our thought of God or of spiritual reality, let us remind ourselves unceasingly that they are neither fully accurate nor definitive" *Heaven and Hell* (New York: Abingdon Press, 1956), p. 23. One should forfeit the reading of the New Testament documents, if the comment of Edward Quinn in his introductory essay to Hans Küng's work is

true. Quinn wrote, "The New Testament . . . has no more than a negative description of heaven: 'Eye hath not seen nor ear heard.'" (p. x, *Eternal Life?*, translated by Edward Quinn).

10. R. T. Kendall, *Once Saved Always Saved* (Chicago: Moody Press 1983, 1985), p. 164.

11. Jürgen Moltmann, *God in Creation*, Gifford Lectures, 1984-1985 (San Francisco: Harper & Row, Publishers, 1985), p. 181.

12. *Theological Students Fellowship Bulletin*, March/April, 1987, vol. 10, No. 4, pp. 35, 36. (Review article by Colin Brown)

13. Ibid.

14. University of Maryland lecturer in history, Colleen McDannell, and professor of religion, Bernhard Lang, of the University of Paderborn, Germany, in their comprehensive history of ideas on heaven, *Heaven: A History* did not take the position that Scripture was a final authority. Old Testament afterlife views, in their opinion, grew slowly from ancestor veneration, to sky god concepts, to thinking of God alone as the prime significance (Ibid., pp. 1, 8, 10, 19). Plato's view of the netherworld as "up" was an improvement, as they see it, of the Hebrew view of the place of departed as "down" (p. 17). To suggest that Jesus' antifamilial sayings and his several harsh comments on relatives "contributed to the rise of the story that Jesus had no human father" (p. 31) is simple conjecture. It would seem fairness should dictate that Ernest Renan's (1823-1892) dated view of this should be said to be challenged by respectable scholars since then. The New Testament documents seemed to be below Josephus as a good source of information on Pharisaic views on the hereafter (p. 20). Instead of the gospels' being solid source documents, they "contain legendary accretions. Their wish to give guidance to their contemporaries shaped—and perhaps dis-

torted—the original tradition" (p. 25). The authority of the biblical documents is not due to divine inspiration, but to cultural interaction combined with "inner effervescence" (pp. 19, 47), which is little different from the bubbling up of divine life in mysticism. The best one can get from the New Testament documents, in the eyes of McDannell and Lang is some probable truth: "the reconstruction of a conjectural but plausible outline of Jesus' own teaching on the afterlife" (p. 25). On the issue of the eyewitness element of the Gospels, they mentioned nothing. On the fact that their scissors-and-paste view of the Gospels is more the pronouncement of a school, rather than a universal consensus of modern scholarship, they said nothing. On these matters, their announced eclecticism (p. xiii) narrowed considerably to present one view, a view of Scripture palpable to those who would rather *not* accept Scripture as the final standard in faith. Full recognition of scriptural authority is mentioned in their treatment of Fundamentalism (pp. 335-342), but was not presented as one of or the preferred view point in the chapters on Jewish and early Christian ideas (chapters 1 and 2). It is questionable that "by the mid-nineteenth century, the static, theocentric heaven of the reformers was favored by only a handful of Protestant writers" (Ibid., p. 287). This seems in conflict with their claim (p. 345) that Fundamentalists and Neo-orthodox theologians "have pared away any image which stands between the soul and the divine center." In sum, McDannell and Lang's perception of the biblical writings is that the information contained in the Old and New Testaments was reactive to human influences, rather than the result of divine revelation: self-surgings from human psyches, rather than heavenly inspired words (p. 22).

15. *Time*, July 4, 1969.

16. Küng, *Eternal Life?*, p. 209: ". . . Many sects and fundamentalist groups think they possess [in the images and visions of Revelation] an open treasury of knowledge. But for us these stories cannot be regarded as a script for the last act of the tragedy of humanity. They do not—unfortunately—contain any special divine 'revelations' which might satisfy our curiosity in regard to the end. . . ." If Küng is right, then investigation of valuable commentaries on Revelation becomes an academic exercise with little practical value. The truth, it seems, lies on the other side of the question. The more careful we are to take advantage of linguistic, grammatical, and historical tools at our disposal, the more assiduously we devote ourselves to the reading of carefully researched commentaries on Revelation, the more confidently can we identify differences distinguishing kooky interpretations from the likely and more correct ones.

17. Ibid., p. 220: ". . . The more subtle the dialectic then between experience and abstraction, the more appropriate could an image concept be to express what is meant by consummation. . . ."

18. "To treat [Revelation] as if it were cold prose, to be dissected and analysed and assessed, is to end up with a dead misshapen thing unworthy of the name of literature, far less of revelation" (p. 1, David Syme Russell, *Apocalyptic: Ancient and Modern* (Philadelphia: Fortress Press, 1978). See also, Milton S. Terry, *Biblical Apocalyptics* (Grand Rapids: Baker Book House, 1988), a 510-page, 20-chapter study, mostly on Revelation. In his lengthy introduction, Isbon T. Beckwith, *The Apocalypse of John* (Grand Rapids: Baker Book House, 1919, 1977), pp. 166-196 on apocalyptic literature; more recently, Leon Morris, *Apocalyptic* (Grand Rapids: Wm. B. Eerdmans Publishing Co., 1972).

19. George Ladd, "Apocalypse," *Evangelical Dictionary of Theology* Walter A. El-

well, editor, (Grand Rapids: Baker Book House, 1984), pp. 64, 65. Similarly, D. S. Russell has commented: "The Babylon of Revelation is about the Roman empire in Domitian's reign. But it is about much more than that. It is a description of the reality that exists in each and any nation, city and institution throughout history. In particular it is archetypical of all *nations*"

(p. 65, *Apocalyptic*). *See also*, Morris, pp. 55, 56.

20. Peter J. Kreeft, *Heaven* (San Francisco: Harper & Row, Publishers, 1980), p. 72.

21. John Bradford, *Writings of John Bradford* (Edinburgh: Banner of Truth, 1848, 1979), vol. 1:267.

1. But Isn't Revelation Too Difficult to Follow?

1. Joseph Augustus Seiss, *The Last Times* (Phila.: Smith, English, and Co., 1863), p. 14.

2. The chronological approach: R. H. Charles, *The Revelation of St. John*, International Critical Commentary (Edinburgh: T & T Clark, 1920); popular commentaries on Revelation from a strict chronological approach are those by John Walvoord and Hal Lindsey, *There's a New World Coming* (1973).

The contrapuntal approach: J. Stuart Russell, *The Parousia* (1887), pp. 307, 377, 378, 395, 406, 407; Isbon T. Beckwith (1919), H. B. Swete (1911), and Wm. Hendriksen, *More Than Conquerors* (1940). A good introductory study is by Chuck Colclasure, *The Overcomers* (1981).

3. Christopher Rowland, *The Open Heaven: A Study of Apocalyptic in Judaism and Early Christianity* (New York: Crossroad, 1982), p. 422: Revelation chaps. 7 and 14 (on the last judgment) are proleptic.

4. Donald Guthrie, *New Testament Theology* (Downers Grove, IL: InterVarsity Press, 1981), p. 871.

5. An amillennial recapitulationist: Isbon T. Beckwith, *The Apocalypse of John* (Grand Rapids: Baker Book House, 1919, 1979), p. 322. A postmillennial recapitulationist: B. B. Warfield, *The Works of Warfield*, Biblical Doctrines (New York: Oxford University Press, 1929), p. 645. Leon Mor-

ris, *Revelation*, Tyndale New Testament Commentary (Grand Rapids: Wm. B. Eerdmans Publishing Co., 1983), p. 41. An historic premillennialist recapitulationist: G. Beasley-Murray, *The Book of Revelation*, p. 317: "As the overthrow of the harlot-city had been related in recapitulatory fashion for the encouragement of the saints, so the appearance of the bride-city is portrayed in 21:9ff., again for their comfort." Also, *see Revelation: Three Viewpoints*, (Nashville: Broadman Press, 1977), pp. 28, 44, 57, 67.

6. Austin Farrer, *A Rebirth of Image* (London: A & C Black, 1949). The chart of Farrer's approach was by Graeme Goldsworthy, *The Lamb and the Lion, The Gospel in Revelation* (Nashville: Thomas Nelson, 1984), p. 57, found in Chart C.

7. Bernard Ramm, *Protestant Biblical Interpretation*, 3rd Revised Edition, (Grand Rapids: Baker Book House, 1970), p. 171. Bernard Ramm is an outstanding evangelical theologian. He draws inferences from the Bible. He doesn't go against the Bible, but tries to reflect it without being accused of false reductionism. Though he cautioned against some inference drawing, he undoubtedly agrees with the inference that God created out of nothing, *ex nihilo*. The phrase "out of nothing" does not appear in the Genesis accounts of creation. And two other inferences arise out of Genesis, chapters 1 and 2. (1) There was no one who could stop, modify, or overturn

God's creative command. That is a justifiable inference. Other inferences from God's unoriginated state follow. (2) One is that deity implies preexistence. (3) Another is that God cannot be held responsible for his actions. Since he preceded all forms of life, he could not be responsible to them. It would be inconceivable to imagine that God was responsible to anyone but himself, for there is no being higher than God. These inferences are legitimate, for they are addressed later in the Bible. Moreover, Jesus drew some inferences from Old Testament verses, which rubbed the Jewish hierarchy (especially the Sadducees) the wrong way (Matt. 22:30, 31). "Out of the title, God of Abraham, Jesus deduced the doctrine of the future life that the Sadducees denied" (Gordon Clark, *Biblical Predestination* [Nutley, N.J: Presbyterian and Reformed Publishing Co., 1969]), p. 5.

8. Vincent Bugliosi, *Helter Skelter* (New York: Bantam Books, 1974, 1975), pp. 321-323. The locusts of chapter 9 have produced other indefensible conclusions, as well. Hal Lindsey, author of *The Late Great Planet Earth*, proposed a dubious interpretation of Revelation chap. 9. He proposed that the locusts "might [my underlining] symbolize an advanced kind of helicopter." (pp. xiv, 123, 124, *There's a New World Coming* (New York: Bantam Books, 1975). The locust reference came from the Book of Joel 2:4f. The physical capabilities of locust, speed, resemblance to a horse's head, and seeming armor, appear to match something military. But comparison of this locust reference to a modern attack helicopter, however, is highly improbable, for the following reasons: (a) The nonmechanistic characteristics—"their faces resembled human faces" (9:7), and their hair "like women's hair" (9:8)—are important features not to be minimized; (b) The locusts, like a real locust's lifespan, lived only five months,

and they could only torment, *not* kill (9:5, 6). Therefore, the intention of the figure must be found that gives serious attention to all descriptions in the passage. At any rate, the serious Bible student should be wary of alleged fulfillments which conflict with the original vision in its context. *See* chapter 3 in the present study for the most likely interpretation.

9. *See* the Appendix where the number symbolism is carried further. Also, John J. Davis, *Biblical Numerology* (Grand Rapids: Baker Book House, 1968), 8th printing; Oswald T. Allis, *Bible Numerics* (Phillipsburg, NJ: Presbyterian and Reformed Publishing Co., 1919).

10. Beware of inferences in eschatology presented and passed on as fact. Certain futurists have accepted some inferences as normative of true belief. Anyone who deviates from them is considered rejecting the Word of God, when in fact the only things being rejected are unjustifiable inferences.

Hal Lindsey has said that those who disagreed with a literal approach to Revelation means they are heading "down the primrose path to liberal theology." (*New World*, p. 261). Lindsey was echoing a similar accusation by John Walvoord who wrote in 1959 that adherents of the amillennial viewpoint eventually become theological liberals in *The Millennial Kingdom* (Findlay, Ohio: Dunham, 1959), p. 71. George Ladd responded: "This amounts to the claim that only dispensationalism, with its literal hermeneutic of the Old Testament, can provide a truly evangelical theology" (pp. 19, 20, *The Meaning of the Millennium*, Four Views, 1977). Years earlier G. E. Ladd protested and answered that insinuation in *The Blessed Hope: A Biblical Study of the Second Advent and the Rapture* (Grand Rapids: Wm. B. Eerdmans Publishing Co., 1956, 1983), pp. 139, 140.

George Eldon Ladd, in his seminal work

The Blessed Hope, has convincingly shown that key dispensational inferences are ill-founded and indefensible. In his short, but powerful book, Ladd has given good grounds for rejecting: (1) The notion that the second coming of Christ is two-phased. As he has shown the rapture is the revelation (pp. 70, 102). There is no two-phase return. (2) He has debunked the contention that the rapture will necessarily precede the tribulation (Ibid., p. 76). (3) He has shown that the resurrection of the saints will not take place at the beginning of the tribulation (Ibid., p. 83). Robert Gundry has given greater credibility that the church will be taken to heaven after the tribulation in his *The Church and the Tribulation* (1973).

The Bible teaches a two-stage eschatology (millennium and second coming or realized presence and future presence), but not a two-phased second coming. Some have argued that God will not be judging Christians at the same time as non-Christians, a position which is part of the mix of insisting on a two-phase return of Christ. But Jesus saw the resurrections and judgments of Christians and non-Christians together (John 5:25-29; Matt. 25:31-46). The argument that judgments of Christians and non-Christians will be separate overlooks the fact that the ongoing, present-day judgment of God takes place simultaneously when the gospel is preached. In the preaching of the Word, at the same time, salvation and judgment take place by the same Word (John 3:19, 21, 36; 2 Cor. 2:14-16). God is not opposed to this type of judgment now, and he will use it later as well. For a thorough reply to the two-stage judgment and resurrection theories, see Hoekema's *The Bible and the Future*, pp. 241-244.

The alleged two-phases of Christ's second coming originated, not with the New Testament, but in nineteenth-century En-gland. It has since spread to captivate large segments of contemporary evangelicalism. Many churches and schools accept the rapture as different from Christ's revelation and they strongly contend that the distinction is biblical. This teaching, however, was not part of the teachings of historic premillennialists, who were posttribulationalists (p. 185, R. H. Gundry, *The Church and the Tribulation*).

An excellent survey of the rapture/revelation controversy, with a solid case that the two are identical is found in William R. Kimball's *The Rapture: A Question of Timing* (Grand Rapids: Baker Book House, 1985), 193 pages. See also Note #26, chapter 3, on John 14:2, 3.

The "rapture" phase was traced by David MacPherson to a Scots charismatic, Margaret MacDonald, who in 1830, first put forward the rapture idea. The idea was adopted by Edward Irving (1792-1834) and Irvingite, Robert Baxter, whose views in turn, were picked up by John Nelson Darby (1800-1882), prominent Plymouth Brethren writer (p. 186, R. H. Gundry, Ibid.). Once an adherent of dispensationalism, Clarence B. Bass had been able to trace the concept back only to Darby: *Backgrounds to Dispensationalism* (Baker, 1977). Plymouth Brethren founders and leaders, however, were influenced by the Irvingite prophetic conferences. And the Irvingite teachings on secret rapture came from the locally influential above-mentioned Margaret MacDonald. Gundry cited the research of Dave MacPherson who traced the teaching back to Ms. MacDonald. (Compare with his work, but now out of print, *The Great Rapture Hoax* (Fletcher, NC: New Puritan Library, 1983). Gundry cited an earlier work of MacPherson which was less complete. Now only a condensed version of the above 210-page work is available (*Rapture?*, 71 pages, from New Puritan Library, 91 Lytle Rd., Fletcher, NC

28732). MacPherson continues to welcome interaction: Box 44, Monticello, UT 84535.)

Does the revelation usher in the millennium? Beside reading the Appendix of this book, it would be very profitable to read two useful books that present options by recognized representatives: (1) *The Meaning of the Millennium*, Four Views, edited by Robert G. Clouse, (InterVarsity Press, 1977); (2) Revelation: Three Viewpoints, G. R. Beasley-Murray, Herschel H. Hobbs, Ray Frank Robbins, (Broadman Press, 1977). Before making up one's mind, it is profitable to read all sides of an issue.

11. Hal Lindsey, *The Rapture* (New York: Bantam Books, 1983), p. 9; John F. Walvoord, *The Rapture Question* (Grand Rapids: Zondervan Publishing Co., 1979), p. 111.

12. Lindsey, *The Rapture*, p. 90: "I believe, along with many scholars, that the apostle John's experience here is meant to be a prophetic preview of what the living Church will experience in the Rapture." In his earlier work *New World Coming*, (New York: Bantam Books, 1975) he said virtually the same thing: "[Rev. 4:1] strongly suggests a similar catching away for the Church" (p. 61).

13. Calvin R. Schoonhoven, *The Wrath of Heaven* (Grand Rapids: Wm. B. Eerdmans Publishing Co., 1966), pp. 52, 53. Schoonhoven cites R. Leivestad's *Christ, the Conqueror* (London: SPCK, 1954), p. 264.

14. Hal Lindsey, *There's a New World Coming* (New York: Bantam Books, 1975) p. 165.

15. Walvoord, *Rapture Question*, p. 112: "There is no justification whatever for dragging in the church as individuals composed largely of Gentiles in racial origin."

2. Is There a Heaven?

1. Frank Ransome, Jr., *The Verse by the Side of the Road* (New York: E. P. Dutton & Co., 1966), pp. 77-121.

2. Loyal Davis, M.D., *A Surgeon's Odyssey* (Garden City, NY: Doubleday & Co., Inc., 1973), p. 37. On the occasion of the unveiling of a portrait of Nancy Reagan's foster father, who adopted her when she was fourteen years old, told the Royal College of Surgeons in Dublin, Ireland, "My father was, next to my husband, the most important man in my life" (*Cincinnati Enquirer*, June 5, 1984), D-2.

3. Sir Thomas Browne (1605-1682), *Hydriotaphia: Urne-Buriall*, (1658), chapter 5.

4. Richard Baxter, *A Call to the Unconverted* (Grand Rapids: Zondervan Publishing Co., 1657, 1953), p. 28.

5. Jeremy Rifkin, *Entropy* (New York: Viking Press, 1980), p. 9.

6. Herbert Schlossberg, *Idols for Destruction* (Nashville: Thomas Nelson Publishers, 1983), a 335-page indictment of the new idolatry practiced in modern times.

7. John Calvin, *Institutes of the Christian Religion*, Ford Lewis Battles, editor, translator (Philadelphia: The Westminster Press, 1960), III, 9:2.

8. Paul Tillich, *The New Being* (New York: Charles Scribners' Sons, 1955), p. 168.

9. Hans Küng, *Eternal Life?* p. 82.

10. Gerhard von Rad, *Old Testament Theology* (New York: Harper & Row, 1962), vol. 1:456.

11. Karl Barth, *Word of God and Word of Man* (New York: Harper & Row, 1957), p. 301.

12. Ernest W. Hengstenberg, *Ecclesiastes* (Evansville, IN: Sovereign Grace Publishers, 1860, 1960), p. 121.

13. "*'eth*" is the Hebrew word for "time" in this passage. It occurs 28 times in succession in Ecclesiastes 3 and 297 times in the entire Old Testament. Some would disagree that there is a case for predestination in this passage. "*'Eth*" occurs in Ecc. 8:5, 6 and 9:12 as appointed time and as uncertain time in Ecc. 9:11 (p. 773, F. Brown, S. R. Driver, C. A. Briggs, *A Hebrew and English Lexicon of the Old Testament* (Oxford: Clarendon Press, 1907, 1975). The interesting thing about the latter listing is that whereas in Ecclesiastes 9:11 *'eth* appears as uncertain time, in the following verse (9:12), "*'eth*" is used as appointed time.

I grant that inevitableness, by itself, does not teach determinism. But the case that something more than inevitableness is intended comes through in the coordinated history of all individuals. By the categorical, comprehensive coverage of all phases of life, randomness, usually associated with chance, is ruled out. By implication and inference a divine figure overshadows the twists and turns of life even when man's heart and will are not in their favor.

John R. Wilch, in his *Time and Event: An Exegetical Study of the Use of 'eth* (Leiden: E. J. Brill, 1969), argued that *mo 'ed* is the more deterministic word, which Koheleth never uses (pp. 126, 127). That seems convincing. However to argue this way is similar to the person who says the Bible does not teach predestination unless *predestine* is used. But we know from elsewhere in the Scriptures this approach is unconvincing. As the frequent Hebrew phrase, "and it came to pass," which the RSV generally and regrettably omits from its Old Testament translation, accentuates eventfulness, so "*'eth*" carries an oblique reference to divine election, for in the passage being discussed (Ecc. 3) *all* occasions of life, not just ones that we decide upon

are included. Moreover, in all of the symbolic situations listed, which form seven double pairs, human decisions, with outcomes, are directed, managed, and overruled by a higher will. H. L. Ginsberg, "The Structure and Contents of the Book of Koheleth," *Supplements to Vetus Testamentum* (Leiden: E. J. Brill, 1955) vol. 3:140, supports the identity of "time" as determined time in Ecclesiastes 3. David J. A. Clines, in his essay "Predestination in the Old Testament" (*Grace Unlimited*, edited by Clark H. Pinnock [Minneapolis: Bethany House Publishers, 1975]) wrote, "Ecclesiastes is surely the leading Old Testament exponent of predestination" (p. 117, see pp. 117-120). Although the teaching on predestination in Ecclesiastes lacks the fullness and precision of the apostle Paul, nevertheless, God is assumed to be behind the ordering. Appointment is combined with appropriateness, but it is divine appointment which is frequently down-played by interpreters. While *'eth* may be translated as appropriate time or season, the context of Ecclesiastes chapter 3 and the theological point of God over time in the Old Testament, emphasized the meaning of fixed or set time, for when the question was asked who determined what was, the questioner was thrown back on the reality of God.

On *'eth* Ludwig Koehler and Walter Baumgartner, *Hebräisches Und Aramäisches Lexikon*, Lieferung, III (Leiden: E. J. Brill, 1983), pp. 851-853; L. J. Coppes in *The Theological Wordbook of the Old Testament*, R. Laird Harris, editor (Chicago: Moody Press, 1980), vol. 2:680, 681; Franz Delitzsch, *Commentary on Ecclesiastes* (Grand Rapids: Wm. B. Eerdmans Publishing Co., n.d.), p. 255; Hengstenberg, p. 91f.

On predestination in the Old Testament *see:* Benjamin Breckinridge Warfield (1851-1921), *Works: Biblical Doctrines*

(Grand Rapids: Baker Book House, 1929, 1981), vol. 2:7-28; Gordon H. Clark (1902-1985), *Predestination in the Old Testament* (Phillipsburg, NJ: Presbyterian and Reformed Publishing Co., 1978), 43 pgs.

What I have written on the use of *'eth* will hardly convince someone that Scripture teaches predestination, for despite the hint at its existence in Ecclesiastes, it is incomplete. The case for biblical predestination cannot be based on Ecclesiastes alone, but arises from the total biblical material. *See* the recent works: Paul K. Jewett, *Election and Predestination* (Grand Rapids: Wm. B. Eerdmans Publishing Co., 1985), 147 pgs., and R. C. Sproul, *Chosen by*

God (Wheaton, IL: Tyndale House Publishers, Inc., 1986), 213 pgs.

14. Ralph Wardlaw, *Exposition of Ecclesiastes* (Minneapolis: Klock and Klock Publishers, Inc., 1868, 1982), p. 106.

15. Clarence E. McCartney, *Autobiography* (Great Neck, NY: Channel Press, 1961), p. 127.

16. J. Stafford Wright, "The Interpretation of Ecclesiastes," in *Classical Evangelical Essays*, edited by Walter C. Kaiser, Jr. (Grand Rapids: Baker Book House, 1972), pp. 140, 141. The original article appeared in *Evangelical Quarterly* in January 1945.

17 Peter Kreeft, *Heaven* (New York: Harper & Row, 1980), p. 45.

3. Is Heaven Created?

1. *The Cincinnati Enquirer*, Dec. 19-21, 1986, *USA Weekend*, Supplement, pp. 4, 5. The *Newsweek* poll was a national sample of 750 adults by telephone December 21, 22, 1986, copyrighted. The Newsweek poll, copyrighted 1989, was reported in *Newsweek* (March 27, 1989, p. 53). Incidentally, *Newsweek* contracted Gallup to take this poll. On Gallup poll of 1982, see McDannell/Lang, *Heaven*, p. 307.

2. Emanuel Swedenborg, *Heaven and Its Wonders, and Hell* (New York: Swedenborg Foundation, 1758, 1960), p. 196 (paragraph 340).

3. Stan Hoig, *The Humor of the American Cowboy* (Lincoln, NE: University of Nebraska Press, 1958, 1970), pp. 35, 36. Hoig cited the story of Sam P. Ridings, *The Chisholm Trail: A History of the World's Greatest Cattle Trail* (1936), pp. 316, 317.

Michiko Kakutani considered it a curious and regrettable oversight that Colleen McDannell and Bernhard Lang, in their massive, *Heaven: A History* (Yale Press, 1988), did not include the wealth of after-

life ideas in films, such as: "Stairway to Heaven," "Here Comes Mr. Jordan," "Heaven Can Wait," "Made in Heaven." (*New York Times*, "The Living Arts" Section, December 7, 1988). To this I would mention Westerns, for from Clint Eastwood's "Pale Rider" (1985) to nearly every John Wayne Western the Bible is used, Revelation is cited, eternal destinies are set in motion, and frontier prayers and horse-riding evangelists stimulate the characters to face up to the Christian hereafter.

4. *Newsweek*, January 2, 1978, p. 33.

5. See the standard commentaries, some of which are: Ceslaus Spicq, *Epîtres Pastorales* (Paris: J. Gabalda, 1947), p. 387; William Hendriksen (1900-1982), *New Testament Commentary:* Exposition of the Pastoral Epistles (Grand Rapids: Baker Book House, 1957, 1979), p. 314; Ronald A Ward, *Commentary on 1 & 2 Timothy and Titus* (Waco: Word Books, Publishers, 1974), pp. 210, 211.

6. Philip Edgcumbe Hughes, *Paul's Second Epistle to the Corinthians*, New Inter-

national Commentary Series (Grand Rapids: Wm. B. Eerdmans Publishing Co., 1962), pp. 429-434. Klass Schilder (1890-1952), *Heaven, What Is It?* translated and condensed by Marian M. Schooland, (Grand Rapids: Wm. B. Eerdmans, Publishing Co., 1950), pp. 34-36. Calvin R. Schoonhoven, *The Wrath of Heaven* (Grand Rapids: Wm. B. Eerdmans Publishing Co., 1966), pp. 63, 64. Moltmann, *God in Creation*, p. 159.

7. Edmund J. Fortman, S. J., *Everlasting Life After Death* (New York: Alba House, 1976), p. 209: "Too often the way heaven was presented in the past, it seemed to be merely a 'place of eternal boredom,' with no real 'living,' with no real growth, with no real developmental activity. An eternity of unchanging contemplation and love and nothing else seemed too little suited to offer men, men of every time, a glorious destiny and fulfillment. It is not surprising that many men chose to build their own heaven on earth. That is why these new trends toward a more 'dynamic heaven' are very good. For a heaven of everlasting happiness is man's destiny, and it should not be down-graded. Too much stress in the past on a static and immobile heaven tended to do just that. A more dynamic heaven is worth pondering today. But with a note of caution to today's theologians—not to repeat the error of the past. For if past theologians 'built' a heaven that was too static, all-static, there is a danger that today's theologians will build a heaven that is too dynamic, all-dynamic." McDannell and Lang, *Heaven*, p, 199: ". . . While Aquinas's medieval heaven, devoid of plants and animals, may have been the standard for Catholic theology, the church still permitted a variety of depictions of the other life—especially when these promised to be useful for Counter Reformation concerns. The sensuality of the Renaissance heaven survived the Reformation and the attacks of the Jansenists and other Catholic reformers."

8. W. H. C. Frend, *The Rise of Christianity* (Philadelphia: Fortress Press, 1984), p. 93. Origen specified where he agreed with Platonism in his answer to Celsus. Hans Lietzmann (1875-1942) has further summarized Origen's eschatology to show how Platonic it was: "The soul did not remain here below. It mounted into the upper air, and searched out the secrets thereof. Then the heavens opened before it, and it moved toward Jesus by passing from sphere to sphere. The nature of the stars, their constellations, their paths, and the heavenly equilibrium, now became open to its gaze. The way led higher up into the regions of the invisible: the soul became more and more spiritualized, and grew to perfect knowledge until at last it was no longer soul, but wholly *nous* and spirit, and was able to behold 'face to face,' the world of intelligible being and essence. That was the way towards likeness to God which was dreamed of by philosophers as the highest good, but granted to Christians in order that they might rise from their present bodily condition, and reach pure *nous*, the 'glory of the sons of God when God is all in all,' for purified beings no longer feel or conceive anything else than God alone." (*A History of the Early Church* vol. 2:311 [New York: The World Publishing Company, 1949, 1961]). For other aspects of his eschatology, *see* Ibid., pp. 303-310 and Jaroslav Pelikan, *The Christian Tradition: The Emergence of the Catholic Tradition—100-600* (Chicago: University of Chicago Press, 1971), pp. 48, 49.

9. Carl F. H. Henry, *God, Revelation, and Authority* (Waco: Word Books Publishers, 1976), vol. 1:86. Hebrews 8:2-5 and 10:1, to readers acquainted with Plato's *Republic* (vii) or with his view of reality, may seem a facsimile version of what

Plato taught. Bible commentator William Barclay states a commonly held view that the writer to the Hebrews used Plato's concept (pp. 94, 95, *The Letter to the Hebrews*, The Daily Study Bible (Philadelphia: The Westminster Press, 1957). Also, *see* Lietzmann, *A History*, vol. 2:305-306, 310-311.

Does Plato's concept have biblical backing? The Hebrews passages have a central bearing on this matter. But what we find in Hebrews makes it less an endorsement than a correction. Several points make the resemblance to be superficial: (1) The idea of copies of earth in heaven is evident earlier than Plato. It can be found in Babylonian literature. (p. 81, F. F. Bruce's essay, "A Shadow of Good Things to Come," *The Time Is Fulfilled* (Grand Rapids: Wm. B. Eerdmans Publishing Co., 1978). The same idea can be found in Exodus 25:9, 10; Ezekiel 2:9f. (2) The emphasis in Hebrews is more on differences, however, than similarities, on contrasts more than agreements. F. F. Bruce says, "If the Aaronic priesthood, the earthly sanctuary and the levitical sacrifices are as ineffective as our author argues, then the relation of the shadow to the substance is much more one of contrast than resemblance" Ibid., p. 87. (See pp. 99-102, Ronald H. Nash, *Christianity and the Hellenistic World* (Grand Rapids: Zondervan Publishing Co., 1984). The contrasts in Hebrews are more between past and present, old and new, earlier and later, than higher and lower. (3) Perhaps the sharpest difference relates to the soteriological stress in Hebrews. The thrust of Hebrews is not abstract ontology, but concrete soteriology. Discussion of the temporal and eternal, shadow and reality are within a framework uncongenial to Platonic philosophy. Ronald Williamson has pointed out a crucial difference: "The idea that such a heavenly ministry could begin as a result of an event on earth, the crucifixion of the Word made flesh, is about as

far removed from Platonism as one could wish to get" (p. 158, *Philo and the Epistle to the Hebrews* [Leiden: Brill, 1970]. (*See* the entire discussion of Nash, *Christianity*, pp. 32-35, 96, 99-102, and the relevant end notes, pp. 279-288.)

10. Schilder, *Heaven*, p. 27.

11. Ludwig Feuerbach, *The Essence of Christianity*, translated by G. Eliot, (New York: Harper Torchbooks, 1841, 1957), p. 14.

12. Klaus Bockmuehl, *The Challenge of Marxism* (Downers Grove: InterVarsity Press, 1980), pp. 57, 58, 174 (note #13).

13. Henry, *God, Revelation, Authority*, vol. 3 (1979):216.

14. Moltmann, *God in Creation*, p. 163.

15. Küng, *Eternal Life?* p. 201.

16. Ibid.

17. Austin Farrer, *Saving Belief* (New York: Morehouse-Barlow Co., 1964), p. 144. Herman Bavinck [1854-1921], *The Philosophy of Revelation* (New York: Longmans, Green, and Co., 1909): "When . . . God is represented as dwelling in heaven, he is not thereby placed outside but in the world, and is not removed by a spacial transcendence from his creatures" (p. 21).

18. Moltmann, *God in Creation*, p. 173.

19. Toon, *Heaven and Hell*, pp. 4-7.

20. Moltmann, *God in Creation*, p. 159. The expression "Majesty on high" is a similar periphrasis (a round-about equivalent expression—JLG) for God in the Book of Hebrews (1:3c; 8:1).

21. Gordon Haddon Clark [1902-1985], *Ephesians* (Jefferson, MD: The Trinity Foundation, 1985), p. 7. Toon, *Heaven and Hell*, p. 69: "It appears not to mean simply 'heaven' as 'God's Place,' since at 3:10 and 6:12, the presence of fallen angels is presumed to be there." It is wrong to assume that all angels are good. Scripture talks of evil angels (Jude 6; 2 Peter 2:4) and of how they will need to be judged (1 Cor. 6:3). Angels can be imperfect instruments

and perpetrators of wickedness on earth. Their day of judgment has been delayed. Satan himself is on a leash. Wicked angels can execute wrath as well as good angels administer justice and mercy. For a current bibliography, see vol. 2:615: *The New International Dictionary of New Testament Theology* (Zondervan, 1976). Since then, Wesley Carr's *Angels and Principalities* (Cambridge University Society for New Testament Studies, 1983) has appeared.

22. Schoonhoven, *The Wrath of Heaven*, p. 12.

23. Ibid., p. 109. For further reflection, Karl Barth, *Church Dogmatics* III/1 (1958), p. 167: "On biblical view the end of the world will consist in a passing away of heaven and earth, in cessation of the function of the heavenly bodies and in the extinction of their particular light, but that the heavenly bodies themselves and as such—like the throne of God and the celestial sea and the angels—will not pass away but will be preserved and given a new function." Also, see the work of a former professor of mine: John Reumann, *Creation and New Creation: The Past, Present and Future of God's Creative Activity* (Minneapolis: Augsburg Publishing, Inc., 1974).

24. Moltmann, *God in Creation*, pp. 171, 183. Similarly, Schilder, *Heaven*, pp. 33, 37.

25. H. Haarbeck, H.-G. Link, C. Brown, "new," *The New International Dictionary of New Testament Theology*, ed. Colin Brown (Grand Rapids: Zondervan Publishing Co., 1976), 2:670-674.

26. Most premillennialists say John 14:2, 3 refers to the rapture of the church. (Recall that dispensational eschatology divides the second coming up into two parts: rapture (Christ coming *for* his church) and revelation (Christ coming *with* his church). John F. Walvoord represents those who take John 14 as an early and principal rapture passage. He wrote: "The only interpretation that fits the statements of John 14 is to refer it to the time of the translation [another word they use for rapture— JLG] of the church. . . . [And to say it refers to a Christian going in death] is certainly desperate exegesis" (pp. 71, 72, *The Rapture Question* [Grand Rapids: Zondervan Publishing Co., 1979]).

Several premillennialists, however, disagree with the unbridled confidence of Walvoord that this passage is about the "rapture." The late J. Barton Payne argued that because Peter brought up his death for Christ that the passage in 14:2, 3 refers to believers' deaths (p. 74), *The Imminent Appearing of Christ* [Grand Rapids: Wm. B. Eerdmans Publishing Co., 1962]).

Robert Gundry rejected this interpretation on the lack of specific reference to the death of believers in 14:2, 3 (p. 152, *The Church and the Great Tribulation*). Gundry advanced a view previously intimated by C. H. Dodd (1884-1973) in his *The Interpretation of the Fourth Gospel* (New York: Cambridge University Press, 1953). The promise to return to the disciples after his death was "closely associated, if not identified with the coming of the Holy Spirit" (p. 395). (Dodd didn't see a second coming of Christ in John. How could it be a "vanishing distinction" in John 5:28 and 12:48?) The tense used in 14:2, 3 is definitely present: "I am coming again" or "I come again." Rather than being a reference to the coming of the Holy Spirit, the present tense is used to emphasize the certainty of Christ's coming again. George Beasley-Murray pointed out that the present with a future sense is common in the Fourth Gospel: see 1:15, 30; 4:21, 23, 25, 28; 14:18, 28; 16:2, 23, 25. (Ibid., p. 256; cf. Blass, DeBrunner, Funk, *A Greek Grammar of the New Testament* [Chicago: University of Chicago, 1961]), #323. The futuristic present has the meaning that the event of return was as certain as that moment. The use of "abide" need not mean the Holy Spirit here.

The contextual atmosphere is vital to arriving at the meaning of John 14:2, 3. Jesus referred to his impending death in 13:31, 33, 36. The eleven got the message and they were deeply troubled. Peter reflected the fatalistic defeat of the disciples when he said he would willingly seek martyrdom. Peter's egotistic loyalty claim must have had the effect of making the other ten disciples feel that they would be left in the lurch. They thought that in Jesus' going to death, theirs was not far behind. Peter got them thinking about themselves. Lest they imagined that Peter would get special treatment, Jesus made clear that there was plenty of room for them all.

A governing key in the interpretation of John 14:2, 3 is to see how it followed Jesus' style in the preceding section which deals with his death. In the immediately preceding context, three times Jesus was deliberately ambiguous: (1) Regarding Judas' ominous act (13:18); (2) of not specifying which "one" would turn against him (13:21); and (3) of leaving ambiguous Judas's intent in leaving (13:29). (There was also a touch of ambiguity in 13:31 and 33.) At times Jesus would exercise his right to be vague, whereas generally he was forthright and crystal clear. (It was Jesus' specificity which got him in trouble with the religious authorities.) When his teaching was perceived as unclear it frequently had to do with the moral/mental blockage of the unbelievers (John 8:43; 10:24). John 14:4 testifies to Jesus having made clear the way. There was nothing obscure about his instructions to believers.

Nevertheless, John 14:2, 3 has ambiguity. The verb tense is ambiguous, which is reflected in the variations one finds in translations. "Believe" could be either imperative or indicative. Should the translation be "believe in God, believe also in me," or "you believe in God, believe also in me." Also, these could be placed as questions. Jesus saw nothing tantalizing in offering hope in the midst of some ambiguity. In the same evening Jesus acknowledged an intentional ambiguity in his remarks (John 16:5, 10, 12, 17).

(Nowhere in the New Testament are Christ's heralds encouraged to be fuzzy about man's need of divine grace and of the solution to the human predicament in Christ. Without clarity people are left wondering what to believe and why. Jesus is noted for the simplicity and clarity in his presentation of bedrock spiritual realities. It is important to note what was ambiguous and what wasn't in his teaching.)

There is an unappreciated ambiguity (not ambivalence) in John 14:2, 3. In interpreting John 14:2, 3, it is important to retain its ambiguity, yet, at the same time, to affirm its certainties, lest the comfort factor doesn't get notice or is left to evaporate. With ambiguity was certainty, but it was not the certainty as to the form of his return, so much as to the *fact* of his return. Other certainties were the ample accommodations being prepared, and the certainty of their being rejoined with him on a scale, degree, and length they could not begin to comprehend. What was left ambiguous was the precise time and nature of his return.

One of the certainties of this famous passage is its allusion to multiple possibilities in Christ's coming to us. This fits in with the way other subjects are treated in John. A double perspective in interpreting the focal point of Christ's death is a major characteristic of the Book of John. Unlike the Synoptics, John does not perceive Christ's death as defeat but as victory. Jesus is the victor, more than the victim. Therefore, in John, Jesus left his enthronement openended: His death was a lifting up, so was his resurrection and ascension. It was all one movement (see T. F. Torrance, Space, Time, and Resurrection [Grand Rapids: Wm. B. Eerdmans Publishing Co., 1976], pp. 110, 123, 146, 154, 177). In the same way, the coming of the Spirit to them, after his departure, was as much Christ's coming to them (14:18) as the Spirit's coming to them. We know it theologically to mean that to receive Christ is to receive the Spirit. Therefore one cannot interpret John accurately without a recognition of this multiplicity in "coming." Leon Morris noted, "It is not impossible that John wants us to see more than one of these ways—he often uses language that can be taken in more ways than one and seems to want his readers to accept the multiple meanings" (vol. 3:490, Reflections on the Gospel of John [Grand Rapids: Baker Book House, 1988]). Traditional exegesis recognizes both the ambiguity and multiplicity of "coming" in John, but not dispensational exegesis (see also, Hal Lindsey, The Rapture, pp. 42-45).

Gundry's alternate suggestion that Jesus alluded to spiritual abodes in his own person (The Church and the Great Tribulation; p. 154) does not sufficiently honor Jesus' emphasis upon death and upon the importance of his substance. Indeed, Gundry's suggestion amounts to saying the important thing is not his unique presence with them, but their unusual incorporation into him. Gundry's interpretation doesn't fit the text, because to say their consolation was in their localization, spiritually, in Jesus' person would confuse them more than comfort them. At this point the intent was not to drive them into an abstract mystical consolation, but to raise them from emotional loss by saying that they would not be forgotten even though he was physically leaving them, and that he would return for them, physically. Barnabas Lindars observed that as

Jesus alluded to his death in his going, so he alluded to his resurrection in his return (The Gospel of John, The New Century Bible Commentary [Grand Rapids: Wm. B. Eerdmans Publishing Co., 1972), p. 471. But the resurrected reappearance of Jesus couldn't have been meant to be the sole sense of his return, for Jesus' resurrection time-on-earth place was a mere forty days, whereas John 14:2, 3 intimates that the arrangement would be a permanent arrangement. Marcus Dods (1834-1909) took the view that the passage was to console grieving Christians today in the loss of their dead in Expositor's Greek New Testament vol. 1:822 (London: Hodder and Stoughton, 1917). While this view cannot be categorically ruled out, two factors would seem to argue that it was intended to apply to the second coming of Christ:

(1) The concrete factor in the consolation is strong. The final fulfillment of Christ's physical presence again with us, must project ahead to the second coming of Christ, for while a Christian's death includes our presence with Christ, it does not have the additional consolation of our physical presence with his physical presence. Donald Guthrie wrote: "This certainly appears to demand a future event to complement the statement about a going away (cf. 14:28)" (New Testament Theology, pp. 800, 801).

Yet in a sense, an Interim State fulfillment anticipates the conclusive actualization in the second coming and eternal state of believers with Christ forever. (Simon, Heaven in the Christian Tradition, p. 216, applies John 14:2 to the Intermediate State.)

(2) David E. Aune (1939-) noted in his The Cultic Setting of Realized Eschatology in Early Christianity (Leiden: Brill, 1972) that the second person plural pronouns in John 14:2, 3 refer to a final coming, not to "an individualized Parousia" (p. 129).

In respect to the dispensational interpretation of making John 14:2, 3 a "rapture" reference, it should be evident to the reader that rapture is a construction dictated by commitment to a system in which rapture is axiomatic. There is no basis in the text for a separate "rapture." George E. Ladd wrote: "Any division of Christ's coming into two parts is an unproven inference" *Last Things* (Grand Rapids: Wm. B. Eerdmans Publishing Co., 1978), p. 56. In his full-scale rejoiner of rapture critics, John F. Walvoord wrote that Marcus Dods was guilty of desperate exegesis (*The Rapture Question*, p. 72). If anything, the evidence shows that John F. Walvoord's statement reflects desperate exegesis, for if, as in the dispensational scheme of things, there is a precise seven years of great tribulation, then it would mean that the abode of John 14:2 and 3 would be only seven years, which, William R. Kimball has rightly said, would make the stay with Jesus "either a mobile home or a temporary residency with a seven-year lease" (p. 116, *The Rapture*). The emphasis Jesus gave to his cohabitation with them, however, was not only that it would be physical, but that it would be permanent. According to the pretributional rapturists, the promise is an interim event, not a lasting state. Therefore, for this reason and for the others mentioned above a rapture-interpretation of John 14:2, 3 must be rejected.

27. Arthur H. Lewis, *The Dark Side of the Millennium: The Problem of Evil in Rev. 20:1-10* (Grand Rapids: Baker Book House, 1980), p. 62: "Some aspects of the thousand-year reign bear a close likeness to the new earth, but others are so contrary as to make the identification impossible. The millennial age is temporal, and its termination point is clearly marked by the revolt of Gog and Magog. But the final state is endless and secure from all forms of evil.

During the millennium the saints join the Messiah in his heavenly realm, but in the final state the Messiah joins the saints in the New Jerusalem on earth. The people of the millennium are a mixed lot—saints and sinners, believers and unbelievers. The people of the final state will all be wholly sanctified and have their names written in the Book of Life (Rev. 21:27)." The New Jerusalem is obviously not the old city of Jerusalem done over. Reumann, *Creation and New Creation*, p. 88: "The view is likely correct that this city is not the old Jerusalem transformed, or the millennial city mentioned at 20:9ff, but a preexistent entity which comes down from above."

28. Anthony A. Hoekema (1913-1988), *The Bible and the Future* (Grand Rapids: Wm. B. Eerdmans Publishing Co., 1979), p. 274. See the entire chapter, pp. 274-287]. Or earlier American Reformed theologian, Charles Hodge [1797-1878] wrote on this feature as follows: "It is true the Bible says: 'Heaven and earth are to pass away,' and by heaven and earth the Scriptures often mean the universe; and it would therefore be consistent with the language of Scripture to hold that the whole universe is to be changed at the last day. . . . Whether the heaven and earth which are to pass away are the whole material universe, or only our earth and its atmospheric heavens, the language of the Scriptures leaves undecided. . . . This earth, according to common opinion, that is, this renovated earth, is to be the final seat of Christ's kingdom. This is the new heavens; this is the New Jerusalem" *Systematic Theology* (New York: Charles Scribners & Sons, 1871), III: 853, 854. It should be pointed out that other reformed theologians see the New Jerusalem to be, not the renovated heavens, but the body of believers, the church of the redeemed. J. Marcellus Kik (1904-1965) in *An Eschatology of Victory* (Phillipsburg, NJ:

Presbyterian and Reformed Publishing Co., 1971), p. 244, wrote: "The Bride, the Church, and the Holy Jerusalem are one and the same thing. Furthermore, it cannot be heaven for it descends out of heaven."

Kik has argued that the New Jerusalem cannot be the consummate state, but is the messianic, gospel, or present earthly state. Kik's view represents postmillennialism. He advanced the following points in support of this position: (1) Regarding the walls (Revelation 21:18, 19): "There would hardly be a necessity for a wall to protect it from enemies if it were the consummate state when all the enemies of the Church are in hell." (Ibid.) He also has argued there is still the mixing of the earthly scenery at several other points: (2) Revelation 21:24 indicates earthly divisions between nations still exist, "which indicates an earthly scene"; (Ibid.) (3) Revelation 21:4 states the removal of tears, and Revelation 22:2c indicates leaves from the tree of life will be for the healing of the nations. Kik asked, "Is that a picture of heaven where healing is needed and medicine provided? The gates are open to those who have as yet not entered. After the description of the Holy City there is still the invitation to come to the river of water of life." (Ibid.) These objections do not require us to abandon the futurism of chapter 21 of Revelation. How we should understand the above three questions is dealt with in chapter 5. It has to be that these items and others similar to them are used anachronistically (the past used in the descriptions of the future), else the whole matter of heaven would never appeal to man. Perhaps this is best seen in the problem of music in heaven, another earthly phenomenon which didn't appear to be a problem to Kik. (See further, chapter 8.)

29. Oscar Cullmann, *Immortality of the Soul or Resurrection of the Dead?* (London: Epworth Press, 1958), p. 37.1. It should be noted that Cullman is more for a bodily transformation than a bodily resurrection. His conception of the outcome of believers is of an "incorruptible lifesustance of the Holy Spirit." (Ibid., pp. 37, 38). Regrettably, some Christian writers denied the recycling of creation. Among these were Joseph Hall (1574-1656) and John Howe (1630-1706). Cited in *Heaven: A History,* pp. 171-173).

30. Rex Downie, *World,* Aug, 31, 1987 (vol. 2, no. 14), p. 15.

31. Fortman, *Everlasting Life After Death,* p. 316. In *The Billings Gazette,* Feb. 4, 1978, p. A-7, Rev. Fortman expanded on his book and speculated that possibly a series of galleries would be in place, where the redeemed could visit and enjoy the world's masterpieces. But the need for old art forms is less inviting than creating new art forms. And creating art forms would hardly be allowed unless the artist made each work a vehicle to worship the Lord. William Cowper (1731-1800) admired raw nature over refined art. He wrote in his poem "The Task," Book 1:

> I admire,
> None more admires, the painter's magic skill,
> Who shows me that which I shall never see.
> Conveys a distant country into mine,
> And throws Italian light on English walls.
> But imitative strokes can do no more
> Than please the eye—sweet Nature every sense
> The air salubrious of her lofty hills,
> The cheering fragrance of her dewy vales,
> And music of her woods—no works of men
> May rival these; these all bespeak a power
> Peculiar and exclusively her own.

(*The Works of William Cowper* Grimshawe edition [New York: W. I. Pooley, 1848], p. 56.) According to Cowper's outlook, paintings are unnecessary when there is access to the complete works.

32. Fortman, *Everlasting Life,* p. 310.

33. Colleen McDannell and Bernhard Lang, *Heaven: A History* (New Haven, CT: Yale University Press, 1988), pp. 353-358, plus the Subject Index: "Heaven" subdivided. This work is easy on Fundamentalism's strident eschatological stances. While Fundamentalism may fizzle in giving specifics on the Intermediate and Eternal States, McDannell/Lang failed to point out the overweening confidence they express regarding eschatological time lines (Ibid., pp. 336-340). By the same token, it is heartening to see a flexibility, openness, and revisionist temperament within the last decade of dispensational theologians (*see* Craig A. Blaising, "Development of Dispensationalism by Contemporary Dispensationalists," *Bibliotheca Sacra*, July-September, 1988, pp. 254- 280).

34. Ibid., pp. 377. *See also*, pp. 172, 178.

35. Ibid., pp. 353, 354. McDannell and Lang seemed more willing to credit the corporeal aspects of the final heaven to secular, rationalistic writers rather than to Scripture itself. This appears as a premature plug for rationalism. In fact, the thrust of rationalism was not to make heaven more attractive with action, but to make it unnecessary. They wrote: ". . . While Calvin might have originated the idea of progress in heaven, it was theologians influenced by Enlightenment notions of earthly progress who changed heaven from a place of rest to a center of activity . . ." (Ibid., p. 205). In fact, they have not shown/documented the specific dependence on Enlightenment writers. Even in the cases of Joseph Hall and John Howe (pp. 171-173), who kept heaven noncorporeal, they provided no direct link with skeptical writers (technically, these two predated the Enlightenment). Therefore, it seems their opinion (stated above) was their conjecture, devoid of concrete evidence on the point. Regarding Calvin, it should be noted that he wrote very little on the hereafter, except to argue against the need for purgatory and attack soul-sleep. He did not venture to comment on the Book of Revelation and generally, he avoided going into the specifics of eschatology.

36. Ibid., p. 355; on Irenaeus, pp. 51-53. Found in later Augustine, pp. 65, 66, 68.

37. Ibid., pp. 19, 47.

4. Where Is Heaven?

1. Moltmann, *Creation*, pp. 173, 174. Moltmann's account of why heaven as place has vanished in Lutheranism is reflected in American Lutheran theologian Francis Pieper's, *Christian Dogmatics* (St. Louis, MO: Concordia Publishing House, 1950-57), vol. 3:553. The location of heaven "can no more be fixed than the location of hell. Every attempt to locate heaven geographically is folly. As the *pou damnatorum* [somewhere of the damned] is wherever God manifests His eternal wrath, so the *pou beatorum* [somewhere of the blessed] is wherever God reveals Himself in His uncovered glory, face to face."

McDannell and Lang, *Heaven* (p. 195), cite the departure of one Lutheran writer from the nonspatial view of heaven. Philipp Nicolai (1556-1608) wrote, that in the future state, earth will be restored, except the sea.

2. Austin Farrer, *Saving Belief* (New York: Morehouse-Barlow, Co., 1964), p. 145.

3. William G. Pollard, *Physicist and Christian* (New York: The Seabury Press, 1961), p. 99. The once-influential Baptist theologian, Augustus Hopkins Strong [1836-1921], interestingly, expressed a view compatible with Pollard's conception: "Where heaven and hell are, is not revealed

to us. But it is not necessary to suppose that they are in some remote part of the universe; for aught we know, they may be right about us, so that if our eyes were opened, like those of the prophet's servant (2 Kings 6:17), we ourselves should behold them" (p. 231, *Systematic Theology*, 6th ed. New York: A. C. Armstrong and Son, 1899). Dr. Gordon Haddon Clark's insight, quoted on page 80, near the end of his comment, is to the same effect.

4. "Above" and "Below" references in John (3:13, 31; 6:32f; 8:23). *See* Barth, *Church Dogmatics* III/3, (1961), pp. 436, 437. Schilder, *Heaven*, p. 42: "'above' and 'below' lie in one field of vision; they are one realm." Wolfhart Pannenberg, *Jesus—God and Man*, 2nd ed., translated by L. L. Wilkins and D. A. Priebe, (Philadelphia: The Westminster Press, 1968), pp. 35, 36, 405.

5. Bultmann's "demythologizing" has been effectively taken to task by Torrance, *Space, Time, and Resurrection*, p. 134 (cited). *See also*, pp. 4, 13-15, 17 (note), 40, 41, 134. On the facticity of Christ's resurrection *see*, Ibid., pp. 82, 87, 95, 171, 174.

6. Ibid., p. 133.

7. George Herbert, *The Works of George Herbert* (New York: Thomas Y. Crowell & Co., n.d.), p. 141 (Poem "The Holy Scriptures").

8. The Greek expression is *entos 'umōn*. Exegetes who favor "among you" include Henry Alford, Ethelbert Stauffer and Hermann Kleinknecht in *The Theological Dictionary of the New Testament*, vol. 3 (1965):116-118. Those who favor "in you," on the basis of better manuscript evidence, include Alfred Plummer, A. T. Robertson, and Frederich Godet.

9. Joseph A. Fitzmeyer, *The Gospel According to Luke* (X—XXIV) (Garden City, NY: Doubleday & Company, Inc., 1985), vol. 2:1161.

10. G. E. Ladd, *The Presence of the Future*, p. 156.

11. Pannenberg, Op. Cit. p. 243.

12. Torrance, *Space, Time*, p. 192.

13. Thomas Curtis Clark (1877-1953) "Evidence," *The Mystery Man*, compiled by T. C. Clark (New York: Richard R. Smith, Inc., 1930), pp. 38, 39.

14. In Paul's writings: Rom. 14:17; 1 Cor. 6:9; 15:50; Gal. 5:21; Eph. 5:5; 2 Thess. 1:5; 2 Tim. 4:18.

15. Karl L. Schmidt, *basileús, TDNT*, vol. 1 (1964), p. 579. Karl Barth says, "Jesus Christ is himself the established kingdom of God" (*Church Dogmatics*, translated by G. Bromiley, [Edinburgh: T & T Clark, 1957], II/2, p. 177). *See also Church Dogmatics* I/1 (1975), pp. 352ff; IV/2, (1958), p. 784.

16. Schilder, *Heaven*, p. 26. *See also* Moltmann, *The Church in the Power of the Spirit*, p. 192.

17. Schoonhaven, *Wrath*, p. 124.

18. Shirley MacLaine, *Dancing in the Light* (New York: Bantam Books, Inc., 1985), p. 350. More on MacLaine's views in chapter 20, "Is Heaven Reincarnation?"

19. Shirley MacLaine, *It's All in the Playing* (New York: Bantam Books, Inc., 1987), p. 222.

20. Warfield, *The Works of B. B. Warfield*, vol. 7 (1931): 86; *see also* Pannenberg, *Jesus*, p. 45.

21. H. R. Mackintosh, *Types of Modern Theology* (London: Fantana, 1933, 1964), p. 149. Process theology, which I believe is going to be the dominant Protestant theology of the future, holds to a similar universalism. For more on process theology see chapter 16 "Growth in Heaven?"

22. Peter J. Kreeft, *Everything You Ever Wanted to Know about Heaven (But Never Dreamed of Asking)* (San Francisco: Harper & Row, 1982), pp. 96, 97, 111.

23. Ibid., p. 97, and Smiley Blanton, *Readers' Digest*, August, 1966, p. 94.

24. Ulrich Simon, *Heaven in the Christian Tradition* (New York: Harper & Row, 1958), p. 30.

25. Peter Taylor Forsyth, *The Cruciality of the Cross*, 2nd edition, (London: The Independent Press, Ltd., 1948), p. 31.

26. Ladd, *Presence*, p. 193.

27. Pannenberg, *Jesus*, 373.

28. Ladd, *Presence*, p. 262.

29. Jeremiah Burroughs, *The Rare Jewel of Christian Contentment* (London: The Banner of Truth Trust, 1648, 1964), p. 75.

30. *Philadelphia Inquirer, Today,* July 29, 1979, pp. 12, 13.

31. D. L. Moody, *Heaven*, p. 91.

32. Kreeft, *Heaven* (San Francisco: Harper & Row, 1980), p. 106.

33. Herbert Lockyer, *The Gospel of the Life Beyond* (Westwood, NJ: Fleming H. Revell Company, 1967), p. 56. Lockyer cited

Reginald Wallis's series of couplets summarizing heaven:

> The light of heaven will be the face of God
> and of the Lamb,
> The joy of heaven, the presence of the
> Lord,
> The beauty of heaven, the perfection of
> God,
> The duration of heaven, the eternity of
> God,
> The warmth of heaven, the love of the
> Lord,
> The harmony of heaven, the name of
> Jesus,
> The theme of heaven, the work of Jesus,
> The authority of heaven, the service of
> Jesus,
> The fullness of heaven, the unsearchable
> God in person.
>
> (ADAPTED)

5. What Is Heaven Like?

1. C. S. Lewis, *Miracles* (New York: The MacMillan Company, 1947), pp. 162, 163.

2. Hoekema, *The Bible and the Future*, p. 226.

3. E. Beatrice Batson, in her article, "Dante: a Poet to Discover," *Christianity Today,* Sept. 24, 1965, wrote in support of the theological worth of the *The Divine Comedy:* "Only the most petulant will overlook the basically Christian vision that underlies the poem" (p. 7). She appealed to Canto 7 of *Paradise* as clearly revealing salvation through the death of Christ. Her interpretation fails to take into account, however, the nulling effect of Dante's semi-Pelagianism in the same Canto. *See* p. 342, Dante, *The Divine Comedy*, Louis Biancolli translation (New York: Washington Square Press, 1968). (Semi-Pelagianism taught that man has the willpower to turn to Christ.)

4. Augustus Hopkins Strong, *Great*

Poets and Their Theology (Philadelphia: Judson Press, 1897), p. 145.

5. Ibid., p. 147.

6. D. R. Davies, *The Two Humanities* (London: The Religious Book Club, 1940), p. 32. (This little noticed book is about the two humanisms.)

7. K. Schilder, *Heaven*, p. 13.

8. G. B. Caird, *The Revelation of St. John the Divine* (San Francisco: Harper & Row, 1966), p. 271. Similarly, Thomas F. Torrance, *The Apocalypse Today* (Grand Rapids: Wm. B. Eerdmans Publishing Co., 1959), pp. 146, 147. Ray Frank Robbins wrote: "To come down out of heaven simply means this is what God does. It is not what man has worked up. It is what God has achieved" (p. 221, Revelation: Three Views).

9. Augustus Hopkins Strong, *Systematic Theology* 6th edition (New York: A. C. Armstrong and Son, 1899), p. 582.

10. Jacques Ellul, *The Meaning of the City* (Grand Rapids: Wm. B. Eerdmans Publishing Co., 1970), pp. 109, 110.

11. Ibid., p. 101. Compare 2 Samuel 7:11.

12. J. Ellul, Ibid.

13. H. Haarbeck; H.-G. Link; C. Brown, "kainos"; *The Dictionary of New Testament Theology,* ed., Colin Brown (Grand Rapids: Zondervan Publishing Co., 1976), 2:670-674 Ibid., vol. 2: 674-696, on *neos* by H. Haarbeck; William Barclay, *The Letter to the Hebrews* (Philadelphia: The Westminster Press, 1957), p. 100. Johannes Behm, *The Theological Dictionary of the New Testament* (Grand Rapids: Wm. B. Eerdmans Publishing Co., 1976), vol. 3:447. Richard Chenevix Trench, *Synonyms of the New Testament* (Grand Rapids: Wm. B. Eerdmans Publishing Co., 1880, 1958), pp. 219-225.

14. G. E. Ladd, *A Commentary on the Revelation of John* (Grand Rapids: William B. Eerdmans Publishing Company, 1972), p. 283, wrote: "Usually in ancient cities the gate was built into the wall itself as part of a tower; so each pearl is larger than the wall itself, constituting both the gate and its tower. Such pearls are beyond our imagination."

15. Moody, *Heaven,* p. 31.

16. Franz Delitzsch, *Biblical Commentary on the Prophecies of Isaiah,* (Grand Rapids: Wm. B. Eerdmans Publishing Co., 1877, 1954), vol. 2:348-350.

17. *iaspis* (jasper) occurs in Rev. 4:3; 21:11. W. Arndt, F. W. Gingrich, W. Denker, W. Bauer, *A Greek-English Lexicon of the New Testament,* 2nd edition (Chicago: University of Chicago Press, 1979), p. 368: "jasper, a precious stone found in various colors, mostly reddish, some green, brown, blue, yellow, and white. In antiquity the name was not limited to the variety of quartz now called jasper, but could designate any opaque precious stone. . . . 21:11

(cf. Isa. 54:12); perhaps the opal is meant here; according to some, the diamond." *See also* pp. 75, 76, 79, Ruth V. Wright and Robert L. Chadbourne, *Gems and Minerals of the Bible,* Harper & Row, 1970, 148 pages. According to George B. Caird, the best source on the gems in Revelation is J. L. Myers in the *Encyclopaedia Biblica* IV. 4,799—4,812. Since his commentary came out, in addition to the works above, *see* Russell P. MacFall, *Minerals and Gems* (Crowell).

18. Jacques Ellul, *Apocalypse (The Book of Revelation)* translated by George W. Schreiner (New York: The Seabury Press, 1977), p. 227.

19. D. L. Moody (1837-1899) is the source of this abbreviated/altered quote. The complete version is found on page 444 of William R. Moody's *The Life of D. L. Moody* (New York: Fleming H. Revell Company, 1900).

20. G. R. Beasley-Murray, Herschel H. Hobbs, Ray Frank Robbins, *Revelation: Three Viewpoints* edited by David C. George (Nashville: Broadman Press, 1977), pp. 139, 221, 237, 238.

21. J. Marcellus Kik, *An Eschatology of Victory* (Phillipsburg: Presbyterian and Reformed Publishing Co., 1971), p. 244: The New Jerusalem "cannot be heaven for it descends out of heaven."

22. Anthony A. Hoekema, *The Bible and the Future,* p. 285. Also, Anthony A. Hoekema in *The Meaning of the Millennium* edited by Robert G. Clouse (Downers Grove, IL: InterVarsity Press, 1977), p. 184.

23. Graeme Goldsworthy, *The Lamb and the Lion:* The Gospel in Revelation (Nashville: Thomas Nelson Publishers, 1984), p. 105.

24. George Eldon Ladd, *A Commentary on the Revelation of John* (Grand Rapids: Wm. B. Eerdmans Publishing Co., 1972), p. 275. Ray Summers, however, cannot be so definite. On this passage he wrote: "This

view is not limited to one particular approach to eschatology. Men who are as far apart in their eschatological views as (Clarence) Larkin and (B. H.) Carroll both hold to this idea. New Testament references of this nature are sufficient for interesting speculation about the future but insufficient for such building of definite ideas or conclusions" *The Life Beyond* (Nashville: Broadman Press, 1959), pp. 202, 203.

25. Edmund J. Fortman, *Everlasting Life* p. 311.

6. Who Will Be in Heaven?

1. Paul Tournier, *The Healing of Persons* (New York: Harper & Row Publishers, 1965), p. 96.

2. Kreeft, *Heaven*, p. 106.

3. John Calvin, *The Institutes of the Christian Religion* Ford Lewis Battles editor (Philadelphia: The Westminster Press, 1960), III, 9:4.

4. Ladd *The Presence of the Future*, p. 303.

5. Ibid., p. 327.

6. Thomas Chalmers (1780-1847), *Sermons and Discourses* (New York: Robert Carter and Brothers, 1881), p. 58.

7. Schilder, *Heaven*, p. 27.

8. Revelation has been called "A Throne Book" because of the frequent appearance of the word. The word *thronos* (throne) occurs sixty-two times in the New Testament. In Revelation alone it occurs forty-seven times. "The emphasis he gives the term may be gauged from the fact that in *Matthew*, the book with the next highest number, the word occurs only four times. John's readers were familiar with earthly thrones, and they were troubled by all that Caesar's throne meant. John will not let them forget that there is a throne above every throne." (Morris, *Revelation* (p. 86).

Marcellus Kik criticized the view that the "throne of glory" in Matthew 25:31-46 was an earthly throne set up in a material city, Jerusalem. To contend that a material city is meant is to mistake the shadow for the reality, the earthly for the eternal, the type for the antitype (pp. 170, 171, *An Eschatology of Victory*; in the one-volume edition of his study of Matthew 24, pp. 112, 113).

9. Karl Barth, *Church Dogmatics*, II/1, pp. 474, 475.

10. G. C. Berkouwer, *The Providence of God* (Grand Rapids: Wm. B. Eerdmans Publishing Co., 1952), p. 124.

11. Simon, *Heaven in the Christian Tradition*, pp. 134, 135.

12. C. S. Lewis, *Miracles*, p. 169.

13. George Dennis O'Brien, *God and the New Haven Railroad* (Boston: Beacon Press, 1986), p. 15.

14. Pierre Berton, *The Comfortable Pew* (Philadelphia: J. B. Lippincott Co., 1965), p. 2.

15. Bradford, *The Writings of John Bradford*, vol. 1:359-362.

16. C. S. Lewis, *The Problem of Pain* (New York: The Macmillan Co., 1962), p. 137.

17. Ibid., p. 140. *See also* his *Letters to an American Lady* in correspondence for 8/18/56 and 10/26/62. The absurdity of elevating animal rights is seen among those who suggest that they should have say as to what form heaven should take. Rupert Brooke (1887-1915), an English poet with some sailing background, wrote, "Somewhere beyond space and time is wetter water slimier slime. . . . And in that heaven of all their wish, there shall be no more land, say fish!"

7. Is Heaven Delayed at Death?

1. Dante Alighieri, *The Divine Comedy* translated by Louis Biancolli (New York: Washington Square Press, 1968), p. 159.

2. Geoffrey Nuttall, *The Faith of Dante Alghieri* (London: SPCK, 1969), p. 38.

3. John Calvin, *Institutes of the Christian Religion* Ford Lewis Battles, translation (Philadelphia: The Westminster Press, 1960), III., 5:6.

4. John Owen, *The Works of John Owen* William H. Goold edition (Edinburgh: Banner of Truth, 1965), vol. 3:435.

5. J. A. Motyer, *After Death* (Philadelphia: The Westminster Press, 1965), p. 57.

6. Philip Schaff, *The Creeds of Christendom*, 6th ed. (Grand Rapids: Baker Book House, 1931, 1983), vol. 2:117.

7. Toon, *Heaven and Hell*, p. 119, who cites R. J. Bastion's article in *The New Catholic Encyclopedia*. The Dutch Catholic *A New Catechism* (New York: The Seabury Press, 1969, 1973) says, "Scripture hardly speaks of it at all" (p. 477).

8. Toon, *Heaven and Hell*, p. 120. Toon also cites the European Dominican Anton van der Walle of Brussels and Karl Rahner of Germany to the same effect.

9. Kreeft, *Everything You Ever Wanted to Know*, pp. 21-23.

10. Ibid., p. 21.

11. Mathias Rissi, *The Future of the World: An Exegetical Study of Revelation 19:11-22:15* (Naperville, IL: Alec. R. Allenson, Inc., 1966), pp. 78, 79: "Revelation knows of no purgatory in which the sufferings of the damned have the effect of erasing sins, nor any other means by which the creature can accomplish his own liberation."

12. Brian Hebblethwaite, *The Christian Hope* (Grand Rapids: Wm. B. Eerdmans Publishing Co., 1985), p. 219. Most of what Hebblethwaite writes is worth reading. He represents a growing tendency in certain evangelical camps to accept postdeath purgatory. The only thing close to postdeath purgatory is a predeath purgatory, both in the life of the Christian after regeneration and in that midland, which Bunyan's *Pilgrim's Progress* referred to as Beulah Land. *See* my discussion of this aspect in the opening pages of chapter 17 Ownership in Heaven?

13. Herman Ridderbos, *The Coming of the Kingdom* (Philadelphia: The Presbyterian and Reformed Publishing Co., 1962), p. 283.

14. Berkouwer, *The Return of Christ*, p. 368.

15. Ibid., p. 377.

8. Time in Heaven?

1. Nelson Pike, *God and Timelessness* (New York: Schocken, 1970). For a reply *see* Norman Geisler's essay, "Process Theology," in the collection of essays, *Tensions in Contemporary Theology* (Moody, 1976).

2. Paper, "Evangelicals and Modern Science," by Robert C. Newman, Ph.D., at "Evangelical Affirmations '89," at Trinity Evangelical Divinity School, Deerfield, IL, May 16, 1989.

3. C. S. Lewis, *Mere Christianity* (New York: The Macmillan Company, 1960), p. 139.

4. Carl F. H. Henry, *God, Revelation, and Authority* (Waco, Texas: Word Books, 1982), vol. 5:240. See his survey of the various views of time on pages 235-251. Oscar Cullmann, *Christ and Time* (Philadelphia: The Westminster Press, 1950), p. 253. (Comments on Cullmann's thesis: *see*

G. H. Clark, *God's Hammer* in his essay, "Time and Eternity" (Jefferson, MD: Trinity Foundation, 1982), pp. 182, 183).

5. P. T. Forsyth, *This Life and the Next*, (London: Independent Press, 1981). p. 40.

6. Simon, *Heaven*, p. 236.

7. Louis Berkhof, *Systematic Theology* (Edinburgh: Banner of Truth, 1941, 1958), p. 60.

8. J. Guhrt, "Time," *The New International Dictionary of New Testament Theology*, ed. by Colin Brown (Grand Rapids: Zondervan Publishing House, 1971), vol. 3:830, 831.

9. Richard Chenevix Trench (1807-1886), *Synonyms of the New Testament* (Grand Rapids: Wm. B. Eerdmans Publishing Co., 1958/1880), pp. 209-212. *See* Oscar Cullmann, *Christ and Time*, translated by F. Filson (Philadelphia: Westminster Press, 1950), pp. 39-44. More recently, consult:

J. Guhrt and H. C. Hahn, *NIDNTT*, vol. 3:849, 850, for ample bibliography on the time words of the New Testament.

10. Sheldon Van Auken, *A Severe Mercy* (New York: Bantam Books, 1979), p. 203.

11. Walter Bauer, William F. Arndt, F. Wilbur Gingrich, F. Danker, *A Greek-English Lexicon of the New Testament*, 2nd ed., (Chicago: The University of Chicago Press, 1979), p. 394.

12. Van Auken, *Mercy*, p. 205.

13. C. Samuel Storms, *The Grandeur of God* (Grand Rapids: Baker Book House, 1984), pp. 66-73.

14. *Ibid.*, p. 72.

15. Paul Davies, *Other Worlds* (New York: Simon and Schuster, 1980), pp. 45-47. For related reading see Robert Jastrow, *God and the Astronomers* (New York: Warner Books, 1980).

16. *Ibid.*, p. 49.

9. What Shall We Do in Heaven?

1. Mark Twain, *Letters from the Earth*, edited by Bernard DeVoto, (Greenwich: Fawcett Publications, 1964), p. 17.

2. O'Brien, *God and the New Haven Railroad*, p. 98.

3. Thomas Chalmers, *Sermons and Discourses* (New York: Robert Carter and Brothers, 1881), p. 58.

4. George B. Caird, *The Revelation of St. John the Divine* (San Francisco: Harper & Row, Publishers, 1966), p. 187.

5. Morris, *The Revelation of John*, p. 100. Statement fits singing from Revelation 5:9, where the words of the song are introduced as "saying." Morris cites one writer who noted that because the angels in question never fell, nor were redeemed, that they have nothing to sing about.

6. Graeme Goldsworthy, *The Lamb and the Lion*, (Nashville: Thomas Nelson Publishers, 1984), p. 54.

7. Caird, *Revelation*, p. 233.

8. *Revelation* 4:8, 11; 5:9, 10, 12, 13, 14; 6:10; 7:10, 12; 11:15, 17, 18; 12:10-12; 15:3, 4; 19:1-4, 6, 7. A devotional study of these hymns is found in Robert E. Coleman's *Songs of Heaven* (Old Tappan: Fleming H. Revell Company, 1980). 159 pages.

9. Twain, *Letters*, p. 17.

10. *People* magazine, April 23, 1979, p. 111.

11. Ibid., 112.

12. Ibid.

13. Ibid.

10. Shall We Rest Eternally in Heaven?

1. Twain, "Capt. Stormfield's Visit to Heaven," *The Golden Road* edited by Damon Knight, (New York: Simon and Schuster, 1973), p. 131.

2. Simon, *Heaven in the Christian Tradition*, p. 234.

3. Ibid.

4. Revelation 1:3; 14:13; 16:15; 19:9; 20:6; 22:7; 22:14.

5. Calvin's first treatise was against soul sleep (*Psychopannychia*, written in 1534; prefaced in 1536; published in 1542), found in vol. 3:413-490 in *Selected Works of John Calvin* edited by Beveridge and Bonnet (Grand Rapids: Baker Book House, 1983). More on this subject in Calvin, *see* his *Treatise Against the Anabaptists and Against the Libertines*, 1544, Benjamin Farley translation (Grand Rapids: Baker Book House, 1982), pp. 119- 158. Calvin draws on the New Testament texts strongly against soul sleep such as Luke 23:43, which implies the continuance of consciousnes after death, and 2 Corinthians 5:8. Walter Künneth, *The Theology of the Resurrection* (St. Louis: Concordia Publishing House, 1965), p. 274: "This 'resting' is not equivalent to some euphemistic phrase about 'being in death,' but denotes, the conscious joy of 'being at home with the Lord.'"

6. David Gregg, *The Heaven Life* (New York: Fleming H. Revell, Co., 1895), p. 65.

7. Baxter, *Saints' Rest*, p. 54.

8. Herbert Lockyer, *The Gospel of the Life Beyond* (New York: Fleming H. Revell, 1967), p. 84.

9. C. S. Lewis, *The Great Divorce* (New York: The Macmillan Co., 1946), p. 80.

10. Henry B. Swete, *The Life of the World to Come* (London: Society for Promoting Christian Knowledge, 1919), p. 105.

11. Roland H. Bainton, *Here I Stand* (New York: Mentor Books, 1950, 1955), p. 231.

12. Schilder, *Heaven*, pp. 117, 118.

13. Swete, *Life of the World to Come*, p. 104. Very similar to Jeremy Taylor (1613-1667), cited by Clarence E. Macartney, *Putting on Immortality* (New York: Fleming H. Revell, 1926), p. 185.

14. Thomas Gataker, M.A. (1574-1654), Puritan preacher at Lincoln's Inn, whose skills with Hebrew and Greek were recognized in his time, was one of the early interpreters in Reformation exegesis to note the feature of judges rising to pronounce sentence (cited in C. H. Spurgeon's *Treasury of David* [London: Marshall Brothers, Ltd., 1874], vol. 4:46). Roland de Vaux, O. P. (1903-1971), *Les Institutions de L'Ancien Testament* (Paris: Les Editions du Cerf, 1961), vol. 1:240—"*Durant les débats, le juge était assis*, Is. 16:5; Dn. 7:9-10; 13:50; cf. Jb. 29:7, *mais il se levait pour pronouncer la sentence*, Isa. 3:13; Ps. 76:10. *Les parties se tenaient debout*, Is. 50:8 (*litteralement: 'Tenons-nous debout ensemble'*); cf. 41:1, *et pour 'comparaître', on disait 'se tenir debout devant le juge'*, Dt. 19:17." During Christ's appearance before Caiaphas, the climactic end was signaled when Caiaphas stood up (Matt. 26:62).

The significance of the physical motions of the Hebrew judge has remarkable bearing on the passage where Jesus dealt with the woman taken in adultery (John 7:53—8:11). (Though not in all of the earliest manuscripts, it is, still, instructional.) A minister friend, the Rev. Harvey Stob, once shared with me his interpretation of this famous passage. Except for one commentary on John, to my acquaintance, no other commentary has noticed Stob's application of the juridical postures, that is, that the down-up positions of Jesus had more theological significance than his finger movements. Stob's opinion was that it was Jesus' movements up and down, rather than his writing on the ground that provided the drama of the event. The Pharisees begin by granting Jesus, unofficially, the role of judge in bringing the woman to him. But Jesus saw they were forcing on him a foregone conclusion (8:4, 5). He would not say anything in the posture of standing, lest it be taken as a verdict by one being considered a judge. John Marsh wrote, "It would appear that Jesus wished to avoid any suggestion that he was taking up the position of a judge" (*Saint John* [Pelican New Testament Commentary Series] London: Pelican Books, 1968, p. 686). Therefore, Jesus knelt down (8:6). He was not going to "play" the law game or be forced by them to rubber stamp their verdict, so he stayed down. But they demanded that he judge, so he stood up (8:7a). They anticipated a clear condemnation of the woman, but what he said was a judgment against *them* (8:7b)! "Again, he stoops down" (8:8) and the Pharisees leave. Then, Jesus rose to pronounce judgment on the woman. And, to the consternation of the vicious critics, what Jesus pronounced was acquittal and an exhortation to her to amend her lifestyle (8:10).

15. Henry B. Swete, *The Ascended Christ* (London: Macmillan and Co., Ltd., 1911), p. 14.

16. John Newton, *"Cardiphonia,"* (Correspondence, *May, 1774), The Works of John Newton* (Edinburgh: The Banner of Truth Trust, 1820, 1985), vol. 2:81.

11. Is Heaven Earned?

1. Jean Becker, "What are your chances of going to heaven?" (Cover Story), *USA Weekend*, Dec. 19-21, 1986, *Cincinnati Enquirer*, pp. 1-4.:

2. *Newsweek*, March 27, 1989, p. 53.

3. *USA Weekend*, Dec. 19-21, 1986, *Cincinnati Enquirer*, pp. 1-4.

4. Herbert Preisker, *misthós, The Theological Dictionary of the New Testament*, vol. 4 (1967), p. 712. This view of Pharisaic soteriology (doctrine of salvation), which represents the positions of F. Weber, Emil Schurer, Joachim Jeremias, and others has been recently challenged by E. P. Sanders. Sanders has argued that the Pharisees did not teach salvation by works, but by the mercy of God. His position amounts to saying that there was no difference between what Jesus said and what the Pharisees said. (See E. P. Sanders, *Paul and Palestinian Judaism* [Philadelphia: Fortress Press, 1977], now in its second printing. W. D. Davies' critique of Sander's work appears in the fourth edition of his seminal work, *Paul and Rabbinic Judaism* (pp. xxviii-xxxviii) [Philadelphia: Fortress Press, 1980]. A valuable review of these matters can be found in Donald A. Hagner's *The Jewish Reclamation of Jesus* (Grand Rapids: Zondervan Publishing Co., 1984), pp. 171-191.

Despite's Sander's insistence that Pharisaic Judaism had a place for God's mercy under the covenant, the Pharisees still retained belief in human ability to do good before a holy God. They still held that the human will had the power to impress God, that repentance was something within the power of the human will. They still believed that good works vs. evil works was a determinative factor in the last judgment. Therefore, our presentation is valid and vital. Sanders has grasped at a straw.

5. Ridderbos, *The Coming of the Kingdom*, p. 218.

6. Ibid.; James Buchanan, *The Doctrine of Justification* (Grand Rapids: Baker Book House, 1868, 1955), p. 57.

7. Ridderbos, *The Coming*, p. 219.

8. Thomas Aquinas, *Summa Theologica*, I-11, q. #114, art. 1.

9. G. C. Berkouwer, *Faith and Justification* (Grand Rapids: Wm. B. Eerdmans Publishing Co., 1954), p. 124: "The Roman doctrine of merit, all casuistry notwithstanding, comes to the same thing as the Judaistic hope of 'reward according to rights.'"

10. Hans Küng, *On Being a Christian* (New York: Doubleday and Company, 1976), p. 401.

11. Ibid., p. 405. An old Catholic writer, Lefèvre d'Étaples (1455-1536), who influenced John Calvin, wrote powerfully against works as meritorious: "It is sheer profanity to speak of the merit of works, especially in the presence of God. For plainly merit does not ask a favour, but demands what is due; and to attribute merit to works is virtually to share the opinion of those who believe that we can be justified by works, an error for which the Jews are most of all condemned. So let us be silent about the merit of our works, which amounts to very little or rather nothing at all, and let us magnify the grace of God which is everything. He who defends merit respects man; but he who defends grace respects God. . . . If merit is to be at-tributed to anyone, it is properly and completely attributed to Christ, who has merited everything for us, while, we confessing that before God we deserve nothing, look to him for grace" (cited by P. E. Hughes, *Commentary on the Epistle to the Hebrews* [Grand Rapids: Wm. B. Eerdmans Publishing Co., 1977], p. 461).

12. Preisker, *misthos, TDNT*, vol. 4: 719.

13. Ibid., p. 728.

14. Ibid., p. 718.

15. Calvin, *Institutes of the Christian Religion*, III. 18:7, Battles translation: "God, to prick our sloth, has given us the assurance that the trouble we have borne to the glory of his name will not be in vain." Paul suggested that there is compensation to Christ's workers in 1 Corinthians 3:5-15 (Preisker, *TDNT*, pp. 714, 718, 722).

16. Ibid., p. 717. *See* David Steinmetz, *Theology Today*, April, 1980 (37:1, p. 34).

17. Ladd. *The Presence of the Future*, p. 301.

18. Martin Luther, *Bondage of the Will*, James I. Packer, O. R. Johnston, translators, (London: James Clarke and Co., Ltd., 1957), p. 184.

19. Ibid., p. 182.

20. Walter Grundmann, *kalos, Theological Dictionary*, vol. 3 (1965): 547.

21. Calvin. *Institutes*, III. 13:2; III. 15:2; III. 18:2.

22. Kreeft, *Everything You Ever Wanted to Know About Heaven*, p. 114.

23. Joseph Hart, Hymn: "Come Ye Sinners Poor and Wretched."

12. Can We Be Sure of Going to Heaven?

1. *Newsweek*, Sept. 16, 1976, p. 56.

2. William Adams Brown, *Pathways to Certainty* (New York: Charles Scribners Sons, 1930), p. 24.

3. John Charles Ryle, *Holiness* (Cambridge, UK: James Clarke & Company, Ltd., 1889, 1959), p. 106, fn. 1.

4. John Calvin, *Institutes of the Christian Religion*, (Battles edition), III, 12:1.

5. Ibid., III. 14:7.

6. James I. Packer, "Justification," *Evangelical Dictionary of Theology* edited by Walter Elwell, (Grand Rapids: Baker Book House, 1984), p. 596: "Paul says that believers are justified *dia pisteos* (Rom. 3:25), *pistei* (Rom. 3:28), and *ek pisteos* (Rom. 3:20). The dative and the preposition *dia* represent faith as the instrumental means whereby Christ and his righteousness are appropriated; the preposition *ek* shows that faith occasions, and logically precedes, our personal justification. That believers are justified *dia pistin,* on account of faith, Paul never says and would deny."

7. Bloesch, *Essentials of Evangelical Theology,* vol. 1:229.

8. Robert S. Candlish, *The First Epistle of John* (Grand Rapids: Zondervan Publishing Co., n.d., 1866), p. 503.

13. Sex in Heaven?

1. Rollo May, *Love and Will* (New York: Dell Publishing, 1969, 1974), pp. 105, 106. *See also,* Ernst Becker, *The Denial of Death* (New York: The Free Press, 1973). Mark Twain, American humorist, though of the Victorian era, was eons away from its spiritual roots. He ridiculed the biblical heaven. The first matter he made fun of was the absence of intercourse in heaven, "the one ecstasy that stands first and foremost in the heart of every individual of his race—and of ours" (p. 15, *Letters from the Earth* edited by Bernard De Voto (Greenwich: Fawcett Publications, Inc., 1964).

2. McDannell, Lang, *Heaven: A History,* pp. 25, 26.

3. Ladd, *Presence of the Future,* pp. 87-100; 311-317.

4. Hoekema, *The Bible and the Future,* p. 252.

5. H. Bietenhard, "angel," *The New International Dictionary of New Testament Theology* edited by Colin Brown (Grand Rapids: Zondervan Publishing Co., 1975), vol. 1:103. For views on sexual activity in heaven without children, see the collected information from the Renaissance, from Milton, from Swedenborg, from William Blake, from Charles Kingsley in McDannell, Lang, *Heaven* (pp. 111-144, 181-275).

6. Elmer T. Clark, *The Small Sects in America* (New York: Abingdon Press, 1965), p. 145. Nardi Reeder Campion, *Ann the Word* (Boston: Little and Brown, 1976), p. 18.

7. N. R. Campion, pp. 18, 31, 59. In a vision she saw Adam and Eve copulate and then she witnessed their expulsion from the garden (Ibid., p. 29).

8. *The New York Times,* October 12, 1980, p. 12. Catholic theologians often appeal to Revelation 14:4 in elevating virginity and celibacy. A controversial interpretation of the origin of original sin by Elaine Pagels, *Adam, Eve, and the Serpent* (New York: Random House, 1988) has advanced the view that belief in inborn sin came about, not because Paul taught it, but because Augustine was hung up on sexual impulses (*see* pp. 98-126). To suppose that Augustine "read back" (p. xxvi) into Paul's letter moral impotence of the human will cannot be supported by evidence from the entire New Testament, for teaching on inborn sin is found in John, 1 and 2 Peter, and Jude as well as in the Synoptic Gospels.

9. Gordon D. Fee, *The First Epistle to the Corinthians* (Grand Rapids: Wm. B. Eerdmans Publishing Co., 1987), p. 254.

10. Ibid., p. 256.

11. James D. G. Dunn, *Jesus and the Spirit: A Study of the Religious and Charismatic Experience of Jesus and the First Christians as Reflected in the New Testa-

ment (Philadelphia: The Westminster Press, 1975), pp. 121, 122; Joseph A. Fitzmeyer, S. J., *The Gospel According to Luke: XXXIV* (Garden City, NY: Doubleday & Co., Inc., 1985), vol. 28A:1577.

12. I. Howard Marshall, *The Gospel of Luke* (Grand Rapids; Wm. B. Eerdmans Publishing Co., 1978), p. 903. John Wenham, *Easter Enigma: Are the Resurrection Accounts in Conflict?* (Grand Rapids: Academia Books, 1984), pp. 106-107.

13. Robert H. Gundry, *Sōma in Biblical Theology: With Emphasis on Pauline Anthropology* (Cambridge, UK: Cambridge University Press, 1976) pp. 89, 90.

14. Thomas Torrance, *Space, Time, and Resurrection* (Grand Rapids: Wm. B. Eerdmans Publishing Co., 1976), p. 136. Torrance follows Barth, his teacher: "What is set aside in the resurrection is not nature itself, but the violation of nature" (Karl Barth, *Church Dogmatics*, III/2 1960, p. 296.

15. Eleanor E. Maccoby and Carl N. Jacklin, *The Psychology of Sex Differences* (Stanford, CA: Stanford University Press, 1974) summarized in *Human Sexuality: A Preliminary Study*, edited by Edward A. Powers (New York: The Pilgrim Press, 1977), pp. 122-126. An interesting challenge to some of the ethical conclusions of *Human Sexuality* is found in *Issues in Sexual Ethics*, edited by Martin Duffy, published by United Church People for Biblical Witness, Souderton, Penna. 1979.

Regarding compliance among males, consider: "While males monopolized political and economic power, they made their domination of women more palatable by surrounding it with an elaborate ritual of deference and *politesse*. They set themselves up as protectors of the weaker sex, and this cloying but useful fiction set limits to their capacity to exploit women through sheer physical force" (Christopher Lasch, *The Culture of Narcissism* [New York: W. W.

Norton, 1979]), p. 189. On understanding the male psychology, *see* Robert A. Johnson, *He* (San Francisco: Harper & Row, 1974, 1986).

16. The fathers who said the resurrected will be sexless include the following: Justin (100-165), *On the Resurrection*, chapter 3; Clement of Alexandria (150-215), *The Miscellanies*, 6/6; Hippolytus (170-236), *Fragments from Discourse on Resurrection;* Jerome (341-420), *Letters*, 108, par. 23; Methodius of Olympus, once an assistant to Origen and later bishop of Lycia [d. 311], *Discourse on Resurrection;* Rufinus Tyrannius (345-410), *Apology in Defense of Himself* 1/8. (Source: Paul Badham, *Christian Beliefs about Life after Death* [New York: Barnes & Noble, 1976], p. 158 (End Note 55)). Badham, lecturer in Theology at St. David's University College, Lampeter, Wales, argued that "a sexless resurrection world would be incompatible with the belief that the man and woman to be re-created would be somatically identical to the men and women now living on earth." (Ibid., p. 82).

A recent evangelical work by Don Baker, *Heaven* (Portland, OR: Multnomah Press, 1983) took the position that the saved are de-sexed (p. 13).

17. Donald G. Bloesch, *Is the Bible Sexist?* (Westchester, IL: Crossway Books, 1982), p. 35.

18. Donald G. Bloesch, *Evangelical Theology* (San Francisco: Harper & Row, 1979), Vol. 2: 229. He also said, "We must not suppose that particular affections will no longer exist, but they must now be seen as having a new basis." (Apparently, Bloesch wants to retain something of earthly marriages!) Ulrich Simon, *Heaven in the Christian Tradition*, p. 217, drew an opposite conclusion from *Mark* 12:25. He wrote: "[*Mark* 12:25] abrogates not only [the] essential human faculty of sexual love and relationship and the need for procrea-

tion, but even the survival of family ties. The earthly relationships do not appear to be translated into heaven." Few feel comfortable holding to the views of William Blake (1757-1827), the mystic, and Charles Kingsley (1819-1875), the Anglican novelist, that sexual activity will survive (pp. 234-245, 261-264, McDannell, Lang, *Heaven: A History*).

19. Hal Lindsey says, "The Church is mentioned *nineteen times* in the first three chapters of the Book of Revelation and isn't mentioned *once* as being on earth from Chapters 4 through 19!" (p. 61, *A New World Coming*, New York: Bantam Books, 1975). He backs down from this blanket statement when he concedes that during the Great Tribulation some will believe in Christ and die for their profession (Ibid., p. 92). The only "church" Lindsey will admit to is the conglomerate of organized religions (pp. 219-224, Ibid.) Essentially the same position is taken by John Walvoord, who taught Lindsey at Dallas Seminary. Walvoord, also, insists the church is not in the same set of chapters because the particular word, *ekklesia* (translated, "church"), does not appear. Walvoord admits the word "saint" and "saints" occurs in the chapters in question, but instead of seeing the church *is* mentioned by another term writes: "This tends to support the concept that the church as the Body of Christ is raptured before events pictured in the book of Revelation beginning in chapter 4" (John Walvoord, *The Revelation of Jesus Christ*), p. 33. The conclusion of Walvoord should make the value of reading Revelation minimal. He wrote: "The peculiar hope of the church, in contrast to that of other saints, is alluded to only obliquely and is not the main substance of the revelations in chapters 4 through 19" (Ibid.).

These claims should be dismissed as incredible, for the church, in the figure of a woman, was promised and given protec-

tion by God. But in specific texts in Revelation "saints" are active on the earth. The 144,000 are the believers who stand loyal to Christ. *They* are the church. Lindsey's comeback would probably be that these were not the church, but tribulation saints. That tack is nothing but a ruse. It has no foundation in the biblical text. It robs the saints of whatever tribulation from being true members of the body of Christ. The church is not taken out to escape tribulation but preserved in it. With God's mark upon his own the saints (the church) were given trouble, but spared the wrath of God. *See* pp. 58-72, G. E. Ladd, *The Last Things* (Grand Rapids: Wm. B. Eerdmans Publishing Co., 1978) and his earlier, *Blessed Hope*, pp. 120-129, in chapter "Wrath or Tribulation?"

20. John Charles Ryle, *The Upper Room* (London: Banner of Truth, 1970, 1988), p. 241.

21. Abraham Kuyper, *The Revelation of St. John* translated by John H. de Vries (Grand Rapids: Wm. B. Eerdmans Publishing Co., 1935, 1963), p. 122.

22. Rollo May, *Love and Will*, p. 113.

23. Ibid., p. 53.

24. Jürgen Moltmann, *The Church in the Power of the Spirit* (San Francisco: Harper & Row, Publishers, 1977), p. 188: "What is being claimed here is not only equal validity, but also equal being in Christ; not only equality in faith before God, but also equality in the fellowship of Christ; not only equal pardon, but also equal rights."

25. The only point this text makes is that the body in its present form, showing the marks of decay and death, as such is "ill-suited for the life of the future" Gordon D. Fee, *The First Epistle to the Corinthians*, p. 799.

26. Proof that C. S. Lewis was deadly serious in the retention of sexuality in heaven is found in his defense of Chris-

tianity, entitled *Miracles* (New York: The Macmillan Company, 1947), p. 166. He had given early formulation to this idea in his space-science trilogy. These are *Out of the Silent Planet, Perelandra* (*see* pages 200, 201 on retention of sexuality) and *That Hideous Strength* (Macmillan, 1946), of which James Packer wrote "despite its fine title, is (to my mind, anyway) hideously bad" (*Christianity Today,* Jan. 14, 1988). (*That Hideous Strength* is about the satanic angelic visitors to earth, members of N.I.C.E., which stands for the National Institute of Co-ordinated Experiments.) Near the end of *That Hideous Strength,* appears an explanation of how the angelic intelligences retained sexual characteristics: "She had been conceiving this world as 'spiritual' in the negative sense—as some neutral, or democratic, vacuum where differences disappeared, where sex and sense were not transcended but simply taken away. Now the suspicion dawned upon her that there might be differences and contrasts all the way but, if this invasion of her own being in marriage from which she had recoiled, often in the very teeth of instinct, were not, as she had supposed, merely a relic of animal life or patriarchal barbarism, but rather the lowest, the first and the easiest form of some shocking contrast with reality which would have to be repeated. . . . 'Yes,' said the Director. There is no escape. If it were a virginal rejection of the male, He would allow it. Such souls can bypass the male and go on to meet something far more masculine, higher up, to which they must make yet deeper surrender. . . . You are offended by the masculine itself: the loud, irruptive, possessive thing—the gold lion, the bearded bull— which breaks through the hedges and scatters the little kingdom of your primness as the dwarfs scattered the carefully made bed. The male you could have escaped, for it exists only on the biological level. But the masculine none of us can escape. What is

above and beyond all things is so masculine that we are all feminine in relation to it" (C. S. Lewis, *That Hideous Strength* [New York: Macmillan Publishing Co., 1946], pp. 315, 316).

27. Karl Barth, *Church Dogmatics* III/2 (1960), p. 296. (*See also,* Ibid., III. 1 [pp. 184, 308, 309]). Augustine believed sexual distinctions were retained, that is, in the resurrection there was no abolition of the sexes (*City of God,* Book 22, Chap. 17 [New York: Modern Library, 1950], pp. 839, 840). Some conservative theologians have questioned Barth's contention of both sexes being in God. Gordon H. Clark, *The Philosophy of G. H. Clark,* edited by Ronald H. Nash [Philadelphia: Presbyterian and Reformed Publishing Co., 1968], p. 74, in the chapter "The Axiom of Revelation" rejects Barth's view of sexuality being the image of God in man. Carl F. H. Henry's reaction: "The theory deserves less plaudits for exegetical fidelity than for ingenious imagination" (vol. 2:138, *God, Revelation, and Authority* [Waco: Word Books, 1976]). Vernard Eller seems to have inadvertently answered the objections of Clark and Henry in his *The Language of Canaan and the Grammar of Feminism* [Grand Rapids: Wm. B. Eerdmans Publishing Co., 1982], pp. 38, 39).

The USA Weekend poll, mentioned in chapter 3 shows that belief in holding God as a man is high—60 percent. Significantly, in their poll, "*no one* thinks of God as a woman; 37 percent say God is neither" (*The Cincinnati Enquirer,* USA *Weekend,* Dec. 19-21, 1986, p. 5).

28. Kreeft, *Everything You Ever Wanted to Know About Heaven,* p. 72. Perhaps the reason why he reflected Barth's conclusion goes back to Carl Henry's criticism (in the preceding note). On page 77, Kreeft has tried to argue that, of course, the image of God in man has to be sexuality, because only humans write love poems, not animals. But he has apparently neglected to

notice ecstasy in animals. What distinguishes them from man is that man has rationality and the mental capacity to devise and use speech to write romantic verse.

29. Bloesch, *Sexist?* p. 66.

30. Ibid., p. 68. Bloesch has done this on pages 25-40 (regarding humans to humans) and pages 61-83 (regarding God).

31. Ibid., p. 70.

32. Ibid., p. 68.

33. G. Bauer, tiktō, *New International Dictionary of New Testament Theology,* edited by Colin Brown (Grand Rapids: Zondervan Publishing Co., 1975), vol. 1:187. See Peter Toon, *Born Again* (Grand Rapids: Baker Book House, 1987), p. 40.

34. Susan T. Foh, *Women and the Word* (Grand Rapids: Baker Book House, 1981), pp. 152, 153. Bloesch, *Sexist?*, p. 117.

35. D. Bloesch, *Sexist?*, pp. 68-70.

36. The Hebrew root *yada,* which occurs a total of 944 times in the Old Testament, has multiple meanings ranging from observation to copulation. It is the word used for the ultimate intimacy of sexual relations in Genesis 4:1; 19:8; Numbers 31:17, 35; Judges 11:39; 21:11; 1 Kings 1:4; 1 Samuel 1:19. Overtones of commitment and love are reflected in its application to obedience, trust, reverence, and service. Jack Lewis, *Theological Wordbook of the Old Testament,* edited by R. Laird Harris (Chicago: Moody Press, 1980), vol. 1:366. E. D. Schmitz, *The New International Dictionary of New Testament Theology* Colin Brown, editor (Grand Rapids: Zondervan Publishing House, 1976), vol. 2:395-400. An important aspect of the experimental side of the word is the actual involvement of the "knower" with or in the object (*Nelson's Expository Dictionary of the Old Testament* edited by Merril F. Unger; William White, Jr., James I. Packer [Nashville: Thomas Nelson Publishers, 1980]), p. 213.

37. R. May, *Love and Will,* p. 112.

38. Kreeft, *Everything You Ever Wanted to Know,* p. 72. He followed C. S. Lewis on this point: cf. Lewis, *Miracles,* pp. 165-166.

39. V. Eller, *The Language of Canaan and the Grammar of Feminism* (Grand Rapids; Wm. B. Eerdmans Publishing Co., 1982), p. x.

40. Ibid., p. 44. Because of space limitations in this chapter I could not show how Eller has taken up on the suggestions of A. C. Thiselton in his seminal work *Two Horizons,* which is a recent hermeneutical text.

41. Karl Barth, *The Theology of Schleiermacher* (Grand Rapids: Wm. B. Eerdmans Publishing, Co. 1968, 1982), pp. 70, 71.

42. Karl Rengstorf, *mathatas, The Theological Dictionary of the New Testament,* edited by Gerhard Kittel (Grand Rapids: Wm. B. Eerdmans Publishing Co., 1967), vol. 4:434.

43. Karl Barth, *Church Dogmatics,* I:1:717.

44. Warfield, *The Works of Benjamin B. Warfield* vol. 8:379. *See also,* pp. 374-381, 388-390, 453-454. Primary sources available in the USA include: *The Autobiography of Madame Guyon* (Moody Press, n.d.); *The Christian's Secret of a Happy Life* by Hannah Whitall Smith (Fleming H. Revell, 1942).

45. Warfield, *The Works of Benjamin Warfield,* 8:539.

46. Richard F. Lovelace, *Dynamics of the Christian Life* (Downers Grove, IL: InterVarsity Press, 1979), p. 116.

47. James I. Packer, *Keep in Step with the Spirit* (Old Tappan: Revell Publishing Co., 1984), p. 157.

48. George W. Knight, III., *The New Testament Teaching on the Role Relationship of Men and Women* (Grand Rapids: Baker Book House, 1977), pp. 14, 20.

49. Lewis, *The Dark Side of the Millennium,* pp. 63, 64. Lewis gives the most credible explanation. Others include Ladd

in *The Blessed Hope*. Ladd mentioned one futurist interpretation which sees Revelation 19:8 as a description of Old Testament saints of restored Israel, not sainted believers today. But that "is an inference which appears to contradict the indications of Scripture" (p. 136). Few futurists, I have found in my reading, believe the bride is Israel. This text is badly handled, as I see it, mostly in reference to the chronological slot assigned to the Marriage Supper of the Lamb. Ladd, who follows sequential chronology of the later chapters of Revelation, says the Marriage of the Lamb must be an event of the redeemed *un*resurrected because Revelation 20:4, as he sees it, puts the millennium afterwards (Ibid., p. 102). The best solution seems to be that the Marriage Supper is described proleptically, that is the event is future, but is described as done in J. S. Russell, *The Parousia* (Baker Book House, 1983), p. 509, and that chapter 20 is not to be viewed as sequentially following Christ's second coming (chapter 19), but that it is a parenthetical explanation of the style of Christ's conquest between the two advents.

50. Kreeft, *Everything You Ever Wanted to Know*, has a view of sexuality in the afterlife similar to his statement "promiscuity of spirit is a virtue" in reference to the Communion of Saints (Ibid., p. 75): "Sex in Heaven? Indeed, and no pale, abstract, merely mental shadow of it either. Earthly sex is the shadow. . ." (Ibid., p. 78). Kreeft's statement is too close to Platonism to be of much comfort. *See* chapter 15, where the limits of this kind of reasoning are discussed.

14. Humor in Heaven?

1. *Newsweek*, March 27, 1989, p. 53.

2. Grady Wilson, *Count It All Joy* (Nashville: Broadman Press, 1984), p. 141.

3. E. Stanley Jones, *A Song of Ascents* (Nashville: Abingdon Press, 1968), p. 341.

4. Three areas of humor should be looked at:

HUMOR IN THE BIBLE

Gary Webster, *Laughter in the Bible* (St. Louis, MO: The Bethany Press, 1960)

Elton Trueblood, *The Humor of Christ* (New York: Harper & Row, Publishers, 1964). See page 27 where he has a short bibliography on humor and the Bible.

HUMOR IN THE PULPIT

Douglas Adams, *Humor in the American Pulpit: From George Whitefield through Henry Ward Beecher* (North Aurora, IL: The Sharing Company, 1975, 1976), 2nd edition.

John W. Drakeford, *Humor in Preaching: The Craft of Preaching Series* (Grand Rapids: Ministry Resources Library of Zondervan Publishing Co., 1986).

A THEOLOGY OF HUMOR

Nelvin Vos, *For God's Sake Laugh* (Richmond, VA: John Knox Press, 1967).

Tom Mullin, *Laughing Out Loud: And Other Religious Experiences (Waco, TX: Word Books, 1983).*

5. McDannell, Lang, *Heaven*, p. 214.

6. Ibid., p. 99.

7. Ibid., p. 135.

8. Vos, *For God's Sake Laugh*, p. 70.

9. John F. MacArthur, Jr., *The Gospel According to Jesus* (Grand Rapids: Zondervan Publishing Co., 1988), p. 151.

10. The fellowship of Merry Christians is composed of over 10,000 members. Their bimonthly newsletter is *The Joyful Noiseletter*. Their address is P.O. Box 668, Kalamazoo, Michigan. This group can identify with the confession of Charles H. Spurgeon: "I never knew what the hearty

laugh and what the happy face meant till I knew Christ" (*New Park Street Pulpit*, vol. 3:428, uttered 10/25/1857).

11. Recent works that discuss this issue include:

FOR

Murray J. Harris, *Raised Immortal: Resurrection and Immortality in the New Testament* (Grand Rapids: Wm. B. Eerdmans Publishing Co., 1983, 1985), pp. 98-101, 144, 216, 217, 220-226.

W. D. Davies, *Paul and Rabbinic Judaism: Some Rabbinic Elements in Pauline Theology* (Philadelphia: Fortress Press, 1948, 1980), 4th edition, pp. 309-311.

F. F. Bruce, "Paul on Immortality," *Scottish Journal of Theology*, vol. 24, no. 4, Nov., 1971, pp. 457-472.

Philip Edgecumbe Hughes, *Paul's Second Epistle to the Corinthians* (Grand Rapids: Wm. B. Eerdmans Publishing Co., 1962), pp. 165-167.

AGAINST

Anthony A. Hoekema, *The Bible and the Future* (Grand Rapids: Wm. B. Eerdmans Publishing Co., 1979), pp. 104-108.

Joseph Osei-Bonsu, "Does 2 Cor. 5:1-10 Teach the Reception of the Resurrection Body at the Moment of Death?" *Journal for the Study of the New Testament*, vol. 28, 1986, pp. 81-101.

Peter Toon, *Heaven and Hell: A Biblical and Theological Overview* (Nashville: Thomas Nelson Publishers, 1986), pp. 127, 128.

P. E. Hughes' commentary, mentioned above, goes over the arguments against the view that the passage teaches a resurrection.

12. C. H. Spurgeon's *Autobiography: Compiled from His Diary, Letters, and Records by his Wife and Private Secretary* (London: Passmore and Alabaster, 1899), vol. 3 (1856-1878):56.

15. Equality in Heaven

1. H. Bietenhard, "*people*", *The New International Dictionary of New Testament Theology* edited by Colin Brown, vol. 2:793-796.

2. Ferrell Jenkins, *The Old Testament in the Book of Revelation* (Grand Rapids: Baker Book House, 1976), pp. 22-24. It should be noted that while there are many influences, references, allusions from the Old Testament in Revelation, shockingly, there are no direct citations.

3. Bruce Waltke, "Kingdom Promises as Spiritual," *Continuity and Discontinuity*, Essays in Honor of S. Lewis Johnson, Jr., edited by John S. Feinberg (Westchester, IL: Crossway Books, 1988), pp. 273, 274. Another astonishing omission in Revelation is the teaching of the rapture of the church. "Revelation does not in fact describe a pre-tribulation 'rapture', and this view must be regarded as speculative" (Donald Guthrie, *New Testament Theology* [Downers Grove, IL: InterVarsity Press, 1981], p. 815). Rev. 4:1 cannot be used (though Hal Lindsey, *New World Coming*, p. 161, suggests it), for only John was "caught up" and that only in a vision (4:2).

4. Swete, *Commentary on Revelation*, p. 133.

5. Isbon T. Beckwith, *The Apocalypse of John* (Grand Rapids: Baker Book House, 1919, 1979), p. 590.

6. Mathias Rissi, *The Future of the World: An Exegetical Study of Revelation 19:11-22:6* (Naperville, IL: Alec. R. Allenson, Inc., 1966), p. 64. On Revelation 21:22, he wrote: "This is also something that sets the eschatology of John apart from all Jewish expectations" (p. 61).

7. Norman A. Beck, *Mature Christianity: The Recognition and Repudiation of the Anti-Jewish Polemics of the New Testament* (Selingsgrove, PA: Susquehanna

University Press, 1985), p. 275. The foment of trouble for the church in Revelation is Satan, the red dragon of 12:4, 9, not the Jewish nation. Except for 11:8 (compare with 11:2) "great city" meant Rome (16:19; 17:8; 18:16, 18, 19, 21).

8. J. Stewart Russell, *The Parousia:* A Study of the New Testament Doctrine of the Second Coming of Christ (Grand Rapids: Baker Book House, 1887, 1983), p. 410.

9. Ibid., pp. 395, 407, 410, 424.

10. G. Beasley-Murray, *The Book of Revelation* (London: Oliphants, 1974), p. 320.

11. Austin Farrer, *The Revelation of St. John the Divine* (Oxford: Clarendon Press, 1964), p. 219.

12. Goldsworthy, *The Lamb and the Lion*, p. 101.

13. I made a total reversal/substitution of David L. Turner's clever couplet found in *Grace Theological Journal*, 6/2 1985, pp. 275f, which Bruce Waltke cited in its original form in *Continuity and Discontinuity.*

14. Moltmann, *The Church in the Power of the Spirit*, pp. 140, 141.

15. William Hendriksen, *Israel and the Bible* (Grand Rapids: Baker Book House, 1968), p. 57.

16. Warfield, *The Works of B. B. Warfield*, vol. 9:257.

17. Kreeft, *Everything You Ever Wanted to Know About Heaven*, pp. 73, 74.

18. Ibid., p. 28. Herbert Lockyer: "The people of God will be one, having one language, as the human race had at the beginning," *The Gospel of the Life Beyond* (Westwood, NJ: Fleming H. Revell, 1967), p. 28.

19. Schilder, *Heaven*, p. 81.

20. Frend, *The Rise of Christianity,* p. 30.

21. The word in 2 Peter 1:1 is *isotimos.* William Barclay's translation is "alloted a faith equal in honor and privilege with our own," *The Letters of James and Peter,* Daily Study Bible (Philadelphia: The Westminster Press, 1958), p. 343.

22. Donald MacGavran, *Understanding Church Growth* (Grand Rapids: Wm. B. Eerdmans Publishing Co., 1970), pp. 243, 252, 253.

23. John Gerstner, *Jonathan Edwards on Heaven and Hell* (Grand Rapids: Baker Book House, 1980), p. 20. Baptist theologian, John Gill (1697-1771), *Body of Divinity* (Atlanta, GA: Turner Lassetter, reprint, 1839 ed. [1769 orig.]), pp. 692, 693, argued that the usual texts about rewards belonged to the millennium, not to the final heaven. Gill lists eight reasons why degrees of glory do not belong in the final heaven.

24. Schilder, *Heaven*, p. 53.

25. Those who support this include: John Owen (1616-1683), *The Works of John Owen* (Edinburgh: The Banner of Truth, 1965), vol. 1:239. Jonathan Edwards, *Jonathan Edwards on Heaven and Hell*, pp. 21-23. C. H. Spurgeon (1834-1892), *New Park St. Pulpit*, vol. 1:202. Strong, *Systematic Theology,* p. 585. William Graham Scroggie (1877-1959), *What about Heaven?* (London: Pickering & Inglis, Ltd., n.d.), pp. 110, 111. Louis Berkhof (1873-1957), *Systematic Theology* (London: Banner of Truth, 1941, 1958), p. 737. Herbert Lockyer (1886-1984), *The Gospel of the Life Beyond* (Westwood, NJ: Fleming H. Revell Company, 1967), pp. 79-82.

26. John H. Bernard, *The Gospel according to St. John*, International Critical Commentary (Edinburgh: T & T Clark, 1928, 1976), vol. 2:532.

27. Ibid., vol. 2:533.

28. Rufus Calvin Zartman, *Heaven* (Reading, PA: Daniel Miller Publishers, 1893), p. 117.

29. Abraham Kuyper, *The Work of the Holy Spirit* (Grand Rapids: Christian Classics, 1972), p. 231. Found in vol. 3, chapter 5.

30. G. C. Berkouwer, *The Return of Christ* (Grand Rapids: Wm. B. Eerdmans Publishing Co., 1972), p. 121.

31. Beasley-Murray, *Revelation*, p. 305.

32. Caird, *The Revelation of St. John* p. 188.

33. Ibid., pp. 87, 94; Schilder, *Heaven*, pp. 81, 82.

34. Caird, *Revelation*, p. 178.

35. Ibid., p. 267.

36. Ellul, *Apocalypse*, p. 224.

16. Growth in Heaven?

1. Few books on heaven have addressed the matter of progress in the hereafter in as much length as McDannell and Lang, in *Heaven, A History* (New Haven: Yale University Press, 1988), which devoted one chapter to the subject: pages 276-306.

2. C. S. Lewis, *The Great Divorce* (New York: The Macmillan Company, 1947), p. 30.

3. John Calvin, "Psychopannychia," *Selected Works of John Calvin*, edited by Henry Beveridge and Jules Bonnet (Grand Rapids: Baker Book House, 1851, 1983), vol. 3:463, 464.

4. John Owen, *The Works of John Owen* (Edinburgh: Banner of Truth Trust, 1850, 1965), vol. 1:407, "The Glory of Christ."

5. McDannell, Lang, *Heaven*, pp. 290, 291.

6. Fortman, *Everlasting Life After Death*, p. 313.

7. Bernard, *The Gospel According to John*, vol. 2:532. As mentioned before, this observation should be made on the use of "mansions" in the King James Version. The present-day meaning of *mansions* is different from the 1611 meaning. *Mansions* derives from the Latin *manere*. The root meaning of the Latin *manere* (the root of our *mansions*) meant "to remain." The concept of enormous building, a large and stately residence, was a later use according to the *Oxford English Dictionary* (M135). When we use *mansion* in our day we think of it as a large and stately resi-

dence. But in 1611, the word carried the sense of "to remain."

8. John Charles Ryle, *Holiness* (Cambridge: James Clarke & Co., Ltd., 1889, 1959), p. 85.

9. Bernard, *Gospel According to John*, vol. 2:533. Clement of Alexandria had a defective view of God as well (compare with C. F. H. Henry, *God, Revelation, and Authority*, vol. 2:171. Caution in use of the early fathers strongly recommended by Calvin, *Institutes of the Christian Religion*, II, 2:4; III, 5:10; III, 11:15.

10. Morris, *The Gospel According to John*, p. 638.

11. R. Schippers, *"goal," The New International Dictionary of New Testament Theology*, vol. 2:59-65.

12. David Peterson, *Hebrews and Perfection* (Cambridge: Cambridge University Press, 1982), pp. 24, 136.

13. Kuyper, *The Work of the Holy Spirit*, pp. 231, 232, found in vol. 3, chapter 5. For additional comments of Kuyper, *see* his *The Revelation of St. John*, p. 335.

14. Henry B. Swete, *The Life of the World to Come* (London: Society for Promoting Christian Knowledge, 1919), p. 108.

15. Lewis, *Divorce*, p. 30.

16. Raymond Moody, Jr., M.D., *Life After Life* (New York: Bantam Books, 1976), pp. 64-72.

17. Kreeft, *Everything You Ever Wanted to Know About Heaven*, p. 56.

18. Schilder, *Heaven*, pp. 79, 80.

19. Herbert Lockyer, *The Gospel of the Life Beyond*, p. 88. The citation is from a greeting card from an unknown author.

20. Emanuel Swedenborg, *Heaven and Its Wonders, and Hell* (New York: Swedenborg Foundation, 1758, 1960), p. 197 (paragraph 340). One of the weaknesses of the recent McDannell and Lang's *Heaven: A History* (1988), which in terms of compensating for a neglect can also be a strength of the book, is its excessive attention to the wild ideas of spiritualist Swedenborg. Whereas the book devotes forty-seven pages to Swedenborg, the text gives only thirty-six pages to Protestant and Catholic Reformers *combined*!

21. Ibid., pp. 23, 24 (paragraphs 41-47), 100, 101 (paragraphs 184-186).

22. Gerstner, *Jonathan Edwards on Heaven and Hell*, p. 39.

23. *Newsweek*, March 27, 1989, p. 53.

24. David Gregg [1846-1919], *The Heaven Life* (New York: Fleming H. Revell, Co., 1895), p. 56. (Gregg was minister of the Lafayette Ave. Presbyterian Church, Brooklyn.) This view was held by Thomas Aquinas (*see* Peter Toon, *Heaven and Hell*, p. 142).

25. "Even those whom Jesus raised up in His lifetime will die again, for they did not receive a resurrection body, the transformation of the fleshly body into a spiritual body does not take place until the End", Oscar Cullmann in *Immortality of the Soul and Resurrection of the Dead?* (London: The Epworth Press, 1958), p. 35.

26. Maurice Rawlings, M.D., *Beyond Death's Door* (New York: Bantam Books, 1979), pp. 79-83. Rawlings did not draw these conclusions, but was suggested to us by the materials on these pages. A recent anthology is Carol Zaleski, *Other World Journeys: Accounts of Near-Death Experience in Medieval and Modern Times* (New York: Oxford University Press, 1987), indexed, 275 pages.

27. McDannell and Lang, *Heaven*, p. 307.

28. Schilder, *Heaven*, p. 109: "[Rev. 21:24] . . . does not mean, cannot mean, that something of culture and civilization will be carried over into eternity. . . ."

29. H. Haarbeck; H.-G. Link; C. Brown, "kainos" *The Dictionary of New Testament Theology*, ed. Colin Brown (Grand Rapids: Zondervan Publishing House, 1976), 2:670-674. G. R. Beasley-Murray; H. H. Hobbs, R. F. Robbins, *Revelation: Three Viewpoints*, p. 221.

30. Stephen Charnock, *The Works of Stephen Charnock*, vol. 4: The Knowledge of God (Edinburgh: Banner of Truth Trust, 1865, 1985), p. 462. Similarly, Charles Haddon Spurgeon, *An All-Round Ministry* (Edinburgh: Banner of Truth Trust, 1900, 1960), p. 167: "We shall continue to learn even in heaven, and shall still be looking deeper and deeper into the abyss of Divine love."

31. Toon, *Heaven and Hell*, p. 155. *See* also John Gerstner, *Jonathan Edwards on Heaven and Hell*, pp. 25, 39.

32. Richard Baxter, *The Saints' Everlasting Rest* (London: The Religious Tract Society, n.d.), pp. 353, 354.

33. Joseph Butler, *The Complete Works of Joseph Butler* (London: William Tegg and Co., 1850), p. 165.

34. H. R. MacKintosh, *The Highway of God* (Edinburgh: T & T Clark, 1931), p. 92.

35. Abraham Kuyper, *The Revelation of St. John*, p. 332.

36. Schilder, *Heaven*, pp. 52, 53.

37. J. J. Duyvene de Wit, "Pierre Teilhard de Chardin," essay, pp. 407-450, in *Creative Minds in Contemporary Theology*, ed. by P. E. Hughes (Grand Rapids: Wm. B. Eerdmans Publishing Co., 1966). Since then, see D. G. Jones, *T. de Chardin*, An Analysis and Assessment (Downers Grove: InterVarsity Press, 1970) and P. Hefner, *The Promise of Teilhard* (Philadelphia: J. Lippincott Co., 1970).

38. McDannell, Lang, *Heaven*, p. 347.

39. Ibid., p. 348.

40. Schubert Ogden, *The Reality of God and Other Essays* (New York: Harper & Row, 1966), pp. 229, 230.

41. Bruce A. Demarest, *General Revelation: Historical Views and Contemporary Issues* (Grand Rapids: Zondervan Publishing Co. 1982), p. 173.

42. Walter Wink, *Interpreting the Powers* (Philadelphia: Fortress Press, 1984), vol. 1:120. This is part of a trilogy. The other volumes are: *Unmasking the Powers* (1986); and *Engaging the Powers* (projected).

43. Norman L. Geisler, essay, "Process Theology," *Tensions in Contemporary Theology* edited by Stanley N. Gundry and Alan F. Johnson (Chicago: Moody Press, 1976), p. 243.

44. Demarest, *Revelation*, p. 170.

45. Wink, *Interpreting the Powers*, vol. 1:122.

46. Ibid., pp. 123, 124.

47. G. C. Berkouwer, *Sin* (Grand Rapids: Wm. B. Eerdmans Publishing Co., 1971), p. 24.

48. Demarest, Revelation, pp. 170-174. *See* his article, "Process Trinitarianism," in *Perspectives on Evangelical Theology* (Grand Rapids: Baker Book House, 1979), pp. 15-36.

49. Hebblethwaite, *The Christian Hope* p. 182. This volume is a history of the doctrine of Christian hope through the centuries. The English spelling is retained from the original English edition, 1984. Hebblethwaite is Dean of Chapel and Director of Studies in Philosophy at Queens College, Cambridge, UK. He is broadly evangelical.

50. Ibid., p. 183.

51. Bloesch, *Crumbling Foundations* (Grand Rapids: Academie Books, 1984), p. 42.

17. Ownership in Heaven?

1. Franz Delitzsch, *Commentary on the Prophecies of Isaiah* (Grand Rapids: Wm. B. Eerdmans Publishing Co., 1877, 1954) vol. 2:436.

2. Bruce Waltke, *ba'al*, root, *Theological Wordbook of the Old Testament* edited by R. Laird Harris (Chicago: Moody Press, 1980), vol. 1:119.

3. Joseph A. Alexander, *Commentary on the Prophecies of Isaiah* (Grand Rapids: Zondervan Publishing Co., 1847, 1953), vol. 2:408.

4. John Bunyan, *Pilgrim's Progress* Sandy Lesberg, editor (New York: The Peebles Classic Library, 1678, 1968), p. 144.

5. H. Van Riessen, *The Society of the Future* (Philadelphia: Presbyterian and Reformed Publishing Co., 1952), p. 45.

6. Simone de Beauvoir, *All Said and Done* (New York: Warner Book, 1975), p. 23.

7. Christopher Lasch, *The Cult of Narcissism* (New York: W. W. Norton, 1979), p. xvi.

8. Jacques Ellul, *The Ethics of Freedom* (Grand Rapids: Wm. B. Eerdmans Publishing Co., 1976), p. 310.

9. Ronald J. Sider, *Rich Christians in an Age of Hunger* (Downers Grove, IL: InterVarsity Press, 1977), p. 88.

10. Graham Hughes, *Hebrews and Perfection* (Cambridge: Cambridge University Press, 1979), p. 72.

11. Christopher Rowland, *The Open Heaven: A Study of Apocalyptic in Judaism and Early Christianity* (New York: Crossroad, 1982), p. 418.

12. Beasley-Murray, *Commentary on Revelation*, p. 181; Caird, *Revelation*, p. 133-140.

13. [no author known], *Theologica Germanica*, LI, cited by Kreeft, *Everything You*

Ever Wanted to Know About Heaven, p. 43.

14. Ibid., p. 44.

15. Ibid., p. 43.

16. Paul Badham, *Christian Beliefs About Life after Death* (New York: Barnes & Noble, 1976), p. 85.

17. Lewis, *The Problem of Pain,* pp. 150, 151.

18. Memory in Heaven?

1. David L. Edwards, *The Last Things Now* (London: SCM, 1969), p. 89.

2. H. H. Price, "Personal Survival and the Idea of Another World," *Classical and Contemporary Readings in the Philosophy of Religion,* edited by John Hick, (Englewood Cliffs: Prentice-Hall, Inc., 1970), pp. 370-393.

3. Shirley MacLaine, *Dancing in the Light* (New York: Bantam Books, 1985), p. 247.

4. Badham, *Christian Beliefs About Life after Death,* p. 73.

5. Paul Tournier, *The Naming of Persons* (San Francisco: Harper & Row, Publishers, 1975), pp. 5, 6, 83.

6. Hick, *Death and Eternal Life,* p. 284.

7. Ibid., p. 385.

8. Badham, *Christian Beliefs,* p. 38.

9. Shirley MacLaine, *It's All in the Playing* (New York: Bantam Books, 1987), p. 168.

10. MacLaine, *Dancing,* p. 40.

11. Ibid., p. 140.

12. Ibid., p. 104.

13. Ibid., p. 311.

14. Ibid., pp. 298, 299.

15. MacLaine, *Going Within: A Guide for Inner Transformation* (New York: Bantam Books, 1989), pp. 89, 90.

16. MacLaine, *Dancing,* p. 305.

17. Ibid.

18. Ibid., pp. 112, 121, 126, 247, 251, 259, 285, 286, 319, 339, 341, 343, 344, 396.

19. MacLaine, *It's All in the Playing,* p. 191.

20. Farrer, *Saving Belief,* p. 140. The view of the soul as separate from body has few advocates today. Anthony A. Hoekema, however, has presented a recent defense of the differentiation between soul and body in his encyclopedic *The Bible and the Future,* pp. 86-95.

21. Sadu Sundar Singh, *With and Without Christ,* Introduction by the Lord Bishop of Winchester (New York: Harper and Brothers Publishers, 1929), pp. 115, 116. Condensed in *Decision* magazine, June, 1962, p. 10.

22. Bliss Carmen, *Bliss Carmen's Poems* (New York: Dodd, Mead, 1929).

23. Kreeft, *Heaven,* pp. 41, 45, 46.

24. William Strawson, *Jesus and the Future,* 2nd ed., (London: Epworth Press, 1959, 1970), p. 210.

25. Anthony A. Hoekema, *Bible and the Future,* p. 101. S. D. F. Salmond in his classic, *Doctrine of Immortality* (Minneapolis, MN: Klock and Klock, 1895, 1984), represents those who deny the parable was intended eschatologically. He wrote, "To suppose it to be our Lord's object here to give a doctrine of the intermediate state is entirely to misunderstand the parable. . . . If [the parable teaches] anything on the subject of the interval between death and resurrection, it is only the broad lesson that the Divine righteousness pursues men after death, and that the estimates of men here and the conditions of men here may be reversed by the moral decisions of the hereafter" (pp. 345, 346).

26. Toon, *Heaven and Hell,* pp. 127,

128, mentioned the hypothesis of F. F. Bruce and Murray J. Harris that those in the intermediate state *have their resurrected bodies!* See F. F. Bruce, "Paul on Immortality," *Scottish Journal of Theology,* vol. 24 (1971): 457-471, and his *1 and 2 Corinthians,* London, 1971, p. 204. Murray J. Harris, *Raised Immortal: Resurrection and Immortality in the New Testament* (London: Marshall, Morgan, and Scott, 1983), p. 40f. See also Joseph Osei-Bonsu "Does 2 Cor. 5:1-10 Teach 'the Reception of the Resurrection Body at the Moment of Death?'" *Journal for the Study of the New Testament,* 28 (1986), p. 81-101. (The latter article is a reply and rebuttal to F. F. Bruce's position.)

27. Owen, *The Works of John Owen,* vol. 1:269.

28. MacLaine, *Dancing,* pp. 203, 249, W. G. T. Shedd, *Sermons to the Natural Man* (Edinburgh: Banner of Truth Trust, 1876, 1977), pp. 335-357; William M. Taylor, *The Limitations of Life* (New York: George H. Doran Company, 1879), pp. 297-311, "Memory as an Element of Future Retribution." Helmut Thielicke (1908-1986), *The Waiting Father* (San Francisco: Harper & Row, Publishers, 1959), pp. 41-51.

William Barclay, *And Jesus Said* (Philadelphia: The Westminster Press, 1970), pp. 92-98.

29. Hans Küng, *Eternal Life?* p. 14.

30. MacLaine, *Dancing,* pp. 203, 249.

31. Ibid., p. 341.

32. Ibid., pp. 93, 298.

33. J. Kik, *The Eschatology of Victory,* p. 259.

34. F. F. Bruce, *Commentary on the Epistle to the Hebrews* (Grand Rapids: Wm. B. Eerdmans Publishing Co., 1964), pp. 75, 76.

35. George Whitefield, *Life and Sermons* (New Haven: Whitmore & Buckingham, and H. Mansfield, 1834), p. 580, in his sermon on Numbers 23:23.

36. Schilder, *Heaven,* p. 105.

37. Ibid., p. 78.

38. N. A. Woychuk, "Will We Have Bodies in Heaven?" *Bibliotheca Sacra,* vol. 108, No. 429, Jan.-March, 1951, p.104.

39. Augustine, *Confessions* Book 12: xiii.

40. Fortman, *Everlasting Life After Death,* p. 312.

41. Hebblethwaite, *The Christian Hope,* p. 208.

19. Recognition in Heaven?

1. Douglas Groothuis, *Confronting the New Age* (Downers Grove, IL: InterVarsity Press, 1988), p. 95.

2. Linda Goodman, *Star Signs* (New York: St. Martin's Press, 1987), pp. 417, 418.

3. MacLaine, *Dancing,* pp. 112, 343.

4. Strangely, *Reunion* was not indexed in McDannell, Lang, *Heaven.* For those interested, see pages: 27, 61, 155, 156, 165, 211, 213, 229, 245, 249, 258, 259, 269, 270, 274, 324, 325, 342.

5. *Life of Henry Alford:* Journals and Letters edited by his widow (London: Rivingtons, 1874), p. 136.

6. George W. Sanville, *Forty Gospel Hymn Stories* [Winona Lake, IN: The Rodeheaver-Hall Mack, Co., 1943], p. 42.

7. *Church Management,* vol. 56, July, 1980, p. 3.

8. William Barclay, *A Spiritual Autobiography* (Grand Rapids: Wm. B. Eerdmans Publishing Co., 1975), p. 64.

9. McDannell, Lang, *Heaven,* p. 27.

10. Ibid., p. 28.

11. Ibid., p. 31.

12. Pannenberg, *Jesus, God and Man,* p. 76.

13. "The most common picture" of eschatological salvation in the gospels is of table fellowship (George E. Ladd, *The Presence of the Future,* p. 208).

14. Hebblethwaite, *The Christian Hope,* Op. Cit., p. 225.

15. Look up the following passages: Drinking wine—Mark 14:25;

Eating and drinking—Luke 22:30;

Table of Old Testament saints—Matt. 8:11, 12; *Luke* 13:29;

A wedding feast—Matt. 22:11-14; 25:1-12;

A large banquet—Luke 14:16-24.

16. G. I. Williamson, *Wine in the Bible and the Church* (Phillipsburg, NJ: Pilgrim Publishing Company, 1976), 53 pages; Andre S. Bustanoby, *The Wrath of Grapes: Drinking and the Church Divided* (Grand Rapids: Baker Book House, 1987), 135 pages; Kenneth Gentry, *The Christian and Alcoholic Beverages* (Grand Rapids: Baker Book House, 1986), 117 pages.

17. Baxter, *The Saints' Everlasting Rest,* p. 354.

18. Strong, *Systematic Theology,* p. 585.

20. Is Heaven Reincarnation?

1. *Newsweek,* March 27, 1989, p. 54.

2. MacLaine, *It's All in the Playing,* p. 68.

3. Ibid., p. 161.

4. Ibid., p. 221.

5. Attorney Constance Cumbey, *The Hidden Dangers of the Rainbow: The New Age Movement and Our Coming Age of Barbarism* (Shreveport, LA: Huntington House, Inc., 1983), pp. 55-58. As of 1983, according to her research, there were approximately 10,000 organizations or their covers in the United States and Canada. In 1988, its proliferation has continued. Douglas Goothuis, in probably the most comprehensive analysis of the New Age movement from the viewpoint of Christianity currently available, *Confronting the New Age,* reported that a three-volume set on channeling had sold 160,000 copies as early as 1975 (Downers Grove, IL: InterVarsity Press, 1988), p. 29. One sign of their emergence into public affairs is their motivational seminars, their educational packets, and their infiltration of corporate America. Although New Age appeals more

to individual investigation and practice (a church they don't wish to be called), in Cincinnati, Ohio, where I live, is what may be representative of what is happening elsewhere: a New Age center is now advertised with other church announcements in the Saturday papers. Although Shirley MacLaine has her base in California, New Age has spread everywhere.

6. Goodman, *Star Signs,* p. 411.

7. Ibid., p. 430.

8. MacLaine, *Playing,* pp. 12, 17. She has had contact with twenty transchannelers up to 1987.

9. Ibid., pp. 17, 18.

10. Ibid., p. 69.

11. Ibid., p. 172.

12. MacLaine, *Going Within: A Guide for Inner Transformation* (New York: Bantam Books, 1989), pp. 71, 72, 90, 91.

13. Ibid., p. 7.

14. Ibid., pp. 9, 12, 186.

15. Ibid., p. 10.

16. Ibid., pp. 63, 75.

17. Ibid., pp. 69, 70.

18. Ibid., p. 72.

19. Ibid., pp. 85, 263.

20. Ibid., pp. 31, 58, 90.

21. MacLaine, *Dancing*, p. 343.

22. MacLaine, *Playing*, p. 122.

23. Ibid., p. 22.

24. MacLaine, *Dancing*, p. 344.

25. MacLaine, *Playing*, p. 15. MacLaine went on later to say: "If each of us creates his own reality, then perhaps each of us creates the characters who people our reality" (p. 121).

26. Goodman, *Star*, pp. 417, 427.

27. MacLaine, *Limb*, p. 98.

28. MacLaine, *Dancing*, pp. 43, 286.

29. MacLaine, *Playing*, p. 6.

30. Ibid., p. 174.

31. Ibid., p. 192.

32. Herman Bavinck, *The Philosophy of Revelation* [New York: Longmans, Green, and Co., 1909], p. 70.

33. Ibid., p. 66.

34. S. Singh, *With and Without Christ*, pp. 111, 112. Leslie D. Weatherhead (1893-1976), the maverick British Methodist, in his *Christian Agnostic* (Nashville: Abingdon Press, 1965), pp. 314, 315, has given an unsuccessful attempt in neutralizing Singh's criticism of Hinduism at this point.

35. MacLaine, *Playing*, p. 24; *see Going*, pp. 45, 169.

36. MacLaine, *Limb*, p. 98.

37. David H. C. Read, *This Grace Given* (Grand Rapids: Wm. B. Eerdmans Publishing Co., 1984), pp. 4, 5.

38. Hans Küng, *Eternal Life?*, pp. 60, 62.

39. Mark Albrecht, *Reincarnation: A Christian Appraisal* (Downers Grove, IL: InterVarsity Press, 1982), p. 113.

40. Cumbey, *The Hidden Dangers*, pp. 189, 192.

41. MacLaine, *Limb*, p. 337.

42. MacLaine, *Dancing*, p. 203.

43. Ibid., pp. 249, 346, 347; MacLaine, *Playing*, p. 161.

44. Ibid., pp. 121, 146, 147, 305; MacLaine, *Dancing*, pp. 112, 242, 247.

45. MacLaine, *Playing*, pp. 304, 305.

46. Goodman, *Star*, p. 122.

47. MacLaine, *Playing*, p. 226.

48. Ibid., p. 226.

49. Ibid., p. 69.

50. Goodman, *Star*, p. 416.

51. Barth, *Church Dogmatics*, II/1, p. 136.

52. MacLaine, *Playing*, p. 161.

53. Ibid., p. 168.

54. Cumbey, *Hidden Dangers*, pp. 33-35. On bibliography: *see* Norman L. Geisler, J. Jutaka Amano, *The Reincarnation Sensation* (Tyndale, 1986); Douglas Groothuis, *Confronting the New Age* (InterVarsity, 1988); and Russell Chandler, *Understanding the New Age* (1988).

55. MacLaine, *Dancing*, p. 341; Goodman, *Star*, p. 123.

56. Ibid., p. 416.

57. MacLaine, *Going*, pp. 178, 179.

58. Ibid., p. 179.

59. Ibid., p. 180.

60. Ibid., p. 181.

61. MacLaine, *Limb*, pp. 182, 210, 235. Groothuis (*Confronting New Age*, p. 103) offered a three-point reply/rebuttal: (1) The Council focused on Origen's writings, not the Bible; (2) Origen's writings are not part of the Bible, therefore, they could not be stricken out of the Bible; (3) Origen's teaching didn't approximate reincarnation.

62. MacLaine, *Playing*, pp. 221, 222.

63. Albrecht, *Reincarnation*, pp. 35-50. Groothuis, *Confronting New Age*, pp. 95-98, on this issue.

64. MacLaine, *Dancing*, p. 341; Goodman, *Star*, p. 123.

65. Albrecht, *Reincarnation*, pp. 36, 37.

66. This admission is recognized by a writer who is sympathetic to belief in reincarnation. *See* Weatherhead, *Christian Agnostic*, pp. 295, 296.

67. Books on Christ's resurrection

should include the standard works of William Milligan and James Orr and recent ones by Gary Habermas, Thomas Forsyth Torrance, and Floyd V. Filson. Complete bibliographies are found in most recent biblical/theological dictionaries.

68. MacLaine, *Limb*, pp. 52, 93, 95, 98, 235; MacLaine, *Dancing*, pp. 42, 43, 114, 363, 404; MacLaine, *Playing*, pp. 161, 174, 192; MacLaine, *Going*, pp. 26, 27, 29.

69. MacLaine, *Playing*, pp. 149, 215, 217; MacLaine, *Dancing*, p. 274.

70. MacLaine, *Limb*, p. 198.

71. MacLaine, *Playing*, p. 337.

72. Arthur Custance, *The Sovereignty of Grace* (Phillipsburg, NJ: Presbyterian and Reformed Publishing Co., 1979), p. 117.

73. *Out on a Limb* enjoyed 15 weeks on the *New York Times* hardcover bestseller list. It has sold more than 2 million copies to date and has been translated into 13 lan-guages. *Dancing in the Light* surpassed all her previous successes: 31 weeks on the *Times* hardcover list and with the fall 1986 release of the paperback edition, there are now more than 2 million copies in print. Further exposure of her views were seen in the television miniseries *Out on a Limb*. (Information from dust cover to *It's All in the Playing*.) *Going Within* (1989), her latest book, which is her shortest, has been marketed with a video tape advertisement titled "Inner Workout."

74. MacLaine, *Going*, pp. 96-98, 134, on chakra; pp. 133-137; on crystals; on colors, pp. 145-147; on body exercises, pp. 53-56; on sound therapy, pp. 145-149; on meditation, pp. 46, 58, 60. A curious modernization of her spelling of chakra is to be noted. Was the later spelling to sepa-rate it from its Indian derivation? Note, she spelled it *chakkra* in *Dancing* (pp. 15, 16) and *chakra* in *Going* (pp. 96-98, 134).

Glossary

Antichrist   Used as both principles and persons and in the sense of in "place of Christ" or "against Christ." In the writings of the apostle John "Antichrist" is a principle; in the writings of Paul "Antichrist" is a specific person; in Revelation both principles and persons constitute Antichrist.

amillennialism   Also known as "historical millennialism," "inaugurated millennium," and "realized millennium." This is the view that one thousand years stands symbolically for the time between Christ's first and second advent.

annihilationism   Two types: (1) The non-Christian, which holds that when you're dead you are dead (no resurrection); and (2) Christians who hold the wicked perish in the full sense of the word (totally destroyed in hell).

anthropology   The study of man. Three types: (a) physical, which studies fossil evidence and so forth; (b) cultural anthropology, which studies cultures; (c) anthropology which replaces theology. It claims man is the only god or that God is idealized man.

anthropomorphic   A description of God in human terms, with physical characteristics such as, "God saw" (Gen. 1:4); or a description of God as if he were limited like humans, subject to our space and time, such as "whom he did foreknow" (Rom. 8:29).

apocalypse   The original title for Revelation. The word means "unveiling," or "disclosure." *Not to be confused* with Apocrypha (books between Old and New Testaments). Apocalypse is a literary genre (form) which features visions and compounded symbols.

beatific vision   The sight of God. From the Latin *visio Dei*. Traditionally ap-

437

plied to seeing God in heaven. Those who know Christ savingly begin to "see" God in time.

chakra system   A New Age word used by Shirley MacLaine. Chakras are alleged centers connecting the soul entity (higher self), the body, and the personality, or so-called energy centers (of which there are seven) that share our character.

channeling   A New Age movement term for contact with previous lives, oneself, or others. The old word was *seance*.

chiliasm   From the Greek word for "thousand" (*chilia*). The Latin counterpart is *millenium*. Millenialists believe that there will be a literal 1,000 years of peace on the earth.

concrescence   A process theology term meaning "coming to be."

context   The surrounding verses (before and after) which explain the usage in a particular verse. Also used of paragraphs and the total book context.

clouds of heaven   A biblical word which describes, not a natural cloud formation, but rather the glory of God, his presence. (*See* Mark 14:62; Matt. 26:64; Dan. 7:13).

cosmic   Relates to universe (world, earth, history of mankind) in terms of issues, nature, effects, and future.

dispensationalism   In eschatology it represents those who espouse the rapture as distinct from Christ's revelation (second coming), a literal seven-year great tribulation (in future), and a literal one-thousand-year millennium on earth.

epexegetical   A grammatical feature where the next phrase explains, describes, or details the meaning of what precedes it.

eschatology   The broad category of future things. The study of end-time events. From *eschatos* which means "last." It stands for all last things. But the last things began when Christ came!

eternal life   Not unending life, but God's qualitative life in man. It begins in time and continues into postdeath.

exegesis   Drawing out the text's meaning, interpreting the Bible linguistically, not mystically. A false exegesis is *eisegesis* (an entirely different word). Whereas exegesis draws out the meaning, eisegesis reads in a meaning that is not there.

firmament   The airy heaven, the heaven of stars, the heaven of atmosphere. In the Bible (Matt. 6:26; Mark 6:41; 13:25; John 17:1; Acts 1:11).

futurist   Two senses: (1) A person holds to a concept of the future, arising from the biblical texts; (2) and sometimes reserved for those who have detailed maps of what's ahead.

genre   Denotes a distinctive group of writings, whose characteristics warrant a separate treatment and conclusions because of the author's style, purpose, and form. *Apocalypse* (another word for the Book of Revelation) is disinctive genre in the New Testament and is distorted when straight prose strictures are applied.

hamartiology   The teaching of the Bible on what sin is and why man is a sinner.

heaven   (in the Old Testament) Appears in plural form *(samayim)*, referring to sky (Gen. 1:6) as well as God's dwelling place (1 Kings 8:30).

heaven   (in the New Testament) Appears as "heaven" *(ouranos)*, 272 times, most frequently in Matthew and as "heavenly" *(ouranios)* over 150 times.

heaven and earth   A combined phrase frequently found designating the earth and outer space beginning with lower atmosphere and stretching into galaxies. The older word for *universe*.

hermeneutics   The science of how to interpret or principles of interpreting the Bible, beginning with the identification of genre (type of literature).

hosts of heaven An Old Testament expression mostly meaning the stars.

idealism An alternative to materialism. It makes mind and ideas. Represented in pantheism, panentheism, spiritualism, and so forth.

Intermediate State A general word for the place of the departed dead, who await the commencement of the final heaven, new heavens and new earth. It is the heaven where believers go at death, before Christ's second coming. It coincides with the time between the first and second comings of Christ.

karma A New Age movement word meaning the law of consequences applied to man's behavior.

kingdom of heaven An equivalent expression of the kingdom of God. *Heaven* is an abbreviation-substitution for *God*. Some futurists (wrongly) attribute it to a restored Jewish kingdom.

literalism Conveniently giving a document a word-for-word concrete meaning when the genre would dictate a consistently symbolic meaning. It is not to be confused with taking the Bible seriously and in historical context.

mantra A New Age word, also peculiar to Buddhism and the occult. It is their word for short "prayer," recited repeatedly, said to themselves as gods.

marriage supper of the Lamb The symbolic expression for the communion between Christ and his church in heaven ahead.

millennium From the Latin, meaning one thousand years. Concept found only in Revelation 20. Some take it as a literal one thousand years on earth. The preferred sense is of an extended period of time in which Christ works His will between His first and second comings.

New Age Associated with reincarnation, channeling, and so forth. An American-based movement which adapts much of Hinduism. The label is different, but the concepts are similar.

new heavens and new earth The final heaven extended to both spheres after God's recreating of the old heavens and old earth, after Christ's second coming.

New Jerusalem The term used in Revelation for the body of believers, the church redeemed by Christ.

oxymoron The shortest paradox, usually two words, such as "living stones," (1 Peter 2:5), or a capsule phrase of contractory words, such as "law of liberty" (James 1:25). In Revelation "first resurrection" and "second death" (20:5, 6) are oxymorons.

pantheism The belief that all is God.

panentheism The belief that God is in all. (Not that all is God). Panentheism is close to pantheism, but not identical with it. For instance, Friedrich Schleiermacher (1768-1834), the founder of Protestant liberal theology was a panentheist.

Platonism Plato's concepts include both belief in man's preexistence, and a World of Ideas having an independent existence, forming the structures of our concrete world.

pluralism The inclusion of many views, even to the point of tolerating contradictory positions.

prehension A process theology term meaning feelings.

premillennialism The belief that Christ returns *before* an earthly millennium.

preterist A school of interpretation which takes Revelation as largely past (although in original readers' future, or applying mostly to past completed action, not to our future). Some grant refulfillments of the past predictions.

pretribulationalism The belief that Christ comes back in a rapture to pull out his church so they do not go through a time of great tribulation.

prolegomenon A technical introduction to an academic topic.

proleptic In Greek grammar a verb tense in which the future is anticipated and talked of. The event is viewed as having already happened, though it hasn't. Found in Hebrew Scriptures in terms of prophetic perfect tense (see Gen. 1:4a; Neh. 9:15a; Dan. 4:6a; Amos 5:2).

purgatory A post-death state in which the punishments and cleansings of moral defilement are removed before entering heaven. An historically Catholic doctrine.

Queen of Heaven A cult of astrological worshiping of planet power.

quietism A school of sanctification that stresses passivity. Largely Quaker in cast. Found in certain branches of Catholic piety and reflected in some forms of evangelical spiritual-life teachings.

rapture Ascribed to an alleged first phase of Christ's second coming by pretribulational premillennialists. Considered by others—such as posttribulational premillennialists, historic millennialists, and postmillennialists—as one and the same as the final revelation of Christ (second coming).

redactor One who edits a document at a later time.

reduplication A school of interpretation which sees the same events repeated but in different symbolic forms. It is characteristic of the Book of Revelation that the same time frames are described progressively and with different perspectives. It is the layered-cake approach in contrast with a linear or chronological approach.

reincarnation The belief that a person has had previous existences in other bodies and that at death the person indwells a new body in repayment for the way he lived in his previous existence.

replication The view that we have a double somewhere in eternity.

Revelation Two meanings: (1) The name of the last book of the Bible. No plural in title; (2) the second coming of Christ described in 1 Thessalonians 4 and elsewhere, such as Revelation 16, 19, and 20.

rewards Associated in popular thinking with earning one's own salvation, resulting from merit. Jesus used the expression as the recognition of human experience *without* the concept of human deserving. In the Bible's usage, it is solely because of God's giving, never because of human achievement.

solecism An irregularity in grammar in which genders are switched and cases are changed. Revelation, for instance, substitutes masculine for feminine gender (11:4; 14:19; 17:3), and nominative for genitive cases (2:13; 3:12; 7:4; 8:9; 14:12). This peculiarity is prominent in the Book of Revelation.

solipsism The rarest form of philosophic idealism which says that the only entity existing is the self.

soteriology The theological term for human salvation. It focuses on questions related to why, how, and when man is saved.

soul sleep The view of Seventh Day Adventists and Jehovah's Witnesses (in our day) and others who contend souls go into a state of unconsciousness at death. A synonym for their position is "mortalism." It takes the figure of death, "asleep"—literally, rather than symbolically.

telepathy The alleged transference of thoughts between people physically separated. Found in the New Age movement.

third heaven The expression used by Paul to describe his encounter with God. It reflects the Jewish view that the heavens were layered.

throne A popular term in the Bible to

denote God's government of the universe. Frequently used in Revelation.

transchanneling The New Age description of using a medium to get a message from the realm of the dead.

treasure in heaven Used in Matthew 6:20; 19:21; Mark 10:21; Luke 12:33 18:22. It does not mean that man can send cash or credit ahead to heaven, but stands for where man's affection is through the vehicle of treasure (compare *rewards*, chapter 11).

tribulation Also known as the great tribulation. A belief held by pretribulational premillennialists that between the alleged rapture and Christ's second coming there is a period of great tribulation. Amillennialists and postmillenialists have traditionally agreed that there is no period of history in which the church of Christ is removed from the scene. Indeed, the church is the object of persecution.

visio Dei The Latin expression for the beatific vision of God.

universe Including the earth and the heavens.

universalism The theological view that everyone will be saved.

(Acknowledgment: use of F. B. Huey, Jr. and Bruce Corley's *A Student's Dictionary for Biblical and Theological Studies* [Grand Rapids: Zondervan Publishing Co., 1983])

Chart A Chapters of Revelation Related to History

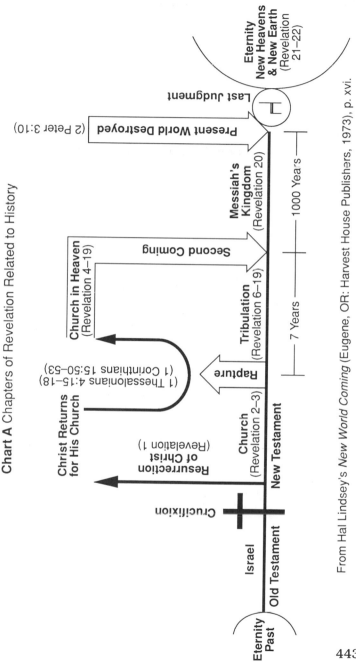

From Hal Lindsey's *New World Coming* (Eugene, OR: Harvest House Publishers, 1973), p. xvi.

443

Chart B The Persecuted Church

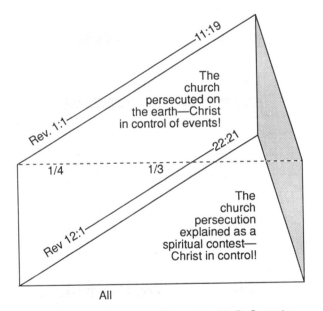

Adapted by J. L. Gilmore and based on H. B. Swete's commentary, *Revelation* (Grand Rapids: Kregel Publications, 1977 repr.), pp. xxix–xliii.

Chart C The View of Austin Farrer

Chapters are shown in brackets

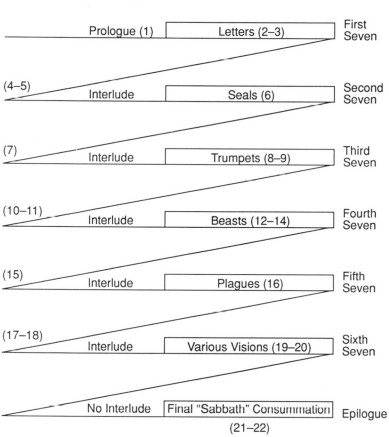

Prologue (1) — Letters (2–3)	First Seven
(4–5) Interlude — Seals (6)	Second Seven
(7) Interlude — Trumpets (8–9)	Third Seven
(10–11) Interlude — Beasts (12–14)	Fourth Seven
(15) Interlude — Plagues (16)	Fifth Seven
(17–18) Interlude — Various Visions (19–20)	Sixth Seven
No Interlude — Final "Sabbath" Consummation (21–22)	Epilogue

Chart by Graeme Goldsworthy, *The Lion and the Lamb*
(Nashville: Thomas Nelson Publishers, 1984), p. 57.

Selected Bibliography

Background

Hoekema, Anthony,
The Bible and the Future (Grand Rapids: Wm. B. Eerdmans Publishing Co., 1979). This is the best resource for understanding the issues, options, and alternatives in eschatology. A must-own, must read book!

McDannell, Colleen, and Lang, Bernhard,
Heaven: A History (New Haven, CT: Yale University Press, 1988). This is the most complete collection of information on heaven, with commentary, currently available. It has Subject, Author, but no Scripture Reference index. It is largely descriptive of heaven, rather than normative: what others have written, not what should be believed. Its strength lies in the breadth of its information (spanning Christian history). Its chief weakness is that Scripture is not finally authoritative.

Interpreting Revelation

Beasley-Murray, George,
The Book of Revelation (Grand Rapids: Wm. B. Eerdmans Publishing Co., 1979). One of the better recent commentaries by a British Baptist. It represents the historical premillennial viewpoint.

Caird, George B.,
The Revelation of St. John the Divine (San Francisco: Harper & Row, Publishers, 1966). An excellent work to be used with care. Easily understandable and without technical detail. Insightful and cautious.

447

Linguistically reliable but without being tedious.

Hendriksen, William,
More Than Conquerors (Grand Rapids: Baker Book House, 1940). This work provides a superb exposition following the reduplication or contrapuntal approach. Strongly recommended. Reprinted many times. If you can afford only one book, buy this one.

Heaven

Kreeft, Peter J.,
Heaven San Francisco: Harper & Row, Publishers, 1980). Some excellent insights. Deals with some modern objections to heaven. Kreeft relies heavily on C. S. Lewis and sections reflect a Roman Catholic view of heaven.

Kreeft, Peter J.,
Everything You Ever Wanted to Know About Heaven: But Never Dreamed of Asking (San Francisco: Harper & Row, Publishers, 1982). The follow-up volume by Kreeft, which deals with detailed questions on heaven. It also deals with hell. Kreeft stimulates and challenges.

Schilder, Klaas,
Heaven: What Is It? (Grand Rapids: Wm. B. Eerdmans Publishing Co., 1950). Abbreviated from the original Dutch edition, this is probably the best book on heaven for theological insight. (Currently out of print.)

Schoonhoven, Calvin R.,
The Wrath of Heaven (Grand Rapids: Wm. B. Eerdmans Publishing Co., 1966). This little-noticed book is a compact and compelling theological examination of infrequently explored areas of the subject of heaven. Well researched and with a masterful use of the biblical texts in their original languages. Any educated Christian can gain much from this work.

Smith, Wilbur,
The Biblical Doctrine of Heaven (Chicago: Moody Press, 1968). This work, despite its many citations of authors from ancient times into early twentieth century lacks perspective. It has interesting information on heaven, but it fails to provide a coordinated theological presentation on heaven. *Heaven: A History,* mentioned above makes Smith's study less valuable than formerly, except for the fact that Wilbur Smith honored Scripture as the Word of God.

Toon, Peter,
Heaven and Hell: A Biblical and Theological Overview (Nashville: Thomas Nelson Publishers, 1986). More current than Schilder, more theological than Smith, and more textual (biblical) than Kreeft. Short without being skimpy. Thought provoking as well as fairly thorough. The next best book on heaven to read after Schilder.

Subject
Index

ability (moral), alleged superior spiritual abilities in females, 238; in Pharisaism, 419 n4; in the New Age, 99, 360; in the New Testament, 359
agelessness, 282–284, 324
agnosticism (*See also* skepticism), nihilistic, 61; reverent, 282
agriculture, 20, 182, 183, 211, 294
aion, 157, 282
amillennialism, 87, 364, 365, 371, 384, 399 n10
angels, archangel Michael, 375; as servants 177; Christ as angel (oblique), 375, 376; fallen angels, 405 n21; guardian angels, 129; humans changed into, 69, 70, 73, 269; in heaven, 28, 130, 284, 288, 406 n23
animals, 49, 50, 57, 61, 123, 130–133, 404 n7, 415 n17
anthropocentric, 86, 88, 89
anthropology, 76, 289
anthropomorphisms, 91, 159, 160, 255, 316
Antichrist, 25, 186, 294, 325
apocalyptic/apocalypticism, 19, 24, 29, 34, 35, 40, 45, 51, 274, 374, 388, 389; Jewish, 97, 220

apostles, 75, 117, 214, 265
Armageddon, 25, 42
art, in heaven 183–184, 410 n31; on heaven, 247–248
atheism, 16, 56, 58, 61, 75, 77

beasts (in Revelation), 25, 46, 50; *See also* Rev. 13:1–8 in Scripture Index
beatific vision (*visio Dei*), 27, 150, 335
Beulah land, 296–298
boredom, 20, 126, 158, 166, 168, 169, 170, 174, 232, 245, 251, 254, 264, 281
born again, 170, 358, 359
Buddhism, 154, 320, 325

Catholicism (Roman), 110, 137, 138, 140, 143, 222, 228, 230, 279, 280, 330, 382, 383, 384
chakra, 361
channeling, 341
children, developed in heaven, 269, 270, 283
chiliasm, *See* millennium
Christ, bride of, 108, 120, 177, 187, 188, 236, 240; as way to God, 104; death of, 96, 135, 170, 262; resurrection of, 39,

Author
Index

Scripture Index

Genesis

1:1—78
2:7—61
4:17—112
15:15—331
22:16—376
25:8—331
35:29—331
47:30—332
49:10—104
49:29, 33—332

Exodus

3:6—389
20:15, 17—299
21:24—357

Leviticus

24:20—357

Numbers

20:24-27—332
27:13—332
32:2—332

Deuteronomy

5:19, 21—299

19:17—418 n14
27:17—299
32:50—332

Joshua

13:33—299

1 Kings

1:21—332
2:10—332
6:20—114
8:27—91
11:21—332

Job

23:10—150
29:7—418 n14

Psalms

2:2-9—369-370
2:4—251, 254
2:8—299
16:5, 6—299
17:15—181
23:4—63
24:1—89, 299
33:26—78

459